HORNCHURCH
DURING THE GREAT WAR

*An illustrated Account of Local Activities
and Experiences.*

BY

CHARLES THOMAS PERFECT,

**Author of "Our Village," "The Souvenir of Anzac Day,"
"Ye Olde Village of Hornchurch," etc.**

ART PAPER EDITION.

COPYRIGHT.

———

Published by Benham and Company, Limited,
24, High Street, Colchester.
1920.

This is a facsimile reprint of
Hornchurch during the Great War
by Charles Thomas Perfect
bequeathed to Havering Museum
by May Clarke

It was published in 2007 by
Havering Museum, Ltd.,
The Brewery Gate, High Street, Romford RM1 1JU

It was prepared for press by
Ian Henry Publications, Ltd.
20 Park Drive, Romford RM1 4LH

Printed by
Athanæum Press, Ltd, Gateshead

ISBN
978 0 86025 927 5

Supported by
The National Lottery®
through Awards for All

BENHAM
&
COMPANY
L.ᵀᴰ
COLCHESTER

Drawn by P. C. Haydon Bacon.

IN THE OLDEN DAYS.

Frontispiece.

PREFACE.

This volume is the result of six years work, and is an endeavour to record the history of our parish during the war—4th August, 1914, to 10th January, 1920—the date on which the war with Germany, our chief aggressor, was officially announced as ended. I have tried to show how Hornchurch responded to " The Call," and in what manner our village helped in the making of war.

While pride of place is, of course, given to those brave men and lads who came forward so unhesitatingly at their country's bidding, and took their places with the fighting forces of the King, it is due to those other parishioners who have taken an active part in the military, semi-military, religious, parochial, and social organizations, which have been so beneficially active during the war, that their services should be suitably recorded. I have also devoted considerable space to the military occupation of Hornchurch, and to the troops quartered here from time to time during the war period, as well as to the many important events and happenings, which have taken place in the parish, some of which have been of a most thrilling and interesting character. In all these directions it has been my earnest endeavour to give a faithful record, so that those now living may have something in their possession which will recall the momentous years of the Great War, and that those who come after may learn something of what their forbears did towards the saving of their country and of the world for God and Right.

With regard to the Rolls of Honour, I do not think it at all possible that, with such a huge and far-reaching parish as ours, absolutely full and complete lists could be compiled of all from Hornchurch who served in H.M. Forces over such a prolonged period. I can only say that no effort or expense has been spared in compiling the lists I have produced, and while expressing my regret for any names which may be missing, I ask at the same time, to be absolved from any blame, having exhausted all the means in my power to make the lists complete. In this part of my work I wish to acknowledge my indebtedness to many friends, without whose help it could not have been accomplished, and I desire to tender my sincere thanks to the Rev. Bernard Hartley, who obtained all the particulars for Harold Wood, and to Mrs. Home, the Misses Muriel Burden, Daisy

Purrett, Doris Searle, Edith Smith, and Messrs. J. T. Attwooll, F. A. Bridge, T. A. Bridges, G. C. Dohoo, Gerald Edwards, Walter Fox, and Arthur Gosling, who rendered valuable assistance in collecting details concerning the other parts of the parish.

I have included in the pages of my book many matters not strictly of a local character, but which seemed to me essential in a record such as this. In compiling the items which come within this category, my object has been to record such information which appeared to me matters of interest connected with the war on which enquiry might frequently arise, so that the volume might constitute a general book of reference. In this connection the articles on " The Control and Rationing of Food," " Daylight Saving," the " Diary of the War," etc., etc., will doubtless be found useful.

I beg to express my great obligation and thanks to Miss Constance Symonds, Mr. P. C. Haydon Bacon, Major A. B. Bamford, Mr. Denis Dunlop, Mr. C. H. Hollinghurst, Mr. William C. Inman, and Mr. Ernest Hicks Oliver for their charming and artistic contributions : and to Messrs. William C. Allen, E. E. Carter, F. Gandon, F. Ford, C. Stanley Holton, F. Kingsford, Luffs, Panora, Ltd., Qualis Photo Company, S. A. Sabine, Sports and General Agency, Bursall Tonge, Underwood and Underwood, Ltd., W. P. Wrack, and W. E. Wright & Sons, for the many beautiful photographs, reproduced in half tones, which have done so much to make the pages attractive and interesting.

My thanks are also due to the Proprietors of " Punch " the " Evening News," and to Lt. Colonel F. W. E. Bendall for permission to reproduce their several contributions, and to Mr. W. Gurney Benham for his beautiful design for the cover of the book, and for his kindly assistance and advice in the production of this volume.

In compiling some of the chapters I have had to rely to some considerable extent on many parishioners for information, and to them I wish also to convey my thanks, and last, but by no means least, I have to express my great obligation to Mr. S. Biddle and to Mr. Ernest Hicks Oliver for their valuable assistance in revising the proofs of my manuscript.

CHARLES T. PERFECT.

" Weylands," Hornchurch.
September 30, 1920.

Hornchurch during the Great War.

" Speak, who began this ? On thy love, I charge thee,
I do not know ; friends all but now, even now,
. . . and then, but now—
As if some planet had unwitted men,—
Swords out, and tilting one at other's breast,
In opposition bloody.
Shakespeare—Othello, II., iii.

INTRODUCTORY.

HORNCHURCH has always had its warriors. When England was Merrie England, and men fought with the simple weapons which gave the fighting man a fighting chance, our old chroniclers tell us that after Mass on Sunday mornings the young men of the parish betook themselves to the spot which is now called Butts Green*, and there disported themselves at the butts with bow and arrow to fit them for the day of battle. From this it may be assumed that the sturdy Essex men of that day were not behindhand in matters military, and many an honest bowman of our village, whose deeds are unrecorded, and whose name is unknown, may have deserved well of his country and of his native place.

Apart from a statement of this general character of a village community preparing for war, there are many individual instances in recorded history of the part the men of Hornchurch have played in the wars of the past. The first was that of the brother-in-law and successor of Edward the Confessor, the kingly warrior Harold, after whom was named Harold, or Harold's Wood, his personal possession, which was then, as now, part of our own parish. The few short months of Harold's reign were full of warlike incident, terminating with two great historic battles in quick succession. He obtained a brilliant victory at Stamford Bridge in Northumbria over the great army of Norsemen and Flemings, led by his brother Tostig and King Harold Hardrada of Norway, on the 25th September, 1066, when both Tostig and Hardrada fell. On the day following that battle,

---

*In the reign of Edward IV., it was enacted that every Englishman should buy a bow of his own height, and that butts for the practise of archery should be erected near every village, where the inhabitants were obliged to shoot up and down on every Feast Day in " penalty of being mulcted a halfpenny." (" How to write the History of a Parish." J. C. Cox, LL.D.)

I

hearing that the Normans had landed in Sussex, he, with an army greatly weakened by losses at Stamford Bridge, at once proceeded south, and by forced marches was able to face the Norman hosts under William, Duke of Normandy, at the battle of Hastings on the 14th October, 1066, when he met his death fighting valiantly at the head of his troops. His march through England from north to south was one of the great military feats of early times.

Anciently the area of the parish of Hornchurch extended far beyond the present boundaries, and included the whole of the Royal Liberty of Havering, stretching from the Thames to Havering and Noak Hill, with its nine miles of fertile and forest lands and its seventeen manors. From one of those manors, that of Mawneys (or Mannys), went forth another great military figure, Sir Walter De Many, the Court favourite of Edward III., and one of the foremost and bravest knights and warriors of that warlike King. He it was who, because of the high esteem in which he was held by the King, made bold to supplicate for the lives of the six burgesses of Calais, and it was his earnestness and eloquence which opened up the way for the beautiful Queen Philippa, whose pleading with the King eventually prevailed, and so averted a tragedy which would have been a reproach to English chivalry for all time.

During the Civil War, two other Manors of the Liberty were occupied by soldiers of great distinction. Colonel Carew Mildmay, of Marks, raised a regiment, and fought on the Parliament side, and was with General Fairfax at the siege of Colchester in June, 1648 ; while from the Manor of Brittons, South Hornchurch, Sir William Ayloffe, High Sheriff of Essex, rode at the head of his Royalist troop of horse to the same historic engagement, and, fighting valiantly in the cause of the King, was, after the siege, sentenced to be shot. That sentence was, however, not carried out, and he was, instead, imprisoned in the Tower and deprived of his lands at Hornchurch. He was afterwards deported to the Barbadoes as a slave, but at the Restoration he regained his freedom and returned to Brittons, and died a Knight of the Shire of the County he had served so well.

During the turbulent period of the Commonwealth, there was probably no individual who had a more remarkable career than one Richard Deane, who became possessor of a portion of the Havering Bower lands. This man served first in the army, and afterwards in the navy, and so distinguished himself in both services that he attained the ranks of General and Admiral. He fought in practically all the principal engagements of the Civil War, and in 1648, while holding the rank of Major-General, he occupied London with Parliamentary troops. In the following year he was prominently concerned in the trial which brought about the execution of King Charles I., and in 1651 became chief of the Navy and Army. It was said of him that "his talents in the battlefield were not inferior to those of Cromwell," and his success at sea was as great as on land. He fell in action in a sea fight with the Dutch, off the North Foreland on June 2, 1653.*

These were men of our parish whose deeds live in the pages of history, but there were others, some of them less exalted, perhaps, who none the less deserved well of their country. Amongst them was Benjamin Harding, of Nelmes, who was born in Hornchurch in 1780, and went out to India in 1794, at the age of 14, as a Cornet in the East India Company's Army. He was present at the battles of Agra, Delhi, and the siege of Seringapatam (Gold Medal). He afterwards exchanged into the 10th Hussars and fought all through the Peninsula, being wounded

Photo]   *[W. P. Wrack*
OLD HOUSES AT THE WESTERN END OF HIGH STREET.

at Vittoria and Orthez, and thus missed Waterloo. He then exchanged into the Queen's Bays, commanded by his cousin, Lord George Beresford, and, attaining the rank of Colonel, subsequently commanded that Regiment. Then there was one, Mason, a veritable giant, who fought in the battle of Waterloo, and who, eighty years ago, was quite a village celebrity. After him were two Crimean veterans—Jasper Smith, who passed the closing years of his life in Appleton's Almshouses in the High Street (where his widow, Mary Ann Smith our oldest inhabitant, aged 93 years, is still living) ; and Sergeant Thomas Betts, for many

*Records of Pyrgo (Montagu Browne, pp. 107-108.)

3

years our village postmaster, who was buried with military honours on March 22, 1908, at the age of 73 years. Then we have still with us Benjamin Laurence Bishop, a veteran of the 92nd Gordon Highlanders, who fought in the Afghanistan War, and participated in Roberts's historic march from Kabul to Kandahar in 1880.

Later there were those brave volunteers of H Company, First Volunteer Battalion, Essex Regiment, whose readiness to respond to the call of the motherland at the time of the South African War is recorded in a later page of this book.

There has, indeed, never been a period in our village history when there has been a lack of men of patriotic spirit and martial enthusiasm to come forward in the day of their country's need and enrol themselves under her banners to fight for her honour and glory and in defence of their own rights and liberties. As it was in the days of the trusty strongbow and ponderous battleaxe, so it was when men fought with pike and lance and sword, and afterwards in the more recent era of musket and black gun-powder. So it is now in the present day, when modern warfare demands vast masses of metal and intricate machinery, when the showers of cannon ball of a by-gone age have given place to furious tempests of steel and chemicals, and when mammoth guns, fed with annihilating ammunition, belch forth death and devastation with every awful blast.

But, while methods have changed from time to time, the fighting spirit of our race has always been the same, and so it came about that in more recent times the inhabitants of our village became prominent in the Volunteer and Territorial movements, and later in the formation of the National Reserve, as well as in those excellent organizations, such as the Church Lads' Brigade, the Cadets, and the Boy Scouts, for the training of lads and boys as yet too young to join the Auxiliary Forces. From these and similar efforts all over the country materialized to a large extent that great citizen army which enabled Great Britain to take her place in this war as one of the great European Military Powers, while retaining her proud position as the greatest Naval Power of the world. That magnificent army, which apparently sprang into being at the touch of Lord Kitchener's magic wand, undoubtedly had its origin in the various voluntary military organizations which existed before the war, as apart from the men who were actually serving in the regular army or in the Territorial forces when hostilities began, there were thousands and tens of thousands throughout the length and breadth of the land who had already served as Volunteers, or had passed through the ranks of one or other of the junior training organizations, and were therefore in great measure trained and ready men.

4

Then there were the war-time organizations, the Volunteer Training Corps and the Cadet Corps, from whose ranks thousands of men were drafted into the regular army.

It would, perhaps, be of interest to recall here how these military and semi-military movements and organizations had their beginnings in Hornchurch, and it will not only serve to inform the latter day inhabitants of what was done in the early days of the British Volunteers, but will probably revive pleasant memories among the older villagers—many, happily, still with us—who had their part in such matters.

HORNCHURCH VOLUNTEERS AND TERRITORIALS.

Although the organised Volunteer movement started only sixty years ago, Hornchurch had its Volunteers as far back as the Napoleonic era. Lord Braybrooke in a report to the Horse Guards‡ at that time mentions seventeen Corps of Cavalry within the County, one of which was raised at Havering-atte-Bower. This Troop, called the Havering Cavalry, was raised by Richard Newman Harding Newman, of " Nelmes," who was Major commanding it, and its roll contained the names of many prominent Hornchurch men.

In June 1798, Mr. Thomas Barrett-Lennard, then of Hactons, (afterwards Sir Thomas Barrett-Lennard, he having been created a Baronet for his patriotic services) received the Commission of King George III. " to raise a Troop of Cavalry of the Association of the Inhabitants of the Parish of Aveley and its vicinity." This was known as The Barstable and Chafford Troop of Volunteer Cavalry and consisted of 38 men, recruited from the following parishes :—Aveley 4, Chadwell 1, Corringham 1, East Tilbury 1, Grays 1, Horndon-on-the-Hill 3, Little Thurrock 3, Mucking 2, North Ockendon 1, Orsett 4, Rainham 4, Stanford-le-Hope 3, Upminster 3, Vange 2, Wennington 2, West Thurrock 1, West Tilbury 2.*.

It will be seen that Hornchurch was not represented in this list, but we are somewhat heartened to learn that, when the Colours of the Troop were consecrated in Aveley Church in August 1799, " *the Coronation Anthem was sung by the Hornchurch Band.*" Later on, in July 1803, Sir Thomas Barrett-Lennard obtained permission from the King to augment his troop to the number of 60, and, when the additional men were added, they were drawn from Navestock, Hornchurch, Laindon, and Little Warley.

A mounted body of this kind was necessarily to some extent exclusive and limited in numbers, but Infantry volunteer corps sprang into being in all parts of Essex during the Napoleonic

‡Victoria History of Essex, vol. 2, section Political History, page 255.
*Essex Review, No. 86, vol. xxii, article by T. Barrett-Lennard, J.P., D.L.;. The Barstable and Chafford Troop of Cavalry.

era, and, though Hornchurch is not specially mentioned, it is stated that "in every small parish a Corps of local warriors, numbering 40 to 100, was raised, and that the military and patriotic spirit ran through baronial halls, homesteads, country houses, and workshops." We may, therefore, confidently assume that the former patriots of our village were no laggards in this movement, and that Hornchurch had its efficient Company of Volunteers.

It was in May, 1859, that the voluntary movement received its impetus in the establishment of the National Rifle Association, and on June 26, 1860, the first Hornchurch Rifles were enrolled, their Company, about 60 strong, forming part of the 15th Essex Rifle Volunteers. The first officers of the Company were :—Captain Peter Esdaile Bearblock ; Lieut. William Mashiter ; and Ensign (and acting Captain) Richard Dendy.

This Company was very successful, and many Hornchurch men, well-known at the present time, were amongst its earlier members.

VOLUNTEERS.

Names of some of the non-commissioned officers and men who first joined the Volunteers in 1860 :—

Q.M.S. : Thomas Mashiter.
Colour-Sergeant : William Dendy.
Sergeants : John Crosse§, William Mitchell, Edward Mitchell, William Bonnett¶ and Thomas Wedlake.
Corporals : J. Pemberton, Arthur Bull‖, E. Shepherd.
Privates : George Dockrill, Robert Dockrill, Isaac Dear, George Dear, James Dear, George Collin, David Lazell, George Kent, J. Johnson, G. Miller, F. Hampshire, G. Hampshire, W. Halls, John Franklyn, Senr., John Franklyn, Junr., George Franklyn, J. Francillan, T. Smith, F. C. Pearce, J. Pearce, W. Pearce, H. G. Pearce, J. Burrell, J. Patmore, G. Patmore, H. Oxley, J. Spencer, J. Beardmore.

VOLUNTEERS AND TERRITORIALS.

The following are the names of some of the officers, non-commissioned officers and men who joined subsequently :—

Captains : H. P. Fry†, R. H. Lyon*, Edwin Savill‡, H. H. Slade.*
Lieutenants :—Shepherd, C. H. Crawley, Champion Branfill Russell, —. Rowley, J. A. McMullen, Arnold B. Beddow, H. H. Hartland, S. W. Williams§.

*Afterwards Major and Lt.-Colonel.
†Captain Henry P. Fry, a son of Mr. Joseph Fry, of Fairkytes, and grandson of the great prison reformer, Elizabeth Fry, had, when he died in December, 1881, been connected with the Volunteer movement for 21 years, for eleven of which he was Captain of the Hornchurch Company. After his death Lieut. R. H. Lyon commanded the Company, and was gazetted Captain 1884.
‖Afterwards Sergeant.
¶Afterwards Q.M.S.
§Afterwards Captain.
‡Afterwards Major.

PIONEERS OF THE 15TH ESSEX RIFLE VOLUNTEERS.

Surgeon : —. Mac Caldin.
Surgeon-Major : Jordison.
Surgeon : Captain Oakley.
Sergeants Instructors : W. Compton, —. Cramp, —. Carroll, —. Dickens, W. Baker, Jas. Young, J. Land.
Sergeants : W. Compton, W. Hook, —. Beckett, T. Howard, G. Howard, Jas. Pearce, C. H. Baker, Senr., Walter Halestrap, F. Fry, W. Tyrrell, J. Dockrill, H. J. Bright, A. G. Sibthorp, H. Hunwicks, G. W. Franklyn, George Collin, C. H. Baker, Junr.
Corporals : Thos. Pearce, F. Playle, A. Halestrap, G. Newman, H. Alexander.
Bandmasters : A. Kingsnorth, —. Foster, M. Larter, W. Reed.
Privates : W. Fry, F. W. Fry, —. Elliston, S. Burrell, G. Hampshire, T. Smith, B. Stone, H. Tyrrell, W. Aldous, P. Smith, H. Alabaster, James Sewell, Albert Collin, A. Gower, G. Adams, Charles Hill, John Pearman, Edward Pearman, F. Franklyn, T. G. Frost, W. G. Frost, Robert Baker, J. Chester, F. J. W. Chester, H. Chester, G. Barlow, C. Barlow, H. Wright, H. Halestrap.

This Company attended many of the great reviews held in the early days of the establishment of the National Rifle Association, which at that time were important and imposing military spectacles. They were present at the great Brighton Review, before the Prince of Wales on April 2, 1866, and at the Grand Review on June 20, 1868, in Windsor Great Park, when Queen Victoria reviewed 28,000 Volunteers. They also attended the Royal Jubilee Review at Aldershot on July 9, 1887, when 60,000 Regulars and Volunteers passed before Her Majesty the Queen. On that occasion *Field Marshal Sir Evelyn Wood, V.C., rode at the head of the Essex Volunteers. They likewise formed part of the Guard of Honour in Hyde Park on March 7, 1863, on the arrival in London of Princess Alexandra of Denmark for her marriage with the Prince of Wales, and later performed a similar service at Chingford on May 6, 1882, when Queen Victoria opened Epping Forest free to the public. At that ceremony 63 non-coms. and men of the Company paraded under Lieut. R. H. Lyon.

The Company became in 1882 part of the 5th Battalion Essex Regiment and in course of time was designated H. Company of the 1st Volunteer Battalion Essex Regiment. When the South African War broke out, practically the whole of the Company volunteered for active service, but only seven of their number were accepted, viz. :—Sergeant Walter Halestrap, Corporal H. Alexander, and Privates F. J. W. Chester, H. Chester, J. Cole, H. Halestrap, and T. Tarling. These men were accepted for active service in February, 1900, and joined the 1st Essex Regiment at Bloemfontein, forming part of Lord Roberts's Army marching on Pretoria. After their term of service all of them returned safely, with the exception of F. J. W. Chester, who died in Pretoria on 4 July, 1900.

*Field Marshal Sir Evelyn Wood, V.C., resided at Upminster Hall.

8

VOLUNTEERS FOR THE SOUTH AFRICAN WAR
(1ST VOLUNTEER BATTALION ESSEX REGIMENT).

The following is a reproduction of the brass tablet in his memory, placed on the South wall of the parish church. This was unveiled on September 8, 1901, by Captain Savill, and dedicated by the Vicar, the Rev. Robert Johnson.

When the Volunteers were superseded by the Territorial Force in 1908, our local Company became part of the 4th Battalion Essex Regiment, and at the outbreak of the Great War the Company was called up for home service, under the command of Major H. H. Slade. Afterwards practically all the men volunteered for foreign service and served in Gallipoli, Egypt

THIS TABLET IS ERECTED BY HIS COMRADES
TO THE MEMORY OF
FREDERICK JOHN WILLIAM CHESTER
AGED 22
PRIVATE IN H COMPANY 1ST V.B. ESSEX REGT.,
WHO, HAVING VOLUNTEERED TO SERVE
HIS QUEEN AND COUNTRY IN SOUTH AFRICA,
DIED IN PRETORIA ON THE 4TH DAY OF JULY, 1900.

9

HORNCHURCH COMPANY, 4TH BATTALION ESSEX REGIMENT (TERRITORIALS).

and Palestine, as a unit of the 4th Essex Regiment. The Battalion sailed for the East on 22 July, 1915, and took part in the following engagements :—The landing at Suvla Bay, August, 1915, serving through the whole of the campaign and participating in the Evacuation of Gallipoli in November, 1915 ; the three Battles of Gaza ; in reserve at Ramleh, River Auga— known as the " Pimple Battle " ; capture of Wilhelma, Mulabbis, and Kafr Kasm, and the advance on Beyrouth (Beirut). Many of the original members of the Hornchurch Company also served with other regiments and in other theatres of war.

HORNCHURCH COMPANY TERRITORIALS DIGGING TRENCHES.

The following are the names of the officers, non-commissioned officers, and men who were called up for service in August, 1914, and moved to their coast defence station at Felixstowe :—

Major H. H. Slade*.

Lieut. S. W. Williams†.

Colour Sergeant : Howard, C. J. *Sergeant Instructor* : Land, H. J. *Sergeants :·* Bright, H. J. ; Earle, W. ; Franklyn, G. W. ; Hunwicks, H. A. ; Paul, ·H. *Lance-Sergeant* : Baker, C. H. *Corporals* : Collin, A. G. ; Earl, L. W. ; Ward, B. F. ; Newman, C. ; Wicks, R. S. *Lance-Corporals* : Bush, H. B. ; Everson, E. G. ;

*Major Slade was gazetted Temporary Lieut.-Colonel, Decr. 29, 1915, and gazetted Substantive Lieut.-Colonel, June, 1916.

†Lieut. Williams, later transferred to the Royal Air Force and served in France in the 46th Squadron with the rank of Captain.

Gower, W. C. ; Monk, A. E. ; Stamp, W. R.   *Bandsman* : Barlow,
C. H.   *Drummer* : Bond, C. E.   *Privates* : Abrams, W. ; Barlow,
W. ; Brockhurst, J. ; Burrell, A. T. ; Blows, W. C. ; Banks, C. ;
Bright, F. T. ; Coulson, C. ; Coulson, P. E. ; Clarke, E. ; Clark, H. ;
Cook, E. ; Cook, C. ; Claxton, A. B. ; Cosby, S. ; Dunk, E. H. ;
Dare, R. ; Dunk, R. A. ; Dawson, A. ; Ellis, A. ; Franklyn, H. A. ;
Francis, F. M. ; Franklyn, J. G. ; Frost, T. G. ; Guy, W. ; Gentry,
A. W. ; Grey, W. H. ; Garrett, E. ; Hill, E. E. ; Hurrell, G. ;
Hutson, A. R. ; Hutson, D. J. ; Hardy, S. E. ; Hardy, C. F. ; Hills,
H. ; Harris, J. ; Knight, B. ; Kemp, F. J. ; Livermore, P. ; Lake,
B. ; London, J. ; London, W. H. ; Lovell, W. ; Lowe, L. ; Martin,
F. ; Minns, W. ; Mills, T. H. ; Newman, G. G. ; North, G. ; Newman,
C. ; Ollington, H. H. ; Oldham, J. W. ; Pemberton, R. ; Parish,
W. A. ; Pridgeon, H. ; Perry, A. T. ; Pomfrett, W. A. ; Purkis,
C. W. ; Rogers, G. ; Stebbing, W. ; Smith, C. G. ; Says, L. A. ;
Tucker, E. ; Talbot, F. ; Tibble. H. G. ; Tyler, R. G. ; Thompson
A. J. ; Tickner, W. ; Wall, A. H. ; Wall, H. ; Wall, S. ; Wood, J. ;
Woods, H. ; Ward. G. J. ; Wellington, D. S. ; Whatling, J. S. ;
Warman, W. A. ; Westgate, L.   *Boys* : Eady, H. ; Huxtable, C. W. ;
Steadman, F. R.

NO. 9 BATTERY FIRST ESSEX ARTILLERY
VOLUNTEERS.

In addition to the Rifle Corps, Hornchurch, in the year 1882,
supplied a Battery (No. 9) to the First Essex Artillery Volunteers.   This Battery was raised by Mr. Henry Holmes,*
who was appointed its first Captain, his Lieutenants being :—

Lieut. Henry Holmes, Junr.,‡ and Lieut. Cliff Gooch.

Among the first Non-Coms. and Men were :—

Sergeant-Major Flower, Q.M.S. F. A. Stratford,† and Sergeants
John Ferguson, G. Sibthorp, J. Bourne and R. W. Derbyshire,
and Sergeant Instructor T. Betts.

The following were Officers, Non-Coms. and Men of a later
date :—

Captain : S. Conron.
Lieutenants :—A. A. Holmes*, Cecil Holmes, Stanley Holmes,
H. E. Ingle.
Sergeant-Major Instructor :—Wilson.
Sergeant-Major .-- Bruce.
Sergeants :—E. G. Bratchell, T. Brutey, G. Crane, F. Le Gassick,
— Eales, A. R. Thorogood.
Corporals :—H. Barker, C. Stillman, T. Goldie, W. Smith.
Gunners :—W. Boyle, A. T. Boyle, W. Reed, — Wheeler,
—. Jenvey, F. Halls, —. Wells, —. Bonnett, —. Kemp, —. Bower-
man, H. J. Harris, C. W. Frost.

No. 9 Battery, in conjunction with No. 8 Battery (Romford),
won several valuable trophies at the various meetings of the
National Artillery Association.   In August, 1895, at Shoebury-

*Afterwards Major and Lieut.-Colonel.
‡Afterwards Captain.
†Afterwards Sergeant-Major.

NON-COMMISSIONED OFFICERS FIRST ESSEX ARTILLERY VOLUNTEERS,
circa. 1890.

ness, under the command of Captain A. A. Holmes, they not only carried off the Queen's Prize for the third time, but also secured the Lords and Commons Prize, and the City and Corporation of London Challenge Cup.

The Battery was at one time 100 strong, and the present Drill Hall in the High Street was built for their accommodation. It was presented by Major Henry Holmes, and was formally opened on the 21st November, 1892. It was then called the Artillery Hall, and had originally a gravelled floor. It is 85 feet long by 45 feet wide.

The Battery attended camp every year, and at the Whitsuntide Camp at Harwich, in 1893, provided one officer—Captain S. Conron, and 56 non-coms. and men ; and in June, 1895, two officers and 50 non-coms. and men attended the Shoeburyness Camp.

The Battery was disbanded in 1898.

THE NATIONAL RESERVE.

" Like an honest man and a soldier."
Shakespeare :—Much Ado about Nothing, II, iii.

Some few years before the war many eminent soldiers viewed with certain misgivings the steady growth of the armed forces on the Continent, and, fearing that we might one day be called upon to take up arms in defence of our Country, those public spirited men—prominent amongst whom was the late Field Marshal Earl Roberts—did everything in their power to bring the Country to a sense of its danger, and to encourage military exercises amongst the civilian population.

One branch of the general idea dealt with the large number of men in this country who had passed through the Navy, Army, or Auxiliary Forces, and having completed their period of service, were entirely lost, so far as any use was made of their military service and experience.

It was eventually decided to form a National Reserve, to be a purely voluntary institution and to embrace in its ranks men who had creditably completed their period of training in any branch of the Service. In less than twelve months from its inception 170,000 men were enrolled.

In the year 1912, Major H. H. Slade, then in Command of the Hornchurch Company, 4th Battalion Territorial Essex Regiment, invited all ex-Service men to a meeting at the White Hart Hotel, with the object of forming a local branch of the National Reserve. About 30 attended the meeting, all of whom expressed their willingness to join the movement. Sergeant Boast was elected Secretary, and was authorized to take command until a commissioned officer could be appointed. Messrs. Haines, James, Shaw, Taylor, and Westley rendered valuable service in the formation of the Company, which made substantial progress, and very soon over 100 men were enrolled. Major J. M. Ewing was then asked to take command, and four section commanders were appointed, viz. :—Colour Sergeant Taylor, and Sergeants Bratchell, Sibthorp, and Shaw.

Many Hornchurch residents will recollect a particular Sunday morning when the various Territorial and other units paraded outside the Parish Church, and were inspected by Edward Murray Ind, Esq., Deputy Lieutenant of the County ; and will also recollect the splendid parade on that occasion of the Hornchurch Company of the National Reserve. In point of numbers they outdid all the other units, there being present one officer, one warrant officer, and 150 N.C.O.'s. and men.

The movement spread, and during 1914 a new Commandant, Major Watkins, was appointed to the Company when Major Ewing retired.

Before very much could be done under the new auspices, and just as the movement was gaining strength and becoming well organized, the war broke out, and such members of the Company who were of military age, and those who could under-take special service, were speedily called to the colours.

THE CHURCH LADS' BRIGADE AND CADETS.

" He must be taught and trained, and
bid go forth."
Shakespeare :—Julius Cæsar, IV, i.

The Hornchurch Company of the Church Lads' Brigade was formed in September, 1903. At the suggestion of Mr. J. M. Ewing, the Rev. Herbert Dale, Vicar, called together a Committee, with the object of establishing a Company for the bene-fit of village lads between the ages of 13 and 19, providing them with a Club of their own, something to interest them in their leisure time on weekdays, and Bible Classes for their religious instruction on Sundays.

The Committee, when formed, consisted of the Rev. Herbert Dale, Messrs. C. Aller, F. H. Barnes, C. H. Baker, J. Breckels, J. Bridges, W. Dendy, T. Donald, C. H. Deering, J. M. Ewing, W. Halestrap, and W. E. Langridge.

The following were the first officers of the Company :—
Captain :—J. M. Ewing. *Chaplain :*—Rev. Herbert Dale. *Lieutenants :*—J. Breckels, C. H. Deering, Percy A. Dunlop and W. E. Langridge. *Staff Sergeant-Major* :—Walter Hale-strap.* *Bandmaster :*—Charles T. Perfect.

The Company, which was attached to the 4th Battalion, St. Alban's Regiment, was equipped with forage cap, belt, haver-sack, and carbine, and was formally inaugurated at the Drill

*Afterwards Lieut.

Photo]   [E. E. Carter, Romford.

HORNCHURCH AND UPMINSTER COMPANIES, CHURCH LADS' BRIGADE, 1904.

Hall, Hornchurch, on Saturday afternoon, September 30, 1903, by the Rev. W. A. Spooner, D.D., Warden of New College, Oxford.

The objects of the Brigade are to train its members in the first principles of military exercises, to inculcate in them the spirit of upright and God-fearing Churchmen, and generally to help them to realise the importance of the Brigade's three excellent maxims, viz :—

1. We being many are one body.
2. What costs nothing is worth nothing.
3. Quality is better than quantity.

The Company was successful from its initiation, winning. in succession, nearly every Battalion trophy for efficiency in military exercises, shooting, sports, etc. It gave the lead to surrounding parishes, and established sections therein, which afterwards became independent Companies, viz :—Upminster, Romford, Dagenham, Rainham and Harold Wood. The photograph here reproduced was taken in 1904, and represents the Hornchurch and Upminster Companies.

In 1908 Captain Ewing resigned the command of the Company, on his appointment as Battalion Major, and Lieutenant J. Breckels was appointed Captain of the Company ; he, at a later date, was succeeded by Captain the Rev. A. C. Kibble, who was followed by Captain Stuart K. Barnes. The Regimental Sergeant-Major during this period was Benjamin L. Bishop, a veteran of the 92nd Gordon Highlanders.

In September, 1911, the local C.L.B. Battalion became a recognised unit of the Territorial Force as an Essex County Cadet Battalion. It was designated the 2nd Chelmsford Cadet Battalion, and the Commandant, Major J. M. Ewing, was appointed Major in the County Territorial Cadet Force, and later, in 1918, was promoted to the rank of Lieut.-Colonel.

After the battalion had become a recognised unit of the Territorial Force, it was inspected every year by a Regular Officer, deputed by the War Office, and on every occasion when this inspection took place, the battalion was complimented on its efficiency. In all official reports, regarding discipline, training and efficiency, it was referred to as " excellent."

In June, 1914, the old C.L.B. equipment was discarded, and the battalion was equipped with the infantry khaki service dress. Early in 1917 it was affiliated to the King's Royal Rifle Corps, and now wears the uniform of that Corps.

At the outbreak of the great war, practically all the members of the Company of military age joined H.M. Forces. Many of them have given their lives in the great struggle, amongst them being the last Captain of the Company, Stuart K. Barnes, who was killed in action on the Western Front while serving with the 2nd Battalion of the London Scottish Regiment, on the 14th July, 1916, and Percy Alexander Dunlop, of the same regiment, who died at Salonica on October 28, 1918. The following is a list, as far as can be ascertained, of the past and present members of the Company who served in the great war, viz. :—

LIST OF C.L.B. WHO SERVED IN H.M. FORCES DURING THE WAR.

Barnes, Stuart, K.* ; Burrell, A. ; Barlow, Walter ; Blanks, W. ; Bishop, A. E. ; Broad, J. ; Boyle, L. ; Bowick, W. ; Brockhurst, S.* ; Burgess, James ; Crowe, E. J. ; Chambers, L. ; Coulson,

Photo]   [Bursall Tonge.
ROUTE MARCH, CHURCH LADS' BRIGADE.

Percy ; Collin, Sidney ; Cressey, Walter* ; Cox, Harold (Canadian Army) ; Davis, Oscar ; Davis, C. H. ; Dare, Reginald ; Deere, F. P. ; Dunlop, Percy A.* ; Dunlop, Denis ; Earle, Sidney ; Ellis, —. ; Franklyn, Alfred ; Franklyn, George ; Franklyn, Sidney ; Franklyn, William ; Gaywood, John E.* ; Goddard, Fred ; Gower, W. ; Hawkins, James Reuben* ; Hardy, —. ; Holdway, W. ; Howell, J. ; Hutson, A. ; Hutson, David ; Hutson, J. ; Humphrey, H. ; Hammond, John Dane* ; Hammond, William George* ; Hills,

*These died for their country.

18

Harry ; Hills, James ; Jensen, C. ; Johnson, Frank ; Kibble, Rev.
A. C. ; Luther, Harold G. ; Luther, Edward A. ; Lowe, S. ; Lam-
port, T. ; Mather, A. A. ; Mortlock, H. ; Nicholls, E. W.* ; Oliver,
Phillip R. J. ; Oliver, George William ; Parish, W. ; Potter, A. ;
Phillips, Major ; Phillips, Barry ; Paveley, Ernest ; Pearman,
Percy ; Rigalls, —. ; Rigalls, —. ; Seccombe, Horace ; South,
Douglas ; Saunders, William ; Saunders, Ernest ; Talbot, Arthur ;
Taylor, Harold Allfrey* ; Turvey, George ; Tyler, Edward ; Tyler,
John ; Tyler, V. ; Tyler, George ; Tyrrell, Harry ; Tyrrell, Louis ;
Unwin, Frank ; Unwin, Herbert ; Wall, E. ; Wall, S. ; Wallace,
W. ; Wells, F. ; Wells, T. ; Wells, W. ; White, D. ; Wood, —.

Mr. Alfred Nunn served as Captain, 5th London Cadet Batt.;
L.D., C.L.B., Head Quarters, St. Anne's Church, Limehouse, from
October, 1915.

N.B :—At the annual meeting of the governing body of the
C.L.B. in 1918, Field Marshal Lord Grenfell, Governor and Commandant, presiding, it was stated that about 250,000 members
and ex-members were serving with the Colours. Among the
honours won by them were :—13 V.C's., One G.C.B., 4 C.M.G's.,
12 D.S.O.s., 72 M.C's., 199 Military Medals. (Vide " Daily
Mail " Year Book, 1919, page 122.)

HORNCHURCH COMPANIES 3RD AND 6TH
ROMFORD BOY SCOUTS.

In the early part of the war the 3rd Romford Troop of Baden
Powell Boy Scouts had a Hornchurch Section attached to it,
of which Section Assistant Scout Master William T. S. Jenkinson
was in charge. In March, 1916, Mr. Jenkinson left for Letch-
worth, where for some time he was employed in munition work,
at a later date joining the R.A.M.C. An endeavour which was
being made to form a new Troop for Hornchurch had to be
abandoned owing to Mr. Jenkinson's departure.

In October, 1917, a new Troop, the 6th Romford, was formed,
to which the Hornchurch Section was attached. This, for a
time, made good progress, but afterwards dwindled so considerably that by the following March there only remained 2 Patrol
Leaders, 2 Seconds and 1 Scout. About that time a New
Zealander, Mr. C. E. Hazell, of Grey Towers Convalescent Camp
(who had been a Scout Master in his own country), heard of the
position and took the Troop in hand. In a few weeks the roll
numbered about 40 boys, and a period of useful activity set in.
Camps were formed, discipline enforced, and hard work rendered
by the Scouts generally, while Scouting games were encouraged.
In the following September Scout Master Hazell went back to
New Zealand as " permanently unfit " for war service, much to
the regret of the whole Troop, as it was realized that had it

*These died for their country.

not been for his services the 6th Romford Troop would not have survived.

Shortly after the departure of Mr. Hazell he was succeeded by Mr. E. Aspinall, from the O.T.C. Camp at Gidea Park, and during the period of his command many badges were presented, and several Patrol Leaders' Conferences took place, the Troop being well maintained. Early in January he left for his home in Liverpool, when another New Zealander from Grey Towers, Mr. C. Wood, became Scout Master, and carried on the good work until May, when, on his resignation, Troop Leader B. Hards was promoted to Assistant Scout Master.

While the 1st Sportsman's Battalion was in training at Grey Towers, and also during the period the New Zealanders were in occupation of that Camp, the boys of these two Hornchurch Sections acted as orderlies and messengers there, particularly in connection with the Camp Post Office. In the New Zealanders' period they also assisted in the work of basket-making, and in many other ways showed their usefulness. Their work was highly appreciated by the officers in command of those units, and they were thanked for their services, and presented with badges for the various periods.

In July, 1918, the Troop did useful work in connection with the Sports held in the grounds of Great Nelmes Mansion for the benefit of St. Dunstan's Hostel, and for this they were presented with a shield.

The following are the names of the members of Hornchurch Section 3rd Troop, as far as can be ascertained, and of those members of the 6th Troop, who served at Grey Towers Camp.

3RD ROMFORD TROOP :—

Patrol Leader : D. Mac Dermott. *Scouts* : B. Fox, B. Schmidt, D. Puddy, S. Edwards, J. Broom, A. Reeves, E. Button, R. Williams, F. Dean, B. Martin, F. Vigis, D. Mason, Albert H. L. Taylor, P. Maidment, C. Dunlop, B. Harper.

6TH ROMFORD TROOP :—

Patrol Leaders : B. Watling and D. Mason. *Second* : F. Wilkinson. *Scouts ;* B. Field, S. Harper, E. Williams, J. Maylor, R. Walker.

WAR-TIME ORGANIZATIONS.

ROMFORD AND DISTRICT DETACHMENT OF THE ESSEX VOLUNTEER REGIMENT.

"I serve here voluntary."*
"By these badges understand the King."†

THE VETERAN'S CHANCE.

Reprinted from " The Volunteer Training Corps Gazette,‡ and Dedicated to the Romford and District Detachment of the Essex Volunteer Regiment (V.T.C.)
By CHARLES THOMAS PERFECT.

I stood at the kerb on a winter's day,
  Watching the soldiers marching away,
And after they'd passed a'down the street,
  I found my heart had a faster beat.

For, where is the man whose soul is right,
  Who is lacking the heart to be in the fight,
To march in the ranks, and to take his stand,
  For the love of his King and the Motherland?

Then I thought of the wife, and the kids, and my job,
  And myself—and my weekly fifty bob;
And I thought of the " Tommy's " pay, and then—
  I thought of my age—two score and ten.

And I knew too well, though the game was fine,
  That a soldier's life was none of mine;
But I turned away with my head erect,
  And a martial step—'twas a neat effect!

At that moment a poster caught my eye,
  Which showed me the way, and the reason why,
I might answer " *The Call* " and some service see,
  By joining the ranks of the " V.T.C."

I saw in a trice I had got my chance,
  And though I never might serve in France,
I could stay at home and do my bit,
  And release a man who is better fit.

For while he is fighting, away at the front,
  Taking his part in the battle's brunt,
I could carry on, and learn squad drill,
  And shoulder a gun, and his number fill.

*Troilus and Cressida, II., i.
†Love's Labour Lost, V., ii.
‡This also appeared, by request, in " On Guard " (Brighton), and the Leicestershire and Rutland Volunteer and Cadet Corps' Gazette.

That's why I'm wearing this uniform,
  That's why I'm learning to do " right form,"
And the time I put in, is done, by the way,
  After the burden and heat of the day.

I'm allowed to pay for my rifle and kit*,
  And my ex'es too, just to show my grit ;
While the War Office *gives* me all it can ;
  " *Advice—on becoming a soldierman.*"

And that is the work which the Volunteer,
  Is doing for all he holds most dear,
It's a veteran's job, but part of the plan
  Which will hasten the end which " The Day " began.

In 1914/15, Volunteer Training Corps were formed all over
the Kingdom.   Towards the end of 1914 some of the residents
of Gidea Park convened a meeting with the object of forming a
Corps for men over military age, and for those who were, or might
become, ineligible for active war service by reason of physical
disability, but who would be quite capable of doing something
useful in case of necessity.   At that meeting it was decided to
call a public meeting at the Artillery Hall, Hornchurch Road,
Romford, and a notice to that effect was published in the local
press by Mr. W. H. Brand, who accepted (pro.-tem.) the position
of Hon. Secretary in connection with the movement.   The public
meeting was accordingly held, about 50 inhabitants, who were
above military age, attending.   Mr. Brand, in explaining the
aims and objects of the Corps, said that, in the event of a hostile
invasion, the only persons allowed to offer armed resistance
were members of the Regular Army, Territorial Force, and
Volunteer Training Corps affiliated to the Central Association.
Other members of the community, who had done nothing to
fit themselves to meet the crisis, would have no opportunity
of striking a blow for their country.   Those joining a Volunteer
Training Corps would receive proper military training in drill
and discipline, so that, should the occasion arise, they would
fight as trained men shoulder to shoulder with his Majesty's
Forces.   The project was favourably received, and the Romford
and District Volunteer Training Corps was duly initiated.   Mr.
W. E. Langridge and Mr. W. T. McGill were the only Hornchurch
representatives at the meeting, but when the Corps was formed
the residents of Hornchurch came forward in large numbers and
formed a most creditable platoon, and took a keen and intelli-
gent interest in their drill and training.

Although the original objects of the Corps were as stated above,
an order was made very early in the history of the V.T.C.
permitting lads under military age to join for preliminary train-

*At a later date uniforms and kits were provided.

Photo]   [W. F. Wright & Sons, Forest Gate.

ROMFORD AND DISTRICT DETACHMENT ESSEX VOLUNTEER REGIMENT.

ing, so that when they arrived at military age they would be, in some measure, trained men. A large amount of very useful ground work was done in this way by the various Corps throughout the country.

The first instruction given to the Company was undertaken by a non-commissioned officer of the Essex Artillery, and afterwards by Mr. S.W. Lewis, of Gidea Park,who had had considerable experience of military drill in the Territorial Force. He eventually became the first officer commanding the Romford Company.

The progress towards efficiency was swift, and as the members increased it was found necessary to form the Company into four platoons, and to appoint Platoon Commanders, of which four were necessary, and also to appoint a Platoon Sergeant, and N.C.O's. to command the four sections in each platoon. Mr. W. T. Mc Gill was appointed Platoon Commander for the Hornchurch Platoon, the section commanders being Messrs. Langridge, Goodbody, James, and Tyler, with Mr. Horsham as Platoon Sergeant. At a later date, owing to the conditions of the Military Act compelling certain of the younger men to resign, the question of N.C.O's had to be revised, and Dr. E. E. Goodbody was appointed Platoon Sergeant in place of Mr. Horsham.

After the Company had been in existence for some few months, a strong Upminster platoon was formed, which added greatly to its efficiency. Mr. W. T. McGill undertook its initial training and for a short time it was under his command, as well as the Hornchurch Platoon. Mr. S. C. Norton was then appointed Platoon Commander, and acted in that capacity until he joined up for active service with H.M. Forces. In addition to the ordinary routine drill, Mr. Norton gave lectures on musketry, and the efficiency of the platoon was very marked during his period of command. Sergeant W. A. Packer succeeded him as Platoon Commander.

Company and Recruit drills took place in the Artillery Drill Hall on week nights, and on Sunday mornings in a field near the Golf Course, Gidea Park, and were very well attended. As the efficiency of the Company progressed, so the advanced movements, as set forth in the drill book, had to be undertaken, and for the purpose of teaching the members extended order drill and field movements, permission was obtained from Mrs. McIntosh to use her grounds at Havering, including a large barn and paddock adjoining. These proved to be admirable for the purpose, and during the summer months full advantage was taken of Mrs. McIntosh's hospitality, the Company holding many field days and instructive parades at Havering.

A bugle band was formed and a full set of band instruments was kindly lent to the Company by the Officers of the Hornchurch Company Church Lads' Cadets. Mr. C. T. Perfect was appointed

Bandmaster, and with the assistance of Mr. C. H. Hollinghurst, Sergeant Drummer, and Mr. Sidney A. Hawkins, Sergeant Bugler, the Band, after a few weeks' practice, was able to lead the Company on march.

In 1915 the whole of the Volunteer Forces in the country were taken over by the War Office, and were attached to the Territorial Force. This necessitated more or less re-organization. The members of the old V.T.C. were asked to sign an under-taking to serve in the new Volunteer Force for the period of the war, and, with the exception of a few of the older members, nearly all of them accepted the obligation. The Company was reformed and attached to the 2nd Battalion for a period, and afterwards to the 3rd Battalion Essex Volunteer Regiment. The officers who received the King's Commission were C. H. Allen, C. L. Brabant, W. A. Packer and P. M. Gunn.

Dr. Storrs Brookfield, J.P., Upminster, was appointed Medical Officer to the Company and himself medically examined all the men who presented themselves for enrolment under the new conditions.

Serious training, both for officers and other ranks, continued, which included special courses on musketry, machine gun, bombing, &c., at various staff training centres. Sergeant W. A. Burrows (Upminster) and Corporal W. Strange (Romford) passed the examination test at Wellington Barracks, Knights-bridge, for Lewis Gun Instructors, and at a later date Sergeant Burrows qualified under the Hythe Travelling School of Mus-ketry, and was appointed Musketry Instructor.

During 1916, 1917 and 1918 Sections from Hornchurch and Upminster assisted the Romford Sections in manning local searchlight and Lewis Gun Stations. On many nights practically all the men were on duty, in turn, at one or other of the stations. This service helped to release many men of the Regular Army for service overseas. For six months the Upminster Section manned entirely the Upminster Common searchlight station, a Sergeant or a Corporal and five men being on duty every night. This Section also took turn with the Romford Section in man-ning the Lewis Gun at Chadwell Heath. The Upminster N.C.O.'s. in this service were Sergeants W. A. Burrows and M. Rayment, and Corporals Phillips, Robbins and Blaver.

During August of each year a number of men attended the Camp at Tadworth for a week or fortnight's training under war conditions, and participated in various field operations against the Guards, who were in the same Camp.

About 120 men were transferred to the Regular Army during the war period. The strength of the Company varied from 90 to 150 of all ranks, the number of new recruits often falling short of the men joining the fighting forces from time to time.

In 1917 the Company attended at Chelmsford for inspection by H.R.H. the Duke of Connaught.

In 1918 the various Battalions of Volunteers were once more re-organized, resulting in the formation of fewer, but stronger Battalions. Consequently, the Company, which had been known as No. 6 Company, 3rd V.B. Essex Regiment, was joined to the Grays Company, which had been No. 7 Company, and the whole then formed the new D. Company, 3rd V.B. Essex Regiment, under the command of Captain C. H. Allen, who was assisted by officers from Romford, Upminster and Grays.

The Upminster Section, in addition to their military activities, formed themselves into a War Charities Committee, properly accredited under the War Charities Act, and in their first effort raised the sum of £125 for a Y.M.C.A. Rest Hut, which was erected on the Western Front, and named the " Upminster Hut." They also raised further sums for various Charities.

Messrs. W. H. Brand, C. H. Balmain, and W. M. Tanfield acted successively as Hon. Secretary to the Company.

The Company was demobilized in November, 1919, and all ranks received a certificate signed on behalf of the King, thanking them for services rendered.

N.B.—Apart from duties of a strictly military character, the V.T.C's. were variously employed in a semi-military and civil capacity. The Daily Mail of May 17, 1916, in an article commenting on the tardy recognition which had been recently accorded the Corps by the Government, and urging a proper and efficient official administration of it, mentioned these activities as follows :—

" Men all over the country, millionaires and labourers alike, have been drilling and route marching since 1914. They have dug trenches, met returning soldiers at Stations and convoyed them, done patrol duties, guarded ammunition factories, and loaded ammunition and military stores into trains. The National Motor Volunteers have provided their own ambulances, met and evacuated trains of wounded, and taken them to hospital. The London Volunteer Rifles have done splendid work as auxiliaries to the London Fire Brigade ; have taken all-night watches at the Fire Stations, have assisted at practically every big fire for a year past, and 600 of them are now qualified firemen. . . . A great percentage of the Corps are fine shots, 400 of their officers have passed theoretical military examinations, and 600 have obtained certificates for drill and field exercises."

MEMBERS OF THE HORNCHURCH PLATOON.

Ashford, Edwin H.* ; Beck, J. T. ; Burden, T. ; Beharell, C T. ; Bridges, C.* ; Bloom, Alfred J. G. ; Brutey, Claude E. ; Bowick, W. A. R.* ; Cogar, William E. ; Cox, C. ; Cooper, A. E. ;

*Went on Active Service.

Catherwood, T. W. ; Cook ; Dale, A. L.* ; Davis ; Dixon, E.* ;
Daniels, Edward Ernest (C.Q.M.S.) ; Dyer, E.* ; Field, Harry V.* ;
Fox, Walter, Foster, Forrester, J. C. ; German, A. E.* ; Goodbody,
Dr. Edmund Ernest ; Goodman, Gregg G. ; Hawkins, Sidney A. ;
Hawkins, Junr. ; Haywood, George Jas. ; Holgate, Harry ; Holling-
hurst, Chas. H. ; Horsham, James E. ; Jackson, B. J.* ; Jarvis, Frank ;
Jones, A. F. ; Jenkinson, W.* ; Lewis, —. ; Langridge, W. E. ;
McGill, W. T. ; Moss, Thos W.*† ; Maidment, George*† ; Oldman,
R. E.* ; Pattison, Percy ; Perfect, Chas. T. ; Ridley, W. G. ; Stoner,
W. B.* ; Storey, —. ; Taplin, J. M. ; Tiddeman, E. S. ; Vigis, —. ;
Wilson, —. ; Wilkinson, E. G.* ; Wright, F. ; Willford, Neville.

MEMBERS OF THE UPMINSTER PLATOON.

Platoon Commanders : S. C. Norton and W. A. Packer.
Medical Officer : Dr. J. Storrs Brookfield.
Rev. H. H. Holden.*
Sergts. : W. A. Burrows and M. Rayment ; *Corpls.* : E. Price,
W. J. Phillips, —. Robbins.
Privates : Ashby, R. Barrett, S. Blaver, Busby, Blackaller,
Briebach, Cant, H. Coe, Champion Russell, * Cresswell, Calvert,
H. E. Cobb, W. J. Derby, *Dear, Furby, Forbes, *Goodwin, Gran-
tham, Gray, Hill, R. Hockley, *R. Humphreys, H. Hagger, W.
Johnson, C. W. Jupp, W. J. Key, Lee, †*Marshall, *A. F. Mawditt,
*Morgan, *McFarlane, *Platt, Poulter, G. F. Prince, Powditch,
†* Reeves, Roome, Rooke, L. Sorrell, Stern, F. C. Sheppey, *C.
Sumpner, Stone, Sharp, Sheidow, R. Thain, W. Tanfield, Turnell,
Tyler, *J. Wise, *L. Warnes, Yarwood, J. W. Young.

V.T.C.

The following is a list of parishioners who joined Corps other
than the Hornchurch Platoon, Romford and District Detachment :—

Banks-Martin, Robert, Captain Essex Motor Volunteer Corps,
    East Ham Squadron.
Flucker, Thos., Sergeant, Romford Platoon, 1915-1919.
Greatorex, G. T., Private 6th City of London National Guard,
    from Feb. 2/16.
Hewitson, Joseph, Major O.C. Bermondsey V.T.C., Nov./14-
    Oct/.16, O.C. 2/11 Batt., C.L.V.R. 1916/1919. Hon. Sec.
    National Relief Fund, Dulwich Division. Joint Hon. Sec.
    Recruiting Committee, Dulwich Division. Official of Min-
    istry of Food at Southend, October, 1917/1920.
Izod, Walter Henry, Sergeant London Volunteer Rifles, Sept./14-
    Jan./17. Served with the London Fire Brigade as Military
    Fireman.
Parker, Charles Leonard, Sergeant-Instructor in Machine Gunnery
    4th Batt. City of London V.R. (National Guard), 1914/1919.
    Served as Sergeant in Charge Anti-aircraft Station, London.
Sayer, George L., Private V.T.C., Essex Regiment. Served in
    Anti-aircraft Defence, 1914/1919.

*Went on Active Service.
†Killed in Action.

Stokes, Alfred Ernest, Sergeant City of London National Guard,
   1914/1919.
Waller, Henry John, Private London Volunteer Rifles, 1914/1918.
   Served in the London Fire Brigade Section.

4th CADET BATTALION ESSEX REGIMENT.

" Let all the ends thou aim'st at be thy country's."
Shakespeare ;—Henry VIII., iii., ii.

Towards the latter part of the year 1915 the Essex Education
Committee formulated a scheme for raising Cadet Corps in connection with the old boys from Elementary Schools, and early
in 1916 a Battalion was formed for Romford and District,
attached to the Essex Regiment and bearing the title of the 4th
Cadet Battalion Essex Regiment. The Battalion was under
the command of Captain and Adjutant A. S. Maskelyne,
and was formed from the following schools :—Mawney Road,
Albert Road, London Road and St. Edward's Schools, Romford ;
Park Lane School and the Village School, Hornchurch ; Beacon-

Photo]   [*E. E. Carter, Romford.*

THE PRESENTATION OF THE COLOURS.

tree Heath School, Whalebone School, Chadwell Heath and Council School, Upminster.

The Committee and first officers were :—

COMMITTEE :

Mr. A. Porter, C.C., Mr. T. Gardner, J.P., C.C., Rev. G. M. Bell, M.A., Mr. W. J. Gay.

Hon. Sec. :—Mr. G. C. Eley, J.P.

Hon. Treasurer :—Mr. A. S. Maskelyne.

OFFICERS :

Honorary Major : J. M. Ewing. *Captain and Adjutant :* A. S. Maskelyne. *1st Lieut. :* G. C. Eley, *2nd Lieuts. :* J. Wackett and G. Barnes. *Battalion Sergeant-Major :* A. Saich. *Battalion Q.M. Sergeant :* H. C. Smith.

The Committee and officers, many of whom were Elementary Schoolmasters, were most enthusiastic in the work of enrolment of members, and before long the Battalion was up to full strength.

On Sunday morning, July 2, 1916, the Battalion, fully equipped and wearing the khaki uniform of the Essex Regiment, held its first Church Parade at Hornchurch Parish Church.

The company, numbering about 120, fell in at the Station Yard, Romford, and divided into four platoons.

The commanding officer (Major Ewing) marched the company away in column of route, headed by the Dagenham and Rainham Bugle Band, attached to the 2nd Chelmsford C.L.B. Cadets, which played the battalion to and from Hornchurch Church.

The preacher was the Rev. Herbert Dale, M.A., who based an eloquent sermon and a stirring appeal on the words of the Apostle St. John, " I write unto you, young men." The preacher welcomed the Romford Cadet Battalion, and pointed out that it was fitting that its first Church Parade should take place at Hornchurch Church, because that was the mother church of the ancient Royal Liberty, from which the Cadets present had been recruited.

At the conclusion of the service the battalion was lined up in the Mill Field and inspected by Mr. Thomas Gardner, J.P., C.C., Major Ewing, and Capt. Dillon.

Mr. Gardner addressed the battalion, and expressed his pleasure, and that of the Essex Education Committee, at the progress the Cadet Movement had made in the Romford district. He thanked Capt. Dillon for kindly bringing the band to assist in the morning's proceedings, and said that he and those associated with him in Cadet matters highly appreciated Major Ewing's kindness in placing his military experience at the disposal of the Romford Cadet Battalion. Mr. Gardner then congratulated Capt. A. S. Maskelyne and Lieut. G. C. Eley,

J.P., upon the fact that they had received commissions from the Lord-Lieutenant of the County, and presented commissions to Lieut. G. Barnes and Lieut. J. Wackett. He added that Mrs. Gardner had stated her intention to present regimental colours to the battalion.

Major Ewing called for three cheers for Mr. and Mrs. Gardner, and these were given with great heartiness.

On Saturday afternoon, 23 September, 1916, the ceremony of the presentation and consecration of the King's Colour, the gift of Mrs. T. Gardner, took place in the Great Eastern Railway Athletic Ground, adjoining Romford Station. The colour was consecrated by the Bishop of Barking, the Right Rev. Dr. Stevens, the presentation being made by Mrs. Gardner. The

Photo]   [*E. E. Carter, Romford.*
THE DEDICATION OF THE COLOURS.

parade was under the command of Major J. M. Ewing, and after the presentation the battalion was inspected by the County Cadet Committee.

The work of the battalion was very vigorous during the war period, and at the time of the Armistice—November, 1918—the officers were as follows :—

Honorary Colonel : The Right Hon. Lord. O'Hagan, *Commanding Officer* : Major A. S. Maskelyne. *Captains* : G. C. Eley, J. Wackett and G. Barnes. *Lieut.* : F. Edwards, and *2nd Lieut.* : R. J. Holloman.

The Hornchurch Company was commanded by Lieut. Edwards, assisted by 2nd Lieut. R. J. Holloman, with W. Earle as Regimental Sergeant Major and J. Douglas MacMillan as Company Sergeant Major. The activities of the Company have been varied. Successful field days were arranged, and an inspection was held annually. The Hornchurch lads carried off the highest percentage of prizes at the Battalion Sports, and are the first holders of the Battalion Musketry Shield presented for competition in 1918, the winning team being R. J. Holloman, W. Earle, J. D. MacMillan and —. Clause.

Evening Classes have been held in various educational subjects, including Military Geography, First Aid and Hygiene, and the Cadets met weekly in the Old Church Lads' Brigade Hall for physical drill and gymnastic exercises.

In connection with shooting practice, valuable assistance was rendered by the Hornchurch Minature Rifle Club, which opened the range to the boys, and Mr. C. L. Parker, the Hon. Sec. of the Club, attended practically every Thursday evening, during three seasons, to instruct the Cadets in the use of the rifle. Many shooting competitions were arranged, including :— The Bell Medal, the Daily Express Medal, S.M.R.C. Medal, Daily Mail Certificate, Daily Telegraph Certificate, and a S.M.R.C. Spoon was competed for every month.

The social side was not neglected, as the Cadets occasionally met for games at the Headquarters at Hornchurch Boys' School, and football matches were arranged and played.

The members who passed through the Hornchurch Company during the war period numbered 86, nineteen of whom joined H.M. Forces, one, S.W. Field, obtaining a Commission as Lieut. in the R.A.F., and one, Flight-Sergeant J. D. Bishop, lost his life whilst flying.

Mr. W. J. Gay, of Dagenham, and a few friends presented the battalion with a full set of brass instruments and drums, and a very efficient band was formed by Bandmaster Ridgewell.

The work of running the battalion was not light. Although recognised by the War Office, and affiliated to the County Territorial Association, no monetary grant was received from either source, and, with the exception of ten shillings, which each Cadet paid towards his uniform, all money had to be raised by the officers. This was done in various ways. Personal appeals were sent out to interested friends in the districts, house to house collections were made, annual flag days were held, and concerts and other entertainments were given for the benefit of the funds. About £700 was raised by the battalion in this way.

The following figures show the battalion's strength at various periods, viz :—31 December, 1916, 243 all ranks ; February, 12, 1918, 275 ; 1919, 185.

In October, 1919, on the resignation of Lieut. Edwards, Major A. F. G. Ruston was appointed to the command of the Company, with the following officers :—2nd Lieuts. R. J. Holloman, E. F. Dixon, and C. L. Parker.

A list of the Hornchurch Company, as far as can be ascertained, is appended.

CADETS.

Allestree, Aley, Alliston,* Anderson, Brazier,* Burrell,* Battson, Borrett, Button, J.L., Button, G. F., Bullock,ᵎ Brockhurst,* Boettjer,* Bishop, J. D.,*† Caldecourt,* Cooper,* Clause, Coker, Cook, Copin, Coulson, Cressey,* Cressey,* Daniels, Dawson, Dunlop, C., Dunlop, —., Dean,* Earle, Earle, Ellis, Emmerson,* Ferguson, Fitch, John, Field, L., Field, E., Field, C., Field, S. W.,* Gillings,* Goodwin, Gower, Grainger, Green, Howard, Halestrap, Hall, Harman,* Hutson, Holloman, Harper, Lungley, Lyons, Maclaren, MacMillan, Mackrow, Manning, Mayne, Medcalf, Medcalf, E., Mortlock, Mohring,* Miller,* Norman, Norris, Oliver, Potter,* Pailthorpe, Parrish, S., Parrish, A., Price, Powell, Saunders, Seach, Spencer, Stillman, Talbot, Tarling, Thorley, Tucker, Tyrrell,* Wall, Whiting, Willard, Wright.

WAR'S ALARMS.

" Now all the youth of England are on fire !
For who is he, whose chin is but enrich'd
With one appearing hair, that will not follow
Those cull'd and choice-drawn cavaliers to France ? "
Shakespeare—Henry V., ii. and iii., Chorus.

I have very vividly in mind the beautifully fine Trinity Sunday morning of June 7th, 1914, only a very few weeks before the outbreak of war, when the Territorials, under Major H. H. Slade, the National Reserve under Major J. M. Ewing, and the Church Lads Cadets under Captain Stuart K. Barnes, paraded after service on the hill outside our ancient Parish Church of St. Andrew's for inspection by Edward Murray Ind, Esq., Deputy Lieutenant of the County. After the inspection the Deputy Lieutenant addressed the men and lads in eloquent terms, and praised them for their smart military bearing. I well remember how he spoke of a time when their services might be required to defend their King, their Country, their homes, and all that they held most dear. While inwardly applauding his high patriotic ideals and sentiments, I, at the same time, thought the need of which he spoke would probably never arise. But in less than two short months commenced the war which was to change the face of the world and affect the destinies of all the

* Joined H.M. Forces.
† Killed on Active Service.

.32

nations of the earth, and in which many of those drawn up before him would take their part, and, alas, not a few would lay down their lives.

I believe it would be quite safe to say that not one of those who undertook the responsibility of training those men and boys, although knowing how important was that training, could have formed the remotest idea how soon the value of their labours would be demonstrated; and few, if any, of the officers who in those later days cheerfully gave so much time and care to their training and preparation, could have imagined that before many months were over they would see those same men and lads depart for the seat of war efficient soldiers, fully armed and equipped to fight shoulder to shoulder with the seasoned men of the regular army, who, with the heroic armies of France and Belgium, had borne the first tremendous onslaughts of the battle in the greatest and most sanguinary war of all time. But so things have turned out, and Hornchurch is to-day proud indeed of her warriors, old and young, for the sailors and soldiers who have gone forth from our village are of all ages, men of mature years, as well as boys in their teens, having willingly offered, or accepted, service as the need arose.

When the blast across Europe began in the last days of July, 1914, and when, a few days later—on that fateful August 4th—England declared war against Germany, our Territorials were away in camp, and were at once called up for active service. On the following Sunday, August 9th, as, after the close of Evensong, there rumbled past the church and down the hill, and on through our quiet village High Street, the heavy transport waggons of the Army Service Corps, and the tramp of soldiers' feet was heard in our hitherto peaceful village, we were able to realize something of what was toward. Even at that very moment the Germans were *hacking their way through Belgium*, and the reports received from the seat of war left no doubt in our minds of the horrors of modern warfare. But its real awfulness was yet to be revealed, and in the massacres of Louvain and Termonde we learned what a cruel, relentless, and despicable foe we had to meet in the German, soon to be known as the " Hun," who was indeed more terribly cruel than his forbears who fought under Attila.

The weeks which followed were big with events. Our army had crossed the Channel and had been in action in France, and when news reached England of the fighting of the British at Charleroi, and later of the masterly retreat from Mons, a great wave of patriotic and martial enthusiasm swept the country. Then began in reality that wonderful voluntary rush to the colours, which was only to end twenty-one months afterwards when our " *contemptible little army* " had reached the enormous total of over 5,000,000. Contemptible little army! Never were words more ill chosen, as the German Emperor, who used them, learned to his cost, when the retreat from the Marne early in September converted his dream of a speedy triumphal entry into Paris into a horrible nightmare, turned the tide of war in favour of the Allies, and brought about that remarkable state of trench warfare which existed for so long a time in Flanders and northern France.

As a fitting memorial of the splendid voluntary effort of this country, I reproduce the King's message to the Nation as it appeared in the Press on the 26th May, 1916, expressing his appreciation of voluntary enlistment and announcing the introduction of Compulsory Service :—

THE KING TO THE NATION.

May 25, 1916.

The Military Service Bill received the Royal Assent yesterday, and is now law. The King issued the following message to his people last night :—

To enable our country to organise more effectively its military resources in the present great struggle for the cause of civilisation, I have, acting on the advice of my Ministers, deemed it necessary to enrol every able-bodied man between the ages of 18 and 41.

I desire to take this opportunity of expressing to my people my recognition and appreciation of the splendid patriotism and self-sacrifice which they have displayed in raising by voluntary enlistment since the commencement of the war no fewer than 5,041,000 men, an effort far surpassing that of any other nation in similar circumstances recorded in history, and one which will be a lasting source of pride to future generations.

I am confident that the magnificent spirit which has hitherto sustained my people through the trials of this terrible war will inspire them to endure the additional sacrifice now imposed upon them, and that it will, with God's help, lead us and our Allies to a victory which shall achieve the liberation of Europe.

GEORGE R.I.

While our great citizen Army was being formed, the United Kingdom was converted into one vast camp. Training grounds and temporary barracks sprang up all over the country, every spare piece of available and suitable ground being used for these purposes.

In our own village Grey Towers Mansion with its beautiful park, in which was the famous pitch of the Village Cricket Club, was turned into a huge camp, Suttons Farm became an Aviation centre, and other fields and meadows were utilized from time to time to accommodate troops moving from one camping ground to another. Most of the houses in the village were at one time or other used as billets, and soldiers in marching order, and when off parade and on pleasure bent, were common and ordinary scenes in our village streets. We were roused in the morning by the stirring bugle blasts of the Reveille, and retired to rest at night—if we were wise—when the plaintive strains of the " Last Post " and " Lights Out " echoed through the village at 10 p.m.

Photo]   [*F. Kingsford, N.Z.E.F.*

ENTRANCE TO MILL FIELD, CHURCH HILL.

The Rolls of Honour.

At the present time the incidents of this war are fresh in the minds of all, but there will come a time when our memories will become clouded, when those things which now concern us so deeply will have partially faded, and when time—that great healer of all wounds—will have toned down the sorrows and losses which now seem to many of us so heavy a burden. It will be then, even perhaps more than now, that our Village Record will be of value. Later on still, the men and lads who now loom so big in our every-day life will have passed away, and it is for us of this day and generation to see to it that their memories are kept green, and their names perpetuated.

Here, then, is the record of their valour, their sacrifice, and endurance. It is for the most part a simple record of the service rendered by those brave villagers, who, with magnificent patriotism, came forward so unhesitatingly at their country's bidding and took their places in the fighting forces of the King, and to whose courage and devotion, after sacrifices and trials innumerable, we owe the happy consummation which has been reached. I doubt not that many deeds of valour, other than those I have been able to record, have been done by these splendid fellows, which will for ever remain unknown, but which would have won for the doers of them a niche in the immortal Temple of Fame. Be that as it may, their names are written in our own Roll of Honour with gratitude and pride, and while we rejoice at the home-coming of the victors who have fought the good fight and prevailed, we bare our heads and silently do homage to the memories of the **HEROIC AND GLORIOUS DEAD.**

Drawn by Denis C. Dunlop.

I.

Asleep they lie—son—husband—father—lover,
　At home, in France, or farther overseas
The earth enfolds them, and the grasses cover,
　Who live in proud and loving memories.

II.

One by the Menin Road, maybe, is lying,
　One where the Somme's bird-haunted rushes wave,
O'er one the uncooled desert wind is sighing,
　One has the deep sea for his silent grave.

III.

Young hearts that held the promise of the morning
　They died, and every single death a gem,
In one great crown, the light of love adorning,
　The clustered jewels of that diadem.

IV.

Aye—you may well be proud—wife, sister, mother,
　Who gave one pearl towards that priceless crown—
For England wears it—and desires no other,
　The coronet of lives laid bravely down.

F. W. E. BENDALL,
Lieut.-Colonel. London Regiment.

[*By permission of the Author.*]

37

Roll of Supreme Honour.

"Their name liveth for evermore."

Abraham, William
Adams, Stanley
Aley, F. R.
Aley, S. A.
Allcock, William
Archer, Frank
Axup, Victor Emmanuel
Aylwin, Ernest Peter
Bacon, Arthur F.
Baker, Charles Henry
Barber, William Charles
Barker, Fred
Barnes, Stuart Kempster
Barrington, L. S.
Beard, J. C. S.
Beer, Lawrence A.
Bennett, Ernest Albert
Bill, Charles Smith
Bill, Frank Keen
Bishop, John Dudley
Blackwell, Harold Fred
Bradley, Reginald John
Bridge, Walter Frank
Brockhurst, John
Brown, E. Denham
Bull, Frank Henry
Burgess, Fred
Card, John Victor
Cardy, G.
Cantle, Fredrick Sipthorp
Chester, Frederick George
Chinnery, George
Clark, Harry
Clyde, Harold
Coe, Frank W.
Cole, Harry
Collin, Frederick William
Collister, W.
Cook, Alfred Charles
Cooke, Christopher
Cox, George William
Creek, Arthur Charles

Cressey, George Joseph
Cressey, Josiah Frederick
Cressey, Walter John
Crow, R. J.
Curtis, Charles
Curtis, Robert
D'Aeth, William Sandle
Daniels, Ernest Joseph
Dawson, Reuben James
Day, Arthur Charles
Dean, Albert
Digby, Alfred Victor
Dix, Herbert Golden
Doe, Frederick George
Downham, Edward
Dunlop, Eric Arthur
Dunlop, Percy Alexander
Eaton, H.
Ellis, Alfred
Fardell, Sydney Ernest
Farrant, Archie R.
Farrant, Hector Reginald
Field, S. D.
Finch, Reginald Thomas
Fitzjohn, William Charles
Flack, J.
Fletcher, C.
Ford, A.
Ford, Harry
Fox, Walter Robert Seymour
Franklyn, George William
Frost Charles Walter
Frost, Timothy Gibson
Frost, William Gibson
Fry, Bertie Robert
Garrett, Ernest Albert
Gaywood, John Edward
Gibson,
Goodrum, Robert Richard
Green, Edward
Grout, Harry
Grout, Leslie A. J.

38

Roll of Supreme Honour.

Guy, William F.
Guymer, Sidney James
Hammond, John Dane
Hammond, William George
Hanson, Arthur
Harvey, Lawrence Henry
Hawkins, James Reuben
Hayward, Percy
Haywood, William Arthur
Hills, Alfred Thomas
Hills, Herbert George
Hitch, H. P.
Hobbs, Nathaniel
Howell, J. R.
Hunwicks, John
Hutchinson, L.
Jarvis, Albert
Kemp, George Henry
Kendall, Frederick Denys
King, Charles Thomas
Kingley, Herbert William
Knight, Alfred Charles
Knight, George Henry
Knight, Henry Charles
Lake, B.
Lazell, Arthur Frank
Leech, Thomas
Letten, T.
Little, C. W.
Little, John
Livermore, Percy
Long, Bertie William
Long, Joseph James
Love, John
Lungley, James Arthur
Macey, Clifford James
Maidment, George
Marrable, Joseph
Marrable, Thomas
Marshall, W. J.
Martin, Horace Charles
Martin, Walter A.
Mason, James
Matthews, Frank Lawson

Mayes, William
Mayne, Thomas
Millard, J.
Miller, A.
Miller, Peter
Moss, Harold Palmer
Moss, Thomas William
Nicholls, Ernest Walter
Nightingale. J. W.
Padfield, Herbert Lawrence
Page, Robert
Pailthorpe, Harold Anderson
Parker, Harry
Parsons, A.
Pearce, A.
Pepper, James
Peto, James
Pewter, B. J.
Poole, A. H.
Powell, Leslie Arthur
Prior, Bertie S.
Purkis, William Ernest
Ramsay, Jesse
Rolfe, Frederick
Saggers, Fred
Sargent, Edward George Thomas
Saunders, G.
Saunders, Henry
Searle, Harry Edwards
Shearman, John
Shelley, G.
Shield, William
Sibthorp, Josiah James
Simpson, John
Sledge, William
Smith, A. H.
South, A. E.
Stebbings, Samuel
Tattersall, Frank
Taylor, Harold Allfrey
Taylor, William Horace
Thorogood. William Harry
Tickner, Walter John
Tucker, Harry Ernest

Roll of Supreme Honour.

Turner, Edwin Syers
Tyler, Richard
Utley, F. C.
Vale, Albert
Veale, Allan Adolphus
Viney, Charles William
Wakeling, George
Wall, Francis J.
Wallis, Edward
Ward, John William
Wardill, George Edgar
Warman, William Alfred
Warren, A. S.

Webb, A. S.
Webb, F.
Webster, George Thomas
Whitams, T. R.
White, George Frederick
White, Jesse Walter Gordon
Wilson, Ernest
Wilson, George Stanley
Wilson, John Thomas
Wright, E.
York, William James
Young, Henry Archie

Former Parishioners, and Descendants of Ancient Families of Hornchurch.

Bearblock, Charles Henry
Bearblock, Walter James
Fulcher, Frank W.
Goodrum, William Henry
Holmes, Albert Arundel

Macklin, Edgar
Pearce, A. C.
Rush, Harry
Wilson, William

Officers and Men belonging to the local Aerodrome and Camps, who lost their lives on Active Service, and were buried in Hornchurch Churchyard.

Lieut. T. R. R. Burns, R.A.F.*
Lieut. W. A. Ellercamp, R.A.F.*
Lieut. W. B. Ferguson, R.A.F.*
Private Filitona, N.Z.E.F.
Lieut. H. Lynn Hopkins, R.A.F.*
Lieut. C. E. Joyce, R.A.F.*
Private J. McRichie,
    1st Sportsman's Battalion
Lieut. Neville Metcalfe, R.A.F.*
Private Prince Moki Rangitira,
    N.Z.E.F.
Lieut. Wilfred Addison Raw*

Private A. Ruffle
— C. R. Sampson, Artists
    O.T.C.
Lieut. J. G. Schmolle, R.A.F.*
Lieut. Hugh Cassilis Smith,
    R.A.F.*
— O. J. Stanton, A.S.C.
Private — Taleva, N.Z.E.F.
Lieut. Aubrey De Teissier, R.F.C.
Lieut. A. E. Trafford, R.A.F.*
Private — Vasau, N Z.E.F.

Those marked * belonged to Suttons' Farm Aerodrome.

ROLL OF HONOUR

"HERE IS THE SCROLL OF
EVERY MAN'S NAME."

Shakespeare :
Midsummer-Night's Dream, I., iii.

ERNEST HICKS OLIVER

Roll of Honour.

Abbey, Alexander, 250 Coy., R.E.

Abraham, William, Pte., 1/4 Essex Regt. (T.F.). ; Egypt ; reported missing.

Adams, Arthur Stanley, Corpl., R.A.F., late R.N.A.S., June 17/16—February 3/18 ; United Kingdom.

Adams, Newton Occleston, Lieut., 4th West Yorks, 8th M.G.C., 1914—1919 ; France ; was wounded 27th October, 1916.

Adams, Stanley, Pte., A.S.C. ; died of pneumonia on July 5/1918, in the General Hospital at Trouville, aged 21.

Adams, Walter L. ; Adams, William George ; Adams, George Frederick, Private, 11/9/15—20/3/19 ; Adams, Frank C. ; Adams, Thos. E.

Allcock, Arthur, Signaller, R.F.A., July/15—March/19 ; England and Ireland.

Allcock, George Frederick, Bombardier, R.F.A., Oct.15—April/19 ; England and France ; was gassed July 14th, 1917 at Ypres ; served overseas 3 years.

Allcock, William, Steward, R.N. Auxiliary Service ; Private A.S.C., and Lancashire Fusiliers, Aug./14—June/18 ; France ; was killed in action near Arras on June 20th, 1918.

Allen, G. ; **Aley, F. R.** ; **Aley, S. H.** ; Aley, George, Private, 22/6/16—24/3/19 ; Aley, Chas. ; Aldridge, Charles ; Allen, Frank ; Allan, Thomas, 54 Canadian Batt. ; Aldous, William ; Alliston, W.

Allen, Herbert George, Gunner, R.G.A., November/15—Feb./19 ; France.

Allsopp, E. A., Driver, R.A.S.C., attached 78th Field Ambulance, January 20, 1915—1919 ; served in France, at Salonika and in Bulgaria.

Ambrose, Alfred John ; Amor, Walter ; Annereau, Charles. ; Appleford, Leonard George ; Archer, Joseph C. ; Arnold, W.

Archer, Frank, Pte., A.S.C. (M.T.), May/15—April/18 ; France ; died of wounds received in action April 7, 1918, in the 2/1st Southern General Hospital, Birmingham.

Archer, Harry, Pte., Middlesex Regiment, Aug. 7/14—January 7/18 ; England ; discharged owing to enteric fever.

Ashford, Edwin Hy., 2/Lieut., Middlesex and Manchester Regiment, May/16—April/18 ; England, France and Italy ; invalided home.

Ashmead, Albert E. ; Aspinall, Horace G.

Attack, Chas. Herbert ; Awbery, Thos. Charles.

Axup, Victor Emmanuel, Leading Signalman, Royal Navy, 1901—1914, ; killed when H.M.S. " Pathfinder " was torpedoed on September 5, 1914 ; age 29 years.

Aylwin, Ernest Peter, Pte., M.G.C., 16/8/16—3/5/17 ; France ; died of wounds, 3/5/17 ; age 28.

Aylwin, Robert Henry, Corp., R.F.A., 16/1/18 · still serving France.

Ayres, H. E., Lance-Corpl., Artists' O.T.C., Home Service, 1918—19.

Ayres, H. F., Lieut., R.E.

Bailey, W. F., Private, 28th T.R. Batt., and 1/4 Essex, 4/12/16—26/10/17 ; Egypt ; was discharged with epilepsy, 26/10/17.

Baker, Arthur, 3rd Essex ; Baker, Horace ; Battson, Henry Charles ; Barker, Percy Charles ; Barber, William ; Barnes, Hedley Mustill ; Barnes, Edward George ; Banks, Donald ; Bateman, Ernest ; Barr, Willock ; Barrett, William Henry ; Barrett, Arthur George ; Batey, Robinson, G. ; Barham, William John ; Barham, Harry ; Barham, John Francis ; Bassett, Samuel John ; Bailes, Arthur Edward ; Bambridge, H. ; **Bacon, Arthur F.** ; **Barrington, L. S.** ; Ballentyne, E. ; Baring, J. H. ; Barlow, Percy R.

Baker, Charles Henry, C.Q.M.S., 4th Essex Regiment (T.F.), killed in action on August 24th, 1915. At the outbreak of war he held the rank of Sergeant in the Hornchurch Company, 4th Essex Regiment (T.F.). When war was declared he was at once called up, and served at Felixstowe, St. Faiths, Drayton, Norwich, Colchester and St. Albans, where he rose to the rank of C.Q.M.S. He afterwards volunteered for active service abroad, and went out with the 54th Division to Gallipoli. He was present at the landing on the 13th August, 1915 and a few days later was with his Company in the front-line trenches on the Peninsula, their only protection being a piled up heap of rocks. On the arrival of some rations, C.Q.M.S. Baker proceeded to issue them out when he was hit by a bullet, causing a severe wound, from the effects of which he died five days afterwards, aged 31 years. He was born in the village on June 19th, 1884 ; was a Sidesman of the Parish Church, and Superintendent of the Sunday School.

Baker, Walter Edward, Pte., 2/5 Buffs, May 31/16—April 12/19 ; Home Service.

Baldock, L. S. J., Pte., R.A.S.C. (M.T.), November 8, 1915—July, 1919 ; served in France.

Baldwin, C. A. T. C., Signalman, H.M.T.B.D. " Rowena," September 17, 1917—January 25, 1919 ; served with the 15th Flotilla, Grand Fleet.

Baldwin, James, Driver, 20/4/15—22/5/19.

Balls, Percy F. J. ; Sergt.-Mechanic, R.A.F., 28/1/15—20/3/18.

Banks, Chas., Private, 1/4 Essex Regiment (T.F.), Gallipoli, Egypt, Palestine and Syria ; re-enlisted in the Guards.

Banks, William, Driver, R.F.A., France, Egypt, Palestine and Syria ; wounded in Palestine ; demobilized March 1919.

Bannister, George, Pte., R.A.O.C., Sept. 4/17—March 14/19, England.

Banyard, Harold Thomas, Lieut., Royal Engineers, 1914-1919 ; France. Enlisted as Motor Despatch Rider, and afterwards became a Signal Officer in the R.E. Awarded the Mons Star and mentioned in Sir John French's first Despatch.

Barber, Cecil Ernest, C.P.O., H.M.S. " Queen Empress," R.N.R., 5/August/14—February 18/19.

Barber, C. H., Company Q.M.S., joined August 28th, 1914, 7th Norfolks ; served in France.

Barber, W., Pte., joined R.N. Lancs. August 6th, 1914 ; transferred to Cheshire Regiment ; wounded in right lung during retreat from Mons ; discharged medically unfit, August 27th, 1916 ; died of consumption, April 3rd, 1918, aged 33.

Barker, Arthur Edward, Gunner, R.H.A., 7/11/15—28/4/19 ; England, Ireland and France.

Barker, Fredk. Chas., L./Cpl., 9th Essex, 4/9/14—8/7/16 ; England and France ; killed and buried at Coillers-la-Boiselle, 8/7/17, aged 28.

Barkham, Albert T., Scout, 10th Canadians, 1915—1919 ; France and Germany ; wounded at Cambrai.

Barkham, Sidney E., Rifleman, London Rifle Brigade, 1917—1919 ; France ; wounded at Cambrai.

Barkham, Stanley C., Trooper, Essex Yeomanry, 1915—1919 ; France.

Barkham, William E., Trooper, Essex Yeomanry, 1916—1919 ; France and Germany.

Barlow, Charles Harry, L./Cpl., 21/6/14—22/4/19 ; Gallipoli, Egypt and Palestine.

Barlow, Percy R., Pte., 3rd Suffolk Regiment, 1/7/18 ; still serving, Rhine.

Barlow, Walter, Farrier, 1/4 Essex and R.A.S.C., 21/6/14—22/4/19 ; Gallipoli, Egypt and Palestine.

Barnard, S. E., Pte., Essex ; joined June 4, 1915 ; served in France ; wounded February, May and September, 1917 ; transferred to Labour Corps, October 24, 1917 ; discharged medically unfit, August, 1918.

Barnes, Clarence Kempster, Corpl., R.A.S.C. (M.T.), Jan./16—August, 1919 ; France, Belgium and Germany.

Barnes, Stuart Kempster, Private, 2nd Battalion London Scottish Regiment, 1914—1916, Ireland and France ; killed in action in France, July 14, 1916, aged 24 years. Upon the outbreak of war he joined the University of London O.T.C., and, after a probationary period, was nominated for a commission, but was, unfortunately, turned down on medical grounds, having developed ear trouble during his course of training. In spite of this physical defect, which, though very serious at the time, was not permanent, he persisted in his endeavours to join up, and was shortly afterwards accepted as Instructor in the 10th Battalion of the Royal West Kent Regiment, stationed at Maidstone, with which Battalion he acted for four months. At the completion of that period he was passed by the Medical Examiners, and in December, 1915, he joined the 3rd Battalion London Scottish Regiment, and went into training at Richmond. He was afterwards transferred to the 2nd Battalion, training at Bishops Stortford and Salisbury. He served with his Regiment in Ireland during the Rebellion in April, 1916. Shortly after the return of the Regiment to England, it was ordered out to France and had only been there three weeks when Private Barnes fell. A comrade in writing of his death said :—" I am sorry to tell you the sad news that Private S. K. Barnes was killed on the 14th July. On the day in question we were holding the first line trenches, and there was a terrific bombardment going on. I was in an advance sap at the time he was on sentry-go. The opposing trenches were only about 100 yards away, and he was killed instantly by a trench mortar, or an aerial torpedo. Sentries are on no account to leave their posts, and he died at his post like a true Briton." He was buried with military honours in the Scottish Cemetery, Merieulle, near Arras. Prior to the war he was Captain of the Hornchurch Company, C.L.B. Cadets. He also raised a Company of the C.L.B. at Rainham.

Bartholomew, Courtney Albert, Pte., 1st Air Mechanic in R.A.F., May/ 1916—January/1919 ; France.

Bass, Leonard William, Signaller, R.G.A., June 3/18—Feb. 25/19, Portsmouth.

Battle, Albert Ernest, Capt., R.E., March 26/17—Sept. 1/19, Admiralty and War Office, Officer in charge of Ship Construction, Paisley Section.

Beales, Joseph, 2/Corpl., R.O.D., R.E., June/16—Feb./19 ; France.

Beard, J. C. S., Private, Middlesex Regiment, March 6/15—Nov. 13/15 ; killed in action in France ; age 21.

Beck, Arnold J. E., Private, R.F.A. and A.S.C. (M.T.), Sept./14—Feb./19 ; France, Egypt and Salonika. He joined H.M. Forces at the age of 17 in Sept./1914. He left with his Brigade for France in Nov./1915, and was in action the following month. In February, 1916, he was in Egypt, where his Brigade was guarding the Suez Canal. In Sept., 1916, he was transferred to A.S.C. (M.T.), and sailed for Salonika that month.

Bennett, Ernest Albert, Canadian Grenadier Guards, served nine months ; Canada and France ; killed in action 9th July, 1917, age 33.

Bennett, George James, Royal Fusiliers, served 12 months ; France ; wounded 9th July, 1917, at the Somme.

Benton, William ; Bennett, Samuel ; Belcher, George ; Bevis, George F. ; Betts, Arthur ; Bewers, Fredk. ; Bennett, Edwin Charles ; Belcher, James T. ; Bell, Fred ; Bennett, Fredk. Edwin ; Bennett, W. P. ; **Beer, Lawrence A.**

44

Berry, Harold Arthur, Capt. 15th Batt. London Regiment (Civil Service Rifles), 4 Aug./14, 17 January/19 ; France ; wounded 30th November, 1917, at Bourlon Wood.

Bettridge, George Arthur, Pte., N.Z. M.G.C.,1916—1919 ; France ; seriously gassed 1917.

Biddick, Ernest James, A.P.C. and M.G.C., Nov./1914 · France.

Bill, Arthur Michael, Sergt.-Major, 3rd Canadian and Army Gymnastic Staff, Feb. 4/1915—25/12/18 ; Belgium, France, England, and Canada. Was wounded in left arm and right shoulder and chest when advancing with Canadians at Ypres, 1916.

Bill, Bernard William, Lt. (A/Capt.), 47 Garrison Coy., 43 Royal Fusiliers, 6/6/13—9/4/19 ; Belgium and France. He was blown up and slightly wounded after attack on Mount Kemmel in May, 1918.

Bill, Charles Smith, Pte., 3rd Toronto Regiment, Canadian Forces. He was in Saskatchewan prior to the war. Enlisted in the City of Regina on February 4th, 1915. Left Canada en route for England on July 1st, 1915. Was transferred and went out to France almost immediately with the 3rd Toronto Regiment. He passed the winter of 1915 in the trenches south of Ypres. Moving up to that town in the spring of 1916 he eventually took part in an advance when the Canadians captured three lines of German trenches. In this advance, whilst acting as Company "Runner," he was killed on the 13th of June, 1916, aged 22.

Bill, Edward Thomas, Bombdr., 271 Bde. R.F.A., Aug. 4/1914—July, 1919 · France, Egypt and Palestine. Contracted Malaria.

Bill, Frank Keen, Pte., 1st H.A.C. He enlisted at the age of 18, with the 1st H.A.C. Was trained at the Tower of London, and a few days after his nineteenth birthday was sent to France. For some time he was travelling with a platoon of selected men for demonstrative purposes. Later he went into the trenches, where he contracted influenza. Pneumonia quickly followed, and he died on Nov. 17/18, and was buried at Etaples, age 20.

Bill, John Hubert, Despatch Rider, R.F.C. He enlisted on Jan. 5, 1916, and went to France early in April of the same year, where he performed his duties as Despatch Rider for two years and ten months. He was in England twice during that period on short leave. On Feb. 2/19, a very severe night, he met with an accident which necessitated his right leg being amputated. After a critical time in hospital he recovered sufficiently to be fitted with an artificial limb.

Bingham, J. T. ; Bickers, —. ; Bird, Chas. ; Bird, George ; Bird, S. ; Bishop, H.

Bird, Albert Edward, Pte., 12th Suffolk Regiment, April 23/16—Feb. 20/19 : France.

Bishop, Albert Edward, Pte,, 2nd South Wales Borderers, 1915—1917 : Gallipoli and Egypt. Was wounded in ankle, knee, hip and left lung, and after treatment in various military hospitals was discharged as unfit for further services.

Bishop, Beresford, Lieut., M.G.C., 4/2/16—14/1/19 ; France and England ; wounded in the head by machine gun bullet at Festubert 9/4/18, and gassed 18/5/18, at Nieppe Forest.

Bishop, George James, Essex Regiment, 1916—1916 ; was discharged owing to ill-health.

Bishop, John Dudley, Flight-Sergt., R.A.F., 9/10/17—July, 1918 ; U.K. ; awarded 1st Class Fighting Scout's Certificate ; killed in Air collision at Manston, Kent, July 17th, 1918, age 18½.

Bishop, John Herbert, Sergt., R.G.A., May 5/16—March 17/19 ; Egypt and Palestine.

Bishop, Laurence Benjamin, Trooper, Surrey Yeomanry and 21st Lancers, 1914—1918 ; France. Was twice wounded in France.

Blackburn, Alfred ; Blair, David ; Blanks, Sydney ; Bland, George
Wm. ; Bloomfield, Robert Henry.

Blackwell, Harold Fred, Signaller, 2nd Essex Regiment, May 9/17—
Aug. 12/18. France. He died on Aug. 14/18, at Wimeraux Hospital,
France, from the result of wounds, age 39.

Blanks, J. W., Private, 13/6/14—8/12/18, gun shot wound left arm ;
disabled.

Blay, James, Corpl., 6th Dragoons and R.A. Veterinary Corps, 5/8/14—
6/5/19, France, awarded French Medal (silver) for special services
rendered in R.A.V.C. Date of award 21/11/18.

Boast, Charles, C.S.M., Essex Regiment, and R.D.C., 3/6/90—10/4/18 ;
England and France ; was invalided from France 12/4/17 and from
the Service on 4/10/18.

Boddington, V., R.A.F.

Bonnett, John Joseph ; Boxall, Harry Stephen ; Bones, Charles Joseph,
Private, 31/7/17—1/5/19 ; Boettjer, Oscar Karl ; Boettjer, Eric R.,
Private, Dec./17—April/19 ; Bowner, F. J. ; Boreham, Percy.

Bonnett, John Joseph, Pte., Queen's R.W.S. Regiment, 1917 ; France
and Belgium.

Bowick, Wm. Alfred Reynolds, Engineer Officer, 1915—1919 ; s./s. " Cros-
by," " Ranawha," " Bolwana," " Montreal," " Montfort," and
" St. George." ; Canada, New Brunswick, New York, France and
Cape Britain. Was torpedoed on 1/10/18, 250 miles from Lands
End on s/s Montfort. Attacked while in convoy on five occasions.

Box, Frederick, King's Own Royal Lancasters.

Brace, Albert James, Pte., R.A.F., April 9/18—Nov. 27/18 : Scotland.

Bradley, Fredk. Charles, Corpl., M.G.C., March 8/16 ; still serving, France
and Germany.

Bradley, John Thomas, Pte., 13th Bedfords, Jan. 12/15—March 14/19 ;
Home Service.

Bradley, Reginald John, Pte., R.M.L.I., H.M.S. " Hawke," North Sea ;
lost on Oct. 15/14, when H.M.S. " Hawke " was torpedoed and sunk.

Bradshaw, Ernest Louis, Pte., Essex Regiment. 9/12/15—12/9/19 ; France.

Bratchell, Edgar George, Signaller, R.G.A., April 3/18—Jan. 15/19 ;
Plymouth.

Brice, John, Rifle Brigade, (Was Prisoner of War.)

Bridge, Walter Frank, Pte., 1st Essex Regiment, Dec. 26/1916—Dec. 5/
1917 ; France. He was wounded in France in 1917, and, returning to
the western front in the August of that year, was again wounded at
Cambrai, from the effects of which he died in No. 5 Casualty Clearing
Station, on Dec. 5/1917, aged 37 years. He was buried at Tincourt
New British Cemetery, about 4 miles East of Peronne. During the
South African War he volunteered for active service, and served as a
private in the 2nd Volunteer Special Service Company, Essex Regiment, being awarded the King's Medal with bars.

Bridges, Alfred Stanley, L/Cpl., City London Yeomanry, 1914/1919 :
Dardanelles, Egypt, Salonika and Mesopotamia.

Bridges, Thomas Clifford, Pte., 1/5 Border Regiment, 1916 ; still serving,
France, Belgium and Germany.

Britton, A., L./Cpl., M.G.C., May/1918—January 1919.

Brockhurst, John, Pte. At the outbreak of war he was in Hornchurch
Company of the Territorials and was immediately called up for Home
Service. He afterwards went to Gallipoli with his regiment, and after
serving there was invalided home, suffering from dysentry. On his
recovery he proceeded to Palestine, where he was killed in action on
November 2/1917, age 27. He was born in Hornchurch and was for
some time a ringer at the Parish Church.

Bromfield, E. Lieut., R.N.

Brooks, J. F., Private, 11th and 21st Middlesex Regiment, June 13/16—
Jan. 25/19 ; France.

Brown, A., enlisted May 25/1915 ; to France December, 1915; demobilised May 27/1919.

Brown, B. W., enlisted May 25/1915 : to Egypt August 18/1915 ; then to Salonika, 1916 ; demobilised May 20/1919.

Brown, E. Pte., 9th Essex, Special Reserve ; called up at outbreak of war ; served in France ; wounded, 1917 ; came home in hospital ship, which was torpedoed ; served in France again, 1918 ; appendicitis, June, 1918 ; discharged medically unfit, February 4/1919.

Brown, E. D., Driver, R.F.A. ; joined January 21, 1915 ; served in France ; killed on the Somme, July 28, 1916.

Brown, Fredk. Wm. ; Brown, R.G. S. ; Brown, W. ; Brittain, Walter ; Bryant, Clifford Fredk. ; Bridge, Thos. R. ; Bryant, Alfred Rolfe ; Bradshaw, Alfred Henry ; Bradshaw John ; Bristow ; Briton ; Bromfield ; Brodrick, Harry E. ; Brooks, John ; Brooks, James ; Bradford, Thos. ; Brodshaw, Wm. ; Brooker, Bertram ; Brockhurst, Isaac E.

Brown, H. L., 2nd Air Mechanic, R.A.F.

Brown, P. J., Rifleman, K.R.R., June 21/15—Feb. /19 ; France.

Brown, W. J., Private, R.A.S.C., Aug. 5/14—May 7/19 ; France ; awarded Mons Star ; gassed.

Brutey, Claude Edward, Pte., M.G.C., 1918 ; England.

Brutey, Ronald Stanley, C.S.M., 1/4 Essex Regiment, 1914—1919; Gallipoli and Palestine.

Bryant, T. E., Capt., Army Pay Department ; joined February 8/1915 ; served in France as Field Cashier with 3rd and 9th Corps ; typhoid fever, April—October 1916 ; demobilised November 13/1919 ; mentioned in Despatches June, 1916.

Bryett, J. E., Regt.-Quarter-Master-Sergt., D.C.L.I. · joined May 29, 1916; to Salonika, November, 1917 ; went through September offensive on Doiran Front, 1918 ; Army of Occupation, Bulgaria : to South Russia, March, 1919 ; invalided out (malaria) October 5, 1919.

Buck, Horace Edwin ; Bullard, Norman Frank ; Bush, George, Driver, 28/12/17—25/10/19 ; Butcher, George ; Burnett, Chas. Laurence ; Burgess, C. ; Burgess, R. ; Burrell, A. ; Burn, Leonard S. ; Butterfield, Chas. ; Butcher, John William ; Burr, Wm. Thos. ; Buck, Percy Cecil ; **Burgess, Fred** ; Bush, Geo. ;

Buckley, Joseph Christopher, Pte., 2/3 London Field Ambulance, Aug./15 —Aug./18 : France. Awarded Military Medal for bravery on the field at Cambrai, after being himself severely wounded.

Bull, Albert Charles, Gunner, R.G.A., Oct. 29/17—Feb. 13/19 ; France.

Bull, Arthur William, Gunner, R.G.A., 2/East Anglian Brigade (Essex), June 9/15—Sept. /18 ; Egypt and Palestine.

Bull, Frank Henry, Pte., 1/4 Essex Regiment, Aug. 4/14—March 26/17 ; Gallipoli, Egypt and Palestine. Wounded at Gallipoli, Aug. 18/15. He was in action at the Battle of Gaza, March 26/1917, and was officially reported wounded and missing, and later a War Office report announced that he died of wounds on or about March 26/1917, age 18.

Bullock, Cecil, Pte., R.A.M.C., Field Ambulance, 1915—1919 ; France ; wounded and gassed during the Retreat, March 21/1918, Somme.

Bullock, Frank Leonard, Pte., 2/23 London Regiment, 1914—1919; France, Egypt, Salonika and Palestine.

Bullock, Percy John William, Capt. Canadian M.G.C., 1914—1919, France. Was wounded during the Battle of Vimy Ridge, and promoted on the field, 1917.

Bullock, Sidney George, Royal Navy, 1914, still serving ; Dardanelles and North Sea on H.M.S. " Impregnable " and " Colussus."

Burrell, Arthur Thomas, L./Cpl., Essex Regiment, Aug. 4/14—Feb./19 ; Home Service.

47

Button, Alfred Edward, Sergt., Suffolk Regiment, 28/1/14—25/8/16 ; France ; discharged disabled 25/8/16.

Button, Charles Henry, Pte., West Yorks Regiment, 7/6/17—12/4/18 ; Reported missing 12/4/18. Since assumed dead, age 18 years.

Cantle, Fredk. Sipthorp, Pte., Queen's Royal West Surrey Regiment, Sept./1914—May 25/1916. He was present at the Battle of Loos in Sept., 1915, was gassed in March, 1916, and killed whilst on patrol duty on May 25/1916, near Ypres and buried at Military Cemetery, Bailleul.

Card, John Victor, Capt., France, Irish Rebellion, Egypt, Salonika, East Africa and North Russia, 1914—1919. Enlisted as a private in the Grenadier Guards in September, 1914, was sent to France in May 1915, and took part in the severe trench fighting near Festubert, where he was injured in consequence of being buried by the explosion of a shell. He returned to England, and after being in hospital for some months, obtained a Commission in the East Surrey Regiment, and was sent to Egypt in May, 1916, and after service there for a short time he joined his Regiment in Salonika, where he took part in several attacks, but, having contracted malaria, was invalided home in December, 1916. On recovering from his illness he was attached to the 1st K.A.R., and went to East Africa in May, 1917, where he took part in the fighting there, under the most trying conditions, climatic and otherwise, but was again a victim to malaria, and in March, 1918, returned to England. In the following September he was sent to Archangel to assist in training Russian Troops, belonging to the British-Slovak Legion. He personally led several attacks on the Onega River front, where he displayed the greatest initiative and bravery, for which he was awarded the Military Cross. His Company was then given the task of cutting a road through virgin forest for 80 versts (60 miles). This was accomplished after the most strenuous work, in a temperature 35° below zero, on insufficient food, and frequently without any tent or other shelter to sleep in. On March 25, 1919, he led an attack on a village held by Bolsheviks, but coming under heavy machine gun fire, he was killed. Age 32.

The following announcement is from the " London Gazette " :—

MILITARY CROSS.

" From December 28th, 1918 to January 2nd, 1919, north of Turchasova, he did excellent work. He personally led the first attack, and by his conduct and courage contributed materially to the steadiness of the attack and counter attack of the Naval Brigade.

Carter, Ernest, Pte., Royal Engineers, July 7/1917 ; still serving, Egypt.

Carter, George Samuel, Sapper, R.E., 3/7/16—14/7/19, France and Germany.

Cash, Harry ; Cast, John David ; Canham, Ernest ; Carder, Francis Chas. ; Tank Corps ; Cane, Walter George ; Callis, Leslie George ; Cavill, James W. ; Catchpole, Robert Wm. ; Carter, Alfred J. T. ; Carrole, Arthur H. ; Cant, John Thomas ; **Cardy, G.**

Catherwood, Arnold, Pte., 1915—1919 ; R.E. (Mining Company), France ; wounded by shrapnel in the arm.

Catherwood, Frank, Q.M.S., R.E., 1915—1918 · Salonika.

Catmull, Alfred Randolph, Pte., K.R.R. and M.G.C., June 14/15—Feb. 22/19 ; France.

Chapman, Frank Joseph, Pte., 3rd Essex Regiment, Aug. 15/18—Jan. 28/19 ; United Kingdom.

Chapman, John Gilbert, Corpl., 6th Batt. Middlesex Regiment, and Mechanical Transport, R.A.S.C., July 28/16—June 6/19 ; England and France.

Chapman, W. F. R., Pte., 1st Gloucester Regiment, Reservist; called up August 4/1914; served in France and Belgium. Retreat from Mons to the Aisne; then on Ypres Front; wounded by shell, October 31/1914; discharged medically unfit, June 8/1915. Employed in examination of cordite and gun-cotton at Royal Arsenal, Woolwich, till 1918; also of Cooper bombs till January 1, 1919.

Chase, P.; Chapman, Clifford W.; Chandler, Edward Chas.; Chandler, David C.; Chaplin, Donald; Chambers, Fredk. John; Chester, Thos.; Christie, Robert Arthur,

Chester, Alfred Robert, Sergt., 1/4 Essex Regiment, June 6/15; still serving, Egypt and Palestine.

Chester, Edward, Sergt., M.G.C., Oct. 29/14—May 6/19; Egypt and Palestine.

Chester, Frederick George, Pte., 7th Buffs, Feb. 28/17—Aug. 8/18; Killed in Action, Aug. 8/18.

Chester, John, Corpl., 3rd Essex Regiment, April 19/18; still serving, Ireland.

Chester, Robert William, A.B., H.M.S. Q.2., May 1/16; still serving.

Chilver, Harold Percy, 2/Lieut., Royal Naval Division, 1915—1919; France and Belgium; awarded M.C. (*See page* 90).

Clare, William, Pte., Ambulance Driver, Dec. 10/15—Jan. 11/19; France.

Clark, Frederick, Horace, Pte., M.T., R.A.S.C., 2/11/15—14/11/18; East Africa. Discharged through malaria and heart disease contracted in East Africa.

Clark, Harold, W., L/Cpl., 1/4 Essex. Was serving in Territorials when war broke out, and saw active service in Gallipoli and Palestine expeditions. Wounded March 26/1917. Demobilized March 6/1919.

Clark, Harry; Clarke, Percy; Clarke, Harry George, Private, 24/4/17—28/2/19; Clark, Arthur; Clayton, B.; Clayton, Wm.; Cloudesley, Clemson Albert; Clover, Clements Fredk.; Claydon, Walter.

Clark, Herbert, Pte., Road Construction Co., R.E., January 11/1917 —April 1/1919. Served in Belgium and France.

Clark, Horace, Driver, R.F.A., October 29/1915 to September 29/1919. Served in India and Mesopotamia.

Clark, Percy, Driver, R.F.A., October 29/1915 to September, 1919. Served in India and Mesopotamia.

Claxton, Alfred Bert., Signaller, R.E., 1914—1919; Palestine.

Clements, Harry Tollemache, Pte., Rifle Brigade, 20/4/18; still serving, France, Belgium and Germany.

Clewes, William John, Pte., R.A.F., 16/1/18—1/11/18.

Clyde, A.

Clyde, H., Pte., joined Middlesex Regiment, November, 1916. Served in France. Wounded December, 1917. Transferred to Dublin Fusiliers. Killed in Action April 23/1918, age 20.

Collin, Albert George, Sergt., 4th Essex Regiment, Aug. 4/14—Oct. 15/18 · Egypt and Palestine. Was wounded in the first attack on Gaza, Palestine, March 26/17 and permanently disabled.

Collin, Frederick William, Pte., 4th Essex Regiment, Nov./15—Nov. 25/17; Egypt and Palestine. Was wounded in the legs at Gaza on March 26/1917, and killed in Action at the north side of Hill (Kerbert Hardra), over the Auja River in Palestine on Sunday, Nov. 25/17, aged 31.

Collin, Sidney Charles, Pte., M.G.C., 11th Company, 4th Division, April 1916—January 1918; France. Permanently disabled. (*See page* 91).

Collins, H., Driver, R.F.A., June 1915—March 1919; France.

Cook, Alfred Charles, Pte., 147 Batt. Overseas Canadian Forces, April /15—Feb. 9/18; France. Was wounded Jan. 20/18 and killed in Action in the advance on the Drocourt-Queant Line, by machine gun bullet, Sept. 2/18, age 34.

49

D

Cook, E. P., Pte., 1/4 Essex, 1914—1919. Served with Egyptian Expeditionary Force whole time. Invalided out January, 1919, after being dangerously ill with dysentery and pneumonia.

Cook, Frederick John, Pte., Essex Regiment, March 2/17—April 6/19; France. Contracted Trench Fever Sept. 5/18.

Cook, Philip James, Pte., M.G.C., March 1/17—Jan. 30/19. France. Gassed on April 25/18.

Cook, George, Gunner, R.G.A., March 21/18; still serving, France.

Cook, Sidney Albert, A.B., H.M.S. "Mohawk," June /17—Sept. /17; H.M.S. "Termagant," Sept. /17—April /19; Dover Patrol.

Cooper, Arthur Arnold, Royal Navy, H.M.S. "President."

Cooper, Arthur Gabbetis, Lieut., R.A.F., 21/3/17—28/5/19 : France, Italy, England (Home Defence). Was awarded Italian "Croce al Merito di Guerra."

Cooper, Ernest Frederick, 2/Lieut., Loyal North Lancs. Regiment, March 1916—Feb. 1919 England and France.

Cooper, Percy, Senr., Sergt., R.A.O.C., Aug. 1914—March 1919; United Kingdom.

Cooper, Percy., Junr., L/Cpl., 2nd Sportsmen's Batt. R.F., Oct. /15—Jan. /19, France and Belgium; wounded by shrapnel in left foot at Cambrai, March /18.

Cooper, Reginald John, Cadet Pilot, R.A.F., 28/8/18—9/1/19; England.

Cooper, S.; Cooper, Percy; Cooke, Eustace; Cooper, Fredk.; Coulson, P.; Copp, John Densem; Coote, George; Collins, George W.; Coke, J. W.; Cowell, Richard; Cooper, James Allenby; Corbell, Wm. James; Cole, A. W.; Cole, Chas. S. D.; Cole, Sydney; Coleman, —.; **Coe, Frank W.**; **Cooke, Christopher**; **Collister, W.**

Copeland, John, Pte., Black Watch, 1915—1919; France.

Corlis, Denis, Sergeant, 1/2/18—25/3/19.

Cornell, George, A./L. Cpl., King's Shropshire Light Infantry, June 21/16—June 28/19; England and France.

Couchman, A. L., Private, R.M.L.I., 4/10/05—7/3/19.

Coulson, C. W., Private 1/4 Essex, 17/6/12—3/4/19.

Coulter, Henry George, Pte., 1st Northamptonshire Regiment, Aug. 5/14—Dec. 10/18 : France. Was wounded on Aug. 18/16, and discharged through sickness, Dec. 10/18. Awarded 1914 star.

Cousens, Alfred Harold, Driver, A.S.C. (M.T.) Jan. 12/16; still serving, France.

Cousens, Harry Leonard, Pte., 3rd Bedfords, Oct. 18/18; still serving, British Isles.

Cousens, Reginald Ernest, 2/Lieut. 2nd R.W.F., Oct. 6/16—April 10/19; France.

Cox, C. H., Trooper, 2nd City of London Yeomanry.

Cox, George, Pte., 13th Essex; served about 15 months France; reported missing.

Cox, George Herbert, Gnr., R.G.A., 1915; still serving, France.

Cox, Percy George, Dvr., R.A.S.C., 1914—1919; Salonika.

Crawford, Daniel, Flight-Cadet, R.A.F., 29/4/18—21/1/19; Home Service.

Creasey, George Joseph, L./Cpl., 7th Glostershire Regiment, Aug. 18/14—Aug. 8/15 · Dardanelles. Was killed in action at the Dardanelles on Aug. 8/1915.

Creek, A. C., Able Seaman, H.M., T.B.D., "Partridge." Joined R.N. August, 1915. Served in the North Sea. Killed in Action December 12/1917, when ship was destroyed, all but 22 lives being lost. Age 20.

Creek, A. E., Sergt., R.F.A., October, 1914—February, 1919; France, Awarded M.M. for courage and devotion to duty on June 6/18. He remained at his post during a violent bombardment and although suffering from the effects of gas shelling he continued, with the help of a comrade, to fire his gun in response to an S.O.S. call.

Cressey, Josiah Fredk., 1st Essex. Killed in Action at Gallipoli, June 4/15, age 29. He enlisted in the Regular Army in 1904, and was in India when the war broke out. He was transferred to Warley Barracks in 1914 and from there went out to Gallipoli with his Regiment.

Cressey, Thos. Sidney, L./Cpl., Sherwood Foresters; France.

Cressey, Walter John, 9th Batt. Essex Regiment, 1916—1917; France. He joined the Essex Yeomanry and went out to France in Dec. /16, and served in the trenches. He was killed in action at Arras on April 9/1 , aged 23.

Cressey, William Henry, Pte., 1/4 Essex Regiment, Oct. 26/14—Jan. 19/19; Egypt. Was wounded in the foot at the first battle of Gaza on March 26/1916 ; also wounded in the left arm at Jaffa, April 17/1916. He was then invalided to England and after being in hospital at Southampton was transferred to the 3rd Reserve Battalion at Felixstowe. He was formerly in the Hornchurch Company C.L.B.

Crick, John H., 2/Lt., R.G.A., May/16—March/19; France, Belgium and Germany.

Crouch, John Robert, Capt., R.N.A.S., and R.A.F., 1915—1919; East Coast Bases, Invested by H.M. the King with D.S.C. 11/4/18, for sinking enemy submarine.

Crow, C. H., Pte., joined March 27/1916, 35 Royal Fusiliers. Transferred to Labour Corps, 1917. Served in France and Belgium two years three months. Invalided out through nephritis, November 8/19.

Crow, F., Pte., 13th Rifle Brigade. Joined September 16/1915, in 18th K.R.R.C. Served in France ; severely wounded (18 wounds : lost leg). Discharged June, 1919.

Crow, John Fredk. · Crow, Henry Charles ; Crabb, —. ; Cross, Chas. John ; Crooke, Ernest Christopher ; Cressey, P. W. ; Crowley, Michael ; Cressey, G. W.

Crow, R. J.

Crowe, Edgar James, Cpl., A.S.C. (M.T.), 27/8/15—16/1/19 ; France.

Cumbers, A. T., Sergt., R.F.A., May, 1915—May, 1919. To France June 19/16. Gassed twice and wounded in jaw.

Cumbers, L. G., Rifleman, 18th K.R.R., November 15/15 to February 28/19. Served in France and Italy. Wounded January 2/1918, in Italy. Previously L./Sergt., Harold Wood Co., C.L.B.

Cutmore, Arthur, Gunner, R.A., Feb. 21/18; Egypt.

Cutmore, George, Pte., Royal West Kents, June 24/18; France and Germany.

Cutmore, J. ; Cumbers, Wm. Edward ; Curtis, Wm. Ernest ; **Curtis, Charles** ; **Curtis, Robert** ; Curtis, Percy ; Cuthbertson, Bruce Anthony ; Culliford, Leonard Arthur.

Cutts, Alfred B., Pte., 17th Royal Fusiliers, 30/6/17—23/1/20; France and Germany.

Cutts, Arthur Wm., Gunner, Anti-Aircraft Artillery, (1st Army), 11/9/16 —6/2/19; France.

D'Aeth, W. S., Pte., joined 2/5 Buffs May 29/1916 ; attached to 3/4 R.W. Surreys; served in France ; wounded and missing at Passchendaele, Oct. 7/1917 ; aged 33.

Dale, Arthur Llewellyn, L./Cpl., R.E.s. (London Electrical Engineers Heavy Bridging Batt.) ; Jan., 1916—Jan., 1919; Bantry Bay, Ireland.

Dale, Austin Fredk., Pte. ; 4th Manchester Regt. and M.G.C. ; Jan./16— April 1918 ; England and France.

Dale, Philip Francis, Capt., 11th Essex and Intelligence Dept., 5th Army., Sept. /14; still serving in 1920 ; wounded Sept. 26/15, in advance on Loos ; England, France and Russia ; Prisoner of War Sept./15— March/18 at Ludwigshafen. (*See page* 92).

Dalton, Ernest Edwin, Pte., Artists Rifles O.T.C.

Daniels, Ernest Joseph, Pte., M.G.C., Sept./17—Oct./18 ; France ; Killed in Action in France 22/10/18. Age 18. Prior to joining H.M. Forces, he was employed in driving a motor tractor plough for the Board of Agriculture.

Dare, Reginald, Cpl., 1/4 Essex Regt., 1914—1919; Gallipoli, Egypt and Palestine.

Davis, Charles Harold, Bdr., R.F.A., Sept. 19/14—Feb. 3/19 ; France and Belgium ; awarded 1914/15 Star.

Davis, Joseph Charles, B.S.M., R.F.A., Sept. 14, still serving ; France and Belgium.

Davis, Norman Archibald George, O.S., Wireless Station, R.N.V.R.

Davis, Oscar Edward, Pte., A.P.C., April 16/17—Oct. 28/17 ; Home Service ; discharged through sickness.

Davis, Robert James, Cpl., R.A.M.C. ; still serving ; Home Service.

Davis, Thos. Henry ; Darwood, Sidney ; Dale, James, Pte., 22/3/16—16/4/19 ; Damant, Walter Leonard ; Damment, Ernest ; Darby, George ; Davey, William ; Darkins ; Davis Thos. W. ; Dawnay C. ; Davis, George.

Dawson, A., Pte., 4th Essex (Hornchurch Coy., Territorials), Aug. 5/1914 —June/1919 ; In hospital 12 weeks through accident at Yarmouth, 1915 ; served in France.

Dawson, Arthur, Pte., Aug. 5/14 ; France.

Dawson, George, Pte., 2/7 Essex Regt., March 6/16, still serving ; Home Service.

Dawson, Henry, Gunner, R.F.A., June/15—May 3/19 ; France.

Dawson, John, Pte., 2nd Batt. N.Z. Rifle Brigade, June 28/16 ; still serving ; France and Egypt. Has lost the sight of one eye through the effects of being gassed.

Dawson, Rueben James, 10th Lincolns, Feb. 29/16—March 22/18 ; France ; reported missing March 22/18 and believed killed.

Dawson, William, Gunner, R.G.A., Jan. 1/17 ; still serving ; Home Service.

Day, Arthur Charles, Signaller, R.F.A., June 15/15—Aug. 11/18 ; France ; was mentioned in Despatches in May, 1917, for repairing telephone wires under heavy shell fire. He died from the effects of gas on Aug. 11/18 in France. Age 22.

Dear, Arthur Henry Albert, Gunner, R.F.A., Jan. 16/16 ; still serving France and Italy ; wounded in the leg in Italy.

Dear, George William Charles, Cpl., A.S.C., Oct. 7/15 ; still serving ; Home Service.

Deere, F. P. ; Dean, A. E. ; Dearman, Wm. James ; Denham, Chas. Ernest ; **Dean, Albert** ; Denham, Sidney E. ; Denham, Wm. C. ; Dellar, Thos. Alfred.

Denning, Herbert Charles, Pte., 31st R.F., drafted to 23rd R.F. (Sportsman's Battalion) in France, Oct. 1916.

Denning, Teddy, Driver, 290th Bde. R.F.A., enlisted 3/9/14.

Desmond, Alfred John, Corpl. Mechanic, 62nd Squadron R.A.F., Nov. 11/16—Feb. 28/19 ; France.

Dice, Ernest Norman, Corpl., Herts Regiment, Sept. 28/16; still serving ; France.

Dickle, Chas. Albert ; Dillworth, L. F. ;

Diebel, Charles Albert, L.-Cpl., A.S.C., Jan. 14/15 ; still serving France.

Digby, Alfred Victor, Pte., M.G.C., May, 1915—Nov., 1917 ; Gallipoli, Egypt and Palestine ; wounded and missing Nov. 25/1917, near Jaffa ; died of wounds Dec. 7/17 in hospital at Damascus.

Dix, H. G., 2nd Lieut., 7th Royal West Kent Regt. Joined University and Public Schools Corps (R.F.) early in 1915 and served in France. He was killed in action at Grandecourt Feb. 14/17 ; age 23. `` Awarded the Military Cross for conspicuous gallantry in action. He led a flank attack on the enemy with great courage and determination. Later, with another officer, he carried out a daring patrol. He set a splendid example throughout." (London Gazette, Jan 10/17.)

Dixon, Ernest Frost, Pte. 1st London Divisional Cyclists F.S.L., in the R.N.A.S., and Lieut. (F.O.O.) in R.F.C., Oct. 10/15—Oct. 14/19 ; North Sea and France.

Doe, Alfred James, Pte., Royal West Kents, 1918 ; still serving France and Germany.

Doe, Frederick George, Pte., 10th Royal Irish Rifles, Oct. 25/16—March 20/19 ; France.

Doe, Frederick George, Pte., 9th Essex, 1916—1917 ; France ; killed in action July 19/17. Age 23.

Doe, William John, Pte., Northumberland Fusiliers, March 1/16—March 1/18 ; France ; wounded in left leg.

Dohoo, Arthur Godfrey, Capt., R.A.S.C., attached General Staff, 16/6/16 —17/2/19 ; France and England.

Dolphin, Chas. Benjamin, Lieut., R.F.C., Sept./14—31/7/19 ; France ; wounded 9/4/17 in Canadian attack on Vimy Ridge.

Donald, Eric Leslie, Pay Sub.-Lieut., R.N.R., Dec./15—Feb./19 ; still serving France and England.

Douse, Francis Walter, Capt., March, 1915—Nov., 1919 ; France and India ; was commissioned in Middlesex Regiment July, 1915 ; served as Brigade Instructor until July, 1916 ; was invalided home from France and promoted to Lieutenant on 1/7/17. In Nov., 1917, he proceeded to India and joined the 2/119th Infantry at Jubblepore, Central India ; was promoted Capt. in May, 1918; he served with this unit until Sept./19 and took part in the Afghan War from May, 1919 to Sept., 1919 on the North Western Frontier. Received wounds at Plug Street Wood near Armentieres, and was recommended for mention in Government of India Dispatches for work during service in India.

Downham, Edward, Pte., Sportsman's Battalion, Jan. /15 ; was killed in action at High Wood on July 20/16, and buried at Bayentine la Petitte.

Dowsett, Jas. Ernest ; Downes, Walter Henry ; Dowsing, Harold ; Dorrington, —. ; Dowsing, Edwin ; Downham, G. ; Downham, Frank E. ; Downham, H. ; Dodd, William.

Drain, F. C., Pte., 10th Essex ; joined April 7/1916 ; to France Nov. 28/1916, where served ; wounded at Poelcapelle Oct. 22/1917 ; invalided home December 6/1917 ; and discharged Sept., 1919.

Drake. Stephen, Farrier, 25/11/15—22/4/19 ; Drew, Victor Lionel ; Drew, Francis M. ; Drake, H. ; Drake, Thos.

Draycott, Lionel George, A.B., Public School Coy., " Hawke " Battalion, R.N.V.R., 13/11/14—17/6/16; Gallipoli ; attached R.N.D. ; wounded in right shoulder and left knee by bullets in Gallipoli Campaign. In consequence of his wounds being of a serious nature, followed by dysentery and pneumonia, he was invalided out of the Service June 17/1916.

Drury, W., Driver, R.F.A. (T.F.), Oct. 28/15—Sept. 30/19 ; Mesopotamia and India.

Dudney, George, Signaller, June /18—Dec. /18, H.M.S.'s " Powerful " and " Diadem " Devonport and Portsmouth.

Duncombe, Frank Percy Edwin ; Durbin, Henry ; Durrant, A. W. ; Durrant, George ; Duncombe, Sidney Edward ;

Dunlop, Aubrey, Pte., Canadian Engineers, 1915—1919 ; France.

Dunlop, Denis, Pte., London Scottish, 1914—1916 ; France ; was gassed by gas shell and discharged with after effects, July. 1916.

Dunlop, Eric Arthur, Pte., Canadian Scottish, 1915—1918 ; France ; died from shrapnel wounds in the head 20/4/18 ; age 23.

Dunlop, Percy Alexander, Corpl., 2nd Battalion London Scottish Transport Section Sept. 12/14—Oct. 28/18 ; Ireland, France, Macedonia, Salonika ; died on active service of malaria fever and nephritis in Salonika on Oct. 28/18 ; age 43. (*See page* 92).

Dunlop, Raymond Everard, Pte., London Scottish, Dec. 11/1915— March, 1919 ; France, Salonica and Palestine and Egypt ; he was present at the capture of Beersheba, Gaza and Jerusalem, and participated in the final allied offensive into Belgium.

Dunlop, Victor R., Sergt., 50th Canadians, 1915—1919 ; France ; received bullet wound in back, and was buried in a dug-out by shell, but was dug out after nearly half an hour had elapsed ; awarded M.M. and D.C.M.

Dyer, Edwin Albert, L./Cpl., A.O.C., 1916—1919 ; Salonika.

Dyke, A.

Earle, William, Sergt., R.E., 18/3/94—Feb. 1915.

Easton, Chas. Thos. ; **Easton, H.** ; Eaton, L./Cpl. ; Earle, Sidney.

Easton, Frederick, Sergt., Army Cyclists Corps, May 30/15—March 20/19 France, Egypt and Palestine.

Easton, John, Sergt., 18th K.R.R. (41st Div.) June 2/1915—June 22/19 ; served in France, Belgium and Italy ; he was wounded on three occasions ; the last time, on March 24/1917 ; he was taken prisoner to Germany, where his right foot was amputated ; he also had a very serious internal wound, which was operated on successfully by German doctors. Sergt. Easton returned to England via Holland on Whit Sunday, 1918, and underwent four more operations. He was awarded the D.C.M. as announced below :—" C/6041 Sergt. J. Easton led his men very gallantly to the attack on 20th September, 1917, across the Basseville Beck to the Tower Hamlets Plateau. By his coolness under heavy machine-gun fire he managed to overcome the resistance of an enemy strong point. After the capture of the objective, his energy and fearlessness were of the greatest value in the consolidation of the position won. In the early morning of the 21st Sept. the posts of his Company were heavily shelled, and both the Officers killed. Sergt. Easton re-established the posts and commanded the remainder of the Company until it was relieved on the morning of 23rd Sept. During this time the positions were heavily bombarded, particularly during the counter-attacks of the 21st September, which he helped to repulse, and all the while were subjected to persistent and accurate sniping, but he always remained cool, and master of the situation. His courage and power of command was most marked."

Edmundson, Walter L.

Edwards, Leonard Joseph, British Red Cross, Salonika.

Elcock, William Henry ; Ellingford, S..

Ellingford, H. C., Pte., Bedfords and Labour Corps ; France ; served Feb., 1918—November, 1919.

Ellingford, T. G., Pte., Royal Fusiliers and Labour Corps ; France ; served June 7/16 to Feb. 16/20.

Ellis, Alfred, Pte., 1st Essex Regiment, 1911—1915 ; Dardanelles ; was wounded in the landing, and was killed by shell June 28/15 ; awarded 1914 star.

Ellis, Harry, Driver, R.E., 1915—1919; Salonica and France ; wounded in France ; awarded 1915 Star.

Ellis, Herbert, Pte., K.R.R., 1918 ; still serving ; Germany.

Ellis, John, Gunner, R.F.A., 1915—1919 ; France ; wounded in 1917.

Ellis, Walter, Pte., Essex Regiment, 1915—1919 ; France ; twice wounded once in 1916 and again in 1918.

Ellis, Walter, Pte., R.M.L.I., H.M.S. " Blenheim," 12/8/12—7/5/19 ; Dardanelles and France ; wounded in France 29/9/18 ; awarded 1914 star.

Ellis, William, Boy, R.A.F., 1917—1919 ; Home Service (under age).
Emmerson, John Fredk., Sergt., Royal Inniskilling Fusiliers, Feb. /16—
    Aug./19 ; France ; gun shot wound in thigh June 7/1917 and sus-
    tained fractured jaw and injury to ear, Oct. 25/1918.
Emmerson, Sidney Arthur, Pte., Royal West Surrey Regiment, June/1918 ;
    still serving, Germany.
England, Chas. Thos.
English, Francis John William, Rifleman, 11th and 12th Royal Irish
    Rifles, June 5/15—Sept. 12/18 ; England and France ; was wounded
    three times and discharged owing to unfitness through wounds.
Errington, Alfred.
Escreet, Hubert John, Lieut., R.F.A., Aug. 9/15—Jan. 27/19 ; France ;
    wounded Sept. 30/1917.
Evans, Clarendon Rees, Corpl., 25/10/15—27/7/19 ; Everson, Leonard ;
    Everson, Ernest Samuel, Sergt., 5/1/09—20/3/19 ; Everett, Arthur
    Benjamin Ellis ; Eves, Wm. ; Everson, F. ; Everson, H.
Evans, Stanley Nevern, Lieut., 19th London Regt., 1915—1919 (3½ years);
    France.
Eve, Alfred William, Pte., M.G.C., March /17 ; still serving, France.
Eves, James, Leading Signalman, Royal Navy, Sept. 26/1911 ; still
    serving ; North Sea and Atlantic in H.M.S. " Antrim," " Calypso,"
    " Boyne," " Cardiff," " Devonshire," " Fearless," " H.M. Sub-
    marine and K.2.

Fancy, C. H., Acting-Corpl., R.E., April 27/17—Oct. 18/19 ; served on
    Western Front ; wounded in left shoulder.
Fardell, Sydney Ernest, Rifleman, 15th Batt. Rifle Brigade, June 18/16—
    April 18/18 ; France ; wounded in forehead and back, and after three
    months in hospital was again sent into the line, and was reported
    killed April 18/18. Aged 32 years.
Fardell, Thomas Charles, Pte., 30th Royal Fusiliers, 7th Royal Sussex
    and R.E.'s, Dec. 7/15—May 17/19 ; France ; was three months in
    24th General Hospital at Etaples ; operation on both feet, then
    transferred to Boulogne.
Farley, John, P.N.R., Royal Engineers, 18/8/15—14/3/19.
Farrant, Archie Raymond, Corpl., 4th Essex and 17th Middlesex Regt.,
    3/12/13—31/7/18 ; Gallipoli and France ; discharged medically unfit
    July 31/18.
Farrant, A. S., Lieut., 3rd Essex ; joined 30th Royal Fusiliers, Nov.
    3/15 ; transferred to 14th D.L.I., December 12/16, and to 3rd Essex,
    Dec. 27/1917 ; took part in attack at Hill 70, April 21/17 ; Second-
    Lieut., Nov. 28/17 ; wounded, May, 1918 ; demobilised, June 27/19.
Farrant, Frederic George, Rifleman, 1st Surrey Rifles, 2/9/14—5/4/19,
    France, Salonica and Egypt.
Farrant, Hector Reginald, 3rd Air Mechanic, R.A.F., 27/10/18—24/11/18 ;
    Home Service ; died of influenza at Blandford Camp on 24th Nov.,
    1918.
Farrant, Henry William, Corpl., Middlesex Regiment, 25/9/05—1/1/19 ;
    France.
Farrant, V. H., Gunner, R.G.A. ; joined November 27, 1915, Royal Fusiliers ;
    served in France ; discharged, August 1/18, with fractured leg received
    while despatch-riding on active service in May, 1917.
Farrant, W. H. ; Fairman, Bertie Harold ; Farmer, E. W. ; Fairman,
    Reginald ; Fairman, Ernest J. ; Fairhead, Arthur ; Fairhead, John ;
    Fayers, Harold A. ; Fairlie, Edward ; **Farrant, Archie R.**
Farrow, T., Stoker, H.M.S. " Diana," Nov. 1915 to Feb. 12/19. In North
    Sea six months ; China 2½ years.
Fennell, W. A. ; Ferguson, D., R.F.A.
Ferguson, D., R.F.A.
Ffitch, Frank E.

Field, Harry Vaughan, A/C.I., R.A.F., 26/2/17—24/2/19 ; England, France, Belgium and Italy.

Field, Stanley Walter William, R.A.F. ; Finchman, Henry T. ; Fisher, C. ; Finch, John F. ; Fisher, G. ; Fisher, Hy. ; Fisher, Percy Wm. ; Fitch, G. ; **Field, S. D.** ;

Fielder, Charles James, H.M.Y. " Amathea," 26/6/17—13/1/18 ; North Sea.

Finch, Reginald Thomas, Sergt., Essex Yeomanry, Aug. 4/14—Dec. 24/18 ; France ; he died in Leicester War Hospital on Dec. 24/18, from illness contracted in France ; age 25 ; interred at Hornchurch.

Fish, A., Acting-Sergt., Essex Regiment, specially enlisted clerk, Record Office, No. 9 District Warley ; served from April 8/15 to 1920.

Fisher, C. E., Pte., Royal Fusiliers, 1914— 17 ; served in France ; disabled through nephritis.

Fisher, G. W., Lieut., Queen Victoria Rifles ; joined Nov. 25/1915, 2/5 The Buffs ; served in France ; shot through arm at Ypres, Nov., 1916 ; disabled through mustard gas shell attack at Arras, March 15, 1918 ; discharged Sept. 23/1918.

Fitzjohn, W., Pte., joined 3rd Essex May 24/1915 ; wounded in knee, July 1, 1916, on the Somme ; to 2nd Essex March, 1917 ; missing from May 3, 1917.

Flint, Ernest John ; Fletcher, Alfred ; **Fletcher, C.**

Floyd, Albert Edward, Pte., 3rd Q.R.W.S., Essex Regiment and A.P.C., Jan. 15/15—July 1/18 ; Guildford, Chatham and London. After training at Guildford he underwent an operation for appendicitis, with complications, and was discharged as medically unfit in Dec., 1915 ; was recalled to the Colours in July, 1917 and posted to Essex Regiment, and afterwards transferred to A.P.C. in consequence of unfitness for active service.

Floyd, Roberts Patrick, Rifleman, 6th Reserve City of London Rifles, April 2/18—May/19 ; Blackdown Camp and Bramley ; Prisoners of War Camp.

Flucker, Maurice Montague, Wireless Operator, R.N., Jan., 1918—May, 1919 ; Grand Fleet.

Flucker, Thomas, Jnr., Steward, Mercantile Marine, May, 1918 ; still serving West Indies.

Folhard, ; Foreman Benjamin ; Forrest, Dennis E. ; Fountain, F.

Ford, Harry, Royal Navy, was killed when H.M.S. " Bulwark " was blown up in the River Medway on Nov. 26/14.

Fountain, F., Middlesex Regt. ; discharged medically unfit, June 1918, after 18 months' Home Service.

Fowler, George, Private, R.M.E., 23/7/18—15/3/19.

Fox, Bernard Roland Valentine, P.F.O., R.N.A.S. (Balloon Sect.), and Civil Service Rifles, Jan. 1/1918—Jan. 14/1919 ; England ; was gazetted P.F.O. at the age of 17½ ; eye trouble, which necessitated hospital treatment, prevented his being dispatched overseas.

Fox, Walter Robert Seymour, Lieut., Royal Air Force, enlisted in the Buffs on attaining the age of 19, in November, 1915, and after completing his training as infantryman took up a specialist course of signalling. In 1917 he saw active service in the trenches in France, and in November of that year he returned to England to take commissioned rank with the Royal Flying Corps, and was gazetted 2nd Lieut. (Observer) on May 18, 1918. Nine days later he was in action over the German lines, and shortly afterwards was severely injured in a crash, but he refused to go into hospital ; he was subsequently wounded in the face by shrapnel, but again declined to quit duty. In the early morning of August 22/1918, Lieut. Fox, whilst carrying out hazardous observations over enemy lines at a low altitude of 600 feet, was shot in the chest by a machine gun from the ground. He never regained consciousness, and died in hospital the same day.

He was considered by his C.O. to be one of the best Observers of his Squadron, and his senior officers placed the greatest confidence and reliance on his work and reports. In addition to the respect which his courage and abilities compelled, he was esteemed by all his comrades for his cheerful willingness, and for the charm of his retiring but sunny disposition, He lies at Gezaincourt (Bagneau), South-west of Dollens.

Franklyn, George John, L./Cpl., Essex Regiment, Aug. 4/14—July 2/19 ; Gallipoli, Egypt and Palestine.

Franklyn, George William, 2nd Lieut., 1/23rd London Regiment :—" At the outbreak of war he held the rank of Sergeant in the 4th Essex Regiment (T.F.), and was immediately called up for home defence. After serving several months in the eastern district, he volunteered for active service abroad, and went out with the 54th Division to Gallipoli. He was present at the landing on the 13th August, 1915, and remained on the Peninsula until November, 1915. On returning to England he obtained a Commission in the 1/23rd London Regiment, and proceeded to France. He was present in many engagements on the Western Front, and was killed in action in the attack of Messines Ridge, June 7, 1917 ; aged 32 years. In announcing his death to his parents, Major-General G. F. Gorringe concluded with the following words :—" Please accept my sincere sympathy with you in the loss you have sustained in this great struggle. Your son was killed whilst leading his men in the recent great battle. He was an excellent Platoon Commander, and was most popular with his men."

Franklin, Henry Albert ; Fryatt, Jeffrey Chalk ; French, A. ; Freeman, Sydney Wm. ; Frisby, George Alfred ; Freeman, John ; Francis, H. ; Fry, L. J.; Franklyn, Alfred ; Franklyn, William.

Franklyn, Sydney Percy, Pte., Essex Regt., Oct. 26/14—April 28/16 ; Great Yarmouth.

Franklyn, William Henry, Pte., Essex Regiment ; Nov. 15/15 ; still serving, Egypt and Palestine.

Freeman, John, Pte., R.E., 1914—1919 ; Ireland, France and Belgium·

French, John, an ex-scholar of Park Lane School ; was awarded the Victoria Cross.

French, Reginald Chas., Sergt., R.A.S.C., 3/10/14—25/5/19 ; France ; awarded 1914 star.

Frost, Chas. Walter, Pte., 2nd Northumberland Fusiliers, 1916—1918 ; India and Mesopotamia ; died of dysentery in Mesopotamia on Nov. 5/18 ; age 44 ; was formerly in No. 9 Battery, 1st Essex Artillery Volunteers.

Frost, Timothy Gibson, Sergt., died of wounds on the field at Gaza, Nov, 3/1917. Was two years and four months on active service at Gallipoli, Egypt and Palestine. He was mentioned in General Allenby's Despatch of Decr. 16/1917, copy of which is appended. It was addressed to Sergt. Frost's widow, and dated 9 May, 1918, from the War Office, Whitehall, and signed by Colonel M. O. Graham :—" I have it in command from his Majesty, the King, to inform you as next-of-kin of the late Sergeant Timothy Gibson Frost, of the Essex Regiment, that this Non-commissioned officer was mentioned in a Despatch from General Sir Edmund Allenby, dated 16th of December, 1917, and published in the Second Supplement to the London Gazette of the 15th, dated 16th January 1918, for gallant and distinguished service in the Field. I am to express to you the King's high appreciation of these services, and to add that His Majesty trusts that their public acknowledgment may be some consolation in your bereavement." Sergt. Frost was formerly in H. Company, 1st Volunteer Battalion Essex Regiment.

Frost, Wm. Gibson, Pte., 9th Essex Regiment, 1915—1916 ; France ; died
of wounds 23/8/16, received in action on Western Front ; was formerly in H. Coy., 1st Volunteer Battalion, Essex Regiment ; age 34.

Fry, Bertie Robert, Pte. ; 4th Essex Regt. ; died on April 4/1916, at
Aylesbury Military Hospital, whilst undergoing military training ;
aged 34 ; interred at Hornchurch, April 8/1916.

Fry Joseph William Albert, Seaman, H.M.S.'s " Saracen," " North Star,"
" Trident " and " Woolwich," June 6/17—July 19 ; Dover Patrol,.
Ostend, Zeebrugge and Scapa Flow.

Fuller, J. L. ; Fulcher, Robert James ; Fuller, Fred.

Gamble, Harry ; Gardner, William George ; Garbe, Gilbert Lewis ; Gamble,.
George Arthur ; Garnham, Ernest A. G. ; Gardner, John Lewis ;
Garrett, E..

Gardner, Arthur William, Corpl., A.P.C., April 1917 ; Salonika and Constantinople.

Gardner, W. G., acting Sergt., R.A.F., Dec. 1/1916—March 8/1919 ; home
service.

Garnham, Ernest Arthur James, Pte., Essex Yeomanry and 9th Essex
Regiment, January 11/15—1919 ; France ; was wounded on March
23/17 in a bombing raid at Arras.

Garrett, E. A., Pte., 4th Essex (Territorials) ; in camp when war broke
out ; drafted to Dardanelles June, 1915 ; invalided home from latter
with dysentery Nov. 6/1915 ; served in France ; missing from April
28/1917 ; age 22.

Garthwaite, F. D., 1st Air Mechanic, R.A.F., 10/10/14—3/3/19.

Gawler, Eric T. H., Sergt., R.A.S.C., 12/1/15—21/2/19 ; England and
France.

Gay, Alfred William, Lieut., R.G.A., March, 1916—Feb., 1919 ; France ;
wounded at the Battle of Arras, April 9, 1917.

Gaywood, John Edward, Wireless Operator, H.M.T. " Redbridge," Aug.
5/1915—Dec. 6/17 ; he was drowned when the " Redbridge " was
torpedoed off Fishguard, Wales, Dec. 6/17.

Gennills, Edward Roland, Rifleman, N.Z. Forces ; Aug. /17 ; still serving ;
France ; seriously wounded in the chest and left shoulder in France,
April 6/1918 ; after treatment in Mile End Military Hospital, London,
and at the N.Z. Hospital, Walton-on-Thames and Hornchurch Convalescent Hospital.

Gentry, A. V., Lieut. 2/23 London Regt., and 11th East Yorks, Sept.
19/1914—July 7/1919 ; England, France and Flanders ; was invalided
home during the summer of 1917 and invalided from the service 1919.

George, F.

Gerken, Frank William, Corpl. 189 Squadron R.A.F., April 2/17—Feb.
27/19 ; Home Service.

German, Alfred Ernest, A.C.I., H.M.S. " Campania " May /17—Nov.
5/18 ; was present when ship was rammed and sunk by H.M.S.
" Glorius " during a gale off Burntisland, Firth of Forth.

Gibson, W. G., joined March 19, 1917, East Surreys ; transferred to 18th
Middlesex ; wounded Dec./17. While in hospital gave blood to two
other comrades in 12 days. Demobilised Nov. 16/19.

Gilbey, F. J., Pte., joined March 28/17, 3rd Queen's R.W.S. ; transf. to
1/19 London Regt. ; served in France ; demob. Jan./19.

Gill, Leonard ; **Gibson,** —. ; Gibson, Albert Wm. ; Gildersleve, Fredk.
Josiah ; Gilbert, Arthur Thos. ; Gipps, Fred ; Gilby, G.

Girling, James Harrison, Pte., 2/7 Devonshire Regt. ; home duty.

Glarse, Thos.

Goddard, A. E., Shoeing Smith, R.H.A., served from outbreak of war..

Goddard, Fred.

Godfrey, F. D., 6th Middlesex Regt. ; joined July, 1916.

Gooday, J., Cpl., R.A.S.C. (M.T.), joined April 27/1915 ; served in France and Belgium ; suffered with pneumonia in 1917 ; demob,. July 14/ 1919.

Goodbody, Terence Edmund, 2/Lieut., Essex Regt., Sept. 18—March, 1919 ; England.

Goodchild, Alfred Thomas, Signaller, 19th Queen's Royal West Surreys and 15th Essex Regiment ; Nov. 6/16—March 13/19 ; England and France (was rejected as medically unfit in 1915).

Goodenough, Ernest Alfred, Sergt.-Major, Australian Imperial Force, Aug. 1914 ; German New Guinea, Egypt and Gallipoli. He joined the Expedition to German New Guinea and was present at the capture of the German possessions. On return to Australia the force to which he belonged was disbanded, and he then joined the Mediterranean Expeditionary Force. He was in Egypt for several months, and landed in Gallipoli in August, 1915. He remained on the Peninsula until the evacuation, when he went into hospital in Egypt. Demobilised Nov. 1919.

Goodrum, Robert Richard, Pte., 4th Essex Regiment ; July 1915 to April 1919. He was invalided home from Gallipoli with dysentery and V.D.H. He was put into training again, and sent to France in Feb., 1918. He was reported missing between 9th and 19th April, 1918, and has not since been heard of ; aged 33 years.

Goodwin, Sydney, Jas., L./Cpl. 11th Royal Scots, Dec./15—Feb. /19 ; France, Belgium and Germany ; wounded on the Somme 9/4/17.

Gould, Walter Henry, Flying Corpl., R.A.F., Sept. /15—March/19 ; France.

Gover, Harold ; Gover, Edward ; Godwin, Harold Arthur ; Goodchild, A. ; Goulden, Sidney Leonard ; Goke, J. W. ; Gould, Dennis ; Goult, G. ; Goates, Lewis ; Goodwin, Wm. Alfred ; Gover, Ralph ; Goddard, A. ; Goldsack,

Gower, F., Private, West Ridings, 29/3/17—2/2/19 ; France.

Gower, Sidney, Notts. and Derby Regt., 1914—1920 ; France and Mesopotamia.

Gower, Wm., Sergt. 4th Essex (T.F.), 1914—1916 ; and cook in R.A.F., to present time ; England and Gallipoli.

Gray, Arthur, Royal Navy.

Gray, H., joined R.F.A. August. 1914.

Gray, W., joined R.F.A. August, 1914.

Green, E., Private, joined Royal Sussex Regiment Dec. 26/1916 ; served in France from March 10/1917—March 23/1918, when he was killed in the German offensive ; age 31.

Green, W. J., Capt., Queen's Westminsters and 1st Royal Berkshires, Sept. 10/14 —Feb. /19 ; England and France ; commissioned 12/5/15 ; promoted Capt. 7/8/16 ; awarded M.C. 10/3/17, and mentioned in Despatches in May /17.

Greenhill, Fredk. Walter, Pte., R.A.O.C., two years ; England and France ;

Greensmith, C. R., Driver, 2A Battery, H.A.C. ; joined Dec. /15 ; served on Western Front ; demob. Feb./19.

Greygoose, Alfred William, S.P.O., H.M.S.'s "Cumberland" and "Ramillies," 1914—1919 ; The Cameroons, German E. Africa, Halifax, Bermuda ; North Sea.

Groot, F. G., R.N.V.R., Naval Schoolmaster at Shotley Barracks.

Grout, L. A. J., Sapper, joined Royal Fusiliers Aug. 1914 ; transferred to Survey Coy., Royal Engineers ; served in France ; killed instantaneously, March 30/1917 ; age 24.

Grummett, Edward ; Grinter, Fredk. George ; Gregory, Walter Fredk. ; Green, Wm. ; Green, Wm. Henry ; Green, A. ; Green, J. T. ; Grout, Herbert ; **Grout. Harry** ; Grover, George ; Gray, U. ; Greenhill, C. ; Grimwood, T.

Guy, W. F., Private, 1/4 Essex (Territorials) at outbreak of war ; Gallipoli June, 1915, where he attained the rank of Corpl. Invalided home Dec., 1916; proceeded to Egypt Feb., 1917, and was killed in action March 27/1917 ; age 21.

Guymer, M., Sapper, R.E., 29/8/16—28/3/19.

Guymer, Sidney James, Pte., R.A.M.C., March 21/16—Oct. 7/18 ; England. He was in Military Hospital with pneumonia and influenza, from which he was discharged on Oct. 1/18, and died at Park Hospital, Hither Green, Lewisham, on October 7/18 ; age 36.

Hall, Benjamin, R.D.C.

Hall, Fredk., Royal Defence Corps.

Hall, Fredk. J., Driver, R.F.A., Oct./16—19/10/19 ; Mesopotamia.

Halls, Sydney William, A.B., Royal Navy ; 1915—April 1919.

Hammond, F. E., Rifleman, 8th City of London Regiment, July 27/14 ; was invalided from service through wounds on 28/1/19.

Hammond, John Dane, L./Cpl., 2nd Norfolks, Aug. 31/14 ; died of wounds in Mesopotamia on 23/4/16 ; age 27.

Hammond, Wm. Geo., Rifleman, K.R.R., June 23/15 ; was killed in action in France on 30/6/16 ; age 28.

Hansen, Lauritz Christian, L./Cpl., 2nd Wellington Regt., N.Z. Forces, Nov. 16/15—March 12/19 ; Egypt and France ; wounded in right foot Sept. 15/16 in Somme battle.

Hare, George, Gunner, R.F.A., 21 May 17 ; still serving ; France and Germany.

Hare, William Henry, 1st Class Stoker, H.M.S. " Blanche " 1914 ; still serving ; North Sea, etc.

Harman, William, Signaller, R.G.A., June 13/17—March 17/19 ; France.

Harold, F. ; **Hanson, A.** ; Hall, Reginald T. E. ; Hamon, Harry ; Harrison, Alfred Francis ; Hart, John Henry ; Hall, Eric ; Hardy, Harry ; Hardy, William ; Hazelton, Hanley William ; Harrington, Harold B. ; Hazelwood, Arthur ; Hammond, Thomas ; Harper, Chas. Albert ; Hart, Arthur ; Hale, J. R. ; Hale, George E. ; Hale, Henry ; Hall, J. R. ; Hall, J. ; Harris, F. ; Harris, G. ; Harris, J. ; Harris, Sidney R. ; Harris, W. ; Harris, S. ; Harber, L. ; Hart, Leslie ; Hasler, John ; Handford, Henry E. ; Hazel, Alfred George ; Hamilton, James.

Harper, Walter, Driver, R.F.A., Tank Corps ; France 1917—1920.

Harrington, Alfred John, Pte., 3rd Northants Regiment ; England ; awarded the O.B.E.

Harrod, Bert David, Pte., 12th Royal Sussex Regiment ; March 8/17 ; still serving ; France.

Harvey, Arthur Bernard, Pte., A.S.C. (M.T.), 1917—1918 ; England.

Harvey, Frank Cecil, Lieut., Staffordshire Regiment, April/15—March /17 ; France ; wounded at the Somme, 30/6/16 ; invalided from service in March/17.

Harvey, George Allen, Sergt., 7th City of London Regiment ; Sept./14—March/19 ; France.

Harvey, Laurence Henry, B.Q.M.S., R.F.A., Aug./14—Feb./19 ; Gallipoli and England ; died of pneumonia 19/2/19, while still serving.

Harvey, Sidney Arthur, Lieut., 7th The Buffs, Nov./14—Feb./19 ; France ; was wounded in France 18/11/16 ; taken Prisoner of War 22/3/18, during German Offensive.

Harvey, T. E., R.A.F.

Hawkins, Frank, A.B., H.M.S. " Courageous," July /17—Feb. 17/19 ; Grand Fleet.

Hawkins, James Reuben, Junr., Pte., 2/1 Durham Light Infantry ; Aug. 10/1916 ; 10th West Yorks Regiment, Sept. 4/1918 ; Home Service and France. He was an old member of the C.L.B., Hornchurch Coy., which he joined about 1910. He was killed in action at Ytres, near Bapaume on Sept. 4/18 ; age 21.

Hawkins, Joseph, Pte., M.G.C., July 28/16; still serving; France; received a gun shot wound in right arm in the summer of 1918.

Hayes, Daniel, L./Cpl., Machine Gun Corps, 1916—1919; France and Italy; 17th and 23rd Divisions.

Hayward, P., Pte., joined Middlesex Regiment, May 5/16; transferred to 7th Royal West Surrey Regiment; to France end of August /16; missing from Sept. 28/16; age 21.

Hayward, William Thomas, Driver, R.A., 29th Division; Dec. 28/14— March 28/18; Gallipoli, Suez, France and Belgium; was a Prisoner of War with the Germans from Nov. 30/17 until the signing of the Armistice.

Haywood, E. J., Pte., Queen's Westminster Rifles.

Haywood, William Arthur, Private, 11th Essex Regiment; Jan. 22/16— Oct. 15/16; France; was reported missing (afterwards presumed killed), Oct. 15/16, on the Somme.

Healing, Alfred Edward; Hewer, Eric Chas.; Head, George C. N.; Head, Albert E.; Heffer, Hy. James; Head, Wm. G.; Heard, Arthur B.; Herwig, George; Hedgecock, Cecil.

Healing, Harold Percy, Cadet, R.A.F., Nov./15—Mar. 6/19; France, Salonika, Egypt; died on Nov. 21/19, from a disease (henkaemia), contracted whilst on active service in the East; age 27.

Hicklin, Joe C. W., 11th Q.R.W.S. Regiment.

Hill, George Henry; Hillier, John; Hill, Thos. H.; **Hitch, H. P.**

Hills, Alfred Thos., Pte., 80th Winnipeg Rifles, Aug./14—May/15; France; wounded 22/4/15, and died in Oxford hospital May 2/1915. age 24; was buried with military honours in Hornchurch Churchyard. He was formerly a choir boy at the Parish Church.

Hills, Herbert George, Royal Navy; drowned on H.M.S. "Hampshire," off Orkneys on June 5/1916.

Hindon, Herbert John, Corpl., R.A.F., Sept./16—Feb./19; England.

Hitch, Harold Reginald, Telegraphist, Royal Navy; April 20/15; still serving; Dardanelles, Salonika, Grecian Islands, Malta, Egyptian Waters, Italian Waters, Dedeagatch and Constantinople.

Holbrook, A. E., Pte., 3rd East Surreys, April 4/18 to Feb. 28/19; Home Service.

Holbrook, Alfred James, Pte., 26th Royal Fusiliers, Jan./18; still serving; France and Germany.

Holbrook, G., Pte., 7th Queen's R.W.S.; joined Essex Regiment June 6/16; transferred to Q.R.W.S. Nov. 23/16; pleurisy and displaced heart March 22/17; trench feet and shrapnel wounds Dec. 16/17; six weeks in hospital 1918, effects of gas; served in Belgium and France; demob. 9/19.

Holbrook, Thomas, Seaman, H.M.S. "Pembroke," (sloop), May 9/18— Feb. 3/19; Coastal Service.

Holbrook, W. C., Pte., R.A.S.C., Jan. 21/15—July 7/19; served in France.

Holbrook, William George, Corpl., 4th Royal Fusiliers, Aug. 4/14—Feb. 4/19; France, Belgium and Germany; Mons Star and rosette.

Holgate, Frederick, Bomb., Essex R.H.A.

Holgate, John, Sapper, R.E.; was wounded at the Dardanelles.

Holgate, Sidney, Pte., Durham Light Infantry.

Hollinghurst, Charles Stanley, M.C., D.S.M., Lieut., R.A.F., 1914 to 1919; Gallipoli, Egypt and France. As a Petty Officer in the R.N.A.S. he served through the Gallipoli Campaign with the 1st Australian Division, and the 29th Division, and was present at the landing at Capa Tepe on the 26th April, 1915. He received the D.S.M. (Gazette, Nov. 9th, 1915), for Machine Gun work. After leaving hospital in Egypt he returned to England and obtained a Commission in the R.F.C. April 15th, 1916. He was subsequently posted to France in July, 1916, and was awarded the Military Cross (Gazette, Nov., 1916) :—"Sec. Lieut. C. S. Hollinghurst, R.F.C., Special Reserve.

For conspicuous skill and gallantry on contact patrol work. On one occasion he was attacked, first by four, and then by three enemy machines, but drove them all off and continued his patrol. On another occasion his observer was hit, and his machine badly damaged, by anti-aircraft fire, but he came back for another machine, and went out again. Two days later he was wounded when flying over the lines at 1,000 feet. He was twice wounded ; once in Gallipoli on July 13th, 1915, and later whilst flying over the Somme on Sept. 13th/16. He was mentioned in Sir Ian Hamilton's Dispatch of Sept. 22/19.

Hollinghurst, Leslie Norman, D.F.C., Capt., R.A.F., 1914 ; still serving in 1920 ; Gallipoli, Egypt, Salonica, France, Germany (Army of Occupation), and India. At the commencement of the war he joined the Royal Engineers, afterwards obtaining a Commission in the 3rd Battalion Middlesex Regiment, and later transferred to the R.F.C., where he obtained the rank of Capt. He was with the 54th Division at Gallipoli, and participated in the Suvla landing in Aug./1915. While holding the rank of Lieut. he was wounded while scouting behind Bulgar lines at Salonica with a small patrol party, consisting of a Sergeant and ten men. He was awarded the Distinguished Flying Cross (Gazette, Oct., 1918), the official announcement being as follows : " Since April 25 this Officer has destroyed four enemy aeroplanes, and driven down one out of control. At all times he displays great determination and cool courage, notably on Sept. 30, when, although his petrol tank had been shot through, and his machine badly damaged, he attacked and destroyed a Fokker biplane that was stalling to fire on another member of the patrol, thereby saving the life of a brother officer. On numerous other occasions Lieut. Hollinghurst, by his gallantry, has saved from disaster other members of the patrol.

Horwood, Archibald Alfred, 2nd Lieut., 6th Batt. Durham Light Infantry ; Dec./15—March 28/18. Trained in the Artists O.T.C., Gidea Park, and went out to France April 1916. Was wounded at Etaples in June 1917, while still a Cadet. Transferred to the H.A.C., and received his Commission Sept./17. He was in action at the Aisne, Ypres and the Somme, and in the Great Offence of March/18, being reported as wounded and missing March 28/18 ; age 24.

Hossack, W. R. C., 2/Lieut., 5th East Surreys ; joined June 18/17, A. and S. Highlanders ; L./Cpl. Sept. 20/17 ; transferred and commissioned May 1/18.

Houghton, Harold, Private, 24/5/17—20/2/19.

Houseman, Ronald ; Hood, George William ; Holby, James ; Horne, William S. ; Horne, John C. ; Holgate, Henry W. ; Hodges, Henry Price, R.A.F. ; Holloman, Frederick ; Horide, Henry Thos. ; Horide, Edward ; Holdway, C. H. ; Holdway, T. W. ; **Howell, J. R.** ; Hooper, S.

Howard, Fredk., Army Pay Corps.

Howe, Thomas Andrew, Corpl., 2nd Coy. K.R.R.C. (Orderly Room Clerk), 1916—1919 ; Winchester.

Howlett, Frederick, Pte., R.A.S.C., June 11/18—Feb. 22/19 ; Home Service.

Hubbard, Francis James ; Hubbard, Jack ; Hunt, Walter Lionel ; Hume, George Henry ; Humphrey, Henry Ernest ; Hum, Henry Charles ; Hutley, Percy ; **Hutchinson, L. ; Hunwicks, John** ; Hudson ; Hunt, L. ; Hunter, A. ; Hurrell, C. ; Hurrell ; Hunsdon, John R.

Hume, G., Pte., R.A.S.C. (M.T.), heavy lorry driver ; joined June 14/17 ; served in France Nov. 1918—Dec. 24/1919.

Hurrell, G., Pte., Essex Territorials ; from outbreak of war to Jan./19 ; served in France.

Ingram, W.
Ireland, R. L.
Isabel, Ernest ; Isbell, Alfred ;

Ivey, George William, Lieut., R.A.S.C., June, 1915—January, 1919. Enlisted as Pte. in Army Service Corps ; promoted to Staff-Sergt.-Major on account of special technical knowledge ; proceeded to France Nov.,1915, with 38th (Welsh) Division ; awarded a commission in the field in January, 1917, and posted to the 4th Division on the Somme in the Horse Transport Section. His Division later moved up to Arras for the Easter offensive, and after a week on special duties in the trenches at St. Laurent Blangy, he was severely wounded by a fragment of 5.9 shell on Easter Saturday. After a year's hospital and convalescent treatment, posted for light duty at the Ministry of Pensions.

Ivey, Gordon, Pte., 5th London Rifle Brigade. Enlisted Sept. 1/15, in the 3/1 East Anglian Division Cyclists, at the age of 16 years, and was discharged as under age on the 24th Dec. of that year. Re-enlisted on 2nd October, 1917, in the 3/15th County of London (Civil Service Rifles), and was drafted to France on 2nd April, 1918, and transferred to the 5th London Rifles Brigade as a Rifleman. He was at the battle of Arras, where he was gassed, and was invalided home to Huddersfield Hospital, suffering from the effects of gas and septic poisoning. Was demobilised on 8th Feb., 1919.

Ivey, Leonard, C.S.M., R.A.S.C., Nov., 1914—May, 1919 ; joined A.S.C. (M.T.) in Nov., 1914, after several medical rejections, and left for France on January 15/1915, with the 28th Division. Was invalided home in January, 1916, for an operation which was successfully performed, and returned to the Western Front June, 1916. He participated in the principal battles at Ypres, Armentieres, and La Basse sectors in 1915. Was promoted Corpl. March 10/1915, Sergt. June 6/1915, C.S.M. March 17/1917. He was wounded on Aug. 11/18, and awarded the Meritorious Service Medal June 16/1918.

Ivey, William Leslie, Lieut., M.C, ; Civil Service Rifles, 1/15th London Regt., Aug. 31st, 1914, to April, 1919. He was drafted to France on 15th August 1915, and was at Loos and Hulloch, where he contracted frostbite at a time when there was no adequate protection against that complaint. He was invalided home and upon recovery obtained a commission in his own Regiment on the 26th April, 1917. Returning to the Western Front on the 15th July, 1917, he was at the battle of Cambrai and the retreat on Dec. 4/6th, 1917. He was in action during the great German offensive of March, 1918, where he acted as Brigade Signalling Officer. Shortly afterwards he was wounded in the arm and leg, and was invalided to England for medical treatment. He was awarded the Military Cross for conspicuous bravery on March 23rd, 1918, and was invested by the King at Buckingham Palace on June 29th, 1919, the following being an extract from the " London Gazette " of 16th September, 1918 :—" Awarded the Military Cross. 2nd Lieut. William Leslie Ivey, London Regt. For conspicuous gallantry and devotion to duty. For six hours, while box respirators had to be worn continuously during a heavy gas and high explosive bombardment, this officer was always on the move, looking after his men, clearing them out of dug-outs that had become gas affected, and superintending as brigade signalling officer the repairing of cables. The third day he was wounded while leading Headquarters company to take up a covering position, but he continud in action, rallying the men of another unit who were retiring, and restored the situation under heavy machine-gun fire."

Izod, Walter Henry, Pte., H.A.C., 26/1/17—27/2/19 ; England.

Izod, William George, 2/Lieut., R.F.A., Aug. 4/14 ; still serving ; France, Belgium and Germany. Previous to the war he was in the Territorial Force, where he gained the T.F. Long Service Medal ; was wounded in August, 1916, and awarded the 1915 Star.

Jackson, B. J., Gunner, R.F.A., Feb., 1917—Sept., 1917; Woolwich; afterwards 2/Lieut. in R.A.S.C. (H.T.) from Oct., 1917—May, 19, at Aldershot and France; returned from overseas owing to active service injury in April, 1918, and retained for Home Service as unfit.

James, Fredk. Hall; Jay, P.; Jay, —.; James, James; Jarvis, John Wm.; Jackson, Arthur S.; Jarrett, Chas. Gordon; James, John; **Jarvis, Albert.**

Jarvis, F., 2/9/15—20/4/18, P.N.R., Royal Engineer.

Jarvis, Norman Wood, Pte., London Rifle Brigade, and 3rd Rifle Brigade, Aug. 4/17—Jan. 30/19; Belgium and France; was wounded in the face in August, 1918, and again in the left ear in October, 1918; was at the Battles of Lens and Cambrai.

Jee, Alfred William, Corporal, 2/3/12—4/3/19.

Jenkinson, Frank.

Jenkinson, Samuel Stewart, L./Cpl., R.E.., Oct./16—March/18; France; discharged through illness contracted on Active Service.

Jenkinson, Wm. Thos. Stewart, Pte., R.A.M.C. and R.A.S.C., July/17—June/19; England.

Jensen, Christian Albert Arthur, Sergt., Royal Engineers (anti-aircraft), April/16/1920; England.

Jensen, George Herbert, 1/Lieut., R.G.A., 2nd Siege Battery and 144th Heavy Battery, April/07—/20; England, Belgium and France; wounded once and gassed; was in the retreat from Mons; awarded Mons Star 1914.

Jenvey, Douglas Walter, Wireless Operator, Royal Air Force, Feb. 1917—Nov. 1919; medically unfit for overseas, served in Home Squadrons as Instructor in Wireless.

Jervis, C. A., Nov. 9/14—March 19/19; Malta, Egypt, Gallipoli and France; Prisoner of War in Germany from March, 1918, to the Armistice.

Johnson, A. E., R.A.S.C. (M.T.); Aug./15—Oct./19; Salonika front.

Johnson, Robert Wm., L./Cpl., 1/4 Essex Regiment, 11/11/14—26/6/19; Egypt.

Johnson, Sidney R. H., Driver, Royal Horse Artillery, May 7/15—April 19/19; France and Egypt.

Jones, Charles Henry Reginald, R.E.

Jones, H., Leading Seaman Gunnery Instructor, Royal Navy, 4/3/03—10/3/19.

Jones, Richard T.; Jones, Harry; Jones, Joseph; Johnson, Frank S.

Joslin, A., Royal Navy.

Judge, Reginald Walter.

Kale, Percy.

Kelly, —.

Kemp, George Henry, Gunner, R.F.A., Sept./17—Nov. 5/18; France; killed in action Nov. 5/18.

Kendall, Frederick Denys, 2/Lieut., Royal Air Force; joined the London Rifle Brigade on reaching the age of 18, and later transferred to the Royal Air Force, obtaining his Commission in June, 1918. He left for Italy on August 7/18, and was killed on the 30th of that month in a bombing raid on Cataro (Dalmatia) from Taranto. He was buried with military honours near Valona, aged 19. The exploit which resulted in his death was thus described by his Commanding Officer:—" Kendall had just carried out an exceedingly trying raid, and by his own skill and pertinacity had won back through shocking weather over the mountains to the Italian lines. Either the strain was too great for him, or he misjudged his landing, but he fell from a small height, and together with his observer, was instantaneously killed. He will be greatly missed in the squadron and by the wing. He was a very clever pilot." He was born at Bangalore, India, but his parents removing to South America, his home for the past seven years has been with his uncle and guardian, Mr. J. W. Crouch, of Edlows, Emerson Park.

Kerslake, Sidney S., Lieut., Civil Service Rifles and 4th Essex Regt. ; 31/8/14—1920 ; India and Ireland.

Kimber, Charles J., Bdr., R.F.A., Nov. 6/16—May 24/19 ; England.

Kimber, Percy V., Corpl., R.F.A., April/15—Jan./19 ; France.

King, A.

King, C. T., Cpl., Hampshire Regt. ; joined June 3/15 ; went to France, March 8/16, where he served until he met his death on the first day of the Somme offensive, July 1/16 ; age 25.

King, D. K., L./Cpl. ; joined R.A.S.C. Oct. 13/14. At Mons ; to Egypt Nov./15 ; afterwards to Salonika ; dysentery and malaria on Struma Front ; in France again until demob. April/19.

King, Harold ; King, Chas. B. ; Kittle, Ernest Edwin ; Kimber, Fredk. George ; Kimber, William Oliver.

King, H. F., Sergt., France and Ireland ; joined Essex Regiment ; transferred to Royal Welsh Regiment ; wounded in shoulder ; bombing instructor ; demobilized 1919.

King, R. W., Essex Yeomanry ; joined Oct. 25/15 ; transferred to 1st Dragoons and to 2nd Co. of London Yeomanry ; served in Egypt and Palestine till June/18 ; then to France to 104th M.G.C., 1st Class Machine Gunner, in charge of a gun team ; demobilized April/19.

Kingley, Herbert William, Pte., Royal Fusiliers, Nov./15—Oct. 7/16 ; France ; was killed in action in France Oct. 7/16 ; age 21.

Kirkman, Henry Cyril, Pte., 2/28 County of London Regt., Artists' Rifles, O.T.C., July /18—Jan./19 ; England.

Kitchener, Harry John, Cadet, Artists' O.T.C., and R.A.F., June/18—April/19 ; training.

Knight, Albert Edward, L./Cpl., R.E., Sept./15—April/19 ; France.

Knight, Alfred Charles, Pte., 10th Essex ; France ; killed March 8/17 ; age 29.

Knight, Alfred Edward, Driver, R.A.S.C., Aug. 30/13—Mar. 24/19 ; England and France.

Knight, Frank Richard, A.P.C. ; Knight, Arthur Claude.

Knight, George Henry, Rifleman, K.R.R., July/16—April/17 ; France ; killed in action near Garelle, N.E. of Arras, April 25/17 ; age 26.

Knight, Henry Charles, Leading Stoker, H.M.S. " Hogue " Aug. 4/14—Sept. 22/14 ; drowned Sept. 22/14 ; age 42.

Knight, Simon, Pte., Royal Marine Engineers, April 10/18—Dec. 17/18 ; Southwick, Sussex.

Knight, Wm. George, Pte., Essex Regiment ; May/16—April/19 ; France ; wounded at Monchy 13/4/17.

Knightbridge, H. B. J., Rifleman ; joined Nov. 14/14 K.R.R.C. ; discharged medically unfit, March 22/15.

Knightbridge, W. W. A. ; joined March 26/17, 23rd Training Reserve Batt. ; transferred to A.P.C., Nottingham, Dec. 8/17 ; demobilized Jan. 16/20.

Knock, Robert Alfred, Rifleman, Rifle Brigade, March/18 ; still serving ; England.

Korriene, C., First Class Gunner, Royal Marine Artillery. In R.N. (H.M.S. Marlborough) when war broke out. Was on that vessel when she was torpedoed ; demobilized May/19.

Lambe, R. Bevis, Lieut., R.F.A. ; was gazetted 2/Lieut. at the age of 17½ years ; served in England until 1918, when he proceeded to France on active service.

Land, Herbert James, C.S.M., Essex Regiment, 24/10/92—7/12/19; England and Ireland; prior to the war he was Sergt.-Instructor to the Hornchurch Coy. 4th Essex Regiment, and previous to 1914 had served in India, South Africa and Malta.

Landors, William George, Pte., A.S.C., April 6/15—April 1S/19; England and France; discharged owing to nervous breakdown and debility.

Lapwood, Chas.William, L./Cpl., Royal Marine Engineers, 4/6/18—12/3/19; France and Belgium.

Lapwood, Herbert A., Sapper, R.E., 4/6/15—10/2/19; France and Belgium; invalided from France with trench fever and nephritis Nov. 29/17.

Lawrence, Henry John; Lambert, Henry T.; Lake, —.; Lane, John; Lane, Thos.; Lazell, E.; Lazell, J.

Lawrence, Leonard A., A./L. Cpl., R.E., I.W. and D.; 20/11/16—11/3/19; Richborough and Sandwich.

Lazell, Arthur Frank, Pte., Duke of Wellington's West Ridings; Oct. 28/14—March 21/18; France; was killed in action on March 21/18; age 27.

Lazell, W. E., Pte., Labour Company; Mar./16—Sept./19; France.

Letten, George Edward, Pte., Scots Guards, May /18—Feb. 2/19.

Letten, J. Pte., 9/2/05—4/4/19.

Letten, John, Stoker, H.M.S. "Natal" and "Electra" 1913; still serving North Sea.

Letten, Joseph, Steward, H.M.S. "Sharpshooter" 1916—March 24/19; England.

Letten, William Henry, Pte., Middlesex Regt.; May 29/18—Jan. 2S/19.

Lewsey, Alfred Harry; Leggett, Albert; Leggett, Alfred W.; Lee, Wm.; Legg, Sydney; **Letten, T.**; Lewis —.; **Leech, Thos.**

Lincoln, Albert James, 1st Class Stoker, H.M.S. "Patrol" Nov. 7/16—Jan. 30/19; Irish Sea Patrol.

Lincoln, Herbert Charles, 1st Class Stoker, H.M.S. "Inflexible," Aug./15; still serving, North Sea Patrol.

Lincoln, William Henry, 1st Class Stoker, H.M.S. "Swale" Feb. 11/15; still serving in Channel Escort Flotilla.

Little, A. F., Stoker, H.M.S. "Marlborough"; joined July 7/18; still serving 1920, Mediterranean Squadron; H.M.S. "Marlborough" brought the Dowager Empress of Russia and her staff to Malta.

Little, C. W., Pte., 6th Royal West Surrey Regt.; joined Jan. 9/18; served in France; killed Sept. 21/18; age 19.

Little, Sidney H.; Little, John H.; **Little, J. J.**

Livermore, P., Pte., 1/4 Essex (Territorials); in camp when war broke out; served at Gallipoli and in Palestine, (Gaza); shell-shock, Nov. 2/17; killed in action on Palestine Front, Sept. 19/18.

Livermore, W., Pte.; joined May 22/17, Royal Fusiliers; transferred to 61st Batt. M.G.C.; served in France; demobilized Nov., 1919.

Lloyd, E. A., Capt., 2nd S.W. Borderers; joined Jan. 25/15, H.A.C. Infantry; Jan. 25/17, gazetted to 6th S.W.B.; April 12/18, taken prisoner near Armentieres; repatriated Dec. 25/18; demobilised June 16/19; accidentally injured, causing loss of sight of left eye.

Lloyd, Llewellyn Samuel; Llewellyn, Robert Lewis; Llewellyn, Alfred.

Lobley, G. H., Pte., 6th Liverpool Rifles; joined Sept. 17/14; sprained ligaments of leg while training; discharged medically unfit, Nov./14.

Lockyer, Donald A., Sergt., Rough Riders and R.E.; Aug./14; still serving; Egypt, Palestine and Syria.

Lockyer, Wm. Henry, Sergt., City of London Yeomanry; Capt. Middlesex Regiment; 5/11/11—9/2/19; England.

Lomax, George Monton, Capt., General List; 14/4/17—28/2/19; Home Forces.

Lomax, R. M., Mercantile Marine, 2nd Officer, s.s. Bechuana. On war service from Feb./15 ; transporting troops on E. African coast from June /15—Jan./18 ; then to Mediterranean under French Government ; released Dec./19.

Long, Bertie Wm., Pte., Royal Fusiliers ; June /15—July/16 ; France ; killed in action July 7, 1916.

Long, George Arthur, Pte., 1st Suffolk Regt. ; Feb. 25/19 ; still serving ; India.

Long, Harold Wilfred, Pte., 2nd Suffolk Regiment ; April/18, still serving ; France and Salonika.

Long, Joseph J., Saddler, R.F.A., Sept. /14—July /18 ; France ; killed in action July 2ʳ, 191ᵗ.

Lovett, C., 2/Lt., R.G.A. ; France and Belgium.

Low, George ; Lockyer, William Hy. ; London, Wm. ; Logan, Frank ; Percy ; **Love, John** ; Lock, —. ; Love, H. ; Love, T. ;

Lowe, George Herbert, Driver, R.F.A. ; Nov./16—March 19 ; France.

Lowe, Louis William, Sergt., 1/4 Essex Regt. ; Aug./14—April/19 ; Egypt.

Lowe, Sidney Albert, Sergt., 1/4 Essex Regt. ; March/15—April/19 ; Egypt.

Ludlow, Arthur Ernest ; **Lungley, Jas. Arthur**.

Luff, Frank, Signaller, Royal Garrison Artillery ; Dec. 9/15—March 3/19 ; England.

Luther, Edward Albert, Corpl., The Rifle Brigade, 20/8/07—13/2/15 ; England, Ireland and France ; awarded 1914 Star ; discharged disabled 13/2/15.*

Luther, Harold George, 2/Lieut., R.E., R.N.A.S. and R.A.F., 10/10/14 —1919 ; England, France and Belgium ; twice wounded. (*See page 94*).

Luther, Sidney James, Pte., 31st Alberta Infantry Battalion, 11 Canadians, Nov./14 ; still serving ; Belgium, France and Germany ; awarded 1915 Star.

Lyons, Harry, Gunner, R.A., 5/3/17—22/1/19.

Macdougal, Joseph George, Corpl., R.N.A.S., May/16—Feb./19 ; Home Service.

Macey, Clifford James, 2/Lieut., 1st Dorset Regt., 4/8/14—25/5/15 ; France ; was killed in action at Hill 60, France, on 25/5/15 ; age 23.

Maidment, Arthur George, Pte., Essex Regt., 28/2/15 ; still serving ; England.

Maidment, George, Corpl., K.R.R., July/15—13/11/16 ; France ; killed on Active Service in France, Nov. 13/16 ; age 44.

Maitland, D. F., Corpl., Army Pay Corps, Essex Regt ; served April/17—April/19.

Makings, George, Coy.-Sergt.-Major, 4th Essex Regt. (T.F.) ; Aug. 4/14—May 30/17 ; Norwich, Stamford and Great Yarmouth ; was discharged on termination of engagement, having served 30 years in Volunteers and Territorial Force.

Mallam, Joseph, L./Cpl., 10/9/14—31/1/19.

Manly, Berry Thos. Chas., 2/Lieut.,Wireless Officer in R.E. Signal Service ; Gallipoli, Egypt and France ; Aug., 1914—1919 ; he was attached to the 29th Division at Gallipoli, and was present at both the landing and evacuation.

Mann, D., Able Seaman ; joined Aug. 15/16, and served on H.M.S. " Miranda " until January 29/19. In the winter of 1917/18 was in hospital at Chatham when the barracks were bombed by German aeroplanes.

Manning, H. F., Pte., R.A.S.C. (M.T.), Supervisor of Army laundry ; May 31/1917—Jan. 24/19 ; Home Service.

*Corporal E. A. Luther wrote a War Diary concerning the operations in which his regiment was engaged, which was highly commended by Colonel Lord Henniker and Major H. G. Parkyn, of the 5th Battalion Rifle Brigade.

Mansfield, A., Gunner, R.F.A.; Oct. 6/16—Dec. /19; Home Service; low medical category.

Mansfield, F. V., Pte., 7th Hussars; joined 15th Hussars and trained with Lord Kitchener's first recruits, Sept./14; France 1916/17; Egypt and Mesopotamia; invalided home with enteritis, Sept./19; still serving 1920.

Mansfield, E. W., Driver, R.A.S.C. (M.T.); March 30/16—Jan. 19/19; served in England, Ireland and France.

Mansfield, H. J., Pte., 7th Royal Warwicks, May /16—Jan./19; France six months; Italy one year and seven months.

Maple, Sydney James, 2nd Class Clerk, R.A.F., 27/8/17—18/11/18.

Marrable, James, Pte., Lancashire Fusiliers; joined Aug. 17/15; France; was twice wounded.

Marrable, Joseph, L./Cpl., 9th Essex, 24/1/16—18/10/16; France; killed in action on the Western Front Oct. 18/16; age 23.

Marrable, Thomas, Rifleman, Rifle Brigade; June 14/15—Sept. 3/16; France; was killed in action on Sept. 3/16, at Beaumont Hamel.

Marrable, William, Pte., Lancashire Fusiliers; joined May 12/18; Home Service.

Martin, C. D.; Maline, —.; Maxim, D.; Matthews, John W.; Matthews, Thos. George; Mathews, Jesse Wm.; Mayhew, Arthur James; Malroy, A.; Maskelyne, John Eric; Masters, George Albert; Mackness, Douglas Chas.; Mason, Samuel; **Marshall, W. J.**

Martin, Chas. Stafford, Sergt., A.P.C., Infantry and Labour Corps, 22/10/14 —8/4/19; Salonica and Egypt; after numerous attacks of malaria and dysentery, invalided home from Egypt suffering from chronic mucus colitis.

Martin, F., Pte., 4th Essex (Territorials), commencement of war—July /19; served on Egyptian front; wounded Dec./18.

Martin, Horace Charles, L./Cpl., Essex Regt., 1914—1917; France; reported missing; age 20.

Martin, J., Driver, R.A.S.C.; Mar. 5/17—Jan./20; served at home until Aug./19; then went to Turkey (Chanak), where he served five months.

Martin, W. A., Pte., 1/4 Suffolks; joined June 1/16; served in France; battle of Arras; wounded April 23/17; died April 26/17.

Mason, Francis Augustus, Capt., Signal Service, R.E.; Aug. 4/14—Feb. 15/19; attached to Staff, Northern Command.

Mason, James, Pte., East Surrey Regt., May 11/16; still serving; France; was a Prisoner of War.

Mason, William David, Bdr., R.F.A., May 26/15—Jan. 8/19; Belgium and France; once wounded.

Mather, Alfred Allervan, Sergt., 17th Royal Fusiliers, 1914—1919; France.

Mather, Richard Robert, Wireless Student, Marconi Co., 1918—1919; England.

Matthews, A. H., Lieut., R.N.A.S. and R.A.F.; Sept./17—/20; France and Egypt; participated in the Aerial Bombardment of Morhange and Lorquin Aerodromes; also the Metz-Sablon triangle during Sept./18; wounded Sept./18.

Matthews, F. L., Pté.; joined Aug. 1914, 10th Royal Fusiliers; served in France; died Nov. 19/16, of heart strain, through excessive fatigue while stretcher-bearing; age 33.

Matthews, G. J. J., 2/Lt., R.A.F.; joined May 17/17, 2nd Artists' Rifles, O.T.C.; transferred to R.A.F., Jan. 10/18, taking commission from that date; Home Service; demobilized Jan. 23/18.

Matthews, J. C., Lieut., R.A.F.; joined Sept. 7/16, 2nd Artists' Rifles, O.T.C.; trans. to R.A.F., May 12/17; Commission June 25/17; to Egypt, Oct. 20/17. On one occasion was two days lost in the desert; graduated as Service Pilot, Dec. 31/17; demob. July 1/19.

Mattock, George William, 601st H.S. Employment Co.

Mayes, Percy Leonard, Air Mechanic, R.A.F., 1916—1919; Fighting Scout Squadron; France.

Mayes, William, R.A.M.C., Field Ambulance, 1914—1918; France; was wounded on May 11/15; mentioned in Despatch to General Headquarters and subsequently killed in action on Oct. 19/18.

Mayne, Thos., Pte., 11th Hussars, attached to R.E. Signals; Sept. 9/14— Mar. 3/16; France; killed in action March 3/16; age 45. He was formerly in the Hornchurch Coy. of the National Reserve. His Section Officer wrote of him as follows:—" I could better have spared half my Section than Tom Mayne. He was always bright, willing and good tempered. He died the death of a true soldier."

McCullum, Donald, 3rd Norfolk Regiment.

McCallum, Francis.

McDermott, Donald William; McAlenan, Wm. Patrick.

McDonald, Angus, Signaller, R.F.A., 10/9/16—24/6/19; France and Belgium.

McDonald, Douglas, Gunner, R.F.A., 1/6/17—10/5/19; France and Belgium; gassed March/18.

McDonald, George Fredk. Handel, Lt.-Col., 6th Batt. Essex Regt. (T.F.).; 1914—1919. Gallipoli, Egypt and Palestine; Mentioned in General Allenby's Despatches. Awarded O.B.E.; Order of the Nile; 1914-15 Star. (*See page* 95).

McDonald, George Jason, L./Cpl. R.E., 10/10/16; still serving; France and Belgium.

McMullen, Donald Jay, Brevet-Major (Commissioned 1911), R.E.; War service from Aug./14; still serving; Staff appointment at War Office; Egypt, Mudros and Palestine; awarded D.S.O. and later promoted Brevet-Major for services in Palestine Campaign.

McMullen, John Alexander, Lieut., M.B.E., No. 4 Motor Ambulance Convoy B.R.C.S., France, Oct. 11/14—April 12/15; Lieut. B.R.C.S. Missing and wounded Enquiry Bureau, Egypt, Mudros, Anzac and Cape Helles, Sept. 23/15—March 10/16; Lieut. R.A.F. (Navigation Instructor in Great Britain), Nov./17—May/19; awarded Military M.B.E. for services in R.A.F.; served at Huddersfield under Ministry of Munitions, April/16—Oct./17. (*See page* 97).

Meades, James; Meloy, John; Mermod, James.

Meehan, W. A., joined Sept. 23/14, R.A.M.C.; transferred Aug. /17, to R.E.; service on many sectors in France; invalided out of the service through wounds, Jan./19.

Merrick, John Albert, Coy.-Sergt.-Major, Border Regt.; Sept. 15/14—. Oct. 11/18; England and Egypt; was invalided from Egypt on Aug. 20/16, and transferred to Home Establishment and discharged disabled on Oct. 11/18; was mentioned in Despatches by Sir John Maxwell, C.-in-C. Egypt, London Gazette, June 21/16; age 52.

Milbank, Walter, Gunner, R.F.A., 4/3/17—9/3/19.

Miller, A.

Miller, Albert Leonard, Sergt., 11th Batt. London Regiment, Sept. 2/14— Oct. 10/16; Great Britain; was discharged in Oct./16 as medically unfit for war service.

Miller, F. J., Pte.; joined Royal Navy Feb./15; Devonport, " Vivid " Barracks, and at sea; discharged from Navy Jan./16 with rheumatic fever. Re-enlisted April 4/18 in 52nd Royal Fusiliers. Went to France in July and was wounded Oct. 23/18; discharged Nov. 29/18 with loss of left arm.

Miller, H., Lieut.; joined Lord Kitchener's Army 1914; transferred to 2/5 Essex 1915.

Miller, Hector, Pte.. M.G.C., June/17—Feb./19; France.

Miller, Herbert; Mitchell, E.; Millbank, Alfred Sidney; Mist, J.; Middleton, Robert; **Millard, J.**; Millard, S. J.

Miller, J. E., Pte., 1st Essex; joined July 2/16; served in France; life almost lost through gunshot wounds in back, left leg and side and right arm; discharged July 25/17.

Miller, Peter, Pte., 2/8 Essex, attached 2nd Royal Sussex; Jan. /16—Sept./16; France; was killed in action at High Wood on Sept. 9/16.

Mills, Arthur James, Gunner, R.G.A., Nov. 7/16—Feb. 8/19; United Paull Point Battery, five months, and Tynemouth Castle one year and seven months.

Mitchel, E., Corpl., Military Foot Police. Had served 21 years in the Army before the war; offered himself Sept. 9/14, and did special services in above Corps in France and Italy; demobilized April 15/19.

Mohring, Albert, O.T.C., Aug./18—Jan./19; Cambridge University.

Moore, G., C.S.M., D.C.L.I.; joined Aug. 9/15, Royal Berks; transferred Aug./16 to 10th D.C.L.I.; Company-Sergeant-Major Oct. 21/17.

Morgan, Charles, 18th Essex; Moss, John; Moody, W.; Moss, Fred. H.; Moore, A. W. P.; Moores, Edward Chas.; Morrison, S. C.; Moore, Harold James; Moorehouse, Earl; Morrison, Cuthbert

Moss, Harold Palmer, L./Cpl., 2/5 Essex Regt., 1st London Regt., and 11th Batt. Royal Fusiliers; Oct./16—Aug. 6/17; home and France. He was a Boy Scout from 12 years of age in Hornchurch Coy. of Romford Troop; joined the V.T.C. early in its career, as a Bugler, where he remained until joining the Army; he was killed in action on Aug. 6/17, at Wimereaux, France, aged 19.

Moss, Thomas William, Sapper, R.E., June 6/16—Oct. 24/17; Chatham and France; was killed in France on Oct. 24/16. Previous to joining the Army, he was a member of the V.T.C.

Mussett, Robert; Mitch, Ernest A.; Munden, Wm.

Mynott, George Henry; Mynett, Wm. John.

Nash, A. C., Writer, R.N.; July 21/16—July 21/19; served on H.M.S. "Duke," Eastern Mediterranean.

Nash, E. H., Pte., A.P.D., Warley; Aug./17—Feb./19.

Neal, Sydney, Pte., 23rd Batt. Royal Fusiliers; Jan./15—March/19; France; was wounded and gassed on two occasions.

Newell, G. H., Staff-Sergt.; joined Aug. 4/14; Mons, Aug. 23/14, and all fighting in France. Made Farrier-Sergt. May 15/15; Staff-Sergt. April 20/18.

Newell, Harvey James A., R.E., Palestine.

Newman, C. B., Sergt., served in 1/4 Essex (Territorials) at outbreak of war; Gallipoli, Egypt; time expired 1916; rejoined same year 12th Essex; France; wounded in knee; discharged medically unfit April/19.

Newman, Francis E.; Newell, C.

Newman, George Gibson, Corpl., Essex Regt., and R.A.F.; Aug. 4/14—April/19; Gallipoli, Egypt and France; was wounded at Gallipoli in thigh.

Newman, James, Store-keeper, Hospital and Troop Ships; Aug. 4/14; still serving; transporting troops to theatres of war; was mined while on H.M.S. "Gookha" in Mediterranean in Oct./17.

Newman, W. J., Pte., 1/4 Essex (Territorials); joined Sept. 17/14, Royal Fusiliers; transferred to Herts Yeomanry and to 1/4 Essex; Gallipoli expedition; Egypt and Palestine (Jaffa Front); Haifa and Beirout; demobilized March 1/19.

Newman, Wm., L./Cpl., K.R.R.; Oct. /14—Jan.19; France; received shrapnel wound in hand in 1916.

Nicholls, Ernest Walter, R.N.; he joined the Navy just before the outbreak of war; served in H.M.S. "Arethusa" and took part in all the brilliant exploits of that ship and perished with her when she was sunk. He was formerly a member of the C.L.B.

Nicholls, Herbert George, 3rd Essex Regt. ; Nov. 6/19 ; England, Egypt, France, Ireland and Malta.

Nightingale, F. V., Gunner, R.G.A. ; twelve years' previous service in R.H.A. ; re-joined March 13/16 ; served in France April 1/16—March 6/19 ; transferred to R.G.A. (28th Anti-Aircraft Section).

Nightingale, J. W., Pte., East Yorks Regt. ; Jan./15—Jan. 15/18 ; served in France ; taken prisoner Nov./16 ; died in Germany Jan. 15/18.

Nightingale, Thomas H., Driver, R.E. Signals, 9/10/16—14/6/19.

Nixon, Herbert ; Nice, S. ; Nice, W.

Norman, John Stanley, Private, 5/5/16—23/2/19.

Norrington, George, 500 R.D.C., North Dublin Union.

Noyes, Thos. Arthur.

Nunn, Fredk. James.

Oakley, W. R., Pte., Headquarters Staff ; joined May 18/18 ; served in France and Belgium ; Salvage Corps, Sept/18—Feb./19 ; demobilized April 30/20.

Oldman, Robert Ellesley, 2/Lieut., 1st Batt. H.A.C., and Essex Regiment ; Jan./17— ; —1920 ; France.

Oliver, Cecil Charles, Stoker, H.M.S. " Inflexible," Nov. 16/15—April 29/19 ; North Sea.

Oliver, George William, Gunner, 1/1 Essex R.H.A. ; Sept./14 to end of war ; Egypt.

Oliver, James Richard, Pte., M.G.C. ; Oct./18 ; still serving ; England.

Oliver, Lewis Edward, Pte:, Duke of Cornwall's Light Infantry ; May/18— end of war ; France ; received gun shot wound in the leg during the advance on the Somme.

Oliver, Philip Richard James, 1st Class Officer's Steward, H.M.S. " Crescent " Feb. 1916—end of war ; with the Fleet.

Oliver, Philip Sidney, Pte., 1/5 Essex Regt. ; Nov./16 ; —still serving ; Egypt ; received a bullet wound through right forearm during the battle of Gaza.

Osborn, Sidney Chas.

Ottley, Wilfred Mark ; Ottley, Wm. E.

Overall, Wm. ; Overall, Sidney G.

Padfield, Herbert Lawrence, Private, London Rifle Brigade, 1914—1915 ; France ; was wounded on June 16/15, from the effects of which he died the following day, June 17/15.

Page, F. D., R.H.A., joined March 17/16, 107 Canadian Batt. ; transferred to 44th ; served on Western Front ; wounded at Amiens, Aug. 11/18.

Page, Robert, Pte., 1st Essex Regiment ; missing ; Gallipoli.

Pailthorpe, Douglas, Capt., R.F.A., 1914—1919 ; France. He was mentioned in Despatches in 1918 and awarded the Military Cross for conspicuous bravery during the same year. The announcement of this appeared in the " London Gazette " for March 26/18, as follows :—" Sec.-Lieut. D. Pailthorpe, R.F.A., Special Reserve. He was in an observation post in the front line, when the enemy attacked under a heavy bombardment. When all his communications were cut by the enemy's fire, he assisted in repelling the enemy's first attack, and in capturing four prisoners. He was driven back by the second wave of the attack, but personally got a Lewis gun in action, and assisted in establishing and maintaining blocks in the communication trenches until supports arrived. He then rendered a most valuable report on the situation and the disposition of the enemy. He showed magnificent courage and initiative throughout."

Pailthorpe, Edward Hugh, Pte., R.A.M.C., 1914—1919 ; France.

Pailthorpe, Halford Noel, Staff-Sergt., Supply and Transport Corps, Indian Army, 1914 ; still serving. At the outbreak of war he was serving at Cawnpore, India, but before the end of 1914 he had landed in France, and was with the Supply Depot Unit in the Indian Reinforcement Camp in Marseilles. He continued to serve in France until the middle of December, 1915, when he embarked for Mesopotamia, and joined one of the Indian Units at that time desperately attempting to relieve our men at Kut. He also participated in the advance to Baghdad and Samarra in Jan./17. He was mentioned in General Sir P. Lake's Despatches, and in addition to receiving the 1914 Star, General Service Medal and Allied Victory Medal, was granted the Meritorious Service Medal, and promoted Sub-conductor in recognition of services rendered in the Field during the war.

Pailthorpe, Harold Anderson, Flight Lieut., R.N. At the outbreak of war he belonged to the Stock Exchange Corps of the R.N.V.R., and was at once mobilized, and after a few days at Headquarters was sent to Chatham and from there to the Dreadnought " Temeraire," where he remained for fourteen months. He eventually obtained a Commission in the Royal Navy, and was appointed to the R.N.A.F. He was stationed at Chingford for training, and was from there transferred to Cramwell, Lincs., and later to Westgate, from whence he was dispatched to France, arriving there on March 17/17. He was soon in the Line, and on May 23 was killed in action, age 27 years. His reports whilst training were excellent, and he was reputed to be a good Air Fighter, and exceptionally clever Pilot. In his last great fight he was attacked by seven German Aviators. He was mentioned in Despatches for this in the " London Gazette " of Oct. 1/17. He was formerly a chorister at the Parish Church.

Palmer, Frederick, 20th Batt. Middlesex Regiment.

Palmer, J. ; Pavitt, Joseph ; Page, George ; Patience, Wm. J. ; Parsons, Benjamin ; Palmer, Henry ; Parrish, Harold ; Patience, Augustus E. ; Parker, Thos. W. ; Palmer, Albert ; Parmenter, Henry Chas. ; Parfitt, W. ; Parsons, George ; **Parsons, A.** ; Parker, C. ; Pamment, John ; Parker, W. ; Park, P. J. ; Parkin, A. ; Page, L., R.H.A.

Palmer, Thos. Edward, Pte., 1/7 Essex Regt. ; 29/7/16 ; still serving ; England, France and Egypt ; was in hospital from Feb. to July/17, suffering from frost bite.

Pamment, Charles Thomas, Stoker, H.M.S. ; Oct./16— April/19 ; North Sea.

Pamment, Joseph Wm., 1st Stoker, H.M.T.B. 35, 15/11/15—16/1/19 ; North Sea.

Pamment, Phillip John, Driver, A.S.C., Horse Transport ; March/17— March/19 ; France.

Parish, John Charles, Sapper, R.E. ; Nov. 15/15—March 28/19 ; France ; discharged through disablement (illness), caused on active service, March 28/19.

Parish, Wm. Arthur, Pte., 1/4 Essex and 1/4 Devon Regt. ; Aug. 4/14 ; Dec. 19, 1919 ; Mesopotamia and India.

Park, P. J., Gunner, Royal Marine Artillery, May 31/16—April 1/19 ; North Sea.

Parker, Harry, Rifleman, London Rifle Brigade, April/16—Oct./16 ; France. Killed October 8th, 1916, by German sniper, while acting as Battalion Scout on the Western Front ; age 15.

Parrish, Leonard Cleugh, Pte., 4th Buffs, 13th Royal Sussex, R.A.S.C. ; 22/1/17 ; still serving ; France and Belgium ; was severely wounded in right thigh, right arm and right shoulder at Zillebecke, near Ypres, on Oct. 19/17.

Parry, Rev. A. J., Chaplain Forces, May/17—Feb. /18 ; Ballykinlar Camp, County Down, Ireland.

Pattison, Stuart Percy, Lieut., 2/20 Batt. London Regt. (attached R.A.F.);
Nov. 11/15—Sept. 11/19 ; France, Salonika and Palestine.
Paul, H. M., Sergt., Essex ; went out with the 4th Essex (Territorials),
at outbreak of war.
Payne, Ernest, 2nd Class Air Mechanic, R.N.A.S., 1916—1919 ; Scotland.
Payne, R. A., Lieut. 1/33 Punjaub Indian Army, 1914 ; still serving.
He joined Civil Service Rifles as Pte. in Sept./14 ; left in /15, and
joined Inns of Court O.T.C. He obtained a Commission in 1916,
and later a permanent Commission in the Indian Army, leaving
England for India in Dec. /18. Was twice wounded while serving in
France.
Pearce, George Henry, 1st Aircraftsman, R.A.F., 10/9/17—18/9/19.
Pearce, Henry George, Pte., 3rd Beds., 9/7/18—28/2/19 ; France.
Pearce, H. J., Pte., R.A.S.C. (M.T.) ; joined May 13/15 ; served in " Butter
fly " Column, France ; contracted dysentry 1917 and demobilised
April 1919.
Pearson, C. H., Pte., 1/7 Essex Regt., 6/11/15—22/3/19.
Pemberton, E. E., Gunner, R.G.A., April/16—Feb./19 ; Home Service.
Pemberton, H., Sergt., Royal Engineers ; joined Aug./14 ; served in
France, Russia, Ireland and Germany.
Pemberton, H. J., Signaller, R.E. ; April/16 to Dec./18 ; Home Service.
Pemberton, R., N.C.O. Pilot, R.A.F. ; outbreak of war in 4th Essex
(Territorials) ; Gallipoli, June/15—Nov./15 ; invalided with dysentery
and enteric ; to France as Despatch-Rider, R.E., March 17/16 ; served
till Aug. 22/18, when transferred to R.A.F. ; qualified pilot, Dec.
20/18 ; demobilized Feb./19.
Pepper, James, A.B., Royal Navy, 1914—1919. He first served on the
cruiser " Doris " and then on the " Aster " mine sweeping, and was
on that vessel when she was mined off Malta. He was then transferred
to another mine sweeper which was also mined immediately afterwards. He then served on the " King Alfred," convoying American
Troops to France, and was torpedoed off the north coast of Ireland,
getting into port under great difficulties. He was discharged from
the Royal Navy in Jan./19 ; volunteered for Russia in May/19, and
was seriously wounded through an explosion on an ammunition
barge, Aug. 23/19.
Percy, Harry Walter, Corpl., R.A.F. (M.T.), 8/1/17—14/1/19 ; Thetford,
England.
Perkins, Wm. Fredk. ; Pearce, James L. ; Paul, H. ; Perkins, John
Harry ; Peear, John Thos. ; Peear, George ; Pettitt, Joseph ; **Pearce,
A.** ; Parker, L. ; Parsons, W. ; **Pewter, B. J.** ; Pewter, S. J. ; Pewter,
A. H. G. ; Periam, Harold R. ;
Petherwick, Walter James, Pte., 28/9/15—19/6/19.
Peto, J., Lancers, killed at a listening post in France ; Jan. 7/16.
Pettican, A. E., Pte., Lancashire Fusiliers ; July 20/16 ; still serving ;
Germany ; has been wounded.
Pettiford, Payne Harry, Capt., 1/12 Loyal N. Lancs. Pioneers, Oct./15—
/19 ; France, Salonica, Egypt, Palestine and Belgium ; mentioned in
Despatches Aug. /18.
Phillips, Barrington, Corpl., R.A.S.C. (M.T.), 1914—1919 ; France.
Phillips, Major Dan., Pte., R.A.S.C. (M.T.), 1915—1919 ; France.
Phillips, Walter C. ; Phillips, Clarence.
Philpot, John Edward, Pte., A.S.C. (M.T.), April 7/15—Feb. 21/19 ; France
and Mesopotamia.
Pinner, E. ; Pitchell, Fredk. Richard ;. Pitts, Wm. J. ; Pike, Cecil Frank.
Pitchers, R. B., Reservist ; joined 3rd Norfolks May/15.
Pomfrett, Ernest Herbert, Leading Seaman, Motor Boat Service, 1913—
1919 ; Devonport, Scotland and Turkey.
Pomfrett, James Alfred, Pte., Northampton Regt., 1918—1919 ; England.

Pomfrett, William Arthur, Pte., Cyclists Corps, 1914—1919 ; Dardanelles and Egypt.

Pond, W., Pte. ; joined Essex Regt. Jan./17 ; went out May 21/17 ; transferred to 13th Royal Fusiliers ; served in France ; trench fever, Oct. /17 ; joined Agricultural Corps, July/18 ; demobilized March/19.

Potter, A. C., K.R.R., Coy.-Sergt.-Major ; France ; awarded D.C.M. for specially gallant conduct at the taking of Flers.

Potter, A. H., Leading Signalman, R.N., H.M.S. " Lowestoft " ; Heligoland and Dogger Bank fights ; also bombardments in Gallipoli Expedition ; on a " Q " boat in Mediterranean for two years ; now serving on H.M.S. " Coventry" ; joined Navy Oct./09.

Potter, Cyril ; Poole, Wm. H. ; Polly, James George ; **Poole, A. H.** ; Pomfrett, S. S. ; Pond, W.

Potter, F. C., C.S.M., 16/10/97—23/2/19.

Potter, J. R., Sergt., R.A.S.C., Dec./14—Jan./20 ; served in France.

Potter, H., Pte., 7/8/18—10/3/19.

Potter, W. H., Royal Navy, Leading Gunner ; Gallipoli Expedition, H.M.S. " Lord Nelson." ; also H.M.S. " Blonde " ; took part in many bombardments and actions, including naval raid on Zeebrugge, April 18/18.

Powell, Fredk. Chas., 1/A.M., R.F.C.

Powell, Leslie A., Flight Sub-Lieut. R.N. ; joined H.M. Forces as a Trooper in the 2nd Dragoon Guards on Sep. 2/14, and after training at Aldershot served in France for a period of nine months. He then returned to England to qualify for a commission, and in Feb./16 was gazetted to the Royal Navy, being attached to the R.N.A.S. He gained his " wings " within three months, and was at first stationed on the East Coast. He was then again despatched to the Western Front, and after serving there for three months as a Pilot was wounded, whilst in flight, on March 4/17, and died of wounds on March 6. As will be seen from his military record he nobly responded to the call of his Country within the first month of the outbreak of war, while still under military age. The following tributes were amongst those received from his brother officers :—" I had the great pleasure of having him under me in my wing, where he proved an excellent officer and a splendid pilot. He was a personal friend of mine, and will be a great loss to his Squadron. Ennis W. R. Chambers, Wing Commander, R.N.A.S., Attached Headquarters, R.F.C." " He was in my Squadron and one of its cheeriest and happiest members. Everyone, officers and men, loved him for everything he did, his happy ways in all troubles, and his grit and nerve when flying and fighting. He was with a number of his friends in a very heavy fight when they were outnumbered by German machines, but he played the game with his comrades, and stood by them in the hour of their trouble. They not only drove off greater numbers than themselves, but in the end his Squadron was still in the air and held the supremacy. He was shot while still in the air, but flew on for another 15 minutes, till he got back to our side of the line, where he brought his machine down." R. H. Mullork, Squadron Comdr., Naval Squadron No. 3, attached No. 22 Wing, R.F.C.

Powell, Thos. George, Pte., Essex Regt.

Pratt, Aubrey James, Gunner, R.G.A., Dec. 9/15—March 8/19 ; France and Italy.

Pratt, George Stanley ; Proctor, George ; Price, Wm. E.

Pratt, James Jonah, Pte., Durham Light Infantry ; Dec. 10/15—Jan. 28/19 ; France.

Prior, Pte., 11th Essex Regt. ; wounded.

Prior, Arthur John, L./Cpl., 10/11/14—9/1/19.

Prior, B. S., Pte., 4th Essex Regt. ; killed at Gallipoli.

Prior, Samuel, Pte., 7/11/14—15/2/19.

Prior, Wm. Joseph ; Probart Chas. Lionel ; Pryke, Robert.

Pudney, W. T., Corpl., Queen's R.W. Surrey ; joined Jan. 24/17 ; served in France, Egypt and Mesopotamia ; had enteric fever and dysentery several times ; demobilized April 24/20.

Purbrook, Charles Arthur, R.A.M.C., B.R.C.S. and Y.M.C.A. ; July 15/20 ; England, France and Belgium ; was discharged from R.A.M.C. owing to strained heart ; resigned from B.R.C.S. for similar reasons, and now with the Y.M.C.A.

Purkis, Arthur, 1st Stoker, H.M.S. " Christopher," 11/6/13 ; still serving.

Purkis, Chas. Edward, 1st Stoker, H.M.S. "Albacore," July/16—Jan/19.

Purkis, Fredk. Walter, 1st Stoker, H.M. Submarines, 11/6/13 ; still serving.

Purkis, William Ernest, Cpl., 1/4 Essex Regt. ; Oct./14 ; Dardanelles and Egypt ; awarded the Military Medal. He was wounded twice in the Gallipoli campaign, and on Nov. 30/17 was reported a Prisoner of War, in the hands of the Turks, since when no further news has been received of him ; assumed to be dead.

Purkiss, George, Pte., Labour Batt., 1917—1918 ; Sussex.

Purkiss, Walter, Petty Officer, H.M.S. " Ure," 1914 ; still serving ; chiefly in the Mediterranean.

Putman, T. F., Corpl., 16th Service (C.L.B.) Batt. K.R.R. ; joined Oct. 17/14 ; served in France ; wounded June 27/16, Sept. 25/17, and Oct. 12/18 ; L./Cpl. June 8/17, Cpl. April 13/18 ; awarded Military Medal for excellent all-round work in machine gun section 1918 ; demobilized March 14/19.

Pye, Alfred James, Pte., M.T., A.S.C., March 13/17 ; still serving ; France.

Rae, C. H., Paymaster-Lieut., R.N. ; was in the Navy at outbreak of war on H.M.S. " Pathfinder " and was one of 51 saved from latter when torpedoed Sept. 5/14 ; also served on H.M.S. " Amethyst " Sept./14 ; " Lowestoft," Oct./14—March/15, and " Calliope," May 15—/19 ; took part in Dogger Bank Action, Jan. 24/15, and Battle of Jutland May 31/16.

Rae, J. I., Pte., 1st London Scottish, 1/14 London Regt. ; Jan. 1/17—Oct. 20/19 ; served in France, Belgium and Germany ; wounded by bayonet thrust on June 8/18, and slightly gassed.

Rae, R., Paymaster-Lieut., R.N.R., granted commission as Assistant-Paymaster and appointed to H.M.S. " Victory " March 13/15 ; served in H.M.S. " Dreel Castle," April 22/15—Nov. 12/19 ; Paymaster-Lieut. March/19 ; on Staff of Rear-Admiral J. S. Luard, C.B., May 1/17—Aug. 15/19.

Rainbird, William Ernest, Gunner, R.F.A. ; May 27/15—June 25/19 ; India.

Rainbow, G. H., Pte., R.A.S.C. (Stores Dept.) ; May 13 /18—Nov./18 ; Woolwich.

Ramsey, Jesse, Pte., 4th Essex Regt. ; killed at Gallipoli.

Randel, Hugh, Lieut., R.N.A.S. and R.A.F. ; Oct./17—Feb. /19 ; Italy and Albania ; awarded Italian Croce di Guerra, announced in " London Gazette " April 5/19 :—" For valuable services rendered in connection with the war, while on service in the Mediterranean area."

Raven, W. A., April 30/17 to Armistice.

Rawlinson, Clarence A. ; Randall, Ernest ; Rayner, Arthur ; Radford, Wm. Peter ; Randall, Godfrey ; Randall, A. ; Raymond, A.

Rayment, W. G., Pte., 8/4/17—3/3/19.

Rea, S. J., Pte. ; joined Sept. 23/15 Middlesex Yeomanry ; transferred to 12th Middlesex (Infantry) Sept. 23/16 ; also to the 11th Royal Fusiliers ; served on all fronts in France. From March 21/18 in charge of Brigade Concert Party, with rank of Sergt. ; demobilized Feb. 7/19.

75

Read, John, Pte., 1st Sportsmen's Batt. and R.E., 1914—1917 ; France.
Reed, Walter John, S./Sergt., R.A.O.C., 10/1/15—23/2/19.
Reeve, Wm. V. ; Reynolds, Fredk. Wm. ; Reynolds, Wm. Robt.
Rhodes, William Henry, Leading Aircraftsman, R.A.F., 26/10/18—20/3/19.
Ridgewen, Arthur ; Richardson, Wm. John ; Richards, Chas. Frank ;
    Rich, W. ;
Riley, Clifford John, Sapper, R.E. Signals, 1916—1919 ; France, Belgium,
    and Germany.
Rippingale, Jack, Sapper, R.E. ; 18/11/15—16/4/19 ; France ; Prisoner
    of War 28/5/18 ; repatriated 1/1/19.
Roast, Chas. Ernest, Pte., Essex Regt. ; Jan./15—April/19 ; France.
Roberts, P. Private, 19/2/17—24/3/19.
Robinson, Edward Henry, Lieut., 2nd and 3rd London Regt., R.F., Aug.
    6/14—Nov. 6/19 ; Malta, Egypt, Dardanelles and France ; was
    wounded at Suvla Bay Dec./15.
Roe, F., Rifle Brigade (Late Lieut., R.N.) ; awarded Distinguished Conduct
    Medal 1915 for carrying out successfully a dangerous and difficult
    scouting operation.
Roffey, Geoffrey Pickering, Lieut., Canadian Cavalry Corps and 19th
    Welsh Regt., Jan. 1915/1919 ; Canada and France.
Roffey, Harold Percy, Lieut., Chinese Labour Corps ; 1917/1919 ; France.
Roffey, Jasper Claud, Private, 6th City of London Rifles, 1915/1919 ;
    France and England ; wounded at Vimy Ridge, 1916, incapacitating
    him from further active service.
Roffey, Myles Herbert, Major, 19th Welsh Regt. and Tank Corps, Jan.
    1915/1920 ; France and Army of Occupation, Germany ; awarded
    D.S.O., January, 1917, mentioned in Despatches three times.
Rogers, Harold Victor, Chief Engineer ; Admiralty Transport No. 50 ;
    1914 ; still serving ; Atlantic service.
Rogers, T., Pte., Royal Fusiliers ; joined June/16 ; served in France ;
    trench fever Dec./16 ; wounded in shoulder April/18 ; demobilized
    March/19.
Rolfe, Fredk., Pte., 1st Essex Regt. ; Gallipoli ; missing.
Rolph, Arthur, Pte., 5/6/19—22/2/19.
Rooke, E. A. ; Rooke, A. V. ; Rooke, C. H. ; Rolfe, Ernest ; Roast, F. ;
    Roast, J. ; Robyns, Eric G. H. ; Rogers, C. ; Rogers, G. ; Rogers,
    A. ; Rogers, Ernest ; Rolfe, Osborne C. ; Roser, Geo. Milton.
Roper, F. V., Cpl ; joined Jan. 24/16, 8th City of London Regt. ; served
    in France ; awarded Military Medal at Ypres, Sept. 20/17, " for cap-
    turing a German concrete farm, fifty prisoners and four machine
    guns, assisted by about eight comrades ; demobilized Feb. 9/19.
Rowe, Wilfred Lewis, Pte., 8th West York Regt. ; May/16—/19 ; served
    at Somme, Ancre Valley, Bullecourt and Passchendaele, Cambrai,
    Bucquoy, Vaux and Marcoing.
Rowlatt, C. N., Major ; at outbreak of war was Captain and Adjutant of
    4th Essex ; Home Service ; appointed to the Staff /15, with rank of
    Major.
Rudken, Charles Joseph, Pte., 16th East Surrey Regt. ; April/17 ; still
    serving ; India.
Rudken, Cyril John, Cadet, Queen's Westminster Rifles and R.A.F. ;
    Feb./17—Jan./19 ; France.
Ruffle, Percy Geo. ; Ruffe, Horace.
Ruhlam, Wm., was Prisoner of War.
Rumsey, George Reymond, Corpl., 22/7/15—1/3/19.
Rush, George T., Pte., 22/8/14—21/2/19.
Russell, Cecil Amos, Leading Telegraphist, R.N.V.R., Mine Sweeper,
    136, 4th F.S.F., 1915/18 ; White Sea, Shetlands and North Coast of
    Scotland.
Russell, C. T. F., Pte., 24 Batt. Royal Fusiliers ; also 1 Batt. Queen's
    R.W.S. ; served in France ; joined Jan. 21/15 ; demobilized Feb. 28/19.

Russell, Walter Stanley, 2/Lieut., R.A.S.C., B.H.Q., 28/9/14—3/5/19 ; France, Serbia, Macedonia, Salonica, Egypt and Palestine ; wounded by shrapnel from high explosive shell in the valley of the River Jordan, March 11/9/18.

Ruston, Alfred Francis Gerald, Major, R.E. (T.F.), 4/8/14—7/3/19 ; England, Gallipoli, Egypt, France, Germany ; mentioned in Despatches 10/4/16 and 9/4/17. (*See page* 99).

Saltwell, C., Signaller, 27th Siege Battery, R.G.A. ; May/17—Feb./19 ; served in France ; gassed April/18.

Sargent, Edward George Thomas, Trooper, King's Own Royal Regt. (Norfolk Yeomanry) and Household Batt., Sept. 6/16—Oct. 10/17 ; United Kingdom and France ; was killed at Poelcapelle on October 10/17 ; aged 20.

Saunders, Henry, Pte., Essex Regt., 1899—1915 ; France ; he was wounded and gassed and killed at St. Jean on May 2/15 ; he served through the South African War with the mounted infantry, and later in India.

Savoy, Joshua ; Saich, Fredk. Wm. ; Saitch, A. ; Savill, G. ; Sarling, Wm. Chas. ; Saggers, Arthur ; Saunders, Albert ; Sawyer, Fredk. ; Salmon, Geo. ; Salmon, Geo. James ; Salisbury, Albert E. ; Sanders, Jeffrey ; **Saunders, G.** ; **Saunders, H.** ; **Saggers, F.** ; Sadler, W. ; Saltmarsh, Frank.

Sawkiss, George, Pte., 8/3/15—20/8/16.

Sayer, Percy J., Pte., 10th Queen's ; March /16 ; still serving ; France.

Sayer, Stanley M., Leading Signaller, H.M.S. " Euryalus," Aug. 2/14 ; still serving ; North Sea, Dardanelles and Mesopotamia.

Says, Leslie Arthur, Pte., 17/6/12—2/5/19.

Schmidt, Bernard C.

Scrine, Horace Bailey, Corpl., A.S.C. (H.T.) ; Sept./14—Jan./19 ; Salonika ; was invalided home with fractured leg.

Scrine, Reginald Orchard, Sergt., Queen's Westminster Rifles ; Dec./14— Jan./19 ; France ; slightly wounded in the neck.

Sealey, Gordon Henry, 1st Class Stoker, Royal Navy and Royal Fleet Reserve ; was taken prisoner at the fall of Antwerp in Oct./14 and remained in Germany for four years and three months.

Searle, Harry Edwards, Corpl., 2nd Oxford and Bucks Light Infantry ; Aug./14—April/16. One of the " Old Contemptibles," " A " Coy., of the 2nd Oxford and Bucks Light Infantry, and of the first Expeditionary Force that landed in Belgium in Aug./14. Served at Mons, the Marne, the Aisne, Ypres, Festubert, and at Kut (Mesopotamia). He was slightly wounded on the Aisne, and was wounded by a shell at Festubert in May, 1915. Returning from the Western Front, from July/15—Dec./15 was Musketry Instructor at Cosham, Portsmouth, to the new Battalion, 3rd Oxford and Bucks ; went out with his draft to Mesopotamia in Jan./16 and was killed in action at the relief of Kut on April 6/16 ; age 29. Prior to joining the Regular Army Feb./08, he served for several years in the Hornchurch Co., 4th Essex Territorials.

Searle, W. ; Sewell, Horace.

Seccombe, James Horace, Lieut., 3rd Monmouth Regt., 24/11/15—15/5/19 ; France and England ; severely wounded at Arras 19/4/17.

Seefels, O. K., Pte., No. 2 Infantry Labour Coy., Middlesex Regt. ; joined June 18/16 ; served in France and Belgium in 1917 as stretcherbearer. Then attached to Canadian Pioneers Batt, for Rail road construction ; demobilized March 27, 1919.

Shave, A. P., Lieut. ; joined H.A.C. Jan. 26/15 ; France ; transferred to S. Wales Borderers, Aug. 3/16, and gazetted 1st. Lieut. April 24/18. Invalided home ; then to Germany and Ireland ; demobilized April 1, 1920.

Shearman, John.

Sheffield, Alan MacGregor, Lieut., Royal Navy; appointed Cadet H.M.S. "Highflyer" Sept./13; at the commencement of the war he was transferred to H.M.S. "Eclipse," one of a Light Cruiser Squadron patrolling the Western entrance to the Channel, and later engaged in escorting the first Canadian contingent from Halifax, N.S., to this country; subsequently he was appointed to H.M.S. "Monarch," one of the Ships forming the second Battle Squadron of the Grand Fleet. On promotion to Acting-Sub.-Lieut he served in Torpedo Boat No. 26, and on promotion to Sub.-Lieut. in H.M. Torpedo Boat Destroyer "Munster," of the 12th Destroyer Flotilla of the Grand Fleet. After two years' service in this ship, during which time he was promoted to Acting Lieut. and Lieut., he was promoted to a new destroyer, the "Trinidad," attached to the same Flotilla. Whilst on this ship he witnessed the surrender of the German High Seas Fleet, and navigated one of the German Destroyers into port. At the conclusion of the war he was appointed to the Super-Dreadnought "Marlborough," of the Mediterranean Fleet, since when he has seen considerable service in the Black Sea and the Mediterranean. In Dec./19 he was appointed to H.M.S. "Stalwart."

Shelley, G.; Shephard, Oliver, A.S.C.; Shephard, Chas. Alfred; Shelley, Wm.; Sheffield, Herbert.

Shepherd, Arthur, Pte., 3rd and 9th Essex; France; was wounded July/16 in back and leg and now suffering from paralysed arm.

Shield, William, Pte., Essex Regt., 1914—1916. Was a veteran of the Essex Regt., having served with the colours for fourteen years before the war. He rejoined the service in 1914, and was invalided out in 1916. He never recovered his normal health and died Sept. 12/18, aged 50 years. He was buried in Hornchurch churchyard with full military honours.

Shipton, H., Pte., 2nd D.C.L.I., June/16—June/19; Macedonia; wounded Dec. 7/16; invalided home May/19.

Sibthorp, Herbert, A.M.I., R.N.A.S., Nov./16—March/19; Dover Patrols; France and Belgium.

Sibthorp, Josiah James, Pte., 5th Canadian Mounted Rifles, Mar./15—Sept. 15/16; France; killed Sept. 15/16; age 38.

Simons, Reginald T.; Simonds, John C. T.; Simons, Burton V.; Simmons Arthur J.; Simpson, George.

Sims, H. F.; joined June/15, 3rd Essex; served in France; wounded; discharged, medically unfit.

Skillicorn, David.

Slade, H. H., Lieut.-Col. Was gazetted 2/Lieut. 1st H.B. Essex in 1897. He was in Command of "H" Company 4th Essex Regiment at the outbreak of war. Was acting Staff Officer Essex Infantry Brigade from Nov./14—Jan./15; 2nd in Command 2/4th Essex from Jan. to May /15. Raised and commanded 3/4 Essex Regiment May/15. Commanded XI Divisional Base Depot in Egypt March—July/16, and 16th Irish Infantry Base Depot in France Aug./16—Dec./17.; promoted Lieut.-Colonel in June/17.

Slawson, Tom Ernest.

Sledge, William, Instructor Gunner, Royal Navy; killed at Gallipoli.

Slyfield, G. W., L./Cpl.; joined Nov. 10/14, Essex Regt.; transferred to 2/6th Gloucesters; served in Belgium and France; severely wounded (fourteen wounds), Aug. 27/17; demobilized March 12/19.

Smith, A.

Smith, A. H., Private, 7th Northants Regt.; joined Sept./16; killed in action April 17/17.

Smith, Albert J. D., Sapper, R.E. 16/1/17—27/10/19; France.

Smith, A. T., 2nd Air Mechanic, R.A.F.; Dec. 27/17—Jan. 26/19; Home Service.

Smith, Chas. ; Smith, D. ; Smith, Albert J. W. ; Smith, James Wm. ;
Smith, John ; Smith, Horace Robert ; Smith, J. A. J. ; Smith,
Archibald T. ; Smith, Henry Clayton ; Smith, Bernard C. ; Smith,
Sidney Leslie ; Smith, Wm. ; Smee, George Henry.
Smith, Frank Henry, West Yorks Regt.
Smith, Percival William, Sapper, R.E., June 7/15—July 7/19 ; France
and Belgium ; awarded 1915 Star and Allies' Medal.
Smith, William Jasper, Corpl., R.G.A. ; France and Germany ; was
gassed.
Smith, William John, Pte., R.E., July/17 ; still serving ; Egypt.
South, A. E.
Spicer, Herbert.
Spurgeon, C. B.
Stalham, Edward, Pte., 2nd Batt. Border Regt. ; Aug. 4/14—May 8/19 ;
France ; was wounded in the left leg during the first Battle of Ypres
and taken prisoner and repatriated on New Year's Day, 1919 ; awarded
1914 Star.
Stanley, F., Royal Navy, Cook's mate ; joined Nov. 6/17, and was placed
with R.A.F. until Feb./19. Then to H.M.S. " Hussar," in which
he was serving in Mediterranean Squadron in 1920.
Steer, Charles, Corpl., S.A. Medical Corps, Oct./15—June/16 ; German
East Africa ; C.F., 9th S.A. Horse, June/16—April/17, German East
Africa ; C.F., 8th Division Artillery, May/17—May/18, France ;
D.A.C.G., XIX Corps, Dec./18—March/19, France. ; awarded
Military Cross in connection with the attack at Zillebeke, 21/7/17 ;
Prisoner of War in Germany May/18—Oct./18. (See page 105).
Stocker, Herbert Frank ; Starling, Wm. ; Steward, Henry ; Stone, Harry
Wm. ; Starr, Thos. ; Stewart, Walter ; Stevens, Chas. B. ; Stukings,
John ; Stringer, Alfred S. ; **Stebbings, Samuel** ; Stroud, R. F. ;
Stanley, F. ; Styles, A.
Stokes, E., 1st class Signaller, 16th K.R.R.C. and Cadet R.A.F. ; joined
Oct. 19/14 ; served in France ; wounded at Passchendaele Oct. 29/
17 ; trench fever March 21/18 ; demobilized Feb./19.
Stokes, H., L./Cpl., 18th K.R.R.C. ; joined July 3/15 ; to France May
2/16 ; service in France and Italy ; demobilized March 6/19.
Stone, J. H., Pte., 3rd E. Surreys ; joined May 12/16 ; discharged on
medical grounds Sept. 15/16 ; subsequently died of pneumonia, Nov.
25/18.
Stone, W., Pte. ; joined 6th Royal Fusiliers ; also in 25th Middlesex and
4th North Hants and acted as Corpl, for a time ; did important road-
making under shell-fire in France and Belgium. Demobilized 4th
Dec., 1918.
Stoner, Wm. Boston, 2/Lieut., 14th Batt. Essex Regt., No. 7, O.C.B.,
11th (S.) Batt. Essex Regt. ; 3/6/16—16/10/18 ; France, Fermoy,
Aldershot ; severely wounded 21/3/18 and invalided from service
permanently disabled Oct. 16/19.
Stukeys, John, Sapper, R.E., 26/6/15—12/2/19.
Styles, A., Corpl., R.E., Road Construction, 1915/1919 ; France.
Sutton, H., Pte., 11th Batt. K.R.R.
Swan, Harry, L./A.C., R.A.F., 23/10/15 ; still serving ; Ireland, England,
Palestine and Egypt ; joined at the age of 16.

Taylor, Arthur ; Taylor, Alfred ; Taylor, C. ; Tanner, Walter ; Tacagni,
Lawrence ; **Tattersall, Frank**.
Taylor, Frederick, C.S.M., 12th Essex Regt., 5th K.R.R., 29th City of
London Regt., and London Regt., 6/8/14—9/2/19 ; England as In-
structor.
Taylor, Harold Allfrey, Pte., 26th Royal Fusiliers, Bankers' Battalion,
Aug./15—June/17 ; France and Belgium. He joined the Public
Schools and Universities' Battalions shortly after the outbreak of the

war, but the Company in which he was employed in civil life applied
for and obtained his discharge owing to business necessities. His
keen patriotism and desire to serve his country, however, prompted
him to seek military service again immediately the opportunity
arose, and during the summer of 1915 he joined the 26th Royal
Fusiliers. After training at Marlow, High Beech, and Aldershot, he
went to France in May/16, with the rank of Corpl, but, consistent
with military custom, reverted to private rank on arrival at the Front.
He remained on active service in " A " Company, first as bomb-thrower,
then in charge of Trench Mortar, and afterwards in the Machine
Gun Section for over a year without leave, having generously given
up to a comrade, whose mother was dangerously ill, his only chance
of returning home on leave. At a little later date he was strongly
recommended for a Commission, and the papers recalling him to prepare
for same were actually in France at the time his death was announced.
He was killed in action at Messines June 7/17, aged 25 years. His
Commanding Officer and Regimental Chaplain spoke in the highest
terms as to his ability and character. He was formerly a choirboy
at the parish church, and was one of the original members of the
Hornchurch Company Church Lads' Brigade.

Taylor, W. H., Corpl., R.E. ; joined Jan./15, technical work in France ;
in charge of bridge-building ship ; also Lewis Gun instructor ; shrap-
nal wound/17 ; died Feb. 25/19, of pneumonia following influenza ;
awarded Military Medal for meritorious service.

Ternouth, Alfred James, Signaller, 1st London Scottish ; 1915—1919 ;
Salonika, Egypt, Palestine and France.

Theobald, J., Pte., Stretcher-bearer, Queen's R.W.S. ; joined June/18 ;
served in France ; demobilized Jan./19.

Thomas, Albert Joseph, Lieut., B.S.A. Police, 14/8/14—19/4/15 ; R.A.S.C.
24/5/15—31/3/18 ; R.A.F., 1/4/18, still serving ; S. Rhodesia, France,
Germany, England.

Thompson, C. W., Pte. ; joined Nov. 30/15, R.A.S.C. (M.T.) ; to France
Sept. 13/16 ; in 1918 offensive ; was with 5th Army ; demobilized
Oct. 22/19.

Thompson, Frank Albert, Pte., Q.R. West Surrey Regt. ; Nov. 16 ; still
serving Flanders ; sustained severe fracture of thigh.

Thompson, Stewart Arthur, Pte., R.A.M.C. ; Sept./15—Mar./19 ; Egypt
and France ; gassed.

Thompson, S. H., Corpl., R.E. (Signal Service), Sept. 3/14—15 April/19 ;
Gallipoli (Suvla landing and evacuation), Egypt, France (March/16
to Armistice) ; awarded 1915 Star ; badly gassed at Ypres Feb./18.

Thorogood, Alfred, 2nd Bedfordshires.

Thorogood, David Valentine, Seaman.

Thorogood, Edward J. ; Thorogood, George E. ; Thomas, John ; Thomp-
son, Richard Henry ; Thornton, Richard ; Thornton, Claude Alfred ;
Thame, Ernest Walter ; Thomson, C. W. ; Thirkettle, Horace ;
Thorogood, H.

Thorogood, E. W., Pte., R.F.A. ; joined Oct. 3/15 ; shell-shock Dec./15 ;
home one year ; volunteered again ; wounded March 25/18 ; served
both periods in France ; demobilized Jan./19.

Thorogood, S., Corpl., Machine Gun Corps ; joined April 10/17 ; wounded
and slightly gassed, March 27/18 ; served in France ; demobilized
Sept. 17/19.

Thoroughgood, Charles, Pte., M.G.C. ; Dec. 29/16—Jan. 23/19 ; France.

Tickner, Sidney Herbert, Sergt.-Instr., 9th Essex Regt., Sept./14—April/19 ;
France.

Tickner, Stanley Thomas, Pte., 9th Essex Regt., Aug./14—Aug./16 ;
France ; invalided from service Aug./16, through internal injuries.

Tickner, Walter John, Pte., 1/4 Essex Regt. (T.), 1st Essex Regt., Aug./14
May/17 ; Dardanelles and France. He was invalided home with

enteric and shell shock from Dardanelles in Oct./15, and on recovery was transferred to the 1st Essex in France, and served in the Lewis Gun Section ; was wounded at the Battle of Cambrai in April/17, and died on May 11/17 ; age 28.

Tiddeman, Edmund Spenser, Lieut. Engineer, H.M.S. " Morea"; 1914—1919.

Tilly, Cyril Norman, Sapper, R.E. ; 1915 ; still serving ; Mesopotamia, Egypt, and Palestine.

Tippin, Ronald, Pte, 4th Royal Fusiliers, and Prisoners of War Escort ; March 2/17—1919 ; France and Belgium.

Todd, Wm. E., Lieut., Queen's Westminsters ; Jan./17—May/19 ; France ; wounded in Aug./18 during offensive at Bullecourt.

Toon, Percy Wm. ; Tokley, James ; Todd, John.

Townsend, Bernard Edmund, Rifleman, K.R.R. ; Dec./16 ; still serving ; France ; gassed.

Townsend, Stuart James, Lieut., R.G.A. ; Sept./14 ; still serving ; France ; gassed.

Townsend, Thomas William Stanley ; Aircraft Hand, R.A.F. ; 15/6/18—12/1/19 ; France, Belgium and Germany.

Trenoweth, Hugh James, Sergt., R.A., 15/5/16—15/10/19 ; England.

Trenoweth, Steffan Bolton, Engineer Lieut.-Comdr.,R.N.,4/8/14—11/11/18 ; North Sea and Mediterranean ; was wounded at Suez Canal on Feb./15.

Trice, Sidney ; Tredget, Wm. Joseph.

Tucker, Ernest, Pte., 1/4 Essex Regt., 7/4/1885—7/2/1919 ; Dardanelles and France ; was wounded in left arm Aug. 21/15 ; returned to England Sept. 1st. Was time expired on April ˅/16 ; joined the Flying Corps July 11/16, and served in France from Oct. 20/17 to Feb. 8/19.

Tucker, H., Pte. ; joined the army at the age of 18, and went out to the Western Front on April 1/19. He was killed in action in France Sept. 13/18, whilst serving in a light trench mortar battery, and was buried in the British Cemetery behind the lines by Capt. Buxton, C.F., in the presence of a number of his Battery comrades. His O.C. wrote of him as follows :—" His loss to the Battery is much felt. He was a splendid lad and was absolutely fearless."

Tucker, Harry Ernest, Pte., 7th Northants, July 10/17—Sept. 13/18 ; France. Was killed in action Sept. 13/18, in France, by explosion of our own trench mortar bombs.

Turner, E. S., Lieut. R.N.V.R., May/15 ; served in trawlers and in H.M. Motor-launches in the North Sea Patrol 1915-16, and in the West Indies Patrol 1917-19. His last Command was H.M.M.L. 360. He died March 6/19, at Fazakerly Hospital, Liverpool, from influenza and pneumonia contracted on his voyage home ; age 41.

Turner, Robert F.

Turvey, G. S., Shoeing Smith ; 6/11/15—24/4/19.

Tyler, Charles Albert, Corpl., 20/4/15—12/7/19.

Tyler, Richard ; Tyler, Wm. Fredk. ; Tyler, John Wm.

Tyrrell, Frank Sydney, Sergt., A.S.C. (M.T.), 6/6/15—6/2/19 ; France and Belgium.

Tyrrell, Henry James, Bombdr., R.G.A., 9/6/17—21/1/19 ; Home Service.

Tyrrell, Louis Edgar, Gunner, R.G.A., 19/11/15—3/3/19 ; France and Belgium ; was wounded and gassed in France and discharged on 3/3/19.

Tyrrell, William Ernest, Rifleman, R.B., 6/6/18—21/10/18 ; Home Service.

Unwin, Francis James, A.B., Royal Navy ; 25/4/15—8/2/19.

Unwin, R. H., Pte., R.A.M.C., 3/11/15—18/3/19.

Urquhart, H. D., Pte., 3rd and 9th Essex ; joined July 16 ; served in France ; wounded Sept. 18/18 ; demobilized Feb. 12/19.

Urquhart, Henry Donald.

Utley, F. C.

Vale, James ; **Vale, Albert.**
Veale, Allan Adolphus, 2/Lieut., R.F.C. ; 1914—1918. During the Gallipoli campaign in 1916 he received a shell and three machine-gun wounds. He was again wounded in France during 1916, by a bomb. Was transferred to England, and in 1917 sustained severe concussion of the brain and spinal injury in Kent through the breaking of the steering rod of the 'plane in which he was flying, which " crashed." He again returned to France, and was killed in action on Jan. 22/18 and buried at Bailleul ; age 23.
Venables, Wm. George ; Verity, B.
Viney, Charles Wm., Pte., 2nd Essex Regt. ; 1914—1915 ; France ; killed 2/5/15 ; age 22.
Viney, Ernest Edward, Bdr., R.F.A. ; 1914—1919 ; France and Palestine.
Vinton, Alfred James, Driver, R.F.A. ; July 26/15—Feb. 8/19 ; France ; awarded Military Medal May 17/18.
Vinton, Ernest Arthur ; Vinten, Edward ; Vinton, Albert Charles ; Viney, E. ; Vinter, Henry.
Vinton, F., Pte., Essex Regt. ; awarded 1914 Star and Croix de Guerre, Belge.

Wager, Ernest, Driver, R.A., 15/11/15—23/3/19.
Wakefield, Thos. ; Wade, Frederick ; Wade, Walter ; Watkinson, George ; Watkinson, William ; Wallace, John ; Wallace, C. ; Wallis, William Harold ; **Wallis, E. E.,** Signaller ; Watson, Anthony William : Warner, B. W. ; Ward, Frank ; Ward, Ernest Chas. ; Waylett, William L. ; Warrington, Fred. ; **Wardill, George E.** ; **Wall, Francis J.** ; Wainwright, E. ; Waite, G. S. ; Waite, E. ; Wakeling, W. G. ; Watkinson, J.
Wakeling, George, Pte., 1st Essex Regt. ; killed at Gallipoli.
Wall, Arthur Henry, L./Cpl., 4th Essex Regt., 17/6/12—4/4/19 ; France ; sustained broken leg at Arras 1917, and was taken Prisoner of War 22/3/18, on Cambrai Front.
Wall, Ernest A., Pte., 2/4 Essex and 2/6 Gloster Regt., 26/10/14—10/5/19 ; France ; was once wounded.
Wall, Frederick, Pte., 26/7/16—3/11/19.
Wall, Herbert John, Pte., 1/4th Essex, 10/6/12—18/2/18 ; France ; discharged with trench feet 18/2/18.
Wall, N. H., Lieut. ; joined Aug. 28/14, Infantry. Then to H.A.C. and became Bombdr. and Sergt. ; sustained serious accident on motor cycle between Canterbury and Margate, while on duty during a Zeppelin attack in Sept./16. Commissioned in R.E. (Labour Batt.). Served in France nine months ; discharged medically unfit Feb. 17/18.
Wall, Sidney Clement, Pte., 4th Essex, 17/6/12—3/2/19 ; Dardanelles and France.
Wall, William, Pte., 2/4 Essex and 46 Machine Gun Corps ; 26/10/14—2/10/19 ; France ; was twice wounded ; awarded Military Medal for conspicuous bravery in the Field on Oct. 3/18.
Ward, Clifford George Washington, 2/Lieut., 6th Reserve Regiment of Dragoons, 2nd City of London Yeomanry, and M.G.C. ; May/15—Feb./19 ; Egypt, Sinia Peninsula, Palestine and France ; awarded 1915 Star.
Ward, John William, Pte., Royal Fusiliers ; June 28/17—Nov. 6/18 ; England ; died of double pneumonia in Warley Hospital ; age 24.
Warman, W. A., 2/Lieut., R.A.F. In camp with 4th Essex (Territorials) at outbreak of war ; to Gallipoli June 23/15 ; on evacuation of latter (Jan. 8/16), drafted to Egypt, 54th Division. Took commission in Royal Air Force ; killed Oct. 13/18, through an accident while flying at Alexandria.
Warren, A. S.
Warren, J. H. ; joined 1915, Royal Fusiliers ; Warren, A. S.

Waskett, William, Gunner, R.G.A. ; March 2/15—April 20/19 ; France.
Watson, Raymond Percival, L./Cpl., Queen's R.W.S. Regt. ; 1916 ; still serving ; France and England.
Webber, A., Pte., Employment Corps ; joined June/17 ; served in France and Belgium ; also 2½ years in Italy ; demobilized Jan./20.
Webster, George Thomas, 2nd Lieut., 203rd Machine Gun Coy., Nov. 29/15—Dec. 7/17, France. He enlisted in the Inns of Courts O.T.C., and after a period of general training for officer's work was specially selected from many competitors for the Machine Gun Corps. Leaving Cambridge Cadet School, he took a special course in machine gunnery at Aldershot, after which he received his Commission. After a short period with a reserve battalion, he was drafted overseas, and was in France early in March, 1917. From that time he was constantly in the firing line, until on the 9th October he received wounds at Passchendaele, which proved fatal. Badly wounded in the thigh, he was taken to a base hospital, and, after much suffering, died on Dec. 7/17, age 29.
Wedlake, Sidney, Staff-Sergt., A.O.C. ; June 15—Feb./19 ; Egypt, Palestine and Libyan Desert ; was mentioned in Despatches 22/1/19.
Weevers, Bert Gower, Corpl., R.N.A.S., and R.A.F. ; June 1/17—Feb , 3/19 ; England.
Weightman, Alfred William, Pte., 1st Norfolks.
Wells, Francis Chas., Pte., A.I.F. ; 1915—1917 ; France ; received shrapnel wounds in back on Dec. 20/16, while in the trenches in front of Armentieres. Was invalided out of Army in 1917 after having had an operation for appendicitis.
Wells, Thomas, Pte., R.A.M.C. ; 1914—1919 ; France ; was gassed on Oct. 23/17, while with the advanced Dressing Station on the Somme ; was in hospital in England and Ireland, and went back to France in Sept., 1918
Wells, William Henry, Sergt., Despatch Rider, R.E. ; 1914—1919 ; France.
Wenn, E. W., Corpl., 12th Royal Fusiliers ; joined Sept. 17/14 ; France ; Sept. /15—March/16 ; wounded March 13/16 ; discharged medically unfit April 17/18.
Wenn, H., R.N., H.M.S. " Drake " in 1914.
Wenn, H. A., Pte. ; joined up December 20/15 ; served with Essex and Norfolks in France ; wounded July 1/16 ; transferred to Labour Corps ; Home Service until discharged medically unfit July 30/19.
Wenn, Harold, Royal Navy, Leading Signalman ; joined 1913 ; served on H.M.S. " Blake " and H.M.S. " Spiraca," North Sea ; still serving.
West, Alfred ; Webb, Henry John ; Wearing, Roland ; Webb, Clement Arthur ; Webb, M. E. ; **Webb, F. ; Webb, A. S. ;** West, Joseph T. ; West, C. ; Weavers, Arthur Henry ; Weller, A.
West, J., Pte. ; joined Essex Regt., A.P.C., Warley, Feb./18 ; transferred to Labour Batt. Aug./18 ; Home service ; demobilized Jan./19.
Westgate, L., Pte., 1/4 Essex (Territorials) ; in Territorials three years before the war ; in camp when war declared ; landing at Suvla Bay and Gallipoli ; discharged, sunstroke and shell shock.
Westley, John Robert, Sergt., British Red Cross Society ; Sept./14—Aug., 1916 ; France ; awarded Mons Star, 1914. (*See page* 108).
Whitams, E. W. C. ; **Whitams, T. R. ;** Wheeler, Harold W. ; Wheeler, George Stanley ; Wheeler, Thos. Arthur ; White, Daniel ; White, Wm. ; Whipp, Wm. A. S. ; Whipps, John ; Whipps, A. ; Whipps, E. ; Whipps, W. Y. ; Whight, Albert ; Whybrow, Bertie.
White, George Frederick, Sergt., 1/18th London Battalion ; 1914—1918 ; Malta and France. He joined the 1st City of London Royal Fusiliers on Sept. 1/14, and served at Malta, and on the Western Front. He was wounded on Oct. 7/16, and invalided to England. After recovery he returned to France on March 31/18, and transferred to the 1/18 London Battalion (attached to the London Irish Rifles), and was

83

killed in action on October 3/18 ; aged 23 years. The following is an extract from a letter received from Lieut. Colin A. Snell, reporting his death :—" He was killed instantaneously, while setting a splendid example to the men in his platoon. To me, his Platoon Commander, he was almost invaluable because he had so much experience, and his loss is felt very deeply by all in the Platoon." He was buried at Radinghem, Armentieres.

White, J. W. G., Corpl., Royal Army Pay Corps ; served at Warley and Nottingham from Aug. 28/16 ; died of pneumonia and phthisis contracted during Service, Feb. 9/19 ; age 33.

Whitehead, Herbert George, Pte., 2nd Royal Fusiliers ; Feb. 22/17— Feb. 20/19 ; France.

Whiting, A. G. ; joined Cyclists' Batt. Dec./15 ; wounded in France.

Whiting, A. J., Bombr., H. A. C. ; Nov., 1915—July, 1919; Belgium and France. Twice wounded.

Whitmore, J. R., Steward, Royal Navy.

Wilkinson, Albert Chas., Boy Mechanic, R.A.F., 23/1/18—23/1/19 ; England ; sustained broken arm at Farnborough, Nov. 20/18.

Wilkinson, Ernest George, Lieut., Artists Rifles and R.A.F. ; 1915— 1919 ; France and England.

Wilkinson, Frank Victor, Gunner, 2nd Royal West Surreys, and Tank Corps ; May 8/16 ; still serving ; France and Belgium ; wounded at Passchendaele 26/10/17.

Willats, Albert Joseph, Pte., Essex Regt., and Middlesex Regt. ; Nov. 4/14—May 16/19 ; France and Salonika.

Willey, S., Pte., H.A.C.

Williams, Arthur Laurence, Lieut.,Mechanical Transport (attached R.G.A.), 15/5/15—10/6/19 ; France.

Williams, Henry Vernon, Sergt., R.A.F. ; Jan./15—Feb./19 ; England and France.

Williams, Samuel Walter, Capt., 4th Essex Regt. and R.A.F. ; 1913— 1919 ; Egypt and France. He was Lieutenant of the Hornchurch Company, 4th Essex Regt. (T.F.), at the outbreak of war, and later transferred to the Royal Air Force. Was a Prisoner of War at Holzminden, Germany.

Wilson, Ernest ; Wilson, Harry Herbert ; Wilson, C. ; Wilson, Albert Timothy ; Wilson Herbert ; Wilson, Ernest D. ; Wllson, Archibald R. ; Wilson, W. ; Willey, Louis ; Wilkinson, H. C. ; Wiffin, Wallace B. ; Winchcombe, Cyril Chas. ; Willmott, George Albert ; Williamson, V.

Wilson, E. J., Royal Navy, A.S., Gunlayer 2nd Class ; joined 1900. Was on H.M.S. " Monarch " from April/14—Jan. 22/19, and took part in all North Sea operations and Battle of Jutland.

Wilson, George Stanley, Pte., Northants Regt. ; Aug. 30/15—Nov. 10/17 ; France ; killed in action Nov. 10/17.

Wilson, J., Corpl., B. Battery, H.A.C. ; joined Aug. 30/15 ; service on Egyptian Front, Battles in Palestine from Beersheba to Jerusalem ; Corpl. Oct./17 ; demobilized May/19.

Wilson, John Thomas, Pte., R.W. Surrey Regt., March/16—Sept. 3/18 ; France ; died of wounds received in action Sept. 3/18.

Wilson, L., June/18—Jan./20 ; Australian Contingent.

Winn, Arthur George Harris, Air Mechanic, R.A.F., Sept./18—29/10/19 ; Salonika.

Wood, William Samuel ; Woodall, Leslie ; Woolley, Francis Leonard ; Woolley, Thomas ; Wolsey, Fredk. Charles ; Wood, J.

Woods, Frederick, Pte., 9/6/15—28/3/19.

Woods, Herbert Richard, Pte., 10/6/12—25/3/19.

Wright, Arthur William John, Corpl., K.R.R. ; June 14/15—Feb. 9/19 ; France ; was wounded and gassed on July 31/17, at St. Jean and again wounded on Oct. 21/17 at Passchendaele.

Wright, Ernest Fredk. ; Wright, Leonard Hy. ; **Wright, E.** ; Wright, H. ; Wright, J. S.

Wright, William, C.S.M., 1/4 Essex ; 16/2/15—21/6/19.

Wykes, Edward B.

Yeltham, Nathaniel ; Yeatman, William.

York, George, Pte., R.D.C. ; 15/4/15—15/2/19 ; Home Service.

York, George Stanley, Driver, R.F.A. ; 4/7/14—5/4/19 ; France, Egypt and Palestine.

York, Wm. James, Pte., 1/4th Essex Regt., 4/7/14—27/3/17 ; Dardanelles, Egypt and Palestine ; reported missing on March 27/17, at Battle of Gaza ; since presumed to have been killed on that date.

Young, F. C., Pte., 3rd Essex ; joined Dec. 6/14 ; transferred to 11th Essex Sept./15, and to 139th Labour Coy., March/17 ; served in France ; wounded Sept. 15/16 ; demobilized Feb./19 ; rejoined June/19, in Labour Coy., and still serving in 1920.

Young, Frederick ; Young, Vivian C. H. ; Young, Patrick ; Young, Harry,

Young, G., Pte., Bedfords and R.A.S.C. ; Home Service ; April/15 1918—February/19.

Young, Henry Archie, Rifleman, 6th City of London Rifles, Aug. 5/15—May 1/16 ; France. He heroically volunteered to join a party to dig out some of his comrades who had been buried in a trench after the Germans had exploded a mine. In this operation he received wounds, from the effects of which he died near Souchez on May 1/16.

TOO LATE FOR CLASSIFICATION.

Boyle, Leslie E., Lieut., Loyal Lancs. Regiment, October, 1914/March 1919 ; France. Enlisted 30 Oct., 1914 as trooper in Essex Yeomanry. Arrived in France 5 Aug., 1915. Gazetted 2nd Lieut. in Loyal Lancs. Regt., 6 June, 1917. Returned to France 25 Aug., 1917, and was wounded in action. Promoted (temporary) Captain 16 May, 1918. Invalided out of the service, owing to ill health caused by wounds, 6 March, 1919.

Clarke, Herbert Leonard, 9th Essex Regiment, 1915/1917 ; France. Enlisted 4 Oct., 1915, and arrived in France 9 March, 1916. He was wounded at Delville Wood 20 July, 1916, and was in hospital at Rouen and Mile End Military Hospital, London. Returned to France 7 Dec., 1916, and was killed by a shell at the Somme 30 April, 1917. Age 22. Buried at Biaches, east of Peronne. He was formerly in the Hornchurch Company, C.L.B.

Cole, Harry, 2nd Air Mechanic R.A.F., 1916/1917. ; France. He volunteered for service at the age of 39, joining the R.A.F. 20 June, 1916. Arrived in France 4 Feb., 1917, and was accidentally shot whilst on duty, a bullet passing through his spine, causing paralysis. He was admitted to No. 3 General Hospital at Le Treport and lingered for four weeks, dying on the 10th April, 1917. Age 40 years.

Lake, B., 4th Essex Regiment (T.F.). Killed in action.

Former Parishioners, and Descendants of Ancient Families of Hornchurch.

Abrahams, Clement Arthur, Lieut., The King's (Liverpool) Regt., 1914—1919 ; France.

Ayres, H. F., Lieut., Royal Engineers, Egypt.

Barker, A. ; Brown, A.

Bearblock, A., Surgeon Sub-Lieut. R.N.V.R., Feb./18—March/19. After serving on H.M.S. " Archer," he was discharged and resumed his studies at University College Hospital, London.

Bearblock, Charles Henry, Lieut., 9th Essex Regiment, Sept. 1914—20/10/15. He was wounded in action near Hullock on Oct. 20/15, and died the same day, age 27 years. Buried at Vermelles Cemetery, France.

Bearblock, Walter James, M.R.C.S., L.R.C.P., Fleet Surgeon, R.N. He was present in H.M.S. " Invincible " on Dec. 8/14, during the Battle off the Falkland Islands. He was killed in action on May 31/16, when the " Invincible " was sunk in the victory off the coast of Jutland ; age 50 years.

Davis, T. H., Royal Navy.

Dennis, F. M., R.G.A.

Ellingford, S.

Fulcher, Frank W., Corpl., 9th Essex Regt., Sept./14—July/15 ; England and France ; was killed in action on July 11/15.

Goodrum, William Henry, Private, R.E. He was invalided from France with shell shock and trench fever, and died at Shoeburyness Military Hospital on Jan. 18/19 ; aged 35.

Gray, Alfred, Royal Navy.

Hammond, B., R.A.F.

Harding Newman, Edward, Colonel, Royal Artillery. Served in France and Belgium during the whole of the war. He commanded the 37th Howitzer Battery, R.F.A. from 1914—1916. Received the D.S.O., 3rd Class of Russian Order of St. Stanislaus ; commanded the 28th Brigade R.F.A. 1916—1917 ; became C.R.A. to 14th Division in 1917 to 1918, C.M.G. Brevet Colonel, and was six times mentioned in Despatches.

Harding Newman, Francis Robert, Major ; served at War Office and Land Agent in the Aldershot Command during the whole war time. He was mentioned in Despatches.

Harding Newman, John Cartwright, Colonel. He commanded the 1st Sherwood Foresters, and was formerly in the Essex Regiment ; served as A.Q.M.G. Aldershot Command from 1914—1916. Was Deputy Director General of Transportation ; G.H.Q., France, Brigadier-General 1916—1917 ; D.A. and Q.M.G. 9th Corps 1917—1919. He is C.B., C.M.G., Officer of the Order of the Crown of Italy, Officer of the Legion of Honour, and was awarded the Croix de Guerre (France). Is Brevet-Major, Brevet-Lieut.-Col. and Brevet-Colonel. Was seven times mentioned in Despatches.

Harding Newman, Thomas, Major, 1st Cambridgshire Regiment. Served as Staff Captain, East Midland Division. A.P.M. Glasgow and in France and Belgium with his Regiment. Received M.C. for the capture of Auby by his Company on Oct. 14/18. Was mentioned in Despatches.

Holmes, Albert Arundel, Capt., 5th Batt. Royal Sussex Regt., Nov. 1914
—May 1915; England. Died of pneumonia contracted while on
active service on May 19/15 ; age 43 years.

Holmes, Albert John, 2nd Lieut., Jan./18—May/19 ; Army of Occupation.

Holmes, Eric Cecil, Lieut., 1916—1918. After serving in the South African
Defence Force, he obtained a Commission in the Durham Light
Infantry, and served in France. He was wounded near Amiens in
the Great Retreat, and died at Rouen April 3/18 ; aged 25 ; buried
at St. Sever Cemetery. He was a grandson of the late Colonel Henry
Holmes, of Grey Towers.

Holmes, Stanley, Capt., 23rd R.F. (Sportsman's Batt.), and A.S.C. Served
in France. Was injured while on duty, and allowed to retire from the
Service in June 1916.

Hunwicks, W. A. ; Hunwicks, H. R.

Jameson, Gilbert A. Joined the 47th Essex V.A.D. (Westcliff) and
performed orderly duties at Overcliff Hospital, V.A.D., from Jan to
Nov./15. In Nov./15 he volunteered for the R.A.M.C., and was
subsequently posted to 11th Field Ambulance, 4th Division, France.
Was demobilized in March/19.

Kimber, F., R.G.A.

King, N. E., Pte ; joined up in Canadian Engineers, in which he served
two years, but owing to illness did not come across.

Korriene, C., Royal Navy.

Leggatt, Leonard Alan, Major, R.A.S.C. (M.T.), 1914—1919 ; France,
Belgium and Russia.

Leggatt, Percy Scott, Lieut.-Comdr., R.N.V.R., 1914—1916; North Sea
and Adriatic. Was invalided from the Service in 1916, owing to
sickness contracted whilst on active service in the Adriatic.

Lillystone, E. C. ; Livermore, T.

Macklin, Edgar, Private, London Rifle Brigade, A.S.C., and Transport
Service 1914 to 1916 ; France and Belgium. After serving on the
Western Front he was invalided home suffering from rheumatism.
On his recovery he joined the Transport Service, and was drowned
on the way to Salonika in the s.s. " Citta de Palermo," which was
torpedoed or mined in the Mediterranean on January 8/16. He was
formerly a choirboy in the Parish Church.

Macklin, Herbert, C.E.R.A., Submarine E7, 1914—Dec. 1918. Was a
prisoner of war in Turkey for 3½ years.

Macklin, Leonard, Lieut., R.A.F., Oct. 19/14—Sept. 19/19. Served as
Observer in France and Ireland. Was twice wounded in France.

Mulley, B. ; Mulley, G. A.

Nash, W. J.

Payne. E. A. R.E.

Pearce, A. C., R.E.

Pudney, A. C., Dorset Regiment.

Rookard, W. E., Private, 312 Training Reserve.

Rush, Harry.

Wall, S. G. ; Wenn, W. G. ; Whiting, J.

Wilson, L., Australian Contingent.

Wilson, W., Australian Contingent.

87

Great War Memorials in Hornchurch Church.

"Thou in this shalt find thy monument."
Shakespeare :—Sonnet cvii.

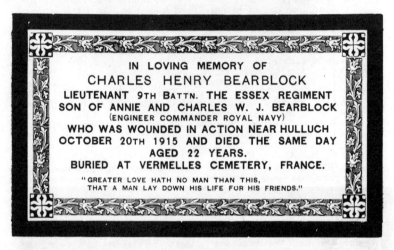

IN LOVING MEMORY OF
CHARLES HENRY BEARBLOCK
LIEUTENANT 9TH BATTN. THE ESSEX REGIMENT
SON OF ANNIE AND CHARLES W. J. BEARBLOCK
(ENGINEER COMMANDER ROYAL NAVY)
WHO WAS WOUNDED IN ACTION NEAR HULLUCH
OCTOBER 20TH 1915 AND DIED THE SAME DAY
AGED 22 YEARS.
BURIED AT VERMELLES CEMETERY, FRANCE.

"GREATER LOVE HATH NO MAN THAN THIS,
THAT A MAN LAY DOWN HIS LIFE FOR HIS FRIENDS."

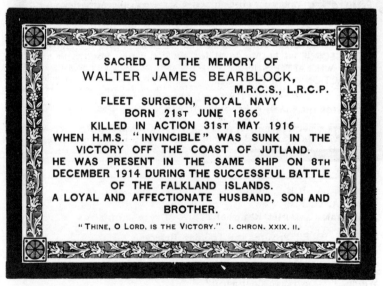

SACRED TO THE MEMORY OF
WALTER JAMES BEARBLOCK,
M.R.C.S., L.R.C.P.
FLEET SURGEON, ROYAL NAVY
BORN 21ST JUNE 1866
KILLED IN ACTION 31ST MAY 1916
WHEN H.M.S. "INVINCIBLE" WAS SUNK IN THE
VICTORY OFF THE COAST OF JUTLAND.
HE WAS PRESENT IN THE SAME SHIP ON 8TH
DECEMBER 1914 DURING THE SUCCESSFUL BATTLE
OF THE FALKLAND ISLANDS.
A LOYAL AND AFFECTIONATE HUSBAND, SON AND
BROTHER.

"THINE, O LORD, IS THE VICTORY." I. CHRON. XXIX. II.

TO THE GLORY OF GOD
AND IN LOVING AND HONOURED MEMORY OF
GEORGE WILLIAM FRANKLYN
2ND LIEUT. 1/23RD LONDON REGIMENT
ONLY AND DEARLY LOVED SON OF
GEORGE WILLIAM AND ROSANNA ELIZABETH FRANKLYN
WHO AFTER SERVICE IN GALLIPOLI WAS KILLED IN
ACTION IN THE GLORIOUS ATTACK ON MESSINES RIDGE
JUNE 7TH 1917 — AGED 32 YEARS.

FOR THEIR WORK CONTINUETH, GREAT BEYOND THEIR KNOWING.

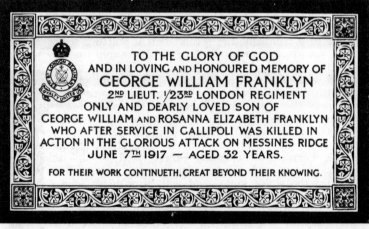

IN LOVING MEMORY OF
ERIC CECIL HOLMES
LIEUTENANT 5TH DURHAM LIGHT INFANTRY WHO DIED OF WOUNDS
RECEIVED NEAR HANGARD IN THE GREAT WAR AND WAS
BURIED AT ROUEN 3RD APRIL 1918 AGED 25
ALSO OF
VIOLET EMILY MARION
WHO DIED IN SOUTH AFRICA AND WAS BURIED AT WARRENTON
11TH AUGUST 1898 AGED 4 YEARS
THE ONLY CHILDREN OF CECIL AND MARION HOLMES
AND GRAND-CHILDREN OF HENRY HOLMES OF GREY TOWERS.
"AND WITH THE MORN THOSE ANGEL FACES SMILE."

SOME PERSONAL WAR RECORDS.

"This story shall the good man teach his son."

Shakespeare :—Henry V., IV., iii.

LIEUT. HAROLD PERCY CHILVER, M.C.

" Valiant . . . . well accomplished "*
" We shall find of him a shrewd contriver "†

Shakespeare.

Lieut. Chilver joined the 1st City of London R.F.A. as a Gunner, in 1915, and was subsequently commissioned in the Royal Naval Division and served in France and Belgium. Just before the last great German offensive, Lieut. Chilver had been slightly gassed, and had been sent down from the front lines to a rear station with about 100 men from the Field Artillery, who had also suffered from a gas attack. He had hardly arrived before he received orders to send back a number of the men and return to his Battery. He despatched one party, but remained behind to accompany the second batch, starting a few hours later. On arriving at his Battery, he discovered that the whole of the first party had become casualties, and found all his senior officers wounded in a dug-out near. His senior officer greeted him with " Well Chilver, what are you going to do ? " " Carry on ! " was the reply, and he immediately rallied his men, laid and fired his guns himself for some time, got his wounded senior officers safely evacuated, withdrew his guns against great pressure, and brought them safely through without capture. Subsequently he was Forward Observation Officer, paid out his telephone wire until surrounded by the enemy and his machine guns, remained the whole night, and sent through his wire valuable information as to the movements of the enemy, which enabled his Brigade to get away. As a reward for his heroic conduct, Lieut. Chilver was awarded the Military Cross, which was bestowed upon him by the King at Buckingham Palace in October, 1918, the following being the official announcement of his decoration :—

> " M.C. 2nd Lieut. H. P. Chilver, R.F.A. For conspicuous gallantry and devotion to duty. He kept a gun in action under heavy shell fire, and firing it himself after most of the detachment had become casualties. Later, as Forward Observation Officer, he laid a wire, though har-

*Two Gentlemen of Verona, IV., iii.
†Julius Cæsar, II., i.

assed by machine-gun fire, thus enabling important information to be sent through. By his energy and courage on the retirement (March, 1918), he kept his Brigade constantly informed."

PRIVATE SIDNEY CHARLES COLLIN, MACHINE GUN CORPS

(11th Company, 4th Division).

" The warlike service he has done, consider ;
Think upon the wounds his body bears."
Shakespeare :—Coriolanus, iii., iii.

It is mainly in consequence of the inhuman and barbarous methods employed by our enemies in this war that we have to-day such a great multitude of stricken heroes in our midst. Many, very many, of them are maimed, blinded, or in some other way disabled for life, whose condition is directly attributable to personal acts of heroism. All of them have looked into the face of death, and, bearing the honourable scars of battle, are now carrying on cheerfully under conditions which by most of us would be considered almost insupportable. Many, too, have been put to tests of endurance in the calm atmosphere of the hospital theatre, which would probably require even more courage to face than the fiery ordeal of the battlefield. It is to one of these valiant men, Private Sidney C. Collin, that this short chapter is mainly devoted. There are surely few finer examples of quiet patient endurance under medical and surgical treatment. Before being finally discharged from hospital, Private Collin underwent no fewer than twenty operations, which resulted in the amputation of both legs just below the thighs :—

Private Collin joined the army in April, 1916, and, after training at Grantham, landed in France two months later. He took part in the battle of the Somme and was with the 4th Division at Beaumont Hamel, Baupaume, Combles, and the Ypres salient. He was badly wounded in both his legs and arms on the right of Combles, on January 25, 1917, after eight months' fighting. The shell which wounded him killed six of his comrades. He was admitted into the 12th General Hospital at Rouen, January 27, 1917, and underwent seven operations, and had his left leg amputated. He was then sent to Craig Head Hospital, Bournemouth, where he remained thirteen months, and underwent twelve more operations and had his right leg amputated. He was afterwards an inmate of the Cluny Red Cross Hospital, Swanage, and of the Pavilion Hospital, Brighton, where one other operation was performed, making twenty in all. He was then transferred to Roehampton to be fitted with artificial limbs, and was eventually discharged from the army on January 30, 1918, at the age of 30 years.

CAPTAIN PHILIP FRANCIS DALE, M.C.

" I do not think a braver gentleman,
More active-valiant or more valiant-young,
More daring or more bold, is now alive."
Shakespeare :—Henry IV., v., i.

Captain Dale, the elder son of the late Rev. Herbert John Dale, Vicar of Hornchurch, 1902-1918, joined the forces in August, 1914 (on leaving school), and was commissioned in the 11th Essex Regt. in October of that year. He went to France twelve months after enlisting, and took part in the Battle of Loos on September 26th, 1915. Unfortunately, on the afternoon of that memorable day he was wounded and taken prisoner, and was one of the eleven officers of his battalion reported " wounded and missing " in that battle. Of these only he and one other survived the battle, both as prisoners. Capt. Dale was imprisoned in the camps of Gütersloh, Fürstenberg in Mecklenburg, Burg, Ingolstadt (Fort 9) and Ludwigshafen. From the last of these he succeeded, *on his fifth attempt,* in making his escape to Holland. He reached home on Sunday, May 12th, 1918— one week after his escape from the camp. He had the honour of being received by the King at Buckingham Palace, and was later awarded the Military Cross for his hazardous venture.

In Sept., 1918, he was sent out to France to join the Intelligence Staff of the 5th Army. He was demobilized as Captain in March, 1919.

After being a month or so in civilian life, Capt. Dale volunteered to join the Relief Force to Russia, but was sent to join the British Military Mission in South Russia in Sept., 1919, where he acted as intelligence officer. He was in the evacuation of Kieff in Dec., 1919, when he received his credentials as Acting British Vice-Consul of Kieff. He was also in the evacuation of Odessa in Feb., 1920.

CORPORAL PERCY ALEXANDER DUNLOP
(2nd Battalion, London Scottish Regiment).

" He hath borne himself beyond the promise of his age."—*
" A better soldier none that Christendom gives out."†
Shakespeare.

Corporal Dunlop joined the 2nd Battalion, London Scottish Regiment. on September 2nd, 1914, within a month of the declaration of War, at the age of 39 years, when no obligation rested upon him, his age being far in advance of the then military age. I well recollect seeing him in the ranks of the battalion in the Lord Mayor's Procession in November, 1914, and recall how greatly I was impressed with the patriotism which prompted him to offer his services to his King and Country in that most

*Much Ado about Nothing, I., i.
†Macbeth, IV., iii.

critical time. After a period of training, he was with his battalion in Dublin during the Irish Rebellion of April, 1915, and shortly afterwards went overseas and served in France, and later in Salonika and Macedonia. In the Macedonian Campaign he went through terrible experiences, culminating in a 92-mile march, when he contracted bronchial asthma, which necessitated his being detained in the 43rd General Hospital at Salonika. His illness rendered him unfit to proceed with his regiment to Egypt, and he was consequently attached to the Fisheries Section in Salonika. In the absence of any testimony from a superior officer concerning his military service and death, the following extracts from a letter received by Mrs. Dunlop from a comrade, Frank Purcell, graphically describing some incidents leading up to a date just prior to his death, are given as some indication of the splendid service rendered by him :—

" I was in the Fisheries (Motor Boats) Section with " Flop " (I was the only man who called him by that name), and we were great pals. We seemed to have something in common, and also we were very lonely men. We were about ten miles away from any camp or body of men, at a place called Lipsaza, hidden up in a gully, into which ran a tiny little bay, where we moored our boats. It was a wild place, and wild people, whose ways and customs have not altered since the days of Christ. So, you see, we were thrown very much together, and had to construct our own world, which, on his side, consisted of his wife, his daughter and his dog, and on my side, my wife and baby boy. He and I once had a great experience. You must understand that I was the motor-boat coxswain, and one day we had to go to Stavros to bring back the Greek fishermen's rations. We got the rations aboard, and started back. I could see bad weather ahead, and told " Flop " to get the tarpaulins covered over them. We made the first headland, and then ran clean into the storm. For about twenty minutes we had a pretty rough time. The waves were continually washing right over us, but we were gaining a little, but after that the sea seemed to go mad, and raved round the little boat. Three times the engine gave out, and three times we got her going just as we were nearly dashed on the rocks. Three hours and odd we fought our way, with people watching us from the cliffs unable to send help, as an ordinary boat would never have lived in such a sea. The Greeks aboard were panic-stricken, and we all thought that it was " Good-bye." I myself simply stuck to the helm (my job), and I can see " Flop " now, in my mind's eye, sitting there in the stern near me, drenched and blown about, waiting for it to end, but calm and smiling. We won through at last, and when we reached the shore I was about " all in." " Flop's " first thoughts were for me, and he had me taken to my tent, and himself (still drenched), brought me blankets and stimulants. He made one proud to be an Englishman !

And now comes the beginning of the end. In September, 1918, all began to drop sick until there was only Lieut. Ormsby, O.C., Corpl. Dunlop and myself, left. First Lieut. Ormsby and then " Flop " went. I carried on for two weeks more, then broke down, but previous to this I went over to Stavros, and saw " Flop " in the Casualty Clearing Station there. He seemed cheerful and looked very well, and was suffering no pains or anything like that. He told me that he was going down to the Base 63rd General Hospital, Salonika. We shook hands, wished each other the best of luck, and parted. Just after this I was taken ill, and continued ill for about three months. I was then drafted to Russia, so, you see, I lost sight of him. When I got " demobbed " he was the first man I thought of, and I wrote. When we said " So long ! " at Stavros, neither dreamed that one was so soon to face his Maker, but " Flop " would calmly go and face the Great Beyond like he lived, a gallant comrade and a white man right through ! "

Corporal Dunlop died in the 63rd General Hospital, Salonika, from malaria and nephritis on October 28th, 1918, about a month after the meeting with his comrade above mentioned. He was buried by the Rev. Kenyon, Chaplain to the Salonika Forces, on October 29th, 1918, at Mikra British Cemetery, age 43.

Prior to the War he was a Lieutenant in the Hornchurch Company of the Church Lads' Brigade.

2ND LIEUT. HAROLD GEORGE LUTHER, ROYAL AIR FORCE.

" You have done a brave deed."

Shakespeare :—Coriolanus, IV., ii.

Lieut. Luther joined the Royal Engineers on 10 October, 1914, and while serving in France as despatch rider, attached to the 2nd Indian Cavalry Division, was wounded at the battle of the Somme, 1916. Rising to the rank of corporal, he transferred to the Royal Naval Air Force on November 17, 1917, and served as probationary Flight Officer, training at Greenwich R. N. College and Eastbourne Aerodrome. He was promoted 2nd Lieutenant, and drafted into the Royal Air Force, 1st April, 1918, serving in Belgium and France with the 65th Squadron R.A.F.

The following is an account of his last fight, in which he had his right hand shot off.

" On the morning of 4 November, 1918, at 8 o'clock, I proceeded with my Squadron upon our usual offensive patrol over the enemy lines. After dropping our bombs upon the targets according to instructions received prior to leaving the ground, we sighted a large formation of enemy aircraft, about 40 in number, made up of single and two-seater Fokkers. There were about 30 of our machines, and a big " dog-fight " ensued. I became engaged with a single-seater Fokker, and after a brief encounter succeeded in getting several good bursts of fire into it. Her pilot appeared to lose control and commenced to spin. I followed him down and saw him crash, and a few minutes later I again became engaged with another machine of the same class. We were flying " nose on " to within ten yards, and I was thus able to get good bursts at point blank range, and the Hun seemed to crumple up and go down. I was about to follow him down when I heard a burst from my rear, and turning my head saw a two-seater Fokker. We immediately became engaged and after a few minutes I was able to dive on him and to obtain a good burst. The Fokker dived vertically and I saw pieces of struts and fabric breaking away. I followed down and saw him crash. I then commenced to climb again, and had gained a height of about 8,000 feet, when my engine commenced to miss, and only gave 900 revolutions per minute, so I turned towards home. I had been flying in a course due west for about ten minutes, when I was heavily shelled by enemy anti-aircraft guns. I immediately commenced the usual tactics, when suddenly I found my right hand practically blown off, and my machine commenced to spin. The engine was also damaged, as it completely " cut out," and I had the greatest difficulty in getting out of the spin, the control or rigging of the machine having been also damaged. However, I was fortunate enough to be able to flatten out sufficiently to make some sort of landing, whereupon the machine turned over on its back and crashed. Here I lost consciousness through loss of blood, and the next I knew was that I was a prisoner of war in a German temporary hospital. Three days later I was moved to another hospital near Brussels, where my right hand was amputated. The following morning I was put on a hospital train for Antwerp.

On the 11 November I was informed that there was an armistice, and that I was no longer a prisoner. The next day all the Allied wounded in the hospital were taken over by the Belgian Red Cross. On the 15th I was removed to a private hospital under the care of a Belgian civilian doctor, and in due course was returned to England."

LIEUT.-COLONEL G. F. H. McDONALD, O.B.E.

" A tall gentleman, by heaven,
And a most gallant leader."
Shakespeare :—2 Henry, III., ii.

Lieut.-Col. G. F. H. McDonald, who was a Captain in the 6th Battalion, Essex Regiment (T.F.), when the war broke out, was mobilised for active service on the 5th August, 1914. The Regiment, a unit of the 54th Division (then the East Anglian Division), proceeded at once to take up its duties as Coast Defence troops, and commenced training hard for foreign service. It took part in the construction of the East Coast Defences, and the hard work that was put in during the autumn and winter of 1914 is shown by the fact that the Division, as a whole, dug over 200 miles of trenches, and mostly in the best quality of sticky clay. In July, 1915, Col. McDonald proceeded with the Division to the Dardanelles as part of the Mediterranean Expeditionary Force. He was then in command of the troops on that ill-fated transport, the " Royal Edward," when he had a narrow escape. Whilst the ship was alongside at Alexandria, he and his staff received orders at the last minute to disembark, and an officer was sent to take over from him. The ship sailed soon after, and the next morning at 9.30 was at the bottom of the sea, the officer who had taken over, being drowned. It may interest the superstitious to know that the ship sailed from England on a Friday, from Malta on a Friday, and was torpedoed and sunk on Friday, August 13th, 1915.

Colonel McDonald, after a few days at Alexandria, proceeded to the Dardanelles, where he remained until the evacuation in 1916. He then returned to Egypt (joining the Egyptian Expeditionary Force), with rather pleasurable feelings, as the Dardanelles could hardly be regarded as a health resort, and sleeping in the open, with the thermometer below freezing point, and the sky for a counterpane, is not exactly a picnic. Egypt, however, is not all that could be desired on active service conditions, but at least the sun is always shining and the temperature warm. Colonel McDonald recollects hearing the troops singing :—

> " The sun has scorched our noses
> And our idea of bliss
> Is for another Moses
> To take us out of this ! "

Whilst in Egypt, Col. McDonald had another lucky escape. He had left his Orderly Room to speak to a passing officer, when in less than a minute afterwards, the Orderly Room was shattered by a bomb. On another occasion, he was going in a car by " road " from Jericho, to the east bank of the Jordan, just north of the Dead Sea, when the Turk amused himself by shelling the road with his " heavies," but the Colonel got through unscathed.

Colonel McDonald took part in the operations in the Islands of the Ægean Sea and Gallipoli, Egypt and the Western Desert, the Suez Canal, and Palestine, and for his services in the East was mentioned in Gen. Allenby's dispatches, and received as rewards the rank of Officer of the Most Excellent Order of the British Empire (Military Division), and was awarded the Order of the Nile by his Highness The Sultan of Egypt.

The Colonel took part in the suppression of the rising in Egypt in the early part of 1919, and returned to England at the end of August, 1919, having been on continuous service overseas for over four years.

Among the appointments held by him may be mentioned :—
Commandant Suez Area (some 500 miles o territory in length),
President of the Board of Control of Labour and Floating Craft,
Joint Authority with the Senior Naval Officer for Control of the
Port, and Authority for convening and confirming the Summary
Military Courts for dealing with crime among the civil population,
Col. McDonald has completed over 35 years Volunteer and Terri-
torial service. His decorations are :—O.B.E., 1914/15 Star,
General Service Medal, Victory Medal, Long Service Medal,
King George's Coronation Medal, Order of the Nile.

LIEUTENANT J. A. McMULLEN, M.B.E.

" Such a man
Might be a copy for these younger times :*
When he speaks not like a citizen,
You find him like a soldier."†

Shakespeare.

With patriotic Britishers, the toast of His Majesty The King
is always the first and most highly appropriate toast at all
public banquets, but long custom has made the proposing of
this toast, however conscious one may be of the high sentiment
embodied in it, a mere matter of form, and it is usually dis-
missed with the words "*Gentlemen ! The King !*". Only once
have I ever heard a real speech connected with this toast. The
occasion was the first annual dinner of the Hornchurch Conservative and Liberal Unionist Association and Club, on the
13th March, 1913, when Mr. J. A. McMullen, the Chairman,
proposed the health of His Majesty in terms of rare eloquence,
full of patriotic and poetic ideals, well worthy of a toast addressed
to the first gentleman of the land, and the Sovereign of our
great Empire. This speech impressed all its hearers in a remarkable way, so much so, that, by request, it was afterwards printed
and distributed. Delivered at a time when too little was said
or thought about that great and inspiring word " Patriotism "
and all that it means, it breathed the love of King and Country
in almost every sentence, and concluded with the following fine
passage, which, in view of the momentous events which followed
so shortly afterwards, was almost prophetic and makes it worthy
of preservation.

" It is difficult to analyse all that is conveyed in the word
' Patriotism.' This love of one's own land, of its traditions,
its successes in art, science and commerce, its victories in war—
even its defeats, leading us often to more glorious victories.
All this is part of us, impossible to analyse or put into words !

*All's well that ends well, I., iii.
†Coriolanus, III., iii.

97

England is not a thing of to-day only. It is of many centuries past, and we trust it will be of many centuries yet to come. Happy is he who leaves it, having done something, however small, for its good, something to increase its influence abroad, or better still something to help in its preservation, to help in handing it down intact to our children who come after !

But above all, let us teach our children all its traditions and its history. These cannot but engender in them the sentiments which I have endeavoured to express.

Gentlemen, rise and toast your King. Toast him first as a man ; then toast him doubly as a symbol—the symbol of—Our Country.

" GENTLEMEN, THE KING! "

Mr. McMullen's contribution of service to his country during the Great War is direct and conclusive evidence of his endeavour to live up to the spirit of the ideals so beautifully expressed by him, and no record of our village would be complete without some special reference to those services.

At the commencement of hostilities he was 51 years of age, but this did not deter him from immediately offering himself for active service. Although unsuccessful at first, he persisted in his efforts, and a little more than two months from the outbreak of the war saw him in France, he having arrived there on the 11th October, 1914, as an Ambulance motor-driver in the service of the British Red Cross Society, who had been asked to send some units right up to the front. He was soon promoted to section leader, and was with his unit during the whole of that terrible winter, when the " Old Contemptibles," gradually reinforced by the Territorials, held off the repeated attempts of the Huns to break through to Calais. His convoy, which was run by the R.A.M.C., hovered just behind the fighting line at Ypres, St. Eloi, Kemmel, Armentieres, Festubert, Givenchy, etc., and at night they carried the poor broken fighting men from the advanced dressing stations (often not more than a few hundred yards from the front trenches) back to the field hospitals, and thence in the daytime to the clearing hospitals, which were generally about ten miles in the rear. The unit was billeted most of the time in the zone of shell-fire, and on one occasion a large fragment of a shell struck the house in which Mr. McMullen had his billet. Six months of this arduous work unfortunately resulted in a return of an old complaint, which brought Mr. McMullen home in April, 1915, on sick leave. The 1914 star was awarded him for his services on the Western Front during this period.

With convalescence, the desire for active service again returned and he rejoined the Red Cross, this time going to Gallipoli—in September, 1915—and was engaged in work connected with the search for the missing and wounded. His wife went with him to Egypt, and whilst he went on to the Dardenelles, she worked in the Red Cross Record Office in Cairo. He spent most of his time in the hospitals at Mudros, but had some interesting opportunities of going round the trenches on the Peninsula, both at the Anzac and Cape Helles positions. Mr. and Mrs. McMullen remained altogether six months in the east, returning to England in March, 1916, after the evacuation at Gallipoli.

One month later Mr. McMullen was appointed engineer to a Government Explosives Factory in the North of England, which work he carried on for eighteen months.

He was then appointed Navigation Instructor, with the rank of 2nd Lieut. (subsequently promoted Lieutenant) in the Royal Air Force, and after passing the necessary examination at the Admiralty Compass Observatory, Slough, he joined a squadron at Newmarket, where training for night bombing raids was carried out. In his system of training he made a point of personally accompanying each of the budding pilots at least once on a cross country flight, carried out by the methods he himself taught, and without reference to the ground. In this way Mr. McMullen made over 80 such flights, of distances ranging up to 90 miles, and it can readily be imagined that with such embryo pilots he had some dangerous experiences. One of these occurred between Hornchurch and Rainham, when the machine finished up on its back in a field, its occupants having a very narrow escape from death.

Towards the end of October, 1918, Lieut. McMullen trained himself to be a " pukka " Observer, and had passed all the aerial, gunnery, and wireless tests. Only the sudden cessation of hostilities prevented him from completing his training for his Observer's " Wings."

Lieut. J. A. McMullen has the satisfaction of having been the oldest officer of the R.A.F. whose regular duties took him almost daily into the air, and that a man of 55 years of age should cheerfully take such risks must surely have been a great incentive and an excellent example to the beginners in the training squadrons to which Lieut. McMullen was attached.

For his services in the Royal Air Force he was awarded the M.B.E. in January, 1919.

MAJOR ALFRED FRANCIS GERALD RUSTON.
" He's a tried and valiant soldier."
Shakespeare :—Julius Cæsar, IV., i.

At the outbreak of war Major Ruston held the rank of Captain in the Kent (Fortress), Royal Engineers (T.F.), commanding No. 3 Company of that unit. He was promoted Temporary Major on 5 July, 1915, which rank was made substantive 1 June, 1916. He served through the whole period of the war, first in England, then in Gallipoli, and afterwards in France. He was twice mentioned in despatches :—first in the Gallipoli Despatch of 10th April, 1916, published 12 July, 1916, and again in Field Marshal Haig's Despatch of April 8, 1917, published 18 May, 1917.

The following personal recollections of the war are of such an interesting character that I reproduce them as written.

When I look back over the $4\frac{1}{2}$ years I spent as an atom in the British Army during the Great War, although, during the whole period, I lived a life not by any means devoid of tension and excitement, I find very few experiences which I can honestly call exciting in the ordinary meaning of the word. I can, however, recall one or two events in which the tension was rather higher than the normal.

Perhaps the most exciting—strange as it may seem—occurred just before the war, on the 30th July, 1914. It was not associated with actual danger or even the promise of danger ; it was simply the departure to its war station of the Special Service Section of the R.E. unit to which I belonged. The Section in question consisted of 25 N.C.O's. and men under one officer, and I was fortunate enough to be that officer. We had had ten days very stiff training at our Annual Territorial Camp, and were promised an easier time for the rest of the fortnight. On the afternoon of the 10th day we were all sitting about after tea talking of the next day's work, which was to be a tactical scheme, and each side was thinking out its plans for getting the better of the other, when there was a strange commotion in the men's mess tents, and the strains of " Onward Christian Soldiers " and " Fight the Good Fight " were wafted to us across the parade ground. A few moments later the mess tents emptied and men were seen in the lines, rolling up great coats and packing kit bags. " Special Service Section " at once came to our minds, and the next moment an order from the C.O. summoning me to the orderly room showed that we were right. In less than an hour we had been medically examined, and inspected, and were marching off to the railway station amid the cheers of our comrades. I shall never forget that march down to Strood Station ; the wives and youngsters of many of the party appeared from no one knows where, and walked beside us, most of them weeping, and I honestly think we felt more like heroes then than we have ever done before or since. Quite a small thing compared with what came afterwards ; but at the time stirring up at least my own emotions, perhaps more than anything I experienced afterwards. It was our first taste of real soldiering.

I will not say much about the far more serious " march off " when the Company marched down to Chatham Station at midnight on 11th October, 1915, for foreign service, with an unknown destination before it, except to say that, exciting as it was, it didn't anything like come up to the mobilisation of the old Special Service Section.

Alas, a large number of the brave fellows who so gallantly marched down Chatham Hill that night were fated never to see the foreign service on which they were so keen.

We had arrived in our transport in Lemnos Bay, and after a few days of idleness were packed on the sweeper "Hythe" with Cape Helles as our destination. The service of sweepers was known at Mudros as "the Ferry," and no one dreamt that we should be up against questions of life and death before we reached the Peninsula, although we knew pretty well what to expect on arrival there.

It was a stormy afternoon, the wind blowing great guns, and few of us were viewing our impending trip with very pleasant expectations. The sweeper on which we were to do the last few miles of our voyage to the front looked but little bigger than a Thames penny steamer, but, with a certain amount of squashing, all were got on board ; a dozen or so details who joined us from H.M.S. "Arragon" just before we sailed made the pressure just about as much as it was possible to stand. Awnings were rigged over the decks fore and aft to protect the men from the spray, and the few officers on board occupied a small upper deck behind the bridge. At four o'clock we set sail, and no sooner were we out of the Bay than we found that we were in for a rough passage indeed. Ninety per cent. of those on board were sea-sick, and few of the remaining ten per cent. felt it quite safe to move about much. Personally, I have the good fortune to be a fair sailor and did not feel any discomfort from the weather. Those on the lower decks found the awnings very necessary, for the spray was blowing over the vessel in regular bucketfuls. After about $3\frac{1}{2}$ hours the wind went down and the sea began to get easier, so I took the opportunity of joining the Ship's Officers at dinner. I had previously discovered that the second engineer was a Barking man, and we had chatted a bit about home, so that after dinner he took me down to the engine room, with all an engineer's pride in his machinery, to show me the engines. I was sitting on a bench with my back to a bulkhead, while he gave some instructions to the men, when suddenly there was a great bump which shook the whole vessel. Knowing that we were not far from our destination I thought at first that we had arrived at our journey's end and had bumped against some pier in getting in, but as we were going at full speed this was of course out of the question, so I thought " Oh, a propellor shaft has burst." Meanwhile, steam was shut off, and thinking that, with engine trouble to see to, the people below would prefer my room to my presence, I went up on deck.

As I was going up the companion way, I saw that we were alongside a fairly large vessel, though it was too dark to see much of it, and fellows were scrambling from ours to her, though many hesitated as though doubtful whether it were not better to stick to the boat they were on. By the time I was fairly on the upper deck the other vessel was slowly moving away from us, or we from her ; a rope which had been thrown to us parted, and we drifted further and further apart. Our vessel showed no signs of being badly hit, so far as I could see, but none the less all on board seemed to regard us as doomed—they had seen more than I had.

Men were by this time cutting the lashings of the awning and clambering on to the upper deck. Poor fellows, most of them had suffered badly from the rough passage, and many of them had already got into their gear in order to be ready to land ; a few lights, not so very far off, showed that we had almost reached Cape Helles, our destination.

I joined the other naval and military officers in trying to keep those on board from panic—though, I am glad to be able to say, there was very little tendency to it—and the next few incidents are rather like a series of pictures than a continuous string of events.

I remember searching for lifebelts or floating benches, but there were none to be found. Then I remember getting a party together to launch the port boat ; we worked with a will and got one end free ; but at the other end the rope jammed and eventually we had to give it up. A similar attempt with the starboard boat was equally unsuccessful. Then I remember seeing the port boat in the water, launched, I think, by some of the crew ; it immediately capsized. Meanwhile, on the Captain's advice, all who could swim had been jumping into the sea and seizing such floating gear as the other vessel had been able to throw overboard. The vessel was now developing a list to port, and we got everyone who could to gather on the starboard side. I was thinking of joining them there, when the list become so pronounced that I could not get up the deck, while my side of the deck was awash. I judged that the only thing to do was to throw myself overboard, which I did in my clothes, boots, and cap, just as I stood, and struck out for a life-buoy, which I saw floating some short distance off. Another fellow reached it at the same moment as I did, so I left it to him, and getting hold of a packed kit-bag, which was floating near by, I struck out for the other vessel, now several hundred yards off and lighted up. Before long the kit-bag became water-logged, so I left it and swam on unassisted. I then saw a boat leaving the other vessel, and succeeded in reaching it, and was pulled in. We picked up a good many more fellows, and then returned to the other vessel, which I found to be H.M.S. "Sarnia."

The "Hythe" must have sunk soon after I left her; I did not see her go down, nor did I hear anything, except, perhaps, the cries of men from the wrecked vessel. From the boat one saw a lot of floating wreckage and heads of men swimming all round the spot where she must have gone down. A number of destroyers were now cruising round, and several boats were engaged in the work of rescue. Batches of men kept coming on board the Sarnia and I thought that a large proportion must have been saved till I went round and made a list. Then I found that out of my own company, about 195 strong, 129 were missing. It was a sad beginning to our foreign service, and it was some time before the remnant quite got over it. The vessel that collided with us was, we found, an auxilary cruiser, and the principal cause was navigating without lights, a necessary precaution against submarine attack. A little Memorial Service held on board the Arragon after our rescue will always be imprinted on my mind. Few of us had more than a shirt and a pair of trousers, and some of us only a blanket—but we meant what we said.

The other two incidents I wish to refer to must be dealt with more briefly.

The evacuation of Helles was an event which did not fail to generate a pretty strong nerve tension in those who took part in it. The most exciting incident, so far as I was concerned, was when several hundreds of us were slowly moving down in pretty dense formation from the back of Sedd-el-Bahr to the old transport "River Clyde," where we were to embark in lighters, and "Asiatic Annie"* saw fit to give us five rounds. The first hit a heap of rails and made no end of a row, but did no damage, a second made a hit on another safe spot, a third fell in the sea, and two were duds. Until after a short time had passed, we all of us had the "wind up" pretty badly, as we felt sure the evacuation had been spotted, and that they would shell the beaches to blazes, a far from pleasant prospect for us, the small remnant who had been left to clear off on the last night. However, we all got away safely, as history relates. It was my fate to go on board H.M.S. "Prince George," a battleship, acting for the nonce as transport. As soon as she was full up—and she *was* full up—she weighed anchor and started slowly steaming off to Lemnos. I had just come on deck after an enormous and very welcome meal in the ward room, when something struck us a very heavy blow. We at once started zig-zagging, and in this slow and rather painful way completed our trip to Lemnos. It was afterwards stated that we had been struck by an enemy torpedo. Fortunately for us, the genius who fired it forgot to release the "gadget" that does duty as a safety

*A very troublesome enemy gun fired from the Asiatic side of the Dardanelles, probably from Fort Chanak.

catch on a torpedo. Having got so far in our adventure, we didn't want to be knocked out at the last moment, and again the "wind had a tendency to the vertical."

Later on I served in France and was unfortunate enough to be taken prisoner, and I will conclude with a few impressions of captivity. My first feeling was one of extreme surprise. I couldn't realise that I had been captured. I had thought of the possibility of being wounded or knocked out, but not of being captured some distance behind the front line! It was in the German break-through on 30th November, 1917, where a good many more of us were surprised to find a German, instead of the postman, knocking at the door while having breakfast in imagined security.

Our captors treated us pretty well, and got us back as soon as it was reasonably safe to do so. We marched into Germany— that is to say into German occupied territory—along a good road with not a shell hole in it, and scarcely a sign of the fierce fight our fellows had had in their endeavour to hold the line.

The trip back to Karlsruhe, the distributing centre, took several days, and what I noticed on the journey went a long way to destroy in my mind the vision of German efficiency. Perhaps all their best men were in the trenches, but those with whom we came in touch seemed fussy, and anything but efficient. This impression was confirmed by my subsequent observations during a year's captivity. I have no complaints to make of my treatment during the captivity. There were, of course, a number of "grouses," but nothing of any real seriousness.

Captivity—for an officer at any rate—is a strange experience to one who is so fortunate as to avoid ill-treatment. Imagine a great boys' school during the holidays, none of the boys having been sent home, and you may get some sort of an idea of the "rags" and the fun, and the fights and the enmities and the friendships, and all the thousand and one incidents of a community life on a large scale, with no work to do. Add to this the fact that we were not allowed out except on walks like those of a school for young ladies of the last generation—en crocodile—, which only occurred about once a week for the individual, and you can perhaps picture the life for yourself.

The adults we saw when we were travelling, or were out on walks, looked, as a rule, puffy and unhealthy, and had very little colour. Not having been in Germany in pre-war days, I cannot say whether this was normal or not. The little children in Baden looked fat and rosy, but in the Harz they looked rather "peaky." The children between 7 and 14 seemed to show the effects of the war most of all, looking pasty-faced and ill-nourished. I never saw any hostility in the people's demeanour ; a certain amount of curiosity sometimes, but in the main sheer apathy. The little children were an exception, an occasional piece of chocolate would quite win their hearts and the appearance of our " crocodile " on a walk was the sign for the gathering of all the little people within reach.

After the armistice there was a certain distinct attempt at friendliness observable in all the people I came across, despite which I cannot say that it was with any regrets that I boarded the Danish vessel " Niels Ebbesen," at Warnemunde, and set sail in half a gale for Copenhagen and home on 13th December, 1918.

THE REV. CHARLES STEER, M.C.

" Why then, God's soldier be he "*
" Whose spirit lent a fire
Even to the dullest spirit in his camp "†

Shakespeare.

The Rev. Charles Steer, formerly Curate of St. Edward's, Romford (1905 to 1910), was for some time prior to the war in South Africa, Vicar of Randfontein, Transvaal. In the summer of 1914 he was on leave, and was in Paris, on the day war with Germany was declared. He immediately came over to England, and endeavoured to obtain a post at the front in the Army Chaplain's Department. Being unsuccessful in this, he returned to South Africa, and for the first year of the war had to console himself with the thought that the work he was doing in the wilds of the Northern Transvaal was in many ways real active service, and that, too, with plenty of hardships. He was placed in charge of the Zoutpansberg district, and his position involved considerable responsibility in the successful endeavours made to avert the Dutch rebellion, which would undoubtedly have proved very disastrous, had it been allowed to develop and spread. In September, 1915, he was summoned to a meeting of the Bishop's Senate, at which a discussion arose as to the attitude the Church had to take with regard to the South African troops shortly to be sent to German East Africa. He put up a strong plea for a certain number of clergy to be allowed to enlist in the ranks, and this project receiving a powerful backing from his brother priests, it was decided, by vote, to adopt that course. On the following day he went to a Recruiting Office in Johannesberg, and enrolled as a private, together with four other priests who saw eye to eye with him. He was called to the Colours in October, and spent a month or two in training at Potchefstroom, with the South African Medical Corps, in which he attained the rank of Corporal, and was placed in charge of the Water Section, attached to the 7th S.A. Infantry.

On December 27th, 1915, he sailed from Durban, arriving at Kilindini on or about New Year's Day, 1916. With his unit, he saw some sharp actions at Salaita Hill, Lumi River, and Taveta,

*Macbeth, v., vii.
†Henry IV., I., i.

under General Smuts' command, and was recommended for the D.C.M. The work of the Water Sections was in those early days extremely arduous, as not only had they to do all the fetching of the water in bullock carts from the tanks, but also the actual rationing of it to the troops both in camp and in action. With an allowance of half a gallon a day for drinking, cooking, and washing, this was no easy matter, under an absolutely vertical sun.

Corporal Steer took part in Van Deventer's forced march to Kondoa Irangi, a matter of 200 miles, in the rainy season, having at times to man-handle the Army Transport carts through black bog up to the axles, the oxen being done up very early in the march. Sleeping out in the open, and in the rains of the tropics, with only a waterproof sheet covering, was a very trying experience, and, as a consequence, fever was rife, and unfortunately medical comforts were few and far between.

The remainder of Mr. Steer's South African War experiences are so interesting, and so graphically told, that I reproduce them as personally narrated.

" On the 1st June, 1916, while at Kondoa Irangi, I was appointed Chaplain to the 9th S. African Horse, then some 300 miles behind us at M'Buyuni. Stealing a ride on the M.G. motor, which had to go back for repairs, I managed to get back to Nairobi, pick up a minimum of kit, and join my new regiment just as it was starting off on its long trek to the front and a very pleasant trek it was. Early in July we pushed forward, fought some sharp actions at T'schunjo Nek and M'Papua, and finally got across the main German Railway after another sharp action, some five miles from the latter place. We thought the enemy would throw in his hand when his railway was lost to him, but we did not know Von Lettow. We had to push him down all the way through the Uluguru Mountains and fight a heavy action for the water outside Kissaki. By this time, though a mounted regiment, we were all on foot again, the horses having all died of tsetse fly. The men, too, were in the last stage of weakness, through lack of food and the ever-recurring fever. So, having captured Kissaki, we proceeded to sit down on one side of the river, with the enemy on the other, until some food and reinforcements could come up. Never shall I forget the stink of the hundreds of dead horses, nor the " delight " with which we, who had been living on donkey and hippo flesh, with now and then a handful of flour as a treat, and some Kaffir corn, pounded into a sort of porridge, received one day a G.R.O., in which it was stated that the *ration of pepper had been reduced from one forty-fifth to one seventy-second of an ounce per man per diem.*

On being relieved here by some Indian troops, we trekked back to Morogoro to refit and rehorse, got our first parcels of the campaign, had two or three square meals at the eating houses there, and then put out for another two hundred miles to Iringa. Long before we got there we were all on foot again, though I myself started out from Morogoro with six horses to my name, and many others had as many. They just died on the roadside, like flies. We were down there in the wilds for Christmas, and a lonesome Christmas it was, with an attempt to surround a large enemy force made on the day itself. Then, being all worn out with fever and dysentery, we trekked back to the railway, some hundred miles, and at the end of February, 1917, had reached Dar es Salam, whence we proceeded to Durban, where the 9th S.A.H. was disbanded.

On arriving in Johannesberg, I was met by my Bishop, and within ten minutes we had drawn up a scheme whereby the Diocese should do its bit in Europe. All the clergy of military age were given permission to go Home, whether as combatants or otherwise, the Bishop undertaking to arrange their work for them in the meanwhile by grouping parishes, etc. Nearly half of the white staff of the Diocese was actually in France by June of that year, 1917, and I am glad to say that I was the first of the bunch, in spite of having been warned by the medical authorities that I was full of malaria and should inevitably die before I reached England, let alone France."

Mr. Steer was mentioned in Despatches, dated May 30, 1917, by Major General A. R. Hoskins, Commander-in-Chief, East African Force.

On arrival in England he was accepted as a Chaplain in the Army Chaplains' Department, and after a fortnight at Aldershot, was sent to France, and attached to the 8th Divisional Artillery, with which he served for a year, going through some heavy fighting with them in the Ypres Salient in July, and again all through the worst of the following winter. He was awarded the Military Cross for conspicuous service in connection with the first advance along the Menin Road. on July 31st, 1917.

In March, 1918, the Division was hastened to the defence of Amiens, and fought all through that retreat.

In the following month Mr. Steer came to England for his marriage with Miss Elizabeth Maud Whitcombe, daughter of the Right Rev. Dr. R. H. Whitcombe, Bishop of Colchester, the ceremony taking place at St. Peter's, Cranley Gardens, London, on April 4th, 1918.

On returning to the Western Front, towards the end of April, he took part in the British reinforcement of the French line, between Chemin des Dames and Rheims, and, unfortunately, fell into the hands of the Germans at the commencement of their attack on May 28th, 1918. He was detained as a prisoner of war in the German Prison Camp at Rastatt and afterwards at Stralsund, whence he was repatriated at the end of October, arriving in London, via Holland, on 1st November, 1918. He, however, only remained in England a few weeks, and just before Christmas was again sent to France, and detailed as Deputy Assistant Chaplain-General, 19th Corps, Headquarters, Cassel, France. He was eventually demobilized on March 31st, 1919, and immediately commenced his duties as Chaplain and Vicar Temporal at Hornchurch.

His decoration of the Military Cross was bestowed upon him by the King at Buckingham Palace on November 7, 1919, the following being the official announcement of the award:

> " Rev. Charles Steer, Army Chaplains' Department :— Notwithstanding the heavy shell-fire, he remained continually in the Batteries, assisting in moving the wounded, and encouraging the men. On a previous occasion, during a long period of heavy shelling, he acted with the greatest gallantry and devotion, by his personal example of cheerfulness, very greatly inspiring all ranks under most difficult conditions."

SERGEANT JOHN ROBERT WESTLEY, BRITISH RED CROSS.

"He hath done good service in these wars."

Shakespeare—Much Ado about Nothing, i., i.

At the outbreak of the war Sergeant Westley was 39 years of age, and was therefore not eligible for active service with the fighting forces, but having served in the South African War in the R.A.M.C.,* his patriotism prompted him to offer his services in the direction in which he considered his experience and ability would be most useful to his country. He therefore volunteered for service in the British Red Cross Society, and was accepted. He arrived in France as early as September 19, 1914. The B.R.C.S. was then forming a Motor Ambulance Convoy at Paris and Boulogne, and this was taken over by the Adjutant-General of the forces, General Macready, at Abbeville, and was immediately attached to the British Army, being the first Motor Ambulance Convoy employed on the western front. Sergeant Westley proceeded with this convoy to Bethune, where it did excellent work in and around Richebourg and Neuve Chapelle, and was mentioned in dispatches by General French in November of that year. The convoy was afterwards shelled out of Bethune, and fell back to Merville, and from that station took part in the engagements of Neuve Chapelle of March and May, 1915. Sergeant Westley continued with the convoy on the British front until March, 1916, and then joined up with a section

*Sergeant Westley served 3 years in South Africa with the R.A.M.C., and was attached to the Ladysmith Relief Column, under General Buller. He was awarded both the Queen's and the King's Medals with clasps for his services.

of 20 cars which proceeded to Paris, where they were taken over by the French Army. At that time the great battle of Verdun was proceeding, the French being very hard pressed by the ferocious and determined attacks of the Germans. The convoy was immediately sent to that front, arriving at Verdun on the 29th March,† and was engaged there with the 2nd and 6th French Armies until the end of the battle, which culminated so gloriously for our gallant and heroic allies. The members of the convoy were daily under artillery fire and in the gas zone, and were awarded for their invaluable service the certificate of the Croix de Guerre, with two stars (gold and bronze). Sergeant Westley's Certificate is dated Verdun, 1916, and is signed by Norman Fletcher and R. Pinget, and contains the following extracts from Orders Nos. 82 and 32 :—

According to regulation, the Director of the Medical Service of the 6th Corps d'Armée cites to the order of the Medical Service of the 6th Corps d'Armée :—

La Section Sanitaire Anglaise, No. 18.

" Under the direction of Lieutenant Pinget and of the O.C. Norman Fletcher, the B.R.C. Motor Ambulance Convoy, No. 18, has for more than two months carried out remarkably well the daily evacuation of the wounded, and in particular has assisted in evacuation of numerous gassed and wounded men during the attacks of the 23rd June and 12th July, 1916, continually passing through the gas zone under considerable artillery fire, in order to carry the wounded as quickly as possible to the ambulances."

The Général de Division, Directeur des Etapes et Services, cites to the order of the D.E.S. :—

La Section Sanitaire Anglaise, No. 18.

" Which, under the joint command of Lieutenant Pinget and Mr. Norman Fletcher and under the general direction of Lieutenant-Colonel Barry A.J., has carried out for many months, with untiring zeal and devotion, the transport of wounded under the most difficult circumstances, and has rendered great service to the army, showing the greatest self-sacrifice in dealing with the wounded in areas which were heavily shelled."

Sergeant Westley was wounded on April 5, 1916 by high explosive shell whilst carrying wounded. After the battle of Verdun he returned to England and received his discharge from the British Red Cross Society in August, 1916, having seen service in France for two years. He holds the Mons Star for 1914.

† The battle of Verdun began on February 21, 1916.

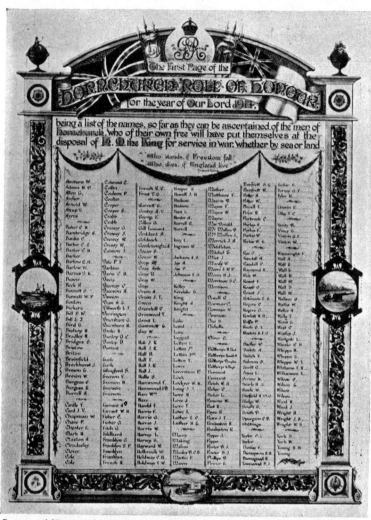

Drawn and Illuminated by H. Noel Pailthorpe.

THE FIRST PAGE OF THE HORNCHURCH ROLL OF HONOUR.

Being a List of Names of some of those Parishoners who first volunteered for Active Service.

Compiled by the Rev. HERBERT JOHN DALE, M.A., Vicar.

Reproduced from the Original which hangs on the South Wall in the Church.

THE BRITISH MERCANTILE MARINE.

"We all that are engaged to this loss
Know that we ventured on such dangerous seas
That if we wrought out life 'twas ten to one ;
And yet we ventur'd——
And since we are o'erset, venture again."
Shakespeare—2 Henry IV., I., i.

"The part in this war which has been played by the officers and men of the British Mercantile Marine is such that some record is imperative." Those are the words of Admiral Lord Jellicoe, and all will heartily agree with them. Although no adequate record of their services can be made in a book such as this, my intention is to make, in grateful recognition, some special reference to that branch of the service which did so much to help win the war, and to make it possible for us to live in comparative comfort, and to maintain our homes during the whole of that terrible period. The story of Captain Fryatt's splendid bravery will for ever remain in the hearts and minds of all true Britons. We know that it was typical of the spirit displayed by the whole of the Mercantile Marine, and that there are few officers and men on its honourable roll about whom something noble and heroic could not be written. In the long list of names in our own roll of Honour are those of several men of our parish who did splendid service in the Transport and Merchant Service, and who thought not at all of the grave risks they were running, and the dangers which almost hourly beset them. One of these brave men, John E. Gaywood, a wireless telegraphist, lost his life when his ship, H.M.T." Redbridge " was torpedoed off Fishguard on 6th Dec., 1917. Another, W.A.R. Bowick, an engineer, whose ship was once torpedoed, and five times attacked while in convoy, and one other, Harold Victor Rogers, who was prominently concerned in one of those stirring dramas of the sea which were almost daily enacted, and which called forth that initiative and heroic devotion to duty of which we are all so justly proud.

The Narrative of the Torpedoing of s.s. " San Eduardo " :—

On the 10th March, 1917, before day had dawned, the s.s. " San Eduardo," on Admiralty Service, having discharged her cargo, was in the Irish Sea, making for a home port. Her Captain, Mr. Griffith, of Pwelheli, and the chief engineer, Mr. Harold Victor Rogers of Hornchurch, had congratulated themselves upon the successful termination of a somewhat venturesome voyage, when, without sign or warning, a German torpedo crashed through the ship's side. The master, imperturbable and ever ready, immediately ordered the engines to be stopped, his object being to induce the belief in the pirates' mind that a vital part had been struck, knowing well that in that case they would be left to their fate. There was no second attack, and the ship was brought safely to port without loss of life. Within a few weeks the " San Eduardo " was made seaworthy, and all hands were ready to carry-on, face fresh dangers and, as it happened, to experience other narrow escapes.

A grateful company notified its appreciation of the courage, initiative and splendid seamanship of its officers, and presented valuable gold watches to the master and chief engineer as souvenirs of the occasion.

A section of the Mercantile Marine was represented in the Victory march in London on 19th July, 1919. The smart and attractive uniforms and colouring, which formed such a great feature in that wonderful spectacle, were conspicuously absent in the case of the men chosen to represent this branch of the service. Nevertheless, they came in for an ovation which equalled or surpassed that given to many of the other splendidly uniformed and equipped sections, as will be seen from the following extract from the " Observer " of July 20th, 1919, describing the event :—

" Before the end of the Naval contingent was reached there was an incident which deserves special mention. Suddenly the martial scene was transformed. The house flags of the chief mercantile lines were borne by, and then came a banner of the sort we are accustomed to in Hyde Park Labour processions, and, after it, 100 men or so in mufti. For a moment the crowd wondered. Then a mighty cheer broke forth as it was realised that these were the simple heroes of the Mercantile Marine whose dogged staunchness in " carrying on " saved us from destruction. There was not a man in that contingent who had not been torpedoed once, and many of them two and three times. Eternal honour to their name ! May they receive the reward of their services in a truer and better realisation of the part they played in the Empire's life ! "

WOMEN'S NATIONAL SERVICE IN THE WAR.

" We have willing dames enough.*
Nay, ladies, fear not,
By all the laws of war you're privileged."†
Shakespeare.

In my article entitled " *The Sportswoman*,"‡, I paid a tribute in a general way to the work of the women during the war, but at that time we were only at the beginning of things, when women's work, apart from the nursing profession, was unorganized, and when all that was done was voluntary, and consisted mainly in the making and supplying of additional comforts for our sailors and soldiers, and in canteen and rest-

*Macbeth, iv., iii.
†Henry VIII., i., iv.
‡See Chapter " Sportsman's Battalion."

Drawn by Constance Symonds.

room work. Later on, when the demands on the man-power of the country were so great, it became necessary for women to enter fields of labour, and upon walks of life, which had hitherto been looked upon as only suitable for the stronger and sterner sex. How well the women of the country responded to the call is one of the outstanding features of the whole war, and it is certainly not too much to say that without their efforts the war could never have been won. Those who replaced the fighting men in Government offices, Banks, Railways, Insurance and Commercial offices, and those who performed the duties of postmen, tram and 'bus conductors, motor drivers, railway porters and ticket collectors, etc., all had their share in this, as did also that great army of women munition workers, who cheerfully risked danger and disease in their daily occupations. All these women workers were content to accept privations and discomfort in the belief that they were helping to " carry on " for the men and lads who were fighting their battles, and in the full knowledge that their own labours were doing much to forward the elements that make for victory.

In addition to these civil occupations many Services were officially instituted and sanctioned in connection with the Navy, Army, and Air Forces, and with the British Red Cross and the Order of St. John of Jerusalem, distinctive uniforms being worn by each unit. In all these Services the women filled the places of men, in the majority of cases with conspicuous success, and won the general admiration of the public for their efficiency. Many of the tasks undertaken by them in the course of their duty entailed hardship and endurance which must have been a serious tax upon their health.

The most prominent of these women's organizations were familiarly known as :—V.A.D.'s, W.A.A.C.'s, W.R.N.S. and W.R.A.F.'s.

THE V.A.D.

The first organized work for women for war purposes was the " Joint Women's Voluntary Aid Detachments Departments " of the British Red Cross, and the Order of St. John of Jerusalem, which came to be known as the V.A.D. These two organizations had for several years previous to the outbreak of war been working hard, and their detachments were in thorough working order, ready to be called up at a moment's notice. The result of this preparedness was that, when the war was declared, both committees were able to assist in a most valuable way. In October, 1914, it was decided to work together as a " Joint Committee." The working members, popularly spoken of as V.A.D.'s, have practically undertaken every branch of hospital work ever since ; as well as running canteens and recreation huts for convalescent and rest stations, thus releasing an immense number of men.

114

Their hospital work was divided into two sections :—(1) Auxiliary hospitals and local work, (2) Special service. While the first was entirely voluntary, the second was sub-divided into voluntary and paid work. Some of the members entered under the section termed " nursing members," and others as " general service members." The latter undertook a variety of work, such as dispensers, clerks, cooks, X-ray attendants, telephone operators, and motor drivers.* The operations of the V.A.D. were not confined to home service, but extended to hospital and other work overseas, where they had to encounter more dangers and risks than would have been the case at home, especially in the latter days of the war, when the bombing of hospitals by the enemy was so indiscriminate and frequent, and when many nurses and V.A.D.'s lost their lives, and many others were seriously wounded.

The V.A.D.'s did a great work, and probably no other form of officially organized women's service was so noble or so self-sacrificing as theirs during the war.

QUEEN MARY'S ARMY AUXILIARY CORPS (W.A.A.C.'s.)

She'll be a soldier too ; she'll to the wars !
Shakespeare :—Henry IV., III., i.

An Army Council instruction was published in 1917, giving approval to the formation of a Women's Army Auxiliary Corps. The object of the Corps was to effect substitution of women for soldiers in certain employment, thereby releasing a very large number of men for the fighting Services.

It is assumed that each member of this Corps definitely released a combatant soldier. Members lived together in quarters, either in camps or barracks, but were attached for work to different Units. Women replaced N.C.O.'s and men in regimental cookhouses, working under the supervision of forewomen. They also acted as waitresses, housemaids, bakers, tailors, clerks, typists, and orderlies. Administrators were placed in charge of hostels.

The uniform was khaki of a neat and effective design.

THE WOMEN'S ROYAL NAVAL SERVICE (W.R.N.S.).

The object of this Service was to displace by women as many men as possible of the naval ratings at the ports. The members enrolled for the period of 12 months, or the duration of the war, whichever was the longer, their occupation being entirely confined to work on shore. The Officers were divided into two Classes (1) Administrative, and (2) Non-Administrative. The former were in charge of W.R.N.S. ratings, and the latter replaced Naval Officers as De-coders and Secretaries at the

*Vide Emily L.B. Forster—Daily Mail Year Book, 1918, page 43.

various Naval bases. The work of the W.R.N.S. began in February, 1918, at Naval bases in the United Kingdom, and later extended to the Mediterranean. The uniform was quite a novel one, but of a very womanly, yet useful kind. The ratings wore blue serge with black crown and anchor buttons, and the officers blue serge with brass buttons.

THE WOMEN'S ROYAL AIR FORCE (W.R.A.F.)

In 1918 another form of Service for women was instituted in the Women's Royal Air Force, which rendered very useful service to the Royal Air Force. The tasks undertaken by these women were, in many cases, arduous, and in the technical branch included the following occupations :—Fitters, Magneto Repairers, Wireless Operators, Motor Drivers, Motor Cyclists, etc. Their uniform was of khaki, which was later replaced by a uniform of blue.

WOMEN'S LAND ARMY.

The formation of the Women's Land Army opened up the way for a very large number of women and girls to release men employed in agricultural pursuits, who had hitherto been exempt from Military Service, but who, in the course of time, through the increasing demand upon the man-power of the Country for the War, had to join H.M. Forces.

The Land Army was divided into three sections :—

1. Agricultural Section.
2. Forage Section.
3. Timber Cutting Section,

and in these were embraced practically all the occupations dealing with labour on the soil.

The women wore distinct uniforms, which were not only suitable, but attractive, viz. :—white smock, slouch hat, breeches and gaiters.

Other official organizations and uniformed Corps were :—

WOMEN'S LEGION, a pioneer corps in connection with the Army services " Cooking and Mechanical and Motor Drivers Section " When the W.A.A.C. was formed, it absorbed the cookery section, but the A.S.C. and other motor drivers at home remained with the Women's Legion.

NAVY AND ARMY CANTEEN BOARD (N.A.C.B.), which took over a large proportion of the organization and work of canteens and did a great deal of useful and necessary war work.

THE WOMEN'S VOLUNTEER RESERVE (W.V.R.)

THE WOMEN'S HOSPITAL CORPS, entirely run by Endell Street Military Hospital, and

QUEEN ALEXANDRA'S IMPERIAL NURSING SERVICE (Q.A.I.N.S.)

LIST OF WOMEN WORKERS.

Allen, Miss, A.P.C., Warley.

Barrett, Miss, A.P.C. Warley, May/16—Jan./18.

Beck, Gladys, V.A.D., Marshall's Park, Romford, 1916—1919, Canteen worker, Y.M.C.A., N.Z. Camp, Hornchurch, and at Hare Hall Camp Romford. 1917—1919

Bentall, Alice Winifred, Postwoman, Hornchurch, 1915—1919.

Bishop, The Misses, A.P.C. Warley.

Bonnett, Sophia Jane, Field Telephone Inspector, Dagenham.

Bradshaw, Miss, A.P.C., Warley.

Brook-Smith, Mrs., Telephonist. R.A.F., Suttons Farm Aerodrome. Hornchurch.

Burrell, Elizabeth Mary, W.A.A.C., England and France, 1916—1919.

Catherwood, Greta, Clerk, Admiralty, 1918—1919.

Catherwood, Gwendoline, Clerk, Admiralty and Ministry of Munitions, 1918—1919.

Catherwood, Maud, Sister, King's College Hospital, London, and Lincoln Hospital, 1914—1919.

Clark, Miss, A.P.C. Warley.

Cockwell, Nina D., Assistant Principal W.R.N.S., Non-Administrative, Portland, and Administrative, Admiralty, Whitehall, 1918—1919.

Cook, E. E., A.P.C. Warley, March/16—Oct./18.

Cook, M. E., A.P.C. Warley April/16—Dec./19.

Cousens, Constance Margaret, Clerk, Ministry of Munitions, Whitehall, 1917—1919.

Cousens, Ethel K., Clerk, A.P.C., 1918—1919.

Cousens, Hilda May, Clerk, Ministry of Munitions, Whitehall, 1917—1919,

Creek, Mrs. (neé Stanley), A.P.C. Warley.

Gerrard, Mrs. (née Lily Mansfield), Munition work at Roneo Works, June/15 to Jan./20.

Guy, E., Government Work at Roneo Works, April/16—Nov./18.

Harris, Enid, Motor Cyclist, W.R.A.F., Suttons Farm Aerodrome, Hornchurch.

Hawkins, Agnes, A.P.C. Warley Barracks, Sept./15—/20.

Hawkins, Susannah Emily, Mobilized Clerk, Warley Barracks, Sept./15—/20.

Hewitson, Dorothea Grace, W.R.A.F., Suttons Farm Aerodrome, Hornchurch 1918—1919.

Holgate, Fanny, V.A.D., 3rd London General Hospital, Wandsworth.

Hollinghurst, Phyllis Madge, Motor Cyclist, W.R.A.F., Suttons Farm Aerodrome, Hornchurch.

Jenkinson, Eveline Mary, Women's Volunteer Reserve, F. Company, 1st London Batt. Hospital, and Canteen Worker and Air Raid duty, London and Woolwich Arsenal, Feb./15—Nov./17.

Kirkman, Elsie, A.P.C. Warley, Nov./17—Oct./19.

Knightbridge, G., A.P.C. Warley, Jan.—July/17.

Lazell, Ellen B., Munition Worker. Stirling Works, Dagenham, 1914 to 1918.

Lester, Doris, Motor Driver, W.R.A.F., Suttons Farm Aerodrome, Hornchurch.

Letten, Emma, Postwoman, Hornchurch, 1915 (6 months).

Lewtas, Miss, A.P.C. Warley.

Lofthouse, Elsie, Motor Driver, W.R.A.F. Suttons Farm Aerodrome, Hornchurch.

Macdonald, Mrs, A.P.C., Warley.

Mallinson, A., A.P.C. Warley.

Manly, Phyllis Ada, Clerk, R.A.F., Aug./18—Dec./19.

Manly, Winifred Rose, Clerk, R.A.F., Aug./18—Dec./19.

Mansfield, Mrs. (née Judd.)

Martin, Rosetta Maud, W.A.A.C.

Matthews, Mrs. (née D. Matthews), A.P.C. Warley.

May, Maud, V.A.D., Romford Military Hospital, and Cook, N.Z. Y.M.CA. Grey Towers.

Mc Mullen, Annie Matilda (Mrs.), B.R.C.S., Missing and Wounded, Enquiry Bureau, Cairo, Sept./15—March/16, and Canteen worker N.Z. Y.M.C.A., Grey Towers.

Merrett, Bessie Frances, W.R.A.F., Suttons Farm Aerodrome, Hornchurch.

Monks, Miss, No. 1 Records, No. 9 District, Warley, Nov./17—March/20.

Nash, Miss, A.P.C., Warley, Sept./15—March/20.

Pamment, Florrie Marie, W.A.A.C., Aldershot Hostel, Sept./17—Mar./18.

Pardoe, Mrs. (née Woodward), A.P.C. Warley.

Payne, Cherry M., Motor Driver, W.R.A.F., Suttons Farm Aerodrome, Hornchurch.

Pemberton, Mrs. H., Making Naval Decorations.

Potter, Mrs., Motor Driver, W R.A.F., Suttons Farm Aerodrome, Hornchurch.

Purbrook, Constance, Masseuse, A.P.M.M.C., N.Z. Convalescent Hospital, Hornchurch, and Military Hospital, Edinburgh.

Rae, Mrs., Hon. worker for London Association for the Blind, from May/18.

Rae, Miss, A.P.C., Warley, Sept./16—Dec./19.

Rainbow, Mrs. (née F. Mansfield), A.P.C., Warley, Dec./17—Oct./19.

Roper, Mrs. (née M. Blundell.)

Seymour, Mrs. (née O. Wilson), A.P.C. Warley, Nov./15—Oct./16 ; also July/17—Oct./19.

Skingley, Daisy, V.A.D., Tottenhall War Hospital, Southgate Branch.

Squire, Mrs., A.P.C. Warley.

Straw, The Misses, A.P.C., Warley.

Symonds, Amy E. C. (Mrs.), Local Registrar, Land Army, 1916—1919.

Symonds, Constance Mary, Enumerator, National Register 1915, and General Service V.A.D. 1916—1917.

Symonds, Margery Doris, Unit Administrator, W.A.A.C., 1918—1919.

Thomas, Ella Dorothea Court, R.A.C. Voluntary Driver, Ministry of Munitions, London, Feb.—Nov./17.

Thompson, Kate (Mrs.), V.A.D. Military Hospital, Romford, 1915 - 9'9.

Tickner, Eva, Munition Worker.

Tickner, Olive, War Office Clerk.

Tiddeman, Gladys Spenser, V.A.D. Military Hospital, Romford, 1915—1919.

Western, Elsie, Telephonist, W.R.A.F., Upminster.

Williams, Dora Margaret Agnes, W.R.A.F., Suttons Farm Aerodrome, Hornchurch.

Woodward, Miss, A.P.C., Warley.

N.B.—For further List of Women Workers see Chapter " The Civil Voluntary Effort."

The Air Raids.

WAR on the HOME FRONT.

Drawn by C. H. Hollinghurst.

"THE AIR RAIDS."

WAR ON THE HOME FRONT.

What a fearful night is this !
There's two or three of us have seen strange sights.
Never till to-night, never till now
Did I go through a tempest dropping fire.*
Some airy devil hovers in the sky
And throws down mischief.†
I heard a humming,
And that a strange one too, which did awake me.‡

Shakespeare.

Hornchurch was in the direct line taken by the German invaders when proceeding by the Essex route to London, and many of the raiders passed immediately over us. On those occasions, although our village was by no means a safe or pleasant place to be in, the inhabitants had many exciting times. The aerodrome at Suttons Farm, established early in the war, was one of the most important of the outer defences of London, and "B" Flight of 739 Squadron,§ which first occupied the Aerodrome, was destined to become famous by reason of the exploits of its pilots.

The dark periods of the month were our most anxious times in the early days of the raids, when Zeppelins were solely employed for the attack, and it was not long before our neighbourhood was surrounded by a cordon of powerful searchlights, which were always a source of interest. Often we were treated to a veritable pyrotechnic display, when those great beams of light were sweeping the skies for enemy airships ; and when, as occasionally happened, they discovered what they were searching for, we were privileged to witness most marvellous sights.

Early in the evenings it was the custom for the searchlights to appear for a short period, and the absence of such displays on a dark night was a fairly sure indication that a raid was anticipated, and that, later on, the searchlights would burst out to some purpose. In these circumstances we all watched with interest, and not a little anxiety, for the silent signals in the sky.

Later on, when the aeroplane was the weapon used by the Germans for the air invasion of this country, the danger period was when the moon was at the full, and the few nights which immediately preceded and followed the full moon.

It would be impossible in a small volume such as this to record all the interesting events connected with the air raids which passed over Hornchurch, and the wonderful doings of the

*Julius Cæsar, i., iii.
†King John, iii., ii.
‡Tempest, ii., i.
§Later, about June, 1917, 78 Squadron became stationed at Suttons, occupying the Aerodrome, and during 1918, 189 (Night) Scout Training Squadron shared the Aerodrome with 78 Squadron.

local squadrons of the Royal Flying Corps, and the Royal Air Force, but I shall try to describe some of the most important. When it is borne in mind that all England rang with exultation by reason of three of these great happenings, viz. :—the bringing down by direct air attack of the first three Zeppelins in England, accomplished by Lieutenants Robinson, Sowrey and Tempest of " B " Flight, Hornchurch, our village may be justly proud of its records, and of being able to claim as fellow parishioners, if only for a brief period of time, the doers of such magnificent and courageous deeds.

MY FIRST SIGHT OF A ZEPPELIN.

On one occasion the searchlights had been exceptionally active quite late in the evening, and we were therefore not surprised when, at about 11.30 o'clock, we heard the deep booming of guns. On looking out of a window at the rear of our house towards London, we immediately saw a bright silvery object, in shape like a huge cigar, in the centre of the rays of a large number of searchlights, probably not less than two dozen. Here, then, was the Zeppelin, the much dreaded monster before our eyes, and only three or four miles away. It apparently knew not which way to turn, for whatever movement it made the searchlights held it fast, a clear target for the guns which were firing incessantly. After a little while it veered slightly to the south and then shot upwards, so that it looked to us almost perpendicular. It then came on to a level keel again, with its nose pointing Londonwards, but the firing appeared to be getting too hot, for it gradually came right round, and then sailed away in a north-easterly direction. All this time the guns were blazing away, and they continued to do so until the huge airship got outside the range of the searchlights. It eventually got away safely, at any rate from our district, but it had failed in its object, which was to reach London, and I have little doubt the Hun sky navigators were well pleased to get beyond the danger zone in which they had found themselves.

Such an episode as this brought the war very close to our doors, and those who witnessed it will not easily forget the sight, which, though awe-inspiring to a degree, was at the same time so entrancing that one forgot altogether the danger involved.

" L 15."

On the night of March 31st, 1916, we experienced a real impression of war in the air. At 9.30 o'clock there was no indication whatever of a raid, no searchlights were visible, and no warning had been given, but suddenly, just about 10 o'clock. we were startled by a succession of most violent explosions, and it was evident that bombs were being dropped at no very great distance. At that moment the searchlights disclosed a Zeppelin, which was heading away from London, and appeared to be unloading her cargo of bombs. Her tail was distinctly seen to dip, and it was thought that she had been hit, and a loud cheer went up all round in the hope and expectation of seeing her descend to earth. She, however, got away, but the following morning, Zeppelin L 15 was discovered in the sea off the Kentish Knock, and this was doubtless our visitor of the previous night. It was assumed that she had either been hit by gun fire, or attacked by an aeroplane, or both. Lieutenant Alfred de Bath Brandon,* the intrepid N.Z. pilot (who was afterwards awarded the D.S.O. for bringing down Zeppelin L 33 on September 23/24th, 1916), and Lieut. H. Stuart Powell* were known to have bombed a Zeppelin in Essex that night, and it was in all probability their attack which caused her to unload and make for home. The actual spot where the bombs fell was Wennington, only four miles from us, where over 20 incendiary and explosive bombs fell in open fields within a very small area, quite close to a farm, but providentially no one was injured, and very little material damage was done.

" L 21."

It is probable that no single incident during the war created a greater sensation than the destruction of L 21, by Lieut. William Leefe Robinson, at Cuffley, on the night of 2nd–3rd September, 1916. For many months, London and other parts of England had been raided by Zeppelins with apparent impunity, and there were many who thought that this state of things might go on indefinitely, and that the Zepps were inviolate. When, however, it became known that one of the flying monsters from Germany had, at last, been brought down in flames, and utterly destroyed, the feeling of relief and restored confidence was very great. It was, therefore, natural that Hornchurch folk learned with extreme satisfaction that the air pilot who had accomplished the magnificent feat was one whose name we all knew, who was personally known to many of us, whose reputation as a night flyer was already established, and whose feats in the air by day had startled and amazed us all.

Lieut. Robinson's fame immediately became world-wide, and honours were showered upon him without stint. Within a

*These daring pilots reported having bombed this Zeppelin, and claimed that their attack was the initial cause of the destruction of L 15, but as the anti-aircraft gunners also put in a claim, the airmen were not allowed the exclusive award. They were, however, both mentioned in a special Despatch by the G.O.C. Home Forces to the G.O.C. of the Royal Flying Corps, and congratulated. Lieut. H. Stuart Powell, who was afterwards awarded the M.C., was stationed at the time at Suttons, but was later transferred to another aerodrome, eventually returning to Suttons as O.C. with the rank of Major.

Photo, Sports and General Agency.

THE ZEPPELIN DESTROYERS:

Captain W. L. ROBINSON, V.C., Lieut. W. J. TEMPEST, D.S.O., and Lieut. FREDERICK SOWREY, D.S.O.

few days of his marvellous exploit he was summoned to Windsor Castle, where the King personally bestowed upon him that most coveted of all honours, the V.C., and he was immediately raised to the rank of Captain and Flight Commander.

He also became the recipient of many valuable prizes and gifts, the money alone which was publicly presented to him amounting to several thousand pounds.

Lieut. Robinson had been up amongst the raiders on several previous occasions, and once only just narrowly missed his quarry and it seemed, therefore, fitting that first honours should have fallen to him.

Several Zeppelins took part in this raid, and they arrived over Essex in the early hours of Sunday morning, 3rd September. Notwithstanding the hour, our village was alive with spectators, and those who watched the progress of the raid were not only rewarded with a sight which, for many months we had all longed in vain to see, but were able to join in that tremendous shout of joy which went up in and around London as the burning monster descended to earth. The following short account by a Hornchurch eye-witness is descriptive of the event :—

" With many of our neighbours I had the unique experience of seeing the first Zeppelin brought down in flames. We had been watching the gun flashes and searchlights, which had by now —about 2 a.m.—receded in a north-westerly direction, when we suddenly saw a red flare light floating in the sky ; gun fire ceased, and then in a few moments the whole neighbourhood was brilliantly lit up, and to our great delight and wonderment we saw the Zeppelin falling down in flames. We could hardly believe the evidence of our eyes, our wonder was so great, but our delight was intensified when we learned a little later that Lieut. Robinson, from our own aerodrome, was the plucky aviator who had accomplished the gallant deed."

In the issue of the " Daily Telegraph " of 6th September, the following account of what took place in mid air was given by an officer of the Royal Flying Corps, who himself assisted in the attack on the Zeppelin. This will convey a fairly good impression of the memorable event :—

" Two other aeroplanes were endeavouring to engage the airship, which was making frantic efforts to get away, at the same time firing her machine guns. The Zeppelin was travelling at top speed, first diving and then ascending, and apparently Lieut. W. L. Robinson, who was the officer piloting the biplane which had first attacked the raider, anticipated the manœuvre. The Commander of the airship threw out tremendous clouds of black smoke which completely hid him from our view, and in which he managed to rise. A few seconds later we saw the airship a couple of thousand feet above us, and at the same altitude was Lieut. Robinson, although a matter of perhaps half a mile away. Immediately Robinson headed his machine for the raider, and, flying at a terrific speed, it appeared that he was going to charge the monster. Away up above the clouds 12,000 feet from the earth, I shall never forget the sight of the blazing airship as it fell. The scene was terrifying in its grandeur. A huge sheet of flame cast a brilliant red glow over the black sky above, tinting to a vivid pink the clouds beneath. As the Zeppelin took fire a second airship was seen approaching, and this now occupied our attention. The Commander of that craft, however, seeing the fate of the first Zeppelin, evidently considered that discretion was the better part of valour, for he turned tail and scurried off as fast as his engines would enable

Photo]   *[Bursall Tonge.*
CAPTAIN W. L. ROBINSON, V.C., IN THE AEROPLANE FLOWN AT CUFFLEY, WITH HIS TWO AIR MECHANICS, AND PORTION OF THE DESTROYED ZEPPELIN.

him to travel. At such a height, and in the darkness, it was impossible to pick him up. He had a good start and made the most of it."

The following is the official announcement of the Secretary of State for War, which appeared in the *Gazette* for 5th September, 1916 :—

His Majesty the King has been graciously pleased to award the Victoria Cross to the undermentioned officer :

Lieutenant William Leefe Robinson,

Worcester Regiment and R.F.C.,

for most conspicuous bravery. He attacked an enemy airship under circumstances of great difficulty and

danger, and sent it crashing to the ground as a flaming wreck.

He had been in the air for more than two hours, and had previously attacked another airship during his flight.

It will be realized how extremely hazardous had been Lieut. Robinson's marvellous achievement when it it is stated (a fact well known to many at the time) that,when he reached " Suttons" after his flight, his petrol was well nigh exhausted, and that a few more minutes in the air might have ended disastrously to him, which would have turned a mighty victory into a tragedy beyond words to describe.

Photo]   [*Luffs, Hornchurch.*
CAPTAIN W. L. ROBINSON, V.C., and LIEUT. F. SOWREY, D.S.O.

On Saturday night, 16 Sept., 1916, a fortnight following the destruction of " L. 31," Captain Robinson was to have made a night patrol over London in the same machine in which he had flown at Cuffley. Some of us were waiting to witness his ascent, but instead, we suddenly saw a bright light in the aerodrome, and concluded that something untoward had happened. We waited on some little while, but no ascent was made, and we afterwards learned that, in attempting to ascend, Captain Robinson's machine struck a hedge, crashed, and immediately caught fire. Captain Robinson, fortunately, managed to get out and away safely, just in time. I saw the wreckage on the following day, and could not help regretting that the machine, which had made such splendid history, had come to such an untimely end. But for this unfortunate happening, it would probably have been preserved in one of our National Museums, as one of the most valuable relics of the great war.

The photograph, here reproduced, shows a part of the wrecked machine, giving its number and the gun-rest which was used by Captain Robinson in bringing down " L 21."

Shortly after his triumph in England, Captain Robinson went to France as a Flight Commander. He was engaged in an aerial fight with the German champion Festner in May, 1917, when, owing to engine trouble, he was forced to descend in a field near Douai. Festner pursued him down, but was prevented from landing by the vigorous use Captain Robinson made of his machine gun. The descent, however, was well within the German lines ; escape was impossible, and he was taken prisoner.

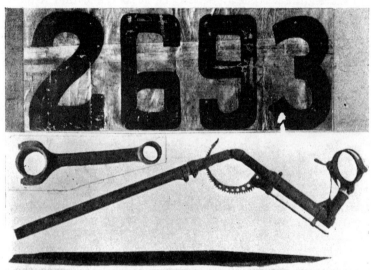

Photo]   [*E. E. Carter, Romford.*
PHOTOGRAPH OF A PORTION OF ONE OF THE WINGS, SHOWING NUMBER, OF THE AEROPLANE FLOWN BY CAPTAIN ROBINSON AT CUFFLEY, ALSO GUN-REST OF THE LEWIS GUN USED BY HIM, AND PART OF THE ENGINE AND PROPELLER OF HIS MACHINE.

He remained in captivity until the signing of the Armistice, when he was released, arriving in England on December 14th, 1918. He had made several unsuccessful attempts to escape, and finally the Germans placed him in solitary confinement. On reaching home he bore evident traces of the harsh treatment he had received at the hands of his captors.

Captain Robinson was engaged to be married to Mrs. Joan Whipple, the young widow of Captain H. C. Whipple, of the Devonshire Regiment, who fell earlier in the war. He was spending Christmas with her, at the residence of his sister,

Baroness Heyking, at Stanmore, and while there was taken ill, and died on the 31st December. The immediate cause of his death was influenza, but his relatives made it known through the Press that when he arrived home he was too tired and broken to resist even the slightest cold. The terrible and unspeakable horrors and privations which he silently and bravely endured had completely sapped his vitality. It was the " refinement of torture " practised upon him with studied heartlessness by Niemeyer, when imprisoned at Holzminden, that sent him to his premature grave. This bully deliberately plotted to take Captain Robinson's life, and sought every means in his power to shatter the nervous system of the airman, and thus reduce him to a physical wreck. At Holzminden, Captain Robinson was known as the English " Redfly " and Niemeyer promised that sooner or later he would avenge the death of Captain Schramm, who perished in L 21.

Such was the tragic end of the young airman, at the moment of his return to home and friends, and on the eve of his marriage. He was buried at Wealdstone on January 3, 1919, with full military honours, borne to his grave by comrades associated with him in the hour of his triumph. Captain Robinson was 23 years of age.

" L 32."

The night of Saturday–Sunday, September 23/24th, 1916, was again a great night for our village. No searchlights had been showing in the early evening, and therefore we felt instinctively that we were about to receive another visit from Germany. The night was very dark with hardly any wind, and shortly before 11 o'clock the searchlights began to get busy, and about three quarters of an hour afterwards the roar of an approaching Zeppelin was distinctly heard. We had not long to wait for its actual presence in our midst, for at about midnight we were startled by six terrific bomb explosions, which shook our houses to their foundations. These bombs we afterwards found had been dropped in the vicinity of Suttons Farm, our own Aerodrome having been attacked. Four of the bombs fell to the east of the Aerodrome and quite close to the farmhouse, one in the Aerodrome itself, and one a few hundred yards to the west of it. Providentially all fell clear of the sheds and buildings, and, with the exception of a slight injury sustained by one of the R.F.C. mechanics, no damage was done.

Captain Robinson was on duty in the aerodrome that night, and the Germans only very narrowly missed a speedy revenge for the destruction of " L. 21."

The Zeppelin then passed over, and some little time afterwards we heard bombs dropping in London, where considerable damage was done to property, and many persons were killed and injured.

Just before 1 o'clock in the morning we were again disturbed by the return of one of the Zepps from London, (it was afterwards announced that three had visited the metropolis), and it was to some purpose that we again looked heavenwards. Heading towards the north-east we saw the airship within the rays of a large number of searchlights. A terrific bombardment then ensued, but the Zepp, rising slightly, continued on its way, and we all began to fear it would escape. It disappeared for a moment from our gaze, and then suddenly we saw a small red light, or lights, which almost instantly burst into a red glare, and we knew that the monster had been hit. It then became one crimson glow, lighting up the country all round as it plunged

Photo]   [*William C. Allen.*

ONE OF THE SHELL HOLES AT SUTTONS AERODROME,
SEPTEMBER 23RD, 1916.

earthwards. As it fell we saw an aeroplane falling away from the stricken airship. A tremendous roar of exultation arose from all quarters, and the delighted onlookers almost went wild with delight that a second Hun raider had been brought down.

Nobody seemed to want to retire to rest after this exciting experience, and apparently very few did. About a quarter of an hour after the destruction of the Zeppelin we heard an aeroplane returning to our Aerodrome, and expectation ran high as to whether one of our pilots had " done the trick " again. We were not kept long in suspense, for at about 2.30 o'clock an exceedingly brilliant glare of white light was seen approaching the village from above the station, and presently Capt. Robinson's car came tearing up the lane filled with officers from the Aerodrome, amongst them being the hero of the night, Lieut. Frederick Sowrey. With him were Captain Robinson, Captain Stammers, Captain Bowers, and Lieut. C. C. Durston. They were on the way to visit the ruins of the burning Zeppelin lying at Billericay, and after receiving our heartiest congratulations, the car proceeded on its triumphant way, followed by Lieuts.

Photo]   *[E. E. Carter, Romford.*

Mallinson and Brock on motor cycles. It was then that we knew that the whole village was astir, for shouts rent the air until the car, ablaze with light, passed away into the countryside.

"L 31."

On the night of Sunday, October 1st, 1916, there were evident signs of another Zeppelin raid. Just before 10 o'clock the first searchlight shot its piercing shaft of light across the sky, and about a quarter of an hour later we heard an aeroplane ascending from our Aerodrome. We then awaited events with a feeling akin to curiosity, as, after the bringing down of the two " Zepps " already recorded, many people thought the Huns would try a safer hunting ground than Essex. However, soon after 11 o'clock the unmistakable sound of an approaching " Zepp" was heard, but this time it was to the N.E. and apparently a considerable distance off, our searchlights failing to discover it, and it passed safely on its way towards London. At about 11.40 we heard the distant sounds of guns and bombs, and we waited with some expectation for what would happen. Suddenly the now familiar red glare again illuminated the heavens to the N.W., and at the same moment a mighty shout rent the air, and we then saw the burning airship slowly descending to earth. At this further exploit by our aerial defence excitement knew no bounds, and, after this had to some extent subsided, we stood about the streets wondering where the airship had been brought down. When it became known that the wrecked Zepp was lying at Potter's Bar, no one dared to hope that the splendid feat had been accomplished by one of our own airmen, but the news at last came through that Lieut. William J. Tempest was the hero of the night, and we almost danced for joy that B. Flight of 739 Squadron, Hornchurch, had done the " hat trick " and had made Our Village famous in aerial warfare for all time.

Lieuts. Sowrey and Tempest were decorated with the D.S.O. for their wonderful achievements.

PRESENTATION TO CAPTAIN ROBINSON AND LIEUTS. SOWREY AND TEMPEST.

On Saturday, 14th October, 1916, presentations were made in the N.Z. Camp, Grey Towers Park, to Captain William Leefe Robinson, V.C., Lieut. Frederick Sowrey, D.S.O., and Lieut. W. J. Tempest, D.S.O., in recognition of their gallantry in destroying Zeppelins, and in grateful appreciation of their splendid services to the country. The presentations took the form of three handsome silver cups, that presented to Capt. Robinson bearing the following inscription :—

" Presented by the residents of Hornchurch, Essex, as a token of admiration and gratitude to Lieutenant William Leefe Robinson, V.C., Worcestershire Regiment and Royal Flying Corps. Lieut. Robinson with conspicuous bravery attacked and destroyed an enemy aeroplane under circumstances of great difficulty and danger during the night of September 2/3rd, 1916."

The other two cups bore similar inscriptions.

Mr. Thomas Gardner, J.P., C.C., presided, and the presentations were made by Mr. W. H. Legg, Chairman of the Parish Council.

Mr. Gardner, in the course of his speech, remarked that everybody in Hornchurch desired to have a part in making the gift to Capt. Robinson, and something between 2,000 and 3,000 individual subscriptions had been received, ranging from 1d. to 2s. 6d. Just as they were getting ready to arrange the presentation, they saw another Zeppelin come down in flames. It was soon known that this monster had been brought down by Lieut. Sowrey, and in a little while, he (the Chairman) received a letter from Capt. Robinson, suggesting that Lieut. Sowrey should share our gift. The Committee decided to fall in with this most generous and sportsmanlike suggestion, and they therefore purchased two silver cups, and while these were being suitably inscribed, down came another Zeppelin, and when they found that this feat had been accomplished by Lieut. Tempest, they all felt they could not do less than present him, too, with a cup.

Photo]   [*Luffs, Hornchurch.*

PRESENTATION OF SILVER CUP TO CAPT. W. L. ROBINSON, V.C,
AT HORNCHURCH, OCTOBER 14TH, 1916.

Capt. Robinson and Lieut. Sowrey were most enthusiastically received when acknowledging their presentations, but Lieut. Tempest was unable personally to receive his cup, being away on duty.

The presentations were made in the presence of a large and most enthusiastic gathering.

"THE SILENT RAID."

The Zeppelin, as an offensive weapon against London, seemed to be a thing of the past before the year 1917 was many months old, although it did not make its final effort on the capital until

October 19th of that year, on which occasion at least four Zeppelins met with disaster. This was known as the " silent raid." I happened to be in London that night and the effect was weird to a degree. We got the warning between 8 and 9 p.m., at which time I was with my wife and daughter in the " Elysee " Restaurant, Coventry Street, close to Piccadilly Circus. We waited there for an hour after the warning had been given, and as nothing seemed to mature we decided to make an attempt to reach home. At that time everybody seemed to be sheltering in the doorways of big buildings, and the streets were practically deserted, the police having warned the public to keep under cover. No guns were firing, and there were no sounds overhead of approaching aircraft, so we decided to make our way to Fenchurch Street Station, and arrived there, only to find that no trains were running. We then went to my office in Lloyd's Avenue, and waited there for some time, but there was still no indication of raiders. Somewhere about midnight we suddenly heard a terrific explosion, and afterwards learned that a bomb had fallen in Piccadilly Circus, within a few yards of the spot we had left earlier in the evening, killing and injuring many people, and doing a great deal of material damage. As may be imagined, we felt extremely thankful that we had risked that passage from west to east.

Only two other bombs were dropped in London that night, and nothing whatever was seen of the raiders. It transpired, however, that the Germans intended it to have been the greatest of all air raids on the capital, but something mysterious intervened which has never been explained, and next day we heard remarkable stories of Zeppelins drifting about in a helpless condition at various places on the Continent, and, as already stated, at least four met with disaster.

We got the " All clear " at about 2.30 a.m., and eventually arrived home about 3.30.

AEROPLANE ATTACKS.

Prior to June, 1917, only three attempts had been made to reach the metropolis by aeroplane. The first was on Christmas Day, 1914, when about midday a single aeroplane got some distance up the Thames, but was turned in the neighbourhood of Erith without doing any damage. The second attempt was on 28 November, 1916, and this met with some success, a single machine dropping six bombs in the west end of London, when nine persons were injured and some damage done to property. This happened between 11.50 a.m. and noon. The third raid was on May 7th, 1917, when, on a moonlight night at about 11 o'clock, a German aeroplane dropped four bombs on the north of London, killing three persons and doing some damage to buildings. On June 13, 1917, however, a determined daylight raid was made in force on London, when a great fleet of aeroplanes attacked, and dropped a large number of bombs in the east end and in the city. I happened at that time to be right in the centre of the city onslaught, and within a very few yards of the spot where the greatest loss of life and the most material damage occurred, and the experience was terrifying in the extreme. The raiders reached the city just before midday without warning, and in consequence there were many casualties—157 killed, and 432 wounded. This raid passed over Essex, and Hornchurch people were able to witness some remarkable sights in the air.

The next daylight raid in force was on Saturday morning, 7th July, 1917, between 10 and 11 o'clock, and this was a much bigger affair than the June raid. Opinions differ as to the number of attackers, the official estimate being twenty-two. I witnessed this air invasion at Hornchurch, and it was an experience that is likely to leave a lasting impression on the memory. I was in my garden when I noticed unusual activity in the air, and looking upwards found that several British aeroplanes had ascended to a high altitude to the north of the village. They certainly appeared as if expecting visitors, and it was not many minutes before a huge hostile air fleet hove in sight, well away to the north, the drone of their engines creating a weird and impressive effect. Our airmen endeavoured to intercept them, but the whole flight proceeded on its way to London, apparently without mishap. The weather conditions were so favourable, and the visibility so good, that the passage to and from London was discernible all the time, the combined enemy and home forces looking like a large flock of birds, showing up bright and silvery in the strong sunlight, with incessant bursts of white puffs of smoke from anti-aircraft shells in their midst. The extreme visibility was so deceiving to the eye that it seemed impossible that the flight could have reached London, and we were very hopeful that the enemy had been turned. Unfortunately that hope was vain, for they not only again reached the heart of the city, but penetrated to the West end and other parts of the capital, and effected much more damage than on the former occasion, though, providentially, owing to the official warning given, the casualties were fewer. Many of us at Hornchurch who were watching the return from London fervently hoped our men would ' bag ' some of the Huns*. From the corner of Stanley Road, Suttons Lane, the flight was distinctly visible, and several of us watched there the oncoming of the Germans, until the gun in our close vicinity opened fire ,and we then thought it prudent to shelter indoors. At that time the flight was apparently over Dagenham, heading straight towards

*It was claimed that four machines were brought down in this raid.

us, but the heavy gunfire evidently decided the enemy to incline to the north-east, and in doing so they passed right over Suttons Lane. I came out of doors again just in time to observe the tail of the flight making towards the direction of Upminster.

No other successful attempt was made on London in day-light, but during the late summer and early autumn months many determined night raids occurred, some of them being of a very serious character. Towards the end of September things reached a climax, owing to the incessant bombing of the capital, and it would scarcely be an exaggeration to say that London was a little panic-stricken, more especially in the East end among the alien population. The same remark would be equally true of some of the East and South-east coast towns, and, as a consequence, thousands of people from those parts and from the London districts migrated to the towns and villages near London in the counties of Surrey, Sussex, Middlesex, and Hertford, which soon became crowded with visitors of many nationalities, a large proportion of whom were Jews. During September and October no less than seven raids were made on the capital, three of them on successive nights.

We shall all have many recollections of the disturbing effect produced by these night raids, most of which passed over Hornchurch. It was generally agreed that the aeroplane raids were far more nerve-racking than those by Zeppelins, and it was seldom, too, that those raids were relieved by a sight of the raiders, although their unwelcome presence in our vicinity was distinctly evident by the ominous and unmistakable drone of their engines. Occasionally, however, a searchlight would discover an enemy plane, and then would follow a terrific bombardment from guns whose proximity was totally unknown to the general public. Now and again, too, machine gun fire in the air, and occasionally a display of explosive bullets, would indicate a fight going on between aeroplanes. This happened more than once almost immediately over our heads.

For some considerable time before the end of hostilities we were immune from air attack, doubtless owing to the perfecting of the aerial defences of London, which rendered raiding by the enemy a very dangerous and risky operation. The last raid* on the metropolis occurred on the night of Whit-Sunday, May 19th, 1918. This raid was the greatest effort made by the Germans on this country, thirty aeroplanes being engaged, seven of which got through to London. The warning was given about 11 o'clock, and the "All clear" at 1.30 o'clock the following morning. The barrage was exceedingly heavy and the defence very effective, four of the raiders being brought down in flames on land, and three others on the coast or at sea. One plane was

*Only one other raid occurred in England, viz., on July 20 on the Kent coast by one solitary plane, but no casualites or material damage were reported.

brought down near Barking, and three bombs were dropped near Bulvan, the shock being severely felt at Hornchurch. The casualties were very heavy on this occasion, 44 persons being killed and 179 wounded. While the raid was at its height a contrast was provided by a nightingale trilling its beautiful song in the Millfield, its sweet notes being distinctly heard between the gunfire. This ended our personal war experiences on the "home front." Those experiences are now, happily, only unpleasant memories, and we are all thankful that we can once more retire to rest at night without the risk and possibility of being awakened by the booming of guns and the roar of aerial war engines overhead.

The principal night raids on London by aeroplane took place on the following dates :—

1917 :—September 4, 24, 25, 29, 30, October 1 and 31, December 6 and 18*.

1918 :—January 29, February 16 and 17, March 7†, and May 19.

AIR RAIDS AND BOMBARDMENTS.

(16th DECEMBER, 1914, TO 17th JUNE, 1918).

No. of Raids	Description.	Civilian Casualties.								Sailors and Soldiers.		Total Casualties.
		Killed.				Injured.						
		Men.	Women.	Children.	Total	Men.	Women.	Children.	Total.	Killed.	Injured.	
51	Airship raids	217	171	110	498	587	431	218	1236	58	121	1913
57	Aeroplane raids	282	195	142	619	741	585	324	1650	238	400	2907
12	Bombardments from the sea	55	45	43	143	180	194	230	604	14	30	791
	Totals ..	554	411	295	1260	1508	1210	772	3490	310	551	5611

Observer, January 12th, 1919.

SUTTONS FARM AERODROME.

Suttons Farm Aerodrome forms part of the Manor of Suttons, and the Farm House itself is built on the site where once stood the ancient Manor House, which was acquired, together with the Manor of Hornchurch Hall, by William of Wykeham in the year 1392 from the Monks of St. Bernard, and presented by him

*This raid occurred quite early in the evening, and London was attacked at about 0.30 o'clock.
†This was known as the "Starlight Raid" and was the only raid made by aeroplanes on a moonless night.

to St. Mary de Winton College (commonly called New College), Oxford. It is situated about a mile south of Hornchurch Church, and was used throughout the Great War as a night and day flying ground, and during 1918-1919 as a night-flying scout training aerodrome.

It is generally admitted that this Aerodrome was one of the best flying grounds in England, the surface being good and the ground flat and spacious. It was, therefore, well adapted for night flying.

During the many raids on London the machines from Suttons ascended and patrolled the sky, the pilots having a unique view of the metropolis, being able to watch the bursting of bombs, and the flashes of our own anti-aircraft guns, and probably often getting mixed up with our " Archie " or bursting shells in their zeal and keenness to " strafe " the Hun raiders. It was a great sight to watch the fast scout machines " taking off " (very often several of them at the same time) into the darkness, and, after a long patrol to see the " Verey " light fired many thousands of feet overhead to indicate the pilot's readiness to descend, and then to watch the answering colour light from the ground, shewing that the Aerodrome was clear for the machine to land.

If Suttons could only lay claim to the Zeppelin strafers, Robinson, Sowrey, and Tempest, it would be fame indeed, but many other distinguished pilots have been stationed at this celebrated Aerodrome during the war, including Captains Mackay, Armstrong, Cockerell, Godfrey, Clapham, and Gran; men who, besides doing great and good work, were amongst the best pilots of the Royal Flying Corps and the Royal Air Force.

The Aerodrome was commanded at various times by young and very able men, who took remarkable pride in upholding for their Squadron the great reputation earned for it in the early days of the war on the home front, and amongst these officers may be mentioned Captains Sutherland Stewart, A. T. Harris, and W. L. Robinson, V.C., Majors Rowden, P. Babington, Allen, H. Stuart Powell, and Truran.

A very large number of young pilots gained their " wings " at Suttons during the time it was a training station, this being largely due to the enthusiasm and great experience of such capable instructors as Captain Harold Hindle James, and Lieut. Victor Chapman, in conjunction with the splendid work of Sergeant-Majors Fulton and Wyatt, and Flight-Sergeants Reid and Martin.

While it is true that Hornchurch folk were privileged to witness some of the most daring and thrilling feats in the air, there was probably never a time when finer exhibitions of flying were seen than during the few weeks which immediately followed the second daylight raid on London of Saturday, July 7, 1917. The day after that raid there was unusual activity at Suttons, the cause being the evacuation of the Aerodrome by the Squadron then occupying it, to make way for another Squadron, which was being transferred from the Western Front, and on July 12 the 46th Squadron, R.F.C. flew over from France and was stationed at Suttons for the daylight defence of London. Major P. Babington was the officer commanding the Squadron, and he it was who evolved the scheme of manœuvring a Squadron of 15 machines in groups of five, by means of signals. Most of us have vivid recollections of the beautiful formations in the air by the whole of this Squadron in three faultless formations of five, headed by the O.C. as leader, which were to be seen almost daily. I do not think any finer flying was ever seen anywhere, and we were all very sorry when, on the 31 August, the Squadron left again for France, the Bosche having discreetly kept away during their short stay of about six weeks. This Squadron greatly distinguished itself in France, but, unfortunately, many of the clever and gallant pilots who had inspired us with so much confidence, and had afforded us so much pleasure, lost their lives shortly after their return. to the Western Front.

Captain S. W. Williams, of Upminster Court, and formerly Lieut. in the Hornchurch Company of the 4th Essex Regiment, was one of the pilots of this " pukka " Squadron.

HORNCHURCH A WAR=TIME CAMP.

3rd EAST ANGLIAN (HOWITZER) BRIGADE, ROYAL FIELD ARTILLERY.

Although armed camps were dotted about all over the country, I do not think any village entertained more soldiery than did Hornchurch during the war period. Within a few days of the commencement of hostilities our first billet arrived, and for about a fortnight the 3rd East Anglian (Howitzer) Brigade, R.F.A., was quartered with us. The Earl of Stradbroke was the Commanding Officer, and he and his staff made their Headquarters at the White Hart, while the men of his Brigade occupied the Council Schools, North Street. The guns were stationed in the field adjoining Mr. Thomas Gardner's residence " Dury Falls," where daily drilling and manœuvring took place.

In those early days of the war the billeting of a Brigade of soldiers in our village was somewhat of a novelty, but, as will be seen by the following pages, it was to become quite a commonplace event.

THE FIRST SPORTSMAN'S BATTALION

(23rd Royal Fusiliers).

" This very day,
Great Mars, I put myself into thy file :
Make me but like my thoughts, and I shall prove
A lover of thy drum "—
Shakespeare :—All's Well that Ends Well, III., iii.

In November, 1914, a new era opened for our ancient village,
owing to the arrival of the First Sportsman's Battalion, the 23rd
Royal Fusiliers, under the command of Colonel Viscount Maitland,
and Hornchurch became for the first time in its history a war-
time camp. The home of the late Colonel Holmes, " Grey
Towers," with its beautiful Park, was selected as the Headquarters of the Battalion. For several weeks before their
arrival, hundreds of workmen had been employed erecting huts
for their accommodation, and when all was completed, Grey
Towers was considered to be quite a model camp, and, at that
time, probably the best in the kingdom.

After a march through London, from Hyde Park to the City,
past the Mansion House—where the Lord Mayor (with whom
was Mrs. Cunliffe-Owen) delivered an address of welcome to the
men—and on to Liverpool Street Station, where they entrained,
the Battalion arrived on the afternoon of November 4 at the
Camp. Their reception in London was of a most enthusiastic
character, crowds of cheering citizens lining the streets, and according them a splendid welcome. Hornchurch folk extended
a similar greeting to them, as, headed by the Cottage Homes
Band, they marched in magnificent order through Grey Towers
gates for the first time. The following verses were written
to commemorate the arrival of the Battalion :

WELCOME TO THE SPORTSMAN'S BATTALION.

November 4th, 1914.

We've waited for you—" *Hard as Nails* "—and now at last you've come,
  We saw you march through London Town, we heard the fife and drum,
We heard the tramp of martial feet, we saw the bunting fly,
  We heard the Lord Mayor's greeting as your ranks went swinging by,
We saw the throng of cheering folk, we heard their mighty shout,
  And then we heard your answering cry :— *"We won't be bothered about !"*

And now *Our Village* welcomes you, yes, every mother's son,
  From the buck " *officially* " forty-five to the lad not twenty-one.
We love you, and we're proud of you, for answering the Call
  Of King and Home and Country—Soldiers and Sportsmen all,
And well we know you'll play the game when guns and cannon roar,
  And, like true Sportsmen, do your bit to make a winning score.

Fame have you won in times of peace on many a playing field,
  Where mimic battles bravely fought but barren victories yield,
But now a sterner fight is yours, where you will show your grit,
  And prove what manly sport can do to make a nation fit.
And when you make your final stand against the German Huns,
  Just keep your wickets up, lads, while they make all the " *runs.*"

CHAS. THOS. PERFECT.

Photo]

GREY TOWERS.

[Frank Luff.

The Sportsman's Battalion was raised by a lady, Mrs. Cunliffe-Owen, daughter of the late Sir P. Cunliffe-Owen, who also obtained a special concession from the King for men up to 45 years of age to join. This opened up the way for a large number of men, hitherto ineligible, to become soldiers of the King. It was a *sine qua non* that a man who joined this Battalion should in reality be an adept in some branch of national sport, and so it came about that men, whose fame was world-wide, were brought together to train for a more serious game than they had ever played before. What better fighting material would you have ? Courage, endurance, patience, bodily fitness, a keen eye, and a bull-dog tenacity are some of the many high qualities acquired in the pursuit of those manly sports which have become part of the Britisher's nature, and, if it be true that the Battle of Waterloo was won on the playing fields of Eton, surely then these Sportsmen of Britain and Greater Britain would acquit themselves right well in the match of " Right v. Might " in which they would ere long be engaged.

I suppose that, in its way, this Battalion was unique in the British Army. The Sportsmen came from all the four corners of the earth, and art, science, literature, and all the professions were represented in the rank and file of this remarkable body of men. Authors, men of letters of all degrees and schools of thought, artists, clergymen, schoolmasters, engineers, doctors, archæologists, journalists, actors, and comedians were all there, and all were exponents of British sport, many of them bearing names which are household words in the realms of sport of to-day. Mighty hunters of big game, cricketers, footballers, boxers, and scullers were amongst the representatives of this remarkable Battalion.

I should like to give a full list of the famous men who first occupied the huts in Grey Towers Camp, and were content to be just ordinary " Tommies," but, as that is quite impossible, I have culled from the pages of the " Sportsman's Gazette " (an excellent magazine, which was published weekly by the Battalion), some of the names, which figured on the first Roll of the 23rd Royal Fusiliers, as giving some idea of this truly heterogeneous body of men :—

Private W. ALBANY. World-famous Champion Sculler.

Private W. E. BATES. Yorkshire County Cricketer.

Private the Hon. B. D. BUTLER (son of Lord Lanesborough), Scratch Golfer, ex-amateur Champion of Sussex, keen Cricketer, member of M.C.C. and I.Zingari.

Lieut. NORMAN A. L. COCKELL. Had the reputation of being the best all-round sportsman in the Battalion. He also had the distinction of being the best shot in the Battalion.

Private C. CAMPBELL RAE BROWN. Author of many novels, and of the celebrated recitation, " Kissing Cup's Race."

Private R. L. CARTER. The well-known Engineer from the Federated Malay States.

Sergeant P. H. COOPER. Anglican Clergyman. (Harrow and Trinity.)

Private J. H. CURLE. Mining Engineer. Was a member of the Johannesburg Force during the Jameson Raid. A great traveller and author. Wrote "The Gold Mines of the World" and contributed many fine articles to the "Sportsmar's Gazette."

Sergeant-Major CUMMING. Champion walker of England.

Corporal C. F. CANTON. Big game hunter and all-round sport. In Matabele Mounted Police. Went through the Jameson Raid and Matabele war.

Lance-Corporal GEORGE DE LARA. Celebrated Actor and Actor-Manager.

Private A. E. DUNN. Late Mayor of Exeter and ex-M.P.

Private F. DARLEY-CROZIER. (Son of Major-General H. Darley-Crozier.) Tropical Planter and crack shot.

Private R. B. DAY. World's Champion Runner.

Private CHARLIE DILLON. Comedian. The incomparable "Dame" of many pantomimes.

Private JERRY DELANEY. Lightweight Champion Boxer of England.

Private J. D. DRIVER. An Irishman and a Quaker. Well-known tennis-player and Umpire. Member of London Stock Exchange.

Private C. C. FREER. Journalist. Sometime on the "Daily Mail" Staff. 2nd Editor of the "Sportsman's Gazette."

Private C. E. GASKELL. One of the finest all-round Sportsman in the North of England. Was known as the "Baby" of Hut 25, "Unity Hall."

Corporal T. W. GREENSTREET. Bachelor of Arts. Lecturer in English History. As a cricketer played for Gentlemen of Essex.

Colonel A. H. GIBBONS. Who afterwards commanded a Battalion of the 5th King's Liverpool was second in Command at Hornchurch. He was one of the best known big game hunters and had killed 5 lions in one day. He also discovered the source of the Zambesi River. He was killed in France.

Private ERNEST G. HAYES. Surrey County Cricket XI.

Private J. W. HITCH. Surrey County Cricket XI. Famous fast bowler.

Private E. H. HENDREN. Middlesex County Cricket XI. and famous footballer, playing for Coventry City, and formerly for Manchester City.

Private J. HENDREN. Durham County Cricket XI. and formerly of Middlesex 2nd XI.

Private JACK HARRISON. Well-known Boxer, Winner of Lonsdale Belt for Middle-weight Championship, 1912. Was in Grenadier Guards 1907-1910.

Private WM. J. HARVEY. First Editor of "Sportsman's Gazette."

Captain STANLEY HOLMES. Son of the late Lieut.-Colonel Henry Holmes of Grey Towers.

Private DOUGLAS HENDERSON. Had ridden across the Andes, S. America, where, previous to the outbreak of war, he had been travelling for six years.

Private RICHARD KENDALL. Actor.

Private J. M. KENDALL. Antiquary. Fellow of the Society of Archæologists, and writer on Archæological subjects.

Lance-Corporal EDWARD LEITH. Song writer and Stage Manager.

Sergeant R. T. NOYES. All-round sport. Born in Winnipeg, was with the Gordon Relief Expedition to Khartoum. A great traveller. Brilliant Raconteur, and affectionately known as " Canada." One of the most popular men in the Battalion.

Private A. SANDHAM. Surrey County Cricket XI.

Lieut. ROBERT DE VERE STACPOOLE. (Cousin of the famous novelist). Previously served in the 6th Dragoon Guards (The Carabineers).

Private DENIS TURNER. Scholar of Pembroke College, Cambridge. Author, and contributor to " Punch," " Vanity Fair." " Onlooker ," etc., etc.

Private A. H. TOOGOOD. Professional Golfer. Champion Midland Counties, Represented England against Scotland, 1904-5-6-7.

Private E. S. VINCER. Marine Engineer. The only Englishman of modern times who has been into the bull ring in Spain and killed his bull in open fight. This was at Carthagena in 1912.

Corporal ALFRED BURDEN WHARTON. Comedian. Well-known London Entertainer, making a speciality of Curate studies. Prominent in entertainments given by the Battalion at Hornchurch.

Private J. J. WILLIAMS (Julian Brandon). Well-known Conjurer and Entertainer, Journalist and Lecturer on Psychology.

Private FRANK WINCHCOMBE. All-round Sportsman. Chairman of Greenwich Branch Junior Imperial League. Wrote many excellent descriptive articles on Celebrated Sportsmen in the " Sportsman's Gazette."

Private D. R. WARNER. (Cousin of General Sir Douglas Haig.) A good Shot and Golfer. Travelled nearly 6,000 miles to join the Battalion.

Hon. BERNARD YORKE. (Son of Lord Hardwicke.) Well-known Sportsman and big game hunter.

I have given the rank of each man as it appeared in the Gazette, and it will be seen what a large proportion of them were " Privates." Their social position was as varied as their avocations, and men of great wealth, sons and kinsmen of Peers, Baronets, Knights, and Merchant Princes shouldered their rifles and drilled side by side with the man who boasted no social position, and whose only qualification for comradeship was that he, in common with his more fortunate brother in arms, was a good sportsman and a patriot.

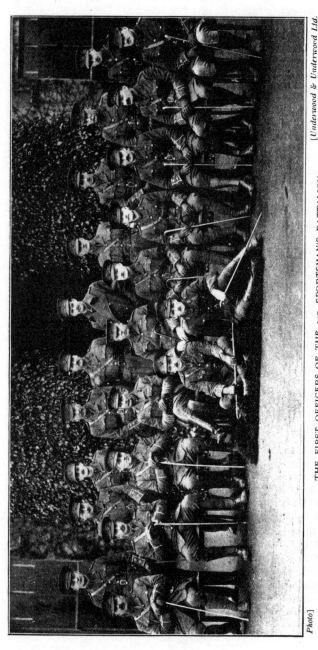

[Underwood & Underwood Ltd.

THE FIRST OFFICERS OF THE 1st SPORTSMAN'S BATTALION.

Back Row (standing) left to right—Lieut. HILL, R.A.M.C., Lieut. WILLIAMS, 2nd Lieut. HILLCOAT, Capt. POWELL, 2nd Lieut. PIRIE, Capt. and Adjt. INGLIS, 2nd Lieut. BEALEY, 2nd Lieut. FOY, 2nd Lieut. RICHARDSON, 2nd Lieut. TAYLOR.

Front Row (sitting)—2nd Lieut. The Honble. B. YORKE, 2nd Lieut. CROSS, Lieut. SUCKLING, Lieut.-Col. GIBBONS, Col. VISCOUNT MAITLAND, Major RICHIE, D.S.O., Capt. CHURCH, Lieut. and Q.-Mstr. de VERE STACPOOLE, Capt. HOLMES, 2nd Lieut. WINTER.

In Front—2nd Lieut. HAYES, 2nd Lieut. MURRAY-THOMPSON.

Photo]

This aspect prompted me to write " *The Sportsman of the King,*" which was published in No. 5 of the " Sportman's Gazette " of January 22, 1915, and which I venture to reproduce here.

" THE SPORTSMAN OF THE KING."

" What I am truly,
Is thine and my poor country's to command."
Shakespeare :—Macbeth, IV., iii.

There was a certain rich man whose ways were cast in pleasant places.

And in those days there was war in all the world, nation warring against nation, and there was a very great slaughter.

And it came to pass that *Bill*, the King of the Huns, made war against the Kingdom wherein the rich man dwelt. And by reason of that God-given gift which men call patriotism, many husbandmen and others (some of them of questionable age), who knew not the art of war, came unto the Captain of the Hosts and said unto him :—" Though we be not skilled in war, and are not cunning in the use of the weapons thereof, and are withal men of peace, yet we pray thee send us against this *Bill*, the despoiler of homes, and the killer of women and babes." And the Captain of the Hosts received them gladly, and after many days his armies increased and multiplied exceedingly.

And the rich man heard the fame thereof, and straightway joined himself unto the Hosts. And behold he was of ancient lineage and had great possessions. Nevertheless, he forsook all that he had, and sorrowed not, but went forth to fit himself for battle.

And whereas in former times he dwelt in high places in great splendour, and possessed many servants, yet was he now constrained to live in a tin tent with a score and nine others like minded.

And, while in the days of his ease men did his bidding with heads uncovered, yet was he now ordered and bothered* about exceeding much (although he said he would not be), and he went whithersoever he was bidden with all humility. And on certain days he became the slave of his comrades, and did menial duties which his soul greatly abhorred.

And moreover, although in past days he possessed many horses, and had automobiles without number, yet had he now but one " pony," which was called " shanks," and verily his foot-gear was of a fearsome and wonderful description.

*Refers to the Battalion's slogan :
We won't be bothered about, We won't be bothered about !
We abso-bloomin'-lootly refuse
To be bothered about—unless we choose,
We won't be bothered about !

145

K

And he lived on the beef which was " bully," and on jam and soup, the taste of which was indescribable and the name thereof unutterable.

His raiment was rough but comely and of a colour akin to mustard, and in it he looked a proper man, and peradventure he knew that this was so. And they gave him a number, and put a label of pure brass upon his shoulder, even " 23rd R.F."

And his country thought well of him and gave unto him spondulics in abundance, even twelve pence per diem, and he was exceeding happy, and waxed strong and fit.

So the rich man became a soldier and was called a " Tommy."

And all this did he in the sacred name of patriotism, and verily he was a " SPORTSMAN " !

But many there were who knew not the ways of the " Sportsman," men who had no let or hindrance, and few possessions, and who, by reason of their youth, and divers other misplaced endowments, should have done their bit and have fought the good fight. These men scoffed at all this sacrifice. They are the slackers who reap where others have sowed, nevertheless they shall have no part in the glory of Victory, and the honour which shall be given unto them who walk in the paths of Duty shall they not know."

———————

Mrs. Cunliffe Owen had every reason to be proud of her great achievement in forming this splendid Battalion, and, as an appreciation of her effort, I wrote for the " Sportsman's Gazette" the following companion sketch to the " Sportsman of the King," which I entitled " The Sportswoman," and in which I incidentally paid a tribute to the magnificent work of the women of Great Britain, in so many and diverse ways, to help the men who were fighting or in training to fight our battles :—

" THE   SPORTSWOMAN."

" Her valiant courage and undaunted spirit,—
More than in woman commonly is seen.
Shakespeare :—1 Henry VI., v., v.

In those days when the kingdoms of the earth were at war, many men went forth to battle and returned not. Yet was not the voice of lamentation heard in the land, and although the hearts of the women sank within them by reason of the slaughter of their valiant husbands and sons, and though peradventure the maidens mourned in secret the loss of their betrothed, nevertheless the people had no knowledge that it was so, for verily they wore not their hearts upon the sleeves of their mantles,

And it came to pass that the women of the land, from those who sat in high places, to the handmaiden who sat at the feet of her mistress, sought how they might serve the men who went to battle against the barbarian Huns. And many and wonderful were the means devised by them to help the warriors who thought not at all of their own comfort, but whose only desire was to war against the oppressor and prevail.

And foremost among the women who were thus constrained were many brave matrons and maids who were verily Sisters of Mercy. These tended the wounded and fallen on the field of battle, and the men whose fighting luck was out blessed them without ceasing.

And, moreover, the sound of the needles which knit was heard in the land, and of a truth there was no peace from the click thereof in the tents of the home dwellers, and even in the market place they were not silent. And great was the joy of those who reaped the fruits of their labours.

And some there were who made ready savoury dishes, and the refreshment which is called light, to set before the men who were making themselves ready for battle. They likewise prepared a place of Rest* for them. These women thought it a pleasant thing to toil diligently to the intent that a glimpse of home might be brought to the men who had cheerfully left wife and children and kindred ; and the while they sat in their chairs of ease, and smoked the pipe of peace (while it was yet time) they thought upon these things, and their hearts were glad within them.

And there was at that time a certain wise woman who was exceeding warlike, and bewailed much that she could not herself go forth to war. And she communed within herself, and after many days she made a proclamation calling upon all those who excelled in feats of strength, and those whose prowess was great in the arena—even those who fought with the fists—and all those who were foremost in the Olympian games, to stand forth and serve the King. And verily her appeal to these men was so exceeding eloquent that a very great legion gathered themselves together to fight under the standard which she had raised.

And there were giants in those days !

And a certain grievous malady attacked many of these men, and the name thereof was "*forgetmyownageitis*" for it came to pass that when they were commanded to declare the day of their nativity, behold they knew it not at all. And many were the errors which they committed in this wise. Nevertheless it was counted unto them for righteousness, and by reason of the enthusiasm which consumed them, they were permitted to join themselves unto the legion, and the decree which should have constrained striplings of over two score years and five to remain men of peace, verily became of none effect.

And it came to pass that not only did the wise woman raise this mighty legion, but she saw to it that tents were builded for them wherein to dwell during the time of their warlike prepara-

*This refers to the " Rest Room " in North Street.

tions. And they were encamped in a very pleasant land, and their joy was exceeding great.

And the wise woman having done all this, was content that it should be so, and she waited patiently for the day and hour of victory.

And the men of the legion which she raised were called the " Sportsmen of the King," and verily she was the first " Sportswoman " in the land, and this shall be spoken of her for a memorial in the days of the Great Peace.

And after her were many " Sportswomen," for were not all those who laboured so abundantly, in many and divers ways for the same end, right good " Sportswomen of the King " ? And as the Widow's mite was rich in charity, even so shall the smallest good deed wrought by the most humble of the daughters of the land be reckoned unto them, for each hath done whatsoever she could.

And verily the generations which shall come hereafter shall rise up and call them blessed.

During the winter months which followed, our sleepy little village became astir with life. The Sportsmen trained hard, and in the intervals of strenuous work and preparation for the grim realities of war, they entered heartily into the social life of " Our Village." It may be said without egotism that Hornchurch threw its doors wide open to the men of the Battalion. The Political Clubs (having sunk all matters concerning politics *for three years or the duration of the war*) offered honorary membership to all who claimed that privilege, and as, unfortunately, Hornchurch has no Public Hall, a Rest Room was opened in the schoolroom at the rear of the Baptist Church in North Street, kindly lent by the Pastor and Deacons, and managed by a Committee of ladies, which room was nightly filled with Sportsmen. There were also very few householders who had not their own little coterie of Sportsmen friends, who were always made welcome. The Sportsmen on their side were not slow in responding to the hospitality they received. Social event followed social event, and barely a week passed without its ball, dance, or concert, and many were the invitations issued to their Hornchurch friends to attend those functions. They also gave a succession of concerts and entertainments in aid of deserving charitable objects, many institutions, such as the Red Cross Society, Dr. Barnardo's Homes, etc., greatly benefiting thereby.

And then came Christmas. The national festival was kept in Camp in right royal fashion. Every hut had its banquet, and the festivities included a football match, a concert in the afternoon, and a ball at night. At the concert the *pièce de resistance* was a highland sword dance and reel by the Colonel, and a very gallant gentleman he looked, too, in his gorgeous highland costume. The " Sports " knew right well how to keep Christmas, and it is hardly likely that any of them will ever forget the Christmas they spent at Grey Towers in 1914. It was certainly a unique experience to some of us to be present at one or other of their entertainments on that day of all the year which is especially dear to us as a home-festival, and when long custom demands that the fireside shall claim the whole of the family circle. But those were abnormal times, and many of us, who would not have dreamt in former years of going outside the homestead on a Christmas Day, were with the Sportsmen in their festivities, and thoroughly enjoyed the novelty of the experience.

The Sportsmen always attended Church Parade at the Parish Church of St. Andrew's on Sunday morning at 9.30 o'clock, and, headed by their splendid band, presented a really fine military spectacle. The village was enlivened also by their early morning exercise, squads and platoons regularly taking their run out before breakfast through the lanes and roads in various directions, and when trenching work had to be done at a distance the march to and from the railway station, with the band and pipers at the head of the Battalion, was a daily delight and mild excitement for our villagers.

The reputation of the Battalion as Sportsmen was fully maintained during their training at Grey Towers, especially in the foremost games of football and cricket. Many important football matches were played at home and away during the season, and a very good beginning was made in cricket. The season was, however, only a few weeks advanced when their occupation of the Camp came to an end. One of the most important and interesting fixtures which took place was a match with the Honourable Artillery Company at Lords on 12 June, 1915, resulting in a splendid win for the " Sportsmen." As will be seen by the undermentioned scores, both elevens included several well-known and famous cricketers :—

HON. ARTILLERY COMPANY v. SPORTSMAN'S BATTALION.
SATURDAY, JUNE 12th, 1915.

HON. ARTILLERY.	First Innings.	
Private O. C. Bristowe	c Hayes, b Bates	53
Private W. A. Batchelor ...	b Penfold	4
Private H. Coverdale	b Hayes	20
Private H. E. S. Skinner ..	b Hayes	1
C.-Q.-M.-S. R. Hargreaves..	b Hayes	37
Private H. B. Kidd	c Smith, b Bates	3
Private A. S. Holland	b Hayes	0
Corpl. D. D. Napper	b Penfold	7
Private W. G. Longden ..	b Marsden	36
Private H. J. Bonsor	l b w b Bates	12
Private N. W. Beeson	not out	2
	B 15. l-b 3	18
		—
	Total	193

SPORTSMAN'S BATTALION.　　　First Innings.

Private E. G. Hayes	b Bristowe	o
Private A. Sandham	l b w, b Bristowe ...:.	21
Private E. Hendren	c Skinner, b Longden ...	35
Private W. E. Bates	c Coverdale, b Bonsor .	57
Capt. H. J. Inglis	c Napper, b Bristowe ..	1
Capt. N. Cockell	c Holland, b Longden .	51
Private A. Webb	b Coverdale	93
Private H. Penfold	not out	30
Lieut. W. A. Rutherford ..	....	
Private A. Smith..........	....	
Sergeant E. L. Marsden ...	....	
	B 15, lb 2	17

Total for 7 Wickets 311

Umpires—Private F. L. Evans and Private J. Cheston.

Scorers—Private R. H. Pavitt and Private W. W. Sawden.

'holo]　　　　　　　　　　　　　　　　　　　　　　　[Underwood & Underwood, Ltd.

FIRST SPORTSMAN'S BATTALION, LORDS, JUNE 12TH, 1915.

　　The day at last arrived, and probably all too soon for many of the " Sportsmen " and their friends, which was to see the departure of the Battalion for Clipstone Camp, there to finish the training, so well begun at Hornchurch, preparatory to being dispatched to the seat of war.

　　Early on the morning of the 26th June, 1915, the Battalion marched out of Grey Towers for the last time, and they were greeted by a larger concourse of people than probably ever before lined our quiet old fashioned streets.

I give below an abridged account of the article which appeared in the "Sportsman's Gazette" describing the departure :—

"GOOD-BYE, HORNCHURCH."

Beautiful weather favoured the dawn of the 26th June, the day when the great majority of the Sportsman's Battalion took their departure from the little Essex village where they had been encamped for the last nine months. They marched away amid enthusiastic cheers from the whole population.

At an early hour, every man, strong and fit, keen and eager, fell into his right place in every section of every platoon. Order prevailed everywhere. Smart in appearance, in fine fettle, they lined up to the roll of the drums. A glow of pride was in the eye of every officer as he surveyed the men before him. The men themselves were swayed with thrilling enthusiasm, which infected the whole surroundings.

It was 6.15 a.m. precisely when marching orders were given at Hornchurch, The band, playing better than they had ever done before, struck up a soul-stirring melody, and one of the finest body of men in training marched out of Grey Towers Barracks, Colonel Viscount Maitland riding at their head, accompanied by his Adjutant, Captain Inglis. As the men swung through the gates rousing cheers greeted them, and they were so robust, and given with such fervour, that the inhabitants of Romford must have been awakened from their slumber.

Notwithstanding the early hour, there stood outside Grey Towers Camp gates a throng of men, women, maids, and boys to cheer the Sportsmen and bid them "Good-bye." A line of motor cars stretched as far as the eye could reach, and these were crowded with smiling women, among whom was Mrs. Cunliffe Owen, who had motored from London to witness the departure. Every member of the D. and E. Companies lined the fences to bid their comrades farewell.

The scene was both wonderful and impressive when Right Flank and C. Companies marched by to entrain for the new camp.

Hornchurch was more crowded than ever when the time came for B. and Left Flank Companies to march in the same tracks as their comrades had done an hour-and-half previously.

At 7.45 the sound of bagpipes and the tramp of men could be heard. Those remaining inside the Camp (D. and E. Companies and hospital staff) were despondent. Friends were now parting, for how long no one could tell. Men lined the drive and eagerly gripped an old Hutmate's or chum's hand as the Companies marched by. They could not speak the word, "Good-bye," for a lump was in their throats which prevented speech—the lump that arises from a throbbing heart. Leaving

DEPARTURE OF THE SPORTSMAN'S BATTALION, JUNE 26TH, 1915.
PASSING THROUGH HIGH STREET.

the old Grey Towers Camp was an ordeal which will never be forgotten by those who witnessed this impressive scene.

B. and Left Flank Companies are now on the road and heading for the Station. Lieut.-Colonel Gibbons rides proudly at the head of his men, with Lieutenant Taylor, Regimental Sergeant-Major Merrick, and Sergeant-Major Blumenthal in attendance.

As the Companies near the Station, the cheering becomes louder, the feeling more intense. Mothers hold up their youngsters for a parting tribute, and Daddy leaves the ranks to give mother and babe a fond embrace. Sweethearts, who had seen these acts, brush aside custom and march side by side with their lovers, and gladly follow the lead of their elder sisters.

It is time to entrain. " Fall in, two deep, March ! " comes the order and away we go. Carriages are allotted to each section, and with snorting steam and screaming whistle, the train slowly begins to move away from Hornchurch Station.

A pause to review the scene. There on the platform is Major Richie, D.S.O., Captain Cockell, and Lieutenant Eeman. They feel the parting keenly. Men's faces are the reflex of a troubled heart. Yet one look more. The crowd stand still. It is mostly composed of women now. We watch. We see them still wave their flags, they still cry out " Good-bye "—and the mother nature asserts her rights. The smiles vanish. The cheerful faces become wan and white. The handkerchiefs which had been so enthusiastically flourished are now used for another purpose.

It has been a soul-stirring scene—a scene never to be forgotten—a memory which will be recalled again and again by those who participated in the separation. The final look round. Yes, it is really " Good-bye, Hornchurch." We are speeding from the " little village " with every revolution of the carriage wheels, and it is safe to say that everyone feels an ache somewhere near his heart at being parted from what he has so long looked upon as home."

And so passed from our midst the wonderful Battalion which will always be looked upon and remembered by Hornchurch folk as " OURS."

It may be permitted to the writer of this book to recall a few of his own personal friends in the Battalion, and if those genial " Sports "—Cook, Denis Turner, Parkes, O'Moore Phillips, John Ward, Shepperson, and Chilmaid—should happen on this page, they will know they are not forgotten.

. Although the majority of the original members of the " 23rd " remained, from choice, privates, preferring, however high their social position in civil life, to fight and march in the ranks, long before the Battalion left Hornchurch it had largely developed into a sort of Officers' Training Corps, so many of them having obtained commissioned ranks*. Many of these became distinguished officers during the war.

The fighting record of the Sportsman's Battalion was honourable and distinguished, and came fully up to the highest expectations. The Battalion went to France with the 33rd Division in November, 1915. Shortly after its arrival it joined the 2nd Division, and served with that Division throughout the war, taking part in the following battles :—Delville Wood, Beaumont Hamel, Vimy Ridge, Attacks on Oppy, First Battle of Cambrai, Bourlon Wood, Miraumont, Greyvillers, and " Lady's Leg " Ravine.

The Battalion also took a prominent part in eventually holding up the enemy in the great and last German offensive of March, 1918. On the 21 August, 1918, it led off for the 3rd Army in the British counter offensive, eventually landing in Germany, and forming part of the Army of Occupation.

Colonel Viscount Maitland, who commanded the Battalion from its formation, proceeded with it overseas. Returning to England in January, 1916, he was succeeded by Lieut.-Colonel H. A. Vernon, of the 1st K.R.R.C. On Lieut.-Colonel Vernon being appointed to the command of a Brigade, he was succeeded in command of the Battalion, in May, 1917, by Lieut.-Colonel E. A. Winter, who originally joined the Battalion as a Private, in 1914. Lieut.-Colonel Winter held command till May, 1919. On his leaving the Battalion to take over the command of the British Camp at Antwerp, Lieut.-Colonel L. F. Ashburner was appointed to command the Battalion.

The Battalion served as part of the Army of Occupation until March, 1920, when it was finally dispersed. It holds the distinction of having had a longer life than any other Service Battalion of the Royal Fusiliers.

The following Honours and Decorations were awarded the Battalion :—4 D.S.O., 1 Bar to D.S.O., 27 M.C., 5 Bars to M.C., 14 D.C.M., 93 M.M., 4 Bars to M.M., 8 M.S.M.

Casualties : - Officers killed 32 ; Other ranks killed 686.

THE NAVVIES' OR PIONEERS' BATTALION
(26th Middlesex Regiment.)

" Canst work i' the earth so fast ?
A worthy pioneer ! "
Shakespeare :—Hamlet, i., v.

For some time after the departure of the " Sportsmen " from Grey Towers, the Camp remained unoccupied, but in the following November the 26th Middlesex Regiment, popularly known as the Navvies' Battalion, arrived under the command of Colonel John Ward, M.P. This fine body of men was

*In the Sportsman's Gazette, No. 22 (Vol. 2) for June 25/15 it was stated that since the Batt. was formed, over 500 men had qualified for officers out of the ranks.

154

drafted into Kitchener's Army for special work, and, as their name implied, was very largely on the manual rather than on the fighting side of warfare ; the Battalion was, however, in nowise lacking in a military sense.

Although their stay with us was short and produced nothing out of the common, it must be said to their credit that their conduct was all that could be desired, and they were in every way quite sensible of their responsibilities as soldiers of the King. Their general bearing was probably somewhat of a reflection of the great example set them by their chief. During the time they were in camp there was no regular Church Parade of the battalion at the Parish Church, but instead a service was generally held on the Parade ground, at which Colonel Ward usually gave a short address, which always contained some sound and good advice to his men. This Service was held at 9-30 o'clock, and those who wished were therefore free to attend service at one or other of our places of worship, and every Sunday morning a commanding military figure might be seen at the service at our ancient Parish Church. This was Colonel John Ward, and with him was always one or more of his officers.

The " Navvies " had a fine band, and, headed by their mascot, a splendid goat, helped to enliven our village during their stay. Afterwards this band did excellent service in assisting recruiting in many of our large midland and northern towns.

Some kind Hornchurch friends were in the midst of making preparations to give the " Navvies " a Merry Christmas, but within a few days of the Christmas festival, the battalion received orders to vacate the Camp, and on December 21st they, too, marched out of Grey Towers en route for the railway station and another camping ground.

THE NEW ZEALANDERS.

" We'll mingle our bloods together in the earth
From whence we have our being and our birth."*
" In brief, a braver choice of dauntless spirits
Than now the English bottoms have waft o'er
Did never float upon the swelling tide."†

Shakespeare.

While the great British Army of five millions was in the making, India and the colonies rallied round the mother country magnificently, and tens of thousands of splendid fighting men from all the British dominions and dependencies came to take up arms against the common enemy. From all the great states of India, fron Canada, Australia, New Zealand, Newfoundland, and South Africa, from North, East, South, and West, wherever the Union Jack proudly floated in the breeze, men came in regular drafts over the whole period of the war, to fight side by side

*Pericles, i., ii.
†King John, ii., i.

155

Photo]

NEW ZEALAND CONVALESCENT HOSPITAL. GREY TOWERS. JULY, 1917.

[Panora, Ltd.

NEW ZEALAND CONVALESCENT HOSPITAL, GREY TOWERS, JULY, 1917.

with the boys at home for the honour and glory of the Empire. Never was there such a marvellous display of unity exhibited before an astonished world, to the consternation and undoing of a disillusioned and disappointed enemy, who had at last discovered the full meaning and significance of those two mighty words, " BRITISH EMPIRE " !

The Canadians and Indians won undying fame in Northern France and Flanders, and the Australians and New Zealanders made imperishable history by their heroic and marvellous fighting at Anzac and Suvla Bay in the operations on the Gallipoli Peninsula.

When, therefore, it became known that " Grey Towers " had been selected as the first depot in England of the New Zealand Contingent, there were few Hornchurch folk who did not feel honoured by the prospect of entertaining those war-worn warriors who had so nobly fought our battles in that terrible inferno at Gallipoli. And so, when the first batches of wounded men were sent here in January, 1916, as convalescents, they soon found a warm corner in our hearts, and before long were as welcome in our homes, and at our local clubs, as were their comrades in arms of the Sportsman's Battalion in the earlier days of the war, and very soon the picturesque slouch hat, with its distinguishing pugaree of the N.Z. Contingent, became as familiar in our streets as previously had been the regulation peaked cap of the 23rd Royal Fusiliers.

A convalescent hospital had been established at Epsom, and men who had been treated there were afterwards drafted to Hornchurch. Grey Towers became a Command Depot for the gathering of all details prior to being returned to their respective fighting units. Lieut.-Col. C. H. J. Brown, D.S.O., was first officer commanding, and was succeeded by Major T. H. Dawson ; Captain H. Short being senior medical officer, and Captain Gordon H. Forsythe adjutant.

Soon after the advent of the New Zealand Division in France at the end of April or beginning of May, 1916, and after their first entry into action on the western front, a large number of wounded, and the usual toll of sick, began to filter through to England.

It was then realised that Hornchurch was far too small for the purposes of a Command Depot, and that, moreover, it was necessary to establish a Convalescent Hospital there. Such " details," therefore, as had been at Hornchurch were now moved *en bloc* to Codford, Salisbury Plain, a certain percentage of the personnel only being left behind to form the staff of the New Zealand Convalescent Hospital. This transition took place on 6 July, 1916.

In the first instance this Convalescent Hospital was commanded by a combatant officer with a senior medical officer to

Photo]   GREY TOWERS CAMP UNDER SNOW.   *[Frank Luff.*

assist him, but it was recognised that, as the unit was intended to be a purely medical unit, it was necessary to put in command a medical officer. This was effected in the middle of September, 1916, when Lieut.-Colonel (then Major) C. H. Tewsley was detailed from duty with a Field Ambulance in France to Hornchurch as Commandant.

The camp, which had hitherto been used entirely as a battalion training camp, however excellent it might have been for that purpose, was found to be quite unsuited, without a very great deal of remodelling, for the purpose for which it was now intended. It may be said that, for all practical purposes, there was nothing beyond sleeping quarters and a training ground.

THE COTTAGE, NORTH STREET.
Occupied by the Nursing Staff of the N.Z. Convalescent Hospital.

If it was to be converted into an effective convalescent hospital, facilities had to be provided in order to meet every demand in this direction that might be made upon it.

It was soon realised that as the New Zealand General Hospitals (three of which had been established in the United Kingdom), had a very limited capacity and were quite unable to cope with the vast numbers of New Zealanders passing from the division to England, a very much larger work was going to be demanded from the Hornchurch Medical Unit than would probably otherwise have been asked of it, and instead of being merely a convalescent hospital it seemed likely to partake more of the nature of a composite unit, partly auxiliary hospital, and partly convalescent hospital. Steps were therefore taken to meet this wider demand.

An up-to-date surgical department was gradually formed wherein all wounds could be treated under perfect aseptic or antiseptic conditions. It was the idea of the Director of Medical Services that the units should furnish a large Electro-massage Department, and that, to a very great extent, cases requiring this particular system of treatment should be concentrated here. To this end a complete electrical equipment was installed and a strong department built up. This grew from very small dimensions to a capacity which was capable of handling with considerable comfort more than 300 cases a day. It was recognised that, in conjunction with such a department, it was necessary to have a proper mecano-therapeutical department. To effect this, one building was set aside as a medical gymnasium, and a large quantity of modern apparatus provided. This soon became one of the most important features of the hospital.

Photo]   [*Luffs, Hornchurch.*

GREY TOWERS ENTRANCE GATES.

An expert instructor was secured from the Army Gymnasium Staff, and suitable N.C.O's. were chosen and detailed for training at the Army Gymnasium Schools. Thus a capable staff of physical instructors was established in this Medical Gymnasium. The programme of the Gymnasium was that men should attend there in half-hour classes. Commencing with about ten minutes of what are commonly known as Swedish exercises, each thereafter used such apparatus as was specially intended for his individual disability. In addition to this, outdoor physical training classes were established on a progressive system, so that the men could be easily passed through a series of classes of an increasing standard of difficulty, finally passing on for further training to the Command Depot. The object was the evacuation of men to the fighting line in France. If men were not likely to be fit after a reasonable time (say 6 months), it was

L

considered economically sound to return them to New Zealand, it being fequently proved that the voyage did more good to them than a lengthy stay in any hospital. These men in most cases returned with later reinforcements for the western front.

It was from the commencement realised that the chief necessity for a convalescent hospital was a proper atmosphere ; if a man could be surrounded by amusements and cheerful occupations, it was pyschologically certain that his cure would be very much quicker than if his surroundings were drab and cheerless. Therefore every encouragement was given to those desirous of doing anything for the men's recreation and amusement. New Zealand had, from the commencement of the war, raised large sums of money, mainly for the benefit of its soldiers, and a Central Committee was established in the Dominion to adminster the whole of these locally-raised subscriptions. In addition, Committees were formed in the United Kingdom and in France, and from these efforts grew up what was known as the New Zealand War Contingent Association, which was practically a body to administer these Patriotic Funds. This association established recreation huts in nearly all the N.Z. camps in England. At Hornchurch a large hut was erected, which contained a canteen, a large hall, billiard-room, and reading and writing room. This was staffed primarily by N.Z. ladies, assisted to a certain extent by ladies of the old country.

In like manner the New Zealand Y.M.C.A. had very large sums at their disposal, and were only too anxious to do anything that was possible in the N.Z. Camps. This Association also established a large hut at " Grey Towers," which was from time to time considerably extended, so that finally it is doubtful whether there was any camp in England with a finer or more up-to-date building. This Y.M.C.A. block consisted in the first instance of a fine canteen, billiard room, a large hall capable of seating from 800 to 900 people, a workshop, which was first known as the arts and crafts department, and a large reading and writing room. Gradually other additions were made, and towards the end of 1918 there were added two large workshops, seven rooms for educational classes and an eighth room to be used as a motor engineering shop. These additional buildings were formally opened on Friday, Dec. 6, 1918* by Brigadier-General Richardson, G.O.C., of the New Zealand Expeditionary Force in the United Kingdom, and completed what was considered the finest New Zealand Y.M.C.A. equipment overseas, and it may be said, in passing, that the educational scheme of the N.Z.E.F. practically started with the Y.M.C.A. Arts and Crafts Depot at Hornchurch.

The Church Army, too, on being approached by one of the Hospital chaplains, immediately consented, contingent on £100 being raised by New Zealand, to build a Church Army Hut. The £100 was immediately forthcoming from one of the N.Z. Dioceses, and the hut was soon afterwards erected, furnished, and dedicated.

The hospital was originally intended for the accommodation of 1,500 patients, but this was soon found to be quite inadequate, and it was therefore raised to 2,000. Even with this accommodation the unit was unable to accept all the New Zealanders that the hospitals had to send, and in consequence men were often distributed among other hospitals throughout the United Kingdom. The establishment was, in consequence, raised to 2,500.

Photo]   *[S. A. Sabine.*
SUNDAY AFTERNOON IN THE CAMP.

It was soon recognised that, in order to prevent such a large number of men from wandering aimlessly about, it was essential to find them some useful occupations. Therefore the scope of what had originated as the arts and crafts department of the Y.M.C.A., was now extended by the addition of Orthopædic workshops, such as were already being established in various parts of England under the able guidance of Colonel Sir Robert Jones. In certain cases, therefore, it was made compulsory for patients to spend some of their time in the workshops. The local secretary of the New Zealand Y.M.C.A., Mr. Horace Fawcett, was appointed as Director, and with him was detailed a medical officer, whose duty it was to go round the workshops and see daily that the patients there were employed on such work as was warranted to assist in the cure of the disability from which they were suffering. Thus, the man with a bullet wound in the forearm, and consequent weakness of his arm and forearm muscles, was detailed to manual work, such as planing and sawing, in which he was not only passing the time pleasantly for himself but, at the same time, exercising the weakened muscles, and therein assisting in his personal cure.

DEMOBILISATION.—The G.O.C. in charge of Administration (N.Z.E.F.) in the United Kingdom, foreseeing that the problems in connection with demobilisation at the conclusion of the war would be considerable, and that the employment of troops during that period would be a very serious matter, issued instructions early in 1918, that, in all units, an educational scheme was to be initiated. An officer in charge of Education was appointed, attached to Administrative Headquarters in London, and educational officers were to be appointed by the local commanding officers to be responsible, under them, for local educational arrangements. It was arranged that a certain amount of education should be carried out during the fighting period, but the main idea was that, immediately an armistice was declared, the machinery would be established for a large educational scheme to be carried on throughout the armistice period, and right on to the end of demobilisation. This was an eminently satisfactory scheme for such a place as a convalescent hospital, and the idea was extensively and enthusiastically taken up at Hornchurch. Able instructors were chosen from the troops themselves, and classes were established, first on a voluntary and afterwards on a compulsory basis.

Amongst the subjects dealt with were the following :—

English, French, Commercial Arithmetic, Shorthand, Book-keeping, Stained Glass work, Building Construction, Carpentry, Cabinet-making, Wood-carving, Basket and Chair making, Agriculture, Wool classing, Dairywork, Fruit Farming, Poultry keeping, Cinema operations, Land Surveying (chiefly for farmers), and Motor Engineering.

FOOD AND RATIONING.—The rationing and shortage of food had also become important questions, and as there was a large tract of land attached to the encampment lying idle, this was gradually got under cultivation, until 40 acres were brought under the plough. Two ends were served here :—In the first place a very considerable addition was made to the food supplies, and in the second place valuable agricultural instruction could be given. A further aid to the food supply was a rabbitry and poultry farm.

RECREATION:—On the recreative side of the hospital work, outdoor and indoor amusements were provided on the widest

Photo]   [*Luffs, Hornchurch.*

N.Z. "BLUE BOYS" ON CHURCH HILL AFTER A MARCH.

scale possible, Numerous excursions were arranged, chiefly through the medium of the N.Z. War Contingent Association and the N.Z. Y.M.C.A., for attending entertainments such as theatre matinées and concerts in London. Every evening also, an entertainment of some kind was arranged in each of the two recreation halls, and a cinema plant was installed in the Y.M.C.A. Hall.

Football, Cricket, Hockey, and Bowling teams were all formed in their proper seasons. A swimming bath was constructed in the stream on the west side of the encampment, and during the summer months swimming and athletic sports were held monthly. During winter a dance was held once a week in the camp amongst the camp personnel.

V.A.D.—In the early days, when the demand for every available man was so insistent, female labour was introduced into the camp, and men were replaced wherever possible ; thus the canteen and mess-rooms were entirely staffed from women belonging to the V.A.D. from Devonshire House, London.

Up to the end of 1918 approximately 20,000* patients passed through this Convalescent Hospital.

NAMES OF OFFICERS CONNECTED WITH GREY TOWERS.

G.O. Commanding the N.Z. Expeditionary Force.—Lieut.-General Sir Alexander Godley, K.C.B., K.C.M.G., &c., who inspected the Camp on several occasions.

G.O. Commanding N.Z. Division, Major-General Sir Andrew Russell, K.C.B., K.CM.G., &c.

G.O. in Charge of Administration, N.Z.E.F. in the United Kingdom. —Brigadier-General C. S. Richardson, C.B., C.M.G.

Officers in Command of the Command Depot at Grey Towers :— Lieut.-Colonel (afterwards Brigadier-General) C. H. J. Brown, D.S.O. (killed in action in France). Major (afterwards Lieut.-Colonel) T. H. Dawson, C.M.G.

Acting Commandant from September, 1916, *after the establishment of the Depot as a Convalescent Hospital.—* Lieut.-Colonel C. H. Tewsley.

Second in Command of Convalescent Hospital.—Captain E. C. Dovey, N.Z.S.E. Major (afterwards Lieut.-Colonel) W. S. Pennycook, N.Z.P.B. (killed in action in France). Major J. M. Rose, M.C., N.Z.S.E.

Senior Medical Officer of the Command Depot.—Captain (afterwards Major) H. Short, O.B.E.

Adjutant of the Convalescent Hospital.—Captain Gordon H. Forsythe, M.B.E.

*This figure is given on the authority of Colonel Tewsley.

Quartermaster.—Captain C. F. Smedley, M.B.E.

Matrons.—Miss F. Wilson, R.R.C , Miss V McLean, R R.C., Miss C. B. Anderson, R.R.C.

Chaplains.—Canon H. D. Burton, O.B.E., Church of England; Captain Garner, Salvation Army ; Rev. Mackenzie Gibson, Church of England ; Rev. Angus Macdonald, O.B.E., Presby-- terian ; Father Richards, M.C., Roman Catholic ; Right Rev. Bishop Neligan, formerly Bishop of Auckland, N.Z.

Camp Secretaries of Y.M.C.A.—Mr. Horace Fawcett, Mr. P. W. Bushnell.

New Zealand Ladies who held permanent positions in the Canteens.— Miss Hilda Williams, O.B.E., Mrs. Warren, Miss Warren, Miss Walsh, Mrs Edmund, and Miss Busby

War Contingent Fund Workers.—Mrs. Fraser, Mrs. West, Mrs. Standish, Miss Macnab, Miss Ross, Mrs. Rough.

Local regular helpers in the Canteens.—Mrs. Robertson, Mrs. Mc- Mullen. Miss May, Mrs. Fraser Parkes, Mrs. Hinton, Miss Cox, Miss Frost, Mrs. Russell, Mrs. Stuttle.

REMINISCENCES.

The long occupation of Grey Towers by the New Zealanders afforded innumerable opportunities for the development of social intercourse with the inhabitants of our village, and, as in the case of the " Sportsmen," many dances and concerts were held at Grey Towers, more especially during their first winter season, to which invitations were extended to Hornchurch folk. In addition, several entertainments on a large scale were given in the Drill Hall, High Street.

Few of those who were fortunate enough to witness it are ever likely to forget that wonderful war dance, or " Haka," performed by the Maoris at the Drill Hall, on March 22nd, 1916. This was given by about 20 magnificent warriors, part of the remnant of the men of their race who fought at Gallipoli, where, as Lieutenant Hæata informed us, in introducing them, they went into battle 500 strong and came out with less than 100 men. They appeared in full war paint and in native costume, and the weirdness of their performance will ever remain a memory with many of us who were held spellbound by the agile and fan- tastic movements of these splendid Maoris, who also sang several songs in their own language. It was all very fearsome and haunting, and one can quite imagine the consternation of the Turks when faced by such a superb body of men, whose war whoops alone must have been enough to strike terror and awe into their hearts.

At the same concert, Miss Rosina Buckman, the New Zealand prima donna, sang five beautiful songs which entirely enchanted her audience. Some of these introduced snatches of Maori, and the tumultous applause with which she was greeted by her brave and gallant countrymen showed how greatly she was appreciated by them as well as by the dwellers in our village. This was altogether a truly wonderful night. The entertainment was given by the New Zealanders to all the village, and all the village came, though, unfortunately, many of our neighbours were unable to obtain admittance, and scores, if not hundreds, had to be turned away from the doors. Those who had seats were lucky, and those who had them not and had to stand the whole evening long, were only a little less fortunate, but how the huge audience was even able to breathe in that crowded Hall during the three hours they were there, will always remain somewhat of a mystery.

How this concert came to be given was in this wise :—Under the chairmanship of Mr. Thomas Gardner, a small committee* was formed, with the Rev. A. J. Parry as hon. sec. for the purpose of providing a series of entertainments for the New Zealand troops, and, as a result, eight entertainments were decided upon. These were of such a high-class character, and so greatly appreciated by the officers and men, that, after the fourth one had been given, the officers, ever on the *qui vive* to return any hospitality accorded to them, kindly offered to provide the programme for the seventh concert and to be the hosts of the village on that occasion. It was a happy idea, and the result could not have been more successful. But oh, that Haka! Many moons after the New Zealanders have departed for their native shores, and the Maoris have gone back to their peaceful pursuits, we shall look back and picture once more that wonderful Maori dance.

The New Zealanders gave many good " shows " afterwards at the Drill Hall in the cause of charity, the most important and interesting being the pantomime of " Achi Baba and the more or less Forty Thieves," which was given on the 30th December, 1916, in aid of the local branch of the Young Helpers' League, in connection with Dr. Barnardo's Homes. The pantomime was arranged and produced by Sapper Theodore Trezise, and was in every way an excellent entertainment. The dresses, scenery, and effects were of a high-class order, and the acting was as good, or even better, than some professional productions. The reserved seats cost 2s. 6d., and I never had a better half-crown's worth of real good fun and laughter. Sapper Trezise had gathered round him some very talented artistes, and in appreciation of the manner in which they acquitted themselves, and in recognition of the very satisfactory monetary result attained for the excellent and deserving institution they benefited, I reproduce the programme in its entirety.

*The Members of this Committee were:—Messrs. F. J. Ashton, E. G. Bratchell, J. M. Ewing, W. Halestrap, W. M. Langton, C. T. Perfect, H. A. Pinney, A. J. Powell, H. L. Symonds, J. M. Taplin.

"ACHI BABA AND THE MORE OR LESS FORTY THIEVES,"

Held in the Drill Hall, Hornchurch, Saturday, Dec. 30th, 1916,

AT 7 P.M.

Achi Baba (a poor Lead Swinger)	Corpl. ALLARDYCE
Cogia (his Wife)	Pte. TED KAVANAGH
Ganem (their Son)	Spr. THEODOR TREZISE
Edward (their Donkey)	Cpl. JUMBO BARNES
Morgiana (their Slave)	Mis. REUBEN THAIN
Hassan (Achi's rich Brother)	Corpl. MURPHY
Mustapha (Hassan's Agent)	Corpl. GUY MARRIOTT
Capt. Fray-Bentos (of the Forty Thieves)	Corpl. BOB ALDRICH
Lieut. See Bee (of the Forty Thieves)	Sergt. WALPOLE
Abdullah (a Lover)	Signr. MAITLAND
Mahomet (a Dancer)	Pte. SNOWY HAMBLING
A Spirit	L.-Corpl. J. COSTELLO

Four Singers .. .. { Sergt. WALPOLE
L.-Corpl. SMITH
Signr. MAITLAND
Pte. D. TAYLOR

A Waiter	Corpl. WEST
A Stuttering Boy	Pte. HOLMES

The rest of us—

Lieut. BEAMISH	S. M. WHITMORE
Sergt. HOWIE	Corpl. FITZGERALD
L.-Corpl. LANBRIDGE	Corpl. J. COSTELLO
Pte. GREEN	Sergt. EMMETT

Two Acrobats .. .. { Sergt. SINCLAIR
Pte. HAMBLING

Assistant Stage Manager	Pte. COSTER.
Scenery	Spr. HORN and Drvr. BURKE
Electrician	Spr. JAMES
Property Master	Sergt. GARVIE

Orchestra.

Pte. McCULLUM   Cpl. MARTIN   Sgt. MALONEY
Mr. WESTON, &c.

Arranged and produced by :—

Sapper THEODOR TREZISE.

NEW ZEALAND PUBLIC AND OFFICIAL CELEBRATIONS AND CEREMONIES.

The grounds of Grey Towers were the scene of an interesting and significant ceremony on Tuesday afternoon, April 4th, 1916, the occasion being the unfurling, by Lady Birdwood, of a New Zealand flag, presented to the Contingent by Lady Allington and friends.

Among the guests were Lady and Miss Birdwood, Admiral and Lady Fremantle, Lady Portman, Lady Thompson, Lady Garvagh, Lady and Miss Lyall, Mrs. Joseph and Miss Beatrice Chamberlain, Lady Codrington, Mrs. Challoner, Mrs. Newman, the Misses Bowen, Miss Graham Hope, Mrs. Newton, Lady

Wingate (wife of the Sirdar of Egypt, Major-General Sir Francis Reginald Wingate, K.C.M.G., K.C.B., D.S.O.), Mrs. Parker (sister of Lord Kitchener), and Miss Richmond.

Lady Birdwood, after performing the ceremony, addressed the troops, and expressed her great pleasure at the opportunity afforded her of visiting the camp. It was, however, left to Miss Chamberlain, daughter of the late great statesman, Mr. Joseph Chamberlain, who had identified himself so largely with Colonial affairs, to give them a message from the women of England, and in doing so she delivered an exceptionally fine patriotic speech, an extract of which is as under. Miss Chamberlain, who was introduced by Major T. W. Dawson said :—

" Men of New Zealand, fellow subjects of King George, fellow citizens of the British Empire,—I have to-day a great privilege, a privilege of thanking you in the name of the women of England for that you offered yourselves, your health and your strength, and your lives, if need be, to guard our Empire and the great cause which it ever defends. We women of England do not wish that you should leave us without having heard our word of thanks. We think of you and we pray for you. We dwell with deep gratitude on that which you have done, but you cannot hear us, you do not know how full our thoughts are of you, and we wish that ere you return to the other side of the world, you should know this. We should also have you thank the women of New Zealand who bravely saw you go. We shall never forget you and we shall teach those who come after us to bless your name. I think, were I not a woman, I might hesitate to give you these thanks. We women cannot fight for ourselves. We must let you fight for us and our hearts are full of gratitude to you who, right on the other side of the world, realised the dangers that threatened us and came here to protect us from the brutality of a remorseless foe. In coming to defend the shores of England," the speaker added, " you were defending your own cause, because it must now be plain to all the world, ' Who touches one of the nations of the British Empire touches all.' They stood together—England and New Zealand, New Zealand and England. Were they not the furthest apart of the lands on which the sun never set ? As they stood together, so did all others. They would defend civilization, they would do right and defend liberty and preserve their glorious heritage. As my father once said to the men of Canada, ' United, we shall be heedful of the great task which Providence has placed upon us. United, no man shall make us afraid.' "

Admiral Fremantle followed with a short address, and the guests were then entertained to tea, after which an entertainment was given, at which the Maoris gave some of their famous war dances.

THE FIRST ANNIVERSARY OF ANZAC DAY CELEBRATIONS.

THE MEMORIAL SERVICE.

" All these were honoured in their generations, and were the glory of their times."—Ecclesiasticus, XLIV., vii.

Of all the New Zealand happenings at Hornchurch there was probably no event of greater importance, or of more historic interest, than the celebrations connected with the first anniversary of Anzac Day.

These celebrations commenced on Easter Sunday morning, April 23rd, 1916, when a special Commemoration and Memorial Service was held in the Parish Church of St. Andrew's, Hornchurch, at 10 o'clock, at which the Vicar, the Rev. Herbert Dale, M.A., officiated.

868 men and 21 officers of the New Zealand Contingent (of these only 46 men fit for active service) under the command of Major T. H. Dawson, marched through the village from their Base Camp at Grey Towers to the Church, headed by their splendid band, under the Regimental Bandmaster, Sergeant-Major Mahoney.

With the exception of the two small Chapels on either side of the Chancel, which were reserved for the general public, the New Zealanders occupied the whole of the Church, and even then, the large building was strained to its utmost capacity to find room for all. Many of the men occupied seats immediately in front of the altar rails, while several officers, failing to obtain seats in the body of the Church, found their way to the ringing chamber of the belfry (which is an open one), where they were able to look down upon a scene, the like of which had never before been witnessed within those ancient walls.

The sight of those war-worn warriors, who had won imperishable fame in Gallipoli on that memorable 25th April, 1915, gathered together on such a unique occasion in the grand old Church, beautifully adorned for the Easter festival with thousands of lovely spring flowers, could not fail to be impressive. But the spectacle was made still more beautiful and impressive by the draping of the pillar adjoining the Chancel on the south side of the Nave, with the large New Zealand flag—recently presented by members of the Allington family, and unfurled at Grey Towers Camp by Lady Birdwood—to which was attached a laurel wreath, with the inscription on purple ribbon :—

" To the memory of those who died for the Empire.— Anzac, 1915."

The service opened with Kipling's Recessional, and, after specially appointed prayers had been offered, the Lesson was read by the Rev. Charles Dobson, Vicar of The Sounds, New Zealand, one of the Chaplains of the New Zealand Expeditionary Force.

There was then enacted the most moving and impressive incident in the whole service. Major Dawson and two of his brother officers, Major A. G. B. Price and Lieut. W. Haeata, left their seats, and advanced to the altar rails, each bearing a memorial wreath, which the Vicar received at their hands, and reverently placed upon the Holy Table. This simple act of public homage by those khaki-clad officers will long live in the memory of all those who witnessed it. It was a most solemn moment, and in it one realised to the full all that those floral emblems stood for, and got a grip of the inner meaning of that silent little ceremony, so eloquent of true comradeship with those heroes who had fought so valiantly, and who, with such unflinching courage, had been faithful even unto death.

One of the wreaths was of gilded palms, the gift of Mrs. Challoner, and bore a similar inscription to that affixed to the New Zealand flag. The other two were sent in memory of the fallen New Zealanders, and of the officers and men of the gallant 29th Division (including the Essex Regiment), which landed at Cape Helles at the same time as the New Zealanders landed at Anzac. These wreaths bore the following inscriptions :—

" To the memory of the fallen (Gallipoli), from the Officers of the New Zealand Depot, Hornchurch."

AND

" To the memory of the fallen (Gallipoli), from the Non-commissioned Officers and men of the New Zealand Depot, Hornchurch."

The first verse of " God Save the King " was then sung, and was followed by the Sermon.

The Vicar took his text from Isaiah xxvi.-4 : " Trust ye in the Lord for ever, for in the Lord Jehovah is everlasting strength." He approached his subject in the full spirit of the text, and recalled the incidents connected with the memorable landing and fighting at Anzac, on the 25th April, 1915. He spoke in eloquent and appropriate terms of the magnificent and glorious service rendered to the Empire by the New Zealand and Australian Contingents, during the whole of the Gallipoli campaign. When referring to the landing, he quoted the words of Mr. Buchan, as follows :—

> " That our audacity succeeded is a tribute to the unsurpassable fighting qualities of our men, the regulars of the 29th Division, the Naval Division, and not least to the dash and doggedness of the Australasian Corps. Whatever may be the judgement of posterity on its policy or its consequences, the Battle of the Landing will be acclaimed as a mighty feat of arms."

" Yes, it was a 'Day that the Lord had made.' Let us rejoice and be glad in it, for what did it mean ? A revelation to the eyes of all men that a force, a new nation had sprung into the world's history ; a grappling of the heart of the Mother Country in her age, to the heart of your lovely and glorious Dominion with hooks of steel ; the striking of a resounding blow for the cause of justice and right-dealing in the world ; a veritable battle for the Kingdom of God.

We cannot fully tell you how the heart of England leapt out to you for the deeds that you had wrought ; but we know that you are right to be determined that the memory of those days shall never die. And we people of Hornchurch are glad, are more glad than we know how to say, that you should be keeping the first Anniversary of that Sunday in our quiet, simple, old village Church, the Parish Church nearly nine hundred years ago of that pathetic figure in our national history, the Patron Saint of our Army for centuries—King Edward the Confessor—before you pass next Tuesday to commemorate, before the eyes of the Nation, the actual date of your Anzac landing, in that same Edward the Confessor's glorious ' Minster of the West,' the life-long dream, the realization of the vision of that ' Poet-King, who thought in stone,' as well as his supreme contribution to the country of his love."

He then paid a touching and pathetic tribute to the comrades of his martial congregation who had died so heroically on that now historic battlefield. In speaking of the men who had made the great sacrifice, he quoted the following words of Cardinal Mercier, the venerable leader of heroic Belgium in its spiritual life :—

" If I am asked what I think of the eternal salvation of a brave man who had consciously given his life in his country's honour, I shall not hesitate to reply that, without any doubt whatever, Christ crowns his military valour, and that death accepted in this Christian spirit, assures the safety of that man's soul. ' Greater love hath no man than this, that he lay down his life for his friends,' and the soldier who dies to save his brothers, and to defend the hearths and altars of his country, reaches the highest of all degrees of charity. He may not have made a close analysis of his sacrifice ; but must we suppose that God requires of the plain soldier in the excitement of battle the methodical precision of the moralist or the theologian ? Can we, who revere his heroism, doubt that his God welcomes him with love ? "

After the Sermon the hymn, " For all the Saints who from their labours rest," was sung in solemn memory of the unreturning brave ; and again the strains of the National Anthem echoed through the grand old Church.

The Vicar then, holding aloft the gilded wreath of palm leaves, pronounced the Benediction, and thus brought to a fitting close one of the most remarkable and impressive services ever held in the history of a Parish Church full of inspiring episodes and memories.

As the soldiers filed out of the Church, a half-muffled peal was rung in honour of the heroic dead.

Mr. H. W. Alden, Organist of the Parish Church, presided at the Organ, and the service was fully choral.

A beautiful Souvenir of the service was presented to every member of the congregation.

ST. ANDREW'S CHURCH was the Church of the New Zealand Depôt in England.

CLERGY AND CHURCH OFFICERS AT DATE OF SERVICE.

Chaplain & Vicar Temporal.—Rev. HERBERT DALE, M.A., New Coll., Oxford.

Assistant Curate.—Rev. ALLEN J. PARRY, A.K.C.

Acting Chaplains to the New Zealand Base Depot.

Churchwardens.—Mr. Walter Dendy and Mr. C. H. Baker.

Deputy-Churchwardens.—Mr. R. Dockrill and Mr. W. E. Langridge.

Sidesmen.—Messrs. Allen, Boulton, E. G. Bratchell, Brooks, T. Burden, Card, J. Dockrill, R. Dockrill, E. Fry, G. Fry, T. Gardner, W. Halestrap, T. Johnson, W. E. Langridge, C. T. Perfect, A. J. Powell, G. Ruston, Sibthorp, H. L. Symonds, and T. W. Wedlake.

DEPARTURE FOR LONDON.

In beautifully fine weather, with the sun shining bright and hot as on any summer day, the Contingent marched out of Grey Towers' Gates at about 8 o'clock on the morning of the 25th April, headed by their mascot, a fine Newfoundland dog, gaily wearing his new regimental coat. The music of the band brought many of our villagers to their doors, or to line the streets to give then a parting cheer, as they passed on their way en route for London, to take part in the march through the streets of the metropolis to Westminster Abbey, where the King and Queen were to join them in their great Commemoration and Memorial service. It was noticed that many of the gallant fellows limped bravely along, and that here and there was seen an armless sleeve, which told its own pathetic tale.

The celebration in London was fully described in all the newspapers and journals throughout the Kingdom, but my record would not be complete without a suitable reference to what took place there, although it is more particularly concerned with the actual doings of the Contingent in our own Village. I therefore mention a few leading incidents, and reproduce extracts from the " *Morning Post*," issue of April 26th, graphically describing in brief the great event, and giving the Order of the Service in the Abbey :—

IN LONDON.

On their arival in London the troops formed up in Aldwych, and, with the Australian Contingent, numbered about 2,000 strong. They then marched by way of the Strand and Whitehall to the Abbey, and never had soldiers a greater or more enthusiastic reception by the London populace. With the New Zealanders was their first V.C., Sergt. Cyril Bassett, of the New Zealand Engineers, and, in addition to the men who went up from Hornchurch, many New Zealanders joined the ranks in London from the various Convalescent Hospitals in and around the metropolis.

Of the number of Anzacs assembled in the Abbey, about 250 were wounded or disabled, including many who had been blinded in action or as the result of wounds. These brave fellows were accorded special seats, in situations favourable for hearing the service.

The New Zealanders carried with them to the Abbey a magnificent chaplet of English roses surrounded by fern leaves, the National Emblem of New Zealand, bearing the following inscription :—

" **To the honour and immortal memory of the Heroic Dead of the 29th Division, from their New Zealand Comrades in arms, Gallipoli, 1915.**"

This beautiful floral emblem was hung on the Chancel rails.

THE SERVICE IN THE ABBEY.

Immediately after the arrival of the King and Queen, who were met at the West Door by the Dean (Bishop Ryle) and Sub-Dean (Bishop Boyd Carpenter), and escorted to the Sacrarium, where they took their seats, the service opened with Dr. Walsham How's hymn, " For all the Saints who from their labours rest," sung to Sir Joseph Barnby's music. This was followed by the Lord's Prayer and the Collects and Wesley's anthem, " Ascribe unto the Lord," after which the Dean, facing the congregation, spoke as follows :—

Let us now unite in praise and thanksgiving for those our brothers who died in Gallipoli for their King and Empire, in the high cause of Freedom and Honour. More especially do we commemorate the names of the following troops who took part in the landing :—

Australian : 1st—4th Brigades of Infantry ; 1st—3rd Brigades of Artillery ; with Engineers, Army Service, Medical, Veterinary, Ordnance, Naval Brigading Corps.

New Zealand : Divisional and Infantry Brigade Headquarters ; The Auckland, Wellington, Canterbury, Otago Battalions ; with Field Artillery, Engineers, Medical, and Army Service Corps.

All these fought most valiantly. Their deeds will be remembered evermore. Their memorial is already inscribed in men's hearts. In future ages the sons of our Empire will seek to emulate the imperishable renown of their daring and bravery. We are resolved that, by God's gracious favour, our brothers shall not have laid down their lives in vain.

" Greater love hath no man than this, that a man lay down his life for his friends."

" The eternal God is thy dwelling-place, and underneath are the everlasting arms."

" Thou wilt keep him in perfect peace, whose mind is stayed on Thee, because he trusteth in Thee."

The Doxology having been sung by the congregation, the Dean offered three special prayers, the congregation kneeling.

All stood to sing " The Recessional " (to the tune " Melita," by J. B. Dykes), which was followed by the National Anthem. The " Last Post " was then sounded by 16 Trumpeters of the New Zealand Contingent.

The congregation then dimissed. As the King and Queen were being escorted to the West Door by the Dean and Sub-Dean, his Majesty stopped to speak to and shake hands with Corporal Geange, a member of the New Zealand Expeditionary Force, who is suffering from paralysis as the result of injuries received in Gallipoli. At the West Door, the Abbey clergy were presented to the King by Earl Kitchener.

The officiating clergy were the Dean (Bishop Ryle), the Sub Dean (Bishop Boyd Carpenter), the Precentor (Rev. L. H. Nixon), Canons Pearce, Carnegie, and Charles, and Minor Canons Perkins, Aikin-Sneath, and Westlake. Sir Frederick Bridge and Dr. Alcock presided at the organ, and the former also conducted the massed band of the Australians and New Zealanders, which played selections fron Handel before the service.

The following are the names of the New Zealand officers who were present at Westminster Abbey :—

Brigadier-General G. S. Richardson, C.M.G. ; Colonel J. G. Hughes, C.M.G., D.S.O. ; Lieut.-Col. C. H. J. Brown, D.S.O. ; Major T. H. Dawson (O.C., N.Z., Base Depot) ; Major A. G. B. Price (Adjutant N.Z. Base Depot), Major J. Brunt, Capts. H. Short, (S.M.O., N.Z. Base Depot), J. H. Herrold, L. Shera, E. Harston, A. Butler, C. Dobson, G. Elliott (Quartermaster N.Z. Base Depot), P. Tahiwi, W. Sinclair, Lieuts. A. E. Alexander, E. H. Beamish, A. C. Boyes, J. W. Bright, L. G. Chaytor, H. A. Christie, F. Codd, A.P.M., J. D. Dryden, J. P. Ferris, G. H. Forsythe, E. H. Gabites, W. Haeata, R. D. Hardie, A. Jack, J. Langridge, F. Milroy, J. McPherson, J. P. Martin, A. Rout, R. J. E. Smith, C. F. Smedley, F. L. G. West, M. J. White, A. J. Wigley, C. E. Wyett, and the Rev. A. J. Parry (Hon. Chaplain to the N.Z. Base Depot).

EN PASSANT.

Anzac Day—the celebration in the heart of the Empire of the anniversary of the landing of the Australian and New Zealand Forces at Gallipoli—has come and gone. It has been an event not readily to be forgotten by those who have been privileged to take part in it. A new day of dignity and honour has been added to the calendar of the Empire. No circumstance was lacking to make the occasion illustrious. The skies, as if in high cabal with Britons, whether at home or from overseas, were benignant. It was a day of warm and genial sunshine such as we have not known in these latitudes since—may one say without mockery ?—mid-January. The London populace, eager to render tribute to their fellow-kinsmen whose gallantry and self-sacrifice in the Empire's cause have moved every heart, were able to throng the streets in comfort and with undimmed spirits and undivided energies, to gaze at and cheer for those whom they delighted to honour. The march of the Australian and New Zealand sections from the Strand to the Abbey was a triumphal progress. The commemoration Service at the Abbey, which was attended by the King and Queen, many Ministers of State, and soldiers of high rank, was one of the most moving and impressive ceremonies that even the ancient Abbey, with all its records of a thousand years, has ever known. No nobler requiem have soldiers ever known ; and the comrades of the fallen, who filled yesterday the shrine of England's highest and most heroic memories, cannot but have felt that henceforward Westminster Abbey is theirs, even as it never was before. Anzac Day has written an inscription on the Abbey rolls which will endure as long as the rolls themselves.

It was a great day—a day, too, of other great happenings. Yet no other events could dim the success and the impressiveness of Anzac Day, the incidents and memories of which must constitute another bond between the Homeland and the Dominions beyond the Seas. Londoners are little likely to forget the experience, in which their hearts were so deeply stirred and engaged. And it is not presumptuous to declare that our kinsmen from Australia and New Zealand, who found themselves so much the heroes of the hour, are as little likely to forget the experience either.

(*Morning Post.*)

THE RETURN TO HORNCHURCH.

The gallant Anzacs looked pleased and happy with their splendid reception in the greatest of all great cities on their return to Hornchurch at about 2 p.m. Many of them were wearing roses and other floral emblems in their hats, which their fair admirers had showered upon them during their triumphal march, and the big drum was decked with a beautiful floral wreath tied with blue ribbon. These men had the proud knowledge of having taken part in one of the most memorable and historic military pageants ever held in the capital, which many of them, but for this war, would probably never have seen. More native New Zealanders have stood on London Bridge than ever Macaulay could have dreamt of in his philosophy ; but, unlike his " solitary New Zealander," they have gazed on the might and magnificence of London, and have looked upon the glories of the great city, and not upon its smoking ruins. That was a fantastic dream of a great writer ; and also the dream and desire of the German Emperor, but its fulfilment is not yet !

At 3.30 o'clock the guests began to arrive at the Headquarters, Grey Towers, and very soon the lawn in front of the Mansion was crowded with friends of the New Zealanders, including many Hornchurch folk. A great number of the visitors came from London and other parts, and the large motor char-a-bancs of the contingent were kept busily engaged bringing party after party from the stations at Hornchurch and Romford.

At 5 o'clock tea was served on the lawn, and immediately afterwards General Sir William Birdwood arrived. He remained in front of the Mansion for some little time, and after receiving the Officers of the Contingent, many of the assembled company were introduced to him.

THE REVIEW.

The General then proceeded to the Parade Ground, accompanied by Sir Thomas Mackenzie, K.C.M.G., High Commissioner for New Zealand, Brigadier-General G. S. Richardson, C.M.G. (Officer commanding the New Zealand Forces in the United Kingdom), Lt.-Col. C. H. J. Brown, D.S.O., Col. J. Hughes, C.M.G., D.S.O., and Lieutenant W. Haeata. On their arrival at the saluting base on the north side of the parade ground, where was unfurled the New Zealand flag, the troops, under the command of Major T. H. Dawson, with the following staff :—Major A. G. B. Price, Captain H. Short, S.M.O., and Captain G. Eliott—presented arms, and the general salute was given.

General Birdwood then moved slowly up and down the long khaki lines, closely inspecting the men, and now and again stopping to chat with them or to shake hands. The inspection over, the troops marched past in column, General Sir William Birdwood taking the salute.

They afterwards formed up into three sides of a square, and Sir Thomas Mackenzie then read the following message from the Prime Minister of New Zealand :—

Convey to all our brave New Zealand soldiers at to-day's gathering hearty good wishes. Their friends and comrades of the Dominion are proud of their gallant deeds, and a hearty welcome awaits them on their return. Express New Zealand's warmest congratulations to those who are to be presented with medals. MASSEY.

The High Commissioner, in the course of his address to the troops, said some people considered that, as the Anzac soldiers were not successful in their enterprise, only loss had resulted. That was a profound delusion. They could not discuss the propriety or otherwise of the line of action taken by the Imperial Government, but they did know that the bringing together of so many men representing the Mother Country and the Dominions in a great enterprise of war had developed a mutual friendliness and cemented a bond, which nothing could sunder either now or in the years to come. In one respect New Zealand seemed to have discovered the coming cloud of sinister events earlier than the home Government. During 1909-10, while those guiding affairs in the centre of the Empire thought that everything made for the maintenance of peace and goodwill among men, New Zealand, on the other hand, was quite sure that the time had not arrived for beating swords into ploughshares. So New Zealand, in common with Australia, set about the passing of an Act to compel their people to train for defence. "We were rather amazed," the High Commissioner continued, "to find afterwards that while we—13,000 miles away—perceived what was threatening, those entrusted with the destinies of the Empire—only 300 miles away from the seat of danger—

did not appear to think that anything possible could go wrong. We are to be consulted with regard to terms of peace. We hope to be consulted also—and that very soon—regarding questions which are of common interest within the Empire. We, for our part, are intensely in earnest on the point that there shall be adequate defence for the British Empire, and this can only be done with land and sea forces commensurate with our enormous responsibilities. The larger questions of trade will, no doubt, engage the attention of our ablest men, and we, for our part, keenly desire to increase our trading relationships within the Empire. I am confident the virility of the British people was never greater. All they require is to be told what is necessary to win the war, and they will respond to the uttermost limits of their power and abilities. We in New Zealand hold that the first duty of citizenship is to defend our country and maintain it for those who will come after us."

At the conclusion of his speech the High Commissioner received a tremendous ovation from the Officers and men, and he then called for three cheers for General Sir William Birdwood, humorously remarking that, although it might not be in accordance with military etiquette for him to do so, he was not under the General's orders, and therefore could not be expected to conform to such restrictions as were involved in military codes. The cheers were given in that hearty and staccato manner so peculiar to the New Zealanders.

Sir William Birdwood then rose to address the men. Before he had been speaking many minutes it was easy to realize how it was he had obtained the inspiring title of the "Soul of Anzac," and when he repeatedly addressed his audience as "lads" and "boys," he appeared more comrade than great General. His sound and good advice was interspersed with such genuine good humour that it was little wonder that he was able to grip them as few men have been able to do. He told them that, although they had done well, and had never failed to rise to the occasion, they had still a lot more hot fighting to do before they got their enemy where they wanted him. All the world had heard of their glorious work. Out on the Peninsula, time after time, he had seen men climbing up the steep hills in the extreme heat, and standing in the trenches under the most trying conditions. On one occasion he met a man carrying two heavy water bottles. "Rather heavy, aren't they?" he asked, "Oh, yes; pretty heavy," was the reply, "They would not be nearly so heavy if they were full of rum." They argued it out and came to the conclusion that if it were rum the bottles would probably be lighter and the man would be heavier, and, possibly, never get on at all. Only on two occasions had he heard grumbling. The first time was from the men who were not in the first line in the landing at Gallipoli, and the same thing occurred in the evacuation.

GENERAL SIR WILLIAM BIRDWOOD ADDRESSING THE NEW ZEALAND TROOPS
IN GREY TOWERS PARK, APRIL 25TH, 1916.

He was going down the trenches on 19th December and heard several men complain that they were not in the rear-guard action. These were the only complaints he heard. He happened to write to the Private Secretary to the King, giving him an account of the evacuation and he replied :—" The part of your letter which gave the greatest pleasure to the King was where you described the men's complaints that they were not the last to leave. With men of that sort you must, indeed, be proud of your Corps "— " *And I am proud of my Corps, and you know it jolly well,*" added the General, " *you are all ' dinkums ' *" He had not the privilege of being born in the Southern Hemisphere, but he was a soldier of Anzac, and he hoped he might continue to be throughout this war.

He went on to speak of the work which lay before them in France, and expressed his confidence in their " carrying on " in a manner which would add still more honour and glory to their records in this war. He then gave them a few practical hints, and emphasized the necessity of training and discipline. He pointed out how much more valuable a soldier was as a fighter when he was thoroughly trained and disciplined, than one who was not efficient in those qualifications, and concluded by saying that there were three great essentials to a soldier :—(1) fighting, (2) training, (3) discipline ; and the greatest of these was discipline, without which no soldier could hope to become a great fighter.

Rousing cheers again greeted the popular General at the close of his speech, and he then distributed the Distinguished Conduct Medals to the following non-commissioned officers and men :—

Sergeant-Major B. S. Boate, Quarter-Master-Sergeant Graham, Sergt. Major A. W. Abbey, Sergeant Tavender, Acting-Sergeant Hill, Sergeants Spencer, Watson, Bennett, Corporal Skinner, Driver Clarke, Sergeant Comrie, Private Stockdell, Private Crawford-Watson.

The Band then played the National Anthem, and brought to a close one of the most unique and eventful ceremonies ever held in our village.

A most pathetic incident connected with the Review was the appearance on the parade ground of Trooper Clutha Mackenzie, of the Wellington Mounted Rifles, son of Sir Thomas Mackenzie, a splendid fellow, standing over six feet high, who had lost his sight in the fighting on the Gallipoli Peninsula.

COMMEMORATION TELEGRAMS.

The Officer commanding the Depot forwarded the following telegrams to the undermentioned Units on Anzac Day :—

" On this the Anniversary of our great adventure, may we New Zealanders tender our tribute to the immortal and glorious valour of the Battalion of your Regiment which we have the Honour to claim as Comrades in Arms." 5TH ROYAL SCOTS, WORCESTER REGIMENT, BORDER

Regiment, Hampshire Regiment, Munster Fusiliers, Lancashire Fusiliers, South Wales Borderers, King's Own Scottish Borderers, Royal Inniskilling Fusiliers, Dublin Fusiliers, Royal Fusiliers, Essex Regiment.

" On this the Anniversary of our great adventure may we the New Zealanders tender our tribute to the immortal and glorious valour of the Indian Troops with whom we had the honour of serving." Indian Troops.

" On this the Anniversary of our great adventure may we the New Zealanders tender our tribute to the immortal and glorious valour of the Royal Naval Division which we have the honour to claim as Comrades in Arms." Royal Naval Division.

CONGRATULATORY TELEGRAMS.

The following replies were received :—

" On behalf of the Indian Army I tender thanks for your timely and happy message of comradeship in arms. That comradeship will further cement the unity of the Empire. I am telegraphing the message to India where it will be warmly appreciated." Secretary of State, India.

" We are proud to be associated with you in an enterprise in which the New Zealanders by their glorious valour earned a reputation which will live with the greatest in the British Army." King's Own Scottish Borderers.

" On behalf of all ranks and battalions of the Royal Inniskilling Fusiliers I beg to thank you for your cordial message, nothing I can say can express our admiration of the wonderful valour of the New Zealanders." Royal Inniskilling Fusiliers.

" Your greetings on the glorious anniversary are reciprocated by all ranks South Wales Borderers who are proud to have been associated with the valiant New Zealanders and look forward to further co-operation to final victory." South Wales Borderers.

" The Essex Regiment have received with pride and pleasure the tribute from their New Zealand Comrades by whose side they consider it an honour to have fought. It will live in their hearts as as undying memento of Comradeship and pride in the solidarity of the Empire that far away sons and themselves are one. Again they thank you." Essex Regiment.

" Edinburgh and Scotland will join us in the warm reciprocation of your telegram which will bind us close to your great Dominion. To you New Zealanders with whose comradeship we were so greatly honoured in the high achievement of a year ago, the Fifth Royal Scots send greetings and remembrances of your undying daring." Fifth Royal Scots.

" On behalf of all ranks of the Battalion Hampshire Regiment I thank you for your telegram tendering your tribute to our Regiment, which message will be sent to that Battalion. I can assure you that they also will ever remember the glorious deeds of the New Zealanders." Hampshire Regiment.

" I have to sincerely thank you on behalf of the 1st Battalion Border Regiment for your kind telegram of to-day's date and it gave me great pleasure to forward same to that Battalion now in France." Border Regiment.

" Thanks for your kind message, proud that the Regiment were associated with the gallant New Zealanders. Wish you all luck in the future." Lancashire Fusiliers.

" The Royal Fusiliers return cordial thanks to their comrades of the New Zealanders for their kind message and tender them the heartfelt thanks attributed on the anniversary of the glorious deed." Royal Fusiliers.

" Please accept my most grateful thanks for the telegram you so kindly sent me on the 25th inst. Your generous words of appreciation have greatly touched me, and I shall have the greatest pleasure in forwarding your wire to the 1st Battalion of my Regiment to whom they refer, and who will, I am sure, greatly value the good opinion of their New Zealand comrades.—B. S. STEWART, Colonel., MUNSTER FUSILIERS.

" TE WHARE PUNI."
(*The Meeting House*).

Te Whare Puni was a continuation of the New Zealanders' Club which was opened in London, at 3, Victoria Street during the last week of November, 1915, and which was known as " The Dug-Out." The latter was initiated by Miss Hilda Williams, and was the outcome of a great desire to provide a quiet place, where the lonely and still weak soldiers of the New Zealand contingent could rest and obtain good home-made food and refreshment at moderate cost, after leaving Hospital ; the wish of the promoters being to provide as homelike an atmosphere as possible.

When the New Zealand Base was definitely established at Grey Towers, it was decided to extend the efforts of the Club to Hornchurch, and four ladies from the " Dug-Out " came down to the village for that purpose on February 16th, 1916. Their preparation and arrangements succeeded so well that on March 5th, 1916, a Club was opened in Hornchurch with Reading and Writing room, and a small Buffet in a room which could only accommodate about 15 to 20 men at a time.

The erection of the handsome and commodious Hut " Te Whare Puni " in Butts Green Road, was then taken in hand, and after many unavoidable delays in building it, was successfully accomplished. That it was completed early in the month of April was largely due to the help of soldier carpenters, who, unfortunately, had to leave for active service in France before it was opened on April 10th by Major Dawson, the Commandant of the Camp.

At the opening ceremony Major Dawson made some very kind and appropriate remarks with reference to the promoters and the staff of the New Zealanders' Club, and explained to their soldier guests that the money to finance and carry on the work was supplied by private individuals—New Zealanders—who had no connection with the New Zealand Government, or with any Association or Society.

The work connected with the Club was all voluntary, and chiefly done by ladies—English, as well as those of New Zealand birth—and, although a small charge was made for the food supplied, it was calculated on a basis to cover only the cost of the raw material, and did not aim at " making it pay "—as some people put it—the cost of preparation and production, rent, etc., being provided from the funds.

In " Te Whare Puni " there was a full-sized billiard table, a piano and a gramophone. Small games, newspapers and maga-' zines were also provided. A Tennis Court quite close to the Hut added to the many attractions of this ideal club. The cost of this latter was defrayed mainly by a gift received from New Zealand, with instruction that the money be used for whatever might be " the most pressing need of the moment." Knowing the tastes of the giver Miss Evelyn Williams decided that to use it in the renting of a lawn and to provide a Tennis equipment would be the most satisfactory way of spending the money, and very helpful to the soldiers by enabling them to indulge in a pleasant and recuperative form of recreation.

The promoters and workers of this Club had the satisfaction of knowing that the Hut, with its many advantages, was greatly appreciated by the New Zealand soldiers and no praise can be too great to shower upon those noble women, who, with such splendid self-sacrifice, devoted their time and money to bring a glimpse of home to the brave men who, with the highest patriotic motives, left home, wife, children and kindred, so many thousands of miles away.

EMPIRE DAY, 1916.

Empire Day, May 24, 1916, was celebrated in Essex and throughout the country generally, and in most instances the school children were given a half-holiday.

At the Grey Towers Camp the Zealanders and the children from the village schools held a joint celebration. The arrange-' ments were made by the Rev. A. J. Parry. About 800 soldiers paraded in the park, under the command of Col. C. H. J. Brown, D.S.O., and they presented a splendid appearance. The New Zealand flag having been broken at the masthead, there was a march past. Afterwards the troops were formed into three sides of a square, into which the school children were marched, in charge of Mr. F. Edwards, headmaster ; Miss Spragg, head-mistress ; and Miss Jones, infants' mistress.

Major Dawson then addressed the children. He said :— " In New Zealand the children were that day celebrating Empire Day in exactly the same way as the children of England. They were delighted to have had that opportunity of coming to dear old England—a country they all loved so much, and for which their fathers and their grandfathers had fought. They had passed through an English winter and did not like it at all ; but now they had seen an English summer they were satisfied that England was the loveliest country in the world. In Gallipoli they fought with the 29th Division, of which the Essex Regiment formed part, and they were proud to know that they were now among those whose fathers and brothers had fought by the side of New Zealanders. In conclusion, Major Dawson announced that the New Zealanders had decided to present the Hornchurch schools with three pictures to commemorate their stay in the village, and these would be hung on the school walls.

Suitable addresses were also delivered by the Rev. A. J. Parry, Mr. T. Gardner, Mr. W. Varco Williams, and Mr. F. Edwards ; and at the close Col. Brown thanked the speakers for the complimentary remarks they had passed with reference to the New Zealanders. He called for three cheers for Hornchurch and these were heartily given. The proceedings concluded with the signing of the National Anthem.

ARTS AND CRAFTS AT HORNCHURCH.
NEW ZEALANDERS' EDUCATION CENTRE.

On Friday, December 6, 1918, at Grey Towers Camp, Hornchurch, a memorable gathering was presided over by Brigadier-Gen. Richardson, G.O.C. the New Zealand Expeditionary Force in the United Kingdom. The occasion was the opening of an addition to the Y.M.C.A. hut in the camp, erected by the New Zealand Y.M.C.A., at a cost of £5,000. The hut embraces an education office and many workshops and class-rooms, the whole comprising a headquarters of educational work for the Colonists in England. The hut was inspected by a large number of visitors, including many ladies, and much surprise and pleasure were expressed at the astonishing variety of hand-made goods and other exhibits, tastefully arrayed for the occasion. Such work has been long in vogue at Hornchurch, and the men have proved keen students and skilful craftsmen. The aim of the organiser was to render the men expert workers in many fields, so that on their returun to New Zealand they may find no difficulty in returning to their respective trades or adopting new ones.

Gen. Richardson spoke in high terms of the work of the Y.M.C.A. No other organisation, he was sure, had done so much for the troops. In particular, he thanked the Association for the work done by them in regard to the education of the men. With the help of the Y.M.C.A. that educational centre was now provided, and he thought it better, for its particular purpose, than any other in the country. It owed its very existence to the Y.M.C.A. He desired, especially, to thank the ladies who, for so long had worked in the institution. The work was started by Mr. W. T. Williams and the Misses Williams, and these workers had seen their efforts, so inaugurated, grow into a very big thing, and now it was handed over to the Association. They also felt grateful to many people in Hornchurch who had done much to secure comfort for the men, amongst whom were Mrs. Warren, Mrs. Edmund, Miss Walsh, and Miss Busby. He also thanked Mr. H. Fawcett, secretary of the Centre, and Col. Tewsley, their O.C. at Hornchurch, for their great interest in the work ; it could not have advanced so far without the help of their commanding officer. Col. Tewsley had high ideals in matters educational, and had strongly supported the institution. All that was being carried out at the camp was essential to the best interests of the men. Their camp was for convalescents, and with this in view all possible was done to divert the men's minds from what they had endured at the Front. The whole work of the Y.M.C.A. had meant very much to lonely, homeless men.

Mr. W. H. George, Hon. Commissioner of the N.Z.Y.M.C.A., speaking for the National Council of the Association, acknowledged the help given to the Association in every direction by Gen. Richardson and the officers. The relationships in that camp were most happy. They much appreciated the work done by Mr. Fawcett ; it was the character of the men who ran the Y.M.C.A., even more than money, that made their work successful. Mr. Fawcett's work was of a high grade, and was done for love of it and out of true desire to help the men. It was believed that the work would open out farther yet in New Zealand, and Mr. Hughes was returning in order to help the men to continue the work so well carried on at Hornchurch.

Mr. G. W. W. B. Hughes, Supervising Secretary, expressed the hope that in future the Y.M.C.A. would share in the national life of New Zealand, and said that everything possible would be done by himself as by other members of the staff.

A tour of the workshops and class rooms was then made by Gen. Richardson and the guests.

The New Zealanders finally evacuated Grey Towers in June, 1919.

After the departure of the New Zealanders from Hornchurch the following was received by the Vicar of Hornchurch from Sir Thomas Mackenzie, K.C.M.G., High Commissioner for New Zealand. It was printed in the parish Magazine for October, 1919, and in publishing it the Vicar said :—" It obviously refers to the many who helped to entertain the New Zealanders in Hornchurch, and a letter on their behalf has been sent in acknowledgment to His Excellency."

New Zealand Government Offices,
Strand, W.C. 2.

Dear Sir,

The repatriation of the New Zealand Expeditionary Force is nearing completion, and I desire, before the last of our soldiers has left these hospitable shores, to give expression, not only to my own gratitude, but to that which the Government and people of New Zealand feel towards those who, during the recent years of warfare, have showered on our men who came so many thousands of miles to fight for the Empire.

Those of our soldiers who had never seen this country looked forward with pleasurable anticipation when donning khaki to making acquaintance with the Homeland of their Race, and their expectations have been more than realized. To you special thanks are due ; the hospitality you have extended will long be remembered by those who were so fortunate as to share it.

Believe me,

Yours sincerely,

THOS. MACKENZIE,

Commissioner for New Zealand.

Bon Voyage and " Kia-Ora " :—New Zealand Troops, constituting the last contingent to leave England, left Plymouth last night, February 16, 1920, for home. *" Vide "* Daily Telegraph, Feb. 17-1920.

No. 2 TRANSFER CENTRE.

Before the departure of the whole of the New Zealand troops from Grey Towers, part of the Camp was occupied by No. 2 Transfer Centre. This Centre was formed in June, 1918, at Watford, for dealing with certain types of men in the army, who were found unsuitable for their duties in their regiments, and probably more suitable for other corps. A selection board was attached to this Centre, which represented every branch of His Majesty's Forces, and if, for example, an infantry man was found unable to stand the exertion of long marches, owing to physical disabilities, and yet was an expert rider, he was examined by a selection officer representing the cavalry, and if found suitable, was placed in a regiment of cavalry suited to his capabilities. In the same way an artilleryman, who could not stand the physical strain as a gunner, would probably be a most efficient clerk, and was sent to the Army Pay Corps after examination. These duties of the Transfer Centre (which from June, 1918, until March, 1919, was known as the Eastern Command Transfer Centre) continued until after the armistice.

At the end of 1918 the centre was employed directly under the War Office for the purpose of providing all the dispersal and demobilisation centres of the kingdom with their permanent personnel. Men were received from all fronts, i.e. :—France, Egypt, Mesopotamia, and Salonica, and were dispatched for duty, after reporting, so that the work of demobilisation might be quickly and efficiently carried out. This work occupied about four months, and, at the end of May, No. 2 Transfer Centre, as it was then named, was moved to Grey Towers ; the public buildings and schools, which it had occupied at Watford, being urgently needed for civilian requirements.

On arrival at Hornchurch, it took up quarters on the west side of Grey Towers Camp, and the few New Zealand troops which still remained in occupation were soon afterwards dispatched to other units or to their Colony. From this date " Grey Towers " house itself was not further used.

Whilst quartered at Grey Towers the centre was occupied in transferring men to a more suitable corps, and the system previously employed in 1918 was again adopted. In this instance, however, it dealt entirely with soldiers who were not demobilizable during that year (1919), owing to their having volunteered for a further term of service, or through their having joined the army later than the year 1915, A large amount of clerical work being required for the disembodiment of the men, many of these soldiers were appointed to regiments chiefly concerned with organizing duties, so that, in spite of the rapid depletion of the forces at that time, a nucleus was still kept in hand to carry out the necessary administration.

The centre was a small unit, consisting of sixteen officers and a hundred other ranks as permanent staff, the Executive Officers being :—

Commanding :—Lieut. Col. N. E. J. BOURKE, Manchester Regt.
Second in Command :—Major J. MARSHALL, R.A.S.C.
Adjutant :—Captain L. A. LUCAS, Middlesex Regt.

From the commencement of its duties to the date of disembodiment the centre dealt with, approximately, 35,000 men.

There were only two Transfer Centres in England :—No. 1 at Ripon, and No. 2 at Hornchurch, both directly under the War Office. Orders were received towards the end of November, 1919, for these centres to be disbanded, as, owing to the army once again returning to its peace time basis, the temporary men who had previously been dealt with would be demobilised forthwith, and the need for this organisation was therefore no longer necessary.

This brought to an end the military occupation of Grey Towers, and Hornchurch once more returned to a peace-time village.

SPECIAL CONSTABULARY.

HORNCHURCH SECTION—ROMFORD DIVISION.

A night-watch constable . . . .*
When others sleep upon their quiet beds—
Constrained to watch in darkness, rain and cold.†
Shakespeare.

Special Constables were sworn in all over the country to assist the regular police in carrying out their duties, and a large and efficient auxiliary force patrolled our highways from sunset to sunrise, and in other ways contributed to the keeping of public order. Hornchurch was part of the Romford Division

*Love's labour lost, III., i.
†Henry VI., II., i.

Photo]   HORNCHURCH SPECIAL CONSTABLES, 1919.   [F. Gandon.

of the Essex Special Constabulary, and recruiting for this section opened in August 1914. On 4th September, nine residents were sworn in at the Old School Room on Church Hill, and on September 11th a further 46 men were sworn, as well as Mr. Burnett Tabrum, J.P., of Romford, who had recently been appointed Superintendent of the Special Constabulary for the Romford Division. He informed the Special Police at that meeting that they must elect one of their number to act as Parish Officer with the rank of sergeant. Mr. George Marsh Horey was unanimously elected to fill that office, and he appointed as his Squad Corporals, Messrs. F. J. Ashton. G. E. Baker, W. Brander, B. W. Bryan, J. D. Cockwell, W. Dendy, L. H. Hatting, W. Mc Dermott, and H. G. Pearce. The section commenced its duties on Sept. 29th, 1916 by a patrol of the whole of the roads and lanes in the Parish. This was only a link in the chain of patrolling that was carried on all round the coast, and within a 6 mile radius from the coast and the tidal rivers, from Durham to Dorset inclusive. The local patrol duty was worked in three shifts, and three patrols each shift, from 8 p.m. to 5 a.m. and constituted 9 miles of patrolling for each duty, making a total distance patrolled each night of eighty miles.

The total strength of the local force was soon raised to 79 of all ranks, and even with this number, it entailed a duty for each member of three hours every third night. This was carried on for 18 months, and then the hostile air raids commenced, which necessitated considerable alterations in the organization, in order to be in readiness to render any assistance or " first-aid " which might be necessary, or to provide shelter for those who might be rendered homeless. Several householders and the local Nursing Corps came forward for this purpose, but owing to many of its members having taken up other work, and removed from the district, other arrangements had to be made. The New Zealand Convalescent Hospital had, by this time, been well established at Grey Towers, and Sergeant Horey informed the Commanding Officer of the position, and put the possible need of " first aid " before him. As the outcome of this, a properly equipped motor ambulance, with all medical appliances, and the necessary personnel was held in readiness on re-receiving warning of a raid. From that time until the Armistice this provision was strictly carried out, but fortunately actual service was not required.

One of the most important duties required of the Special Constables was to make themselves acquainted with the instructions of the Local Emergency Committee, as, in the event of an invasion on the coast, the population would have had to be removed, housed, and fed ; stores, cattle, horses and transport vehicles to be mobilized and moved to an arranged place ; and the traffic on the roads to be regulated, so as to permit the unhindered passage of the military. This was all arranged in detail, and a test call was made on one occasion, the inspecting officers being Supt. W. T. J. Howlett of the Essex Police, and Chief Supt. A. E. Box of the Special Constabulary, who visited all points in the Parish, and expressed their great satisfaction, every man being in his place, and able to answer correctly all questions put to him as to his duties in the event of a specific emergency arising.

During the 4½ years of their service the public saw very little of the Special Constables, except, perhaps, when a careless householder happened to be showing too much light, and then he was promptly acquainted of the fact by one of them, and duly warned of the consqeuences. Their measured tread was, however, often heard in the dead of the night. Often, too, they were out in strong force awaiting the consummation of a first warning of approaching enemy aircraft, and ready either to take up their air raid posts, or, in the event of a threatened raid not maturing, the order to resume normal conditions, in which case those not on actual patrol duty would be free to go back to their homes and beds, and the general residents would be unaware that anything out of the ordinary had happened.

It was the expressed opinion of the chief officers of the County Constabulary that it was largely due to the diligent manner in which the Special Constabulary enforced the Lighting Order that the county suffered so little by hostile aircraft, although in the direct line of flight of nearly all the enemy aircraft in their passage to London.

In recognition of services rendered a General Order, dated 17 June, 1917, promoted all Sergeants to Inspectors, and Corporals to Sergeants.

The " Specials " paraded for service at the Parish Church or Armistice Sunday, November 17, 1918, and also attended the National Peace Thanksgiving Service on Sunday 6 July, 1918, when over 40 members were present. This was the last parade held by the section. Demobilization took place on Monday, 14 July, 1919.

Forty-seven members qualified by three years service and 150 hours of duty for the special Police Medal.

Mr. and Mrs. T. Gardner invited all the local " Specials " to a smoking concert and social evening at the schoolroom, North Street, on December 15, 1917, and on May 17, 1919, they were entertained to dinner at the White Hart Hotel, Romford, by Mr. W. Varco Williams, J.P., C.C., and Mr. Thomas Gardner, J.P., C.C. On that occasion, while Chief Superintendent A. E. Box, and Superintendent W. T. J. Howlett expressed their complete satisfaction with the efficiency and zeal displayed by the members in carrying out their allotted tasks, and praised them for their unselfish devotion to duty at all times and in all weathers,

Mr. Williams expressed the appreciation of the community for the loyal and willing service rendered by them, and remarked that it was not easy to adequately measure the value of that service which had been so ungrudgingly given over so long a period, and which reflected the greatest possible credit on them individually and collectively, and on the parish to which they belonged.

I feel sure I shall be voicing the views of my fellow parishioners in endorsing those sentiments, and in offering Inspector Horey and his officers and men our heartiest thanks for all the good work done by them for our security and comfort during the strenuous days of the great war, and when it is borne in mind that, in the majority of cases, their police duty had to be done "after the burden and heat of the day," we shall the better realize the full value of their service on our behalf.

This record would be lacking in appreciation if mention were not made of the valuable assistance rendered to the " Specials " by our genial Police Sergeant J. H. Crowe. They found him an able instructor, whose advice was always readily and cheerfully given.

Inspector Horey was not only a most zealous and painstaking officer, but was most popular with his men. The measure of his popularity was shown by the presentation which was made to him by the members of his section, on July 24, 1919, of a handsome cigarette box, inscribed as follows :—

Presented to
INSPECTOR G. M. HOREY
By his Colleagues in the Hornchurch Section
as a Token of their appreciation of his
considerate and tactful leadership
during the period of
the Great War.

MEMBERS OF THE HORNCHURCH SECTION, ROMFORD DIVISION, ESSEX SPECIAL CONSTABULARY, WITH PERIODS OF SERVICE.

1914 to Demobilisation :—*Inspector* G. M. Horey.

Sergeants :—F. J. Ashton, B. W. Bryan, G. E. Baker, J. D. Cockwell, W. Denby, L. H. Hatting, W. McDermott.

Special Constables :—A. E. Alp, W. C. Allen, R. W. Beard, S. A. Bannister, J. Breckels, F. M. Barrington, C. Cheek, T. J. Catherwood, J. T. Childs, W. G. Card, J. R. S. Dixon, C. Dunlop, T. C. Davis, G. Edwards, A. Ferguson, S. Goodenough, F. W. Gillman, C. Green, S. F. Gibson, F. Hall, P. Home, C. H. Hollinghurst, G. Hurrell, J. Lester, W. J. Low, E. H. Robinson, E. S. Robinson, J. H. Searle, F. W. Taylor, S. T. Turner, S. T. Watkinson, C. W. Wheeler, E. Watson.

1915 to Demobilisation :—G. Blake, E. G. Bratchell, W. Clippingdale, T. Crawford.

1916 to Demobilisation :—W. C. Harper, R. J. Pearce, E. C. Robson, J. A. Shears, T. W. Smith, W. H. Woodall.

1918 to Demobilisation :—W. Alliston, H. G. Brown, A. Barker, J. F Stradwick.

Resigned to join H.M. Forces, with period served in Special Constabulary. :—

1914–15 :—F. Harvey, J. Moss.

1914–1916 : A. J. Mills.

1914–1917 :—A. E. Battle, B. J. Cuthbertson, H. V. Field, B. J. Jackson, A. J. Parry.

1914–1918 :—J. B. Conly,* H. G. Pearce, T. W. S. Townsend.

1915–1916 :—J. W. Jarvis, J. G. McDougal.

1916–1917 :—G. Bannister, W. M. G. Comley.

Resignations, with Periods of Service.

1914–1915 :—W. Brander, C. J. Beharell, L. Budd, O. Bentley, H. L. Ewens, S. Home, J. E. Houseman, H. J. Jordan, R. H. Palmer, T. Rookwood, W. Slater, H. Wright.

1914–1916 :—A. A. P. Chalke, L. D'Ascoli, J. R. Hawkins, T. A. Jones, W. Langton, A. E. Palmer, B. Van Trump, W. K. Youlden.

1914–1917 :—A. Gaff, H. Green.

1914–1918 :—C. E. Feast, J. W. Shepherd, W. Smith.

1915–1916 :—S. B. Earle.

1915–1917 :—H. L. Symonds.

1916–1917 :—A. C. Payne.

1916–1918 :—C. L. French.

Deaths, and Periods of Service.

1914–1918 :—Sergeant H. G. Pearce, Constable Leonard Newth.

1914–1917 :—Constable W. L. C. Coxall. Resigned in 1916 owing to ill health, and died February, 1917.

1916–1917 :—Constable S. A. J. Floyd.

The following parishioners served in sections of the Special Constabulary outside the Hornchurch Section, Romford Division :—

Bass, Leonard W.—Wickford, September, 1914.—June, 1918.

Bassett, Herbert Alfred.—Romford, September, 1914, October, 1916.

Bratchell, E. G.—Romford, Emergency Committee, 1914–1919.

Muskett, Herbert Chas. W.—Four years.

Perfect, Charles Thomas.—Orsett Division, Grays Emergency Committee, 1914–1919.

Powell, Arthur John.—Section Commander, City of London Police Reserve, August, 1914—February, 1918.

Harold Wood Special Police will be found under the Harold Wood Chapter.

---

*Resigned on appointment to a Commission in the V.T.C.

PUBLIC MEETING ON THE SECOND ANNIVERSARY OF THE WAR.

"Come the three corners of the world in arms,
And we shall shock them. Naught shall make us rue,
If England to itself do rest but true."
Shakespeare :—King John, Act. v., Sc. vii.

On Friday evening, August 4, 1916, the second anniversary of the declaration of war, a public meeting was held in Fairkytes Meadow, Billet Lane, to pass a resolution declaring inflexible determination to continue the war to a victorious conclusion, similar resolutions being passed at meetings all over the country. Mr. J. R. Robertson presided, and was supported by Sir John Bethell, Bart., M.P., Mr. Thomas Gardner, J.P., C.C., Major Dawson, N.Z.E.F., Rev. Herbert Dale, Rev. Peter Miller, Major J. M. Ewing, etc.

Photo]   *[Luffs, Hornchurch.*

"FAIRKYTES." BILLET LANE UNDER SNOW.

A very large concourse of Hornchurch people gathered together in the picturesque meadow in the centre of our ancient village. The Romford and district detachment of the Essex Cadets, under Captain A. S. Maskelyne was on parade, and the Hornchurch band was in attendance.

After the Chairman had addressed the meeting, Sir John Bethell proposed the resolution, as follows :—

" That on this, the Second Anniversary of the declaration of a righteous War, this Meeting of the citizens of Hornchurch records its inflexible determination to continue to a victorious end the struggle in the maintenance of those ideals of Liberty and Justice which are the common and sacred cause of the Allies."

Major Dawson seconded the resolution, which was carried with great enthusiasm.

The band played the national anthems of the allies, and patriotic songs were sung by Miss Lena Kirkman and Mr. John Challis.

Mr. W. Varco Williams, being unable to attend in consequence of illness, sent a stirring and patriotic letter, which was read in its entirety to the meeting.

A feature of the evening was a persistent echo, which created considerable interest, and which was commented on in the " Romford Times " as under :—

" Emphasis to the declaration of Hornchurch people that they are inflexibly resolved to continue the war to a victorious end was given by an echo, which followed the proceedings with the closest attention. It was insistent in repeating the words of the speakers as distinctly as they were uttered, and the experience was an eerie one, both for those on the platform and for those in the audience. The scene was a pleasant tree-girt meadow, in the cool of the evening, and the words which came back from nowhere were uttered from a flag-bedecked wagon stationed under the branches of a walnut tree. Probably it was the first time in history that the field had been the scene of speech-making, and probably the echo had for the first time been aroused from slumber to reveal its presence at a momentous period of national life. Further testing of its powers may reveal more startling wonders, but never will the echo have the opportunity to be more emphatic on the nation's policy with regard to the war than on the occasion of which it took so full and free advantage. Hornchurch people are loyal and patriotic to the core, and the echo which has its home in their midst is at one with them. Its declaration of its unalterable sentiments was so insistent that it was somewhat disconcerting. It had to be borne with, however, for an order to " turn that fellow out " would have come back from the beyond with all its peremptoriness ; and an echo can laugh at regular police and special constables—if only it will deign to laugh."

THE WINDMILL AND MILL COTTAGE.

THE CIVIL VOLUNTARY EFFORT IN THE WAR.

" I'll employ thee too ;
But do not look for further recompense
Than thine own gladness that thou are employ'd."
Shakespeare :—As you like it, III., v.

INTRODUCTORY.

Those who were imbued with the spirit of the above quotation during the war were legion. Never was there such a time for individual effort! Everybody served!! Everybody worked!!! The civilian contribution to the work of the nation was a veritable triumph of voluntaryism, and was aptly described, while hostilities were in progress, by the " Daily Graphic " in the following words :

"In that retrospective survey of the war which will be possible when peace happily returns, an aspect of outstanding worth will be the marvellous manner in which the nation has 'mothered' our fighting forces. Voluntaryism established an enviable record in recruiting, but has been exhausted and obliged to give place to compulsion. No such necessity has arisen in the realm of philanthropy. The nation has not grown weary, and will not, of ministering in a multitude of ways to the comforts of our troops. In Red Cross and V.A.D. work alone the superb services which have been rendered without the least recompense would suffice to give this war a unique character. But when the full story of countless other activities is told, from the canteens manned by voluntary helpers to the hearty hospitality of private homes, it will be recognised how the conflict has revealed the inexhaustible depths of human sympathy and practical benevolence."

At a later date—when Peace had once more been established —the " Observer," in its description of the Great Victory March through London of July 19, 1919, made the following appreciative reference to the part played by the nation as a whole :—

"What we have to be grateful for is that strength of the modest years, not specialised in gladiators, but possessed of millions of unassuming and obscure individuals. Character, in a word, and a just cause brought to nothing as powerful an agglomeration of mechanical power devices as the world has seen. For Germany the war was a trial of its perverted chivalry. It was to be the apogee of an army steeped in the creed of force, confident in its equipment, and devoted in pitiful loyalty to a stage Alexander in horrific trappings. On us the war descended as a trial not so much of the British forces as of the British people, and, in obedience to necessity, these two became one. Never before have we waged a national war as this was. The army was the people and the people was the army ; some, as their youth allowed, served at the battle front, and the rest, as age or sex insisted, lived and worked along the great lines of communication that ran from the front, back through the war zones and across the water, into their very homes. While the war lasted it could be said of few that they were not " in the service." Those who have served are entitled to regard the march of yesterday as their own parade, though time and space and the Office of Works should forbid a parade of the nation."

—*Observer*, July 20, 1919.

In endeavouring to place on record the public and semi-public work accomplished in our village, I have done my utmost to make it as complete as possible, but I am fully conscious that it cannot be absolutely so. I doubt not there are many who " did their bit " in their own quiet unostentatious way, and no one knew it, and there were probably few who in those troublous days did not place many good actions to their credit, which will for ever go unrecorded. All such have their reward in that inward satisfaction which must always be experienced by the doers of good deeds in secret.

There were, however, many of our parishioners whose self-imposed, and oftentimes arduous tasks, were more or less of a public character, and were of necessity done in the open, and it is of these and their works that this chapter of my book will for the most part be devoted.

One of the first matters which claimed the attention of our parishioners was in connection with the newly-formed camp for recruits at Purfleet. News came that there was a serious shortage of blankets and rugs for the men at that camp, and in consequence a house-to-house collection was immediately made, which resulted in a goodly number of blankets being sent over by motor car the same night. Similar supplies were repeated on several successive days.

Immediately after the declaration of war, measures were taken to ascertain in what ways the civil community could be of assistance to the fighting forces of the King. Meetings were held with a view to the formation of first-aid classes, working parties, and the like, and many useful schemes were set on foot which served their purpose for the time being. I reproduce here the first invitation to the public to join in work of this description in Hornchurch. Some of the ideas which originated at this time developed afterwards on definite lines, as will be found recorded later on in this chapter.

TO THE WOMEN OF HORNCHURCH.

An Appeal for our Soldiers and Sailors in the War.

A hurriedly called informal meeting of ladies was held (through the kind permission of Mrs. Gardner and at her suggestion at her house), on Saturday Afternoon, August 8th, 1914, to consider whether, following the action taken in the parish at the outbreak of the Boer war, a collection of money should not immediately be made from the women of the Parish, to purchase materials, and whether invitations should not be issued to form working parties to make up those materials into necessaries for our Soldiers and Sailors.

The following ladies undertook to try and gather in subscriptions and help in forming working parties and giving advice and information as to the various arrangements from time to time. The Mrs. Aller, Ashton, Attwood, Baker, C. H. Baker, Junr., Bletsoe. Burden, Card, Dale, Dendy, Ewing, Gardner, Ivey, J. D. Johnson, Lambe, McMullen. Miller. Pailthorpe, Parry, Perfect, Purbrook, J. R, Robertson, Sanderson, Savill, Symonds, Tiddeman, Varco Williams and Winn, and the Misses Keighley. Lee, May and Varco Williams. These ladies were therefore formed into a Provisional General Committee, with the Vicar as Chairman, and with the power to add to their number, and a Provisional small Executive Committee was appointed by the meeting with Mrs. Gardner as Chairwoman and Mrs. McMullen Miss Varco Williams as Hon. Joint Secretaries and Treasurers to discharge all administrative offices.

Will you please help the ladies who may call upon you with such con-tributions as you can afford ; and also let them know whether you would help to make up the material into garments, either in working parties or in your own homes.

HERBERT DALE,

August 8th, 1914.　　　　　　　　　　Chairman *(pro. tem)*.

RECRUITING.

In the early days of the war the subject of recruiting com-manded the serious attention of the people of Hornchurch, and several meetings were held to further that most important move-ment. Afterwards a local Recruiting Committee for the Romford Division was formed, and on that Committee Mr. Thomas Gardner J.P., C.C., and Mr. James R. Robertson were the representatives for Hornchurch.

A large number of public meetings followed in various parts of the Division, and very vigorous were Hornchurch activities in this respect. Under the auspices of this Committee a great

Recruiting and Patriotic Meeting was held at the Drill Hall, Hornchurch, on Friday, October 30, 1914. The large audience was intensely enthusiastic, and the influence which went out from that meeting was afterwards known to have been very fruitful in its results.

Mr. Thomas Gardner, J.P., C.C., presided, and was supported by the following gentlemen :—Commander Carlyon Bellairs, R.N. ; Sir Frederick Green, J.P. ; Sir Montague C. Turner, Mr. Cunliffe-Owen, Colonel Carter, Colonel R. H. Lyon, Major H. H. Slade, Rev. Herbert Dale, Mr. W. Varco Williams, J.P., C.C., Mr. J. R. Robertson, Captain Stanley Holmes, Capt. C. F. Dawson, Capt. A. Bryant, Lieut. S. W. Williams and Mr. H. L. Symonds.

Commander Bellairs, who was the speaker of the evening, gave a patriotic and stirring address, and in it made a strong appeal to those men of military age who had not already joined H.M. Forces to come forward and offer their services without delay to their country in its hour of need.

Sir Frederick Green, Sir Montague Turner, Colonel Lyon, Major Slade, Lieut. Williams, and Mr. H. L. Symonds also spoke.

The resolution, which was as follows, was proposed by Mr. W. Varco Williams, and seconded by Mr. J. R. Robertson :—

"That this Meeting of the Parishioners of Hornchurch pledges itself to make every effort to assist in bringing the war to a victorious conclusion, especially by endeavouring to further the enlistment of Recruits in the ranks of His Majesty's Forces."

The resolution was passed with acclamation and was followed by the singing of the National Anthem.

QUEEN MARY'S NEEDLEWORK GUILD.

"Ladies, you deserve
To have a temple built you !"
Shakespeare:—Coriolanus, v., iv.

Queen Mary's Needlework Guild held a very high place in all the good work voluntarily done by the women of England during the War. A local Branch of this Guild was established early in the war period at Dury Falls, the residence of Mrs. Gardner, its organizer, and, as many Upminster ladies associated themselves with the work, it became to be known as the Hornchurch and Upminster War Hospital Supply Depot and Working Parties.

Apart from the Nursing profession itself, probably no other women's work stands out so prominently, or was so splendidly carried on, as that associated with Queen Mary's Needlework Guild, and as everything connected with it was of a purely volun-

tary character, it deserves the highest appreciation of the community in general, and there are few Hornchurch and Upminster folk who will not feel proud of the record of their local branch.

The money collected amounted to the handsome total of £1,166 10s. 3d., and when it is considered that this was, for the most part, spent in the purchase of material, which, when worked up, numbered 65,528 articles, and included surgical dressings and bandages, as well as a large variety of comforts for the men of H.M. Forces, it is probable that the value of the finished articles amounted to not less than £5,000.

The history of the work and scope of the branch was outlined in a farewell letter addressed by the organizer to the members, and is here reproduced. This letter formed part of a beautiful little brochure, compiled by Mrs. Gardner, a copy of which she presented to every member at a garden party given by her to the members and their husbands, at Dury Falls, on Peace Day, Saturday afternoon, July 19th, 1919. In consequence of the decision of the parish to hold their official celebration of Peace Day at a later date, this was the most important local semi-public function of the day, the attendance being very large.

All full members wore the badge of the Guild, and at their last gathering Mrs. Gardner gave, and personally presented, the official guild ribbon and bars to those members who had made the full attendance in each working year ; many of the recipients receiving the full complement of bars.

The complete list of members, and detailed information connected with the work, are appended to Mrs. Gardner's letter :—

Dury Falls,
Hornchurch.

July 19th, 1919.

Ladies,

As this is our last gathering, I think it is only right that I should briefly sketch a short history of our work here during the last four years.

You will remember that war with Germany was declared on August 4th, 1914. In that same week, on Friday, August 8th, a meeting was called here of the Ladies of Hornchurch, to consider if it would be desirable at once to form working parties and to collect money for the purchase of materials for the making of Hospital necessaries for our Soldiers and Sailors.

The result of that meeting was that working parties were at once started in the Village and on Emerson Park, money was collected, and materials bought. The various articles were all cut out here, then sent to the different working parties, who returned them again to me when finished. These articles were then sorted and marked, packed in big bales, and sent away to various Hospitals at home and abroad, Hospital Ships, The Red Cross Society, and St. John's Ambulance Depot.

This worked well for a time, but as the War progressed the demand for every kind of Hospital Bandage and Dressing was so great that we felt we must try to do more to help, and it was then decided to open a Hospital War Supply Depot in Hornchurch.

Now such a thing as an empty house or suitable room was not to be found, and therefore we have had to do all our work in my Drawing Room.

We began our work here on Monday, October 6th, 1915, as a Branch Depot of Queen Mary's Needlework Guild (Surgical Branch), the Head Depot being at No. 2 Cavendish Square, London ; and we are registered as a War Charity under the Essex County Council.

We commenced with 13 Members, and we end with 148 names on our books.

The working days have been every Monday, Tuesday and Thursday afternoons from 2 o'clock to 5 o'clock.

We have worked in the room three years and six months, and during that time we have made every kind of Bandage and Surgical Dressing, besides many other things required for the comfort of our wounded men. The work was kept up to a very high standard of perfection, and we very soon earned a good name for efficiency at the Head Depot.

The finished work has been sent away at the rate of two hampers full per week. Sometimes we have managed three hampers when extra pressing requests came down from Head Quarters.

We have sent direct to Hospitals at home and abroad, to some of the Clearing Stations at the Front, to Hospital Ships, and many other places, besides what we have sent to the Head Depot.

CHILDREN'S PROCESSION, RED CROSS SOCIETY,
HORNCHURCH BRANCH.

We have worked with a small Committee of five ladies, viz. :—Mrs. Dendy, Mrs. A. Williams, Mrs. Lambe, and Mrs. McMullen, the two latter being Joint Treasurers and Secretaries, with myself as Organiser. The materials which we have used have been of the best, but at the same time we have bought our goods as carefully as we could, and we have wasted nothing. The clothes we sent to the Belgian Refugees were made entirely from the odd pieces from our work room.

Again a quantity of odd pieces were used up for making children's clothes for the Plain Needlework stall at our Red Cross Sale of Work in 1917.

A good many pieces were used up in this way for the Sunday School Guild Bazaar at Christmas—1918.

The selvedges from all materials have been used to tie up our parcels and also knitted into dish cloths.

Old linen sheets were turned into pillow cases, glass cloths, medicine cloths, etc. ; old table linen into face towels and feeders ; old pillow cases and body linen into soft handkerchiefs ; old towels made good dusters or sterilizing towels. Gentlemen's old white shirts made splendid nightshirts, and the hard fronts and cuffs turned into labels for the treasure bags, the very small pieces which we could not use being sold to the local rag merchant, and the money obtained in this way went into the funds for materials.

We have made and sent away a total of 65,528 articles, and the large amount of work accomplished is entirely due to the regular attendance made, for no matter what weather we had, wet or fine, the members have always attended well.

Financially we have done well, and with the assistance of so many kind friends in the neighbourhood, our little Depot has been entirely self-supporting. Every penny we have received in any way has been spent on materials, etc. ; we have had no expenses whatever, and all the charges for carriage and postage have been defrayed by Members of the Committee.

In addition to the funds collected for the Depot, the members have given the following :—

Christmas, 1914—103 plum puddings, which were sent to the 4th Essex Regiment and to the Navy. Christmas, 1915 and 1916—the money to pay for 100 plum puddings.

We have also sent each Christmas time a parcel containing one pair of socks and one shirt to every Hornchurch man whose name we could ascertain serving at the time in France and Egypt or in the Navy.

A spinal carriage was sent to the 3rd London General Hospital, Wandsworth, on October 25th, 1917, by a few of the workers, who subscribed and paid for the same.

The sum of £3 15s. was subscribed in the room, and sent to Cavendish Square towards the Queen's Silver Wedding Gift of Blankets in July, 1918.

Ladies, the good-bye brings with it a tone of sadness ; sadness that you and I, who have been working here together, have now to part. Our work is finished, and we can lay aside our needles and thimbles, feeling that we, who have met here each week, have done our little bit to help others during this sad war and anxious time. I think, in times to come, many of us will look back with pleasure on the work we have done here, and to our bright, happy little meetings—meetings which I trust have made us all fast friends for life—but I cannot say good-bye without first thanking you one and all for the kind and willing help you have all given me during these past years. Without your help this little Depot could not have been the success it has proved to be ! My thanks are due to all those who helped financially, and to those, *especially the children of this Parish and the Cottage Homes*, who have helped me by working at home for this Depot, for without the kind help and assistance I have received from everyone I could have done nothing.

My grateful thanks to one and all,

I remain,

Yours very truly,

M. GARDNER.

Organiser :—Mrs. GARDNER.

Committee :—

Mrs. DENDY
Mrs. A. WILLIAMS
Mrs. LAMBE ⎫ *Joint Secretaries*
Mrs. McMULLEN ⎭ *and Treasurers.*

Mrs. Aller, Mrs. Alp, Mrs. Ashton, Mrs. Allen, Mrs. Anderson, Mrs. Abraham, Mrs. Axell, Miss Asplin, Mrs. Baker, Mrs. Burden, Mrs. Battle, Mrs. Bartholomew, Mrs. Bletsoe, Mrs. Bishop, Mrs. Bratchell, Mrs. Brittain, Miss Beck, Miss Brown, Miss M. Brown, Miss Beard, Mrs. Card, Mrs. Clarke, Mrs. Carthew, Mrs. Cross, Mrs. Conly, Mrs. Cuthbertson, Mrs. Cundle, Mrs. Crow, Miss Crouch, Mrs. Dendy, Mrs. Douse, Mrs. Dale, Mrs. Donald, Mrs. Dockrill, Mrs. Escreet, Mrs. Earle, Mrs. Elbington, Mrs. Eve, Miss Escreet, Miss D. Escreet, Mrs. Forrester, Miss Fisher, Miss Farquah, Miss Frost, Mrs. Gardner, Mrs. Greatorex, Mrs. Gilbray, Mrs. Gibbon, Mrs. Goodchild, Mrs. Gibbs, Mrs. Gidden, Mrs. Gotts, Miss N. Gidden, Miss D. Gibbon, Mrs. Holmes, Mrs. Harris, Mrs. Humphrey, Mrs. Hazard, Mrs. Ibbertson, Mrs. Irlam, Mrs. James, Mrs. Johnson, Mrs. Jobson, Mrs. Joslin, Mrs. W. Johnson, Mrs. Jenking, Miss Joslin, Miss Jenkinson, Miss Jarvis, Mrs. Kerslake, Miss Keighley, Mrs. Lambe, Mrs. Langton, Mrs. Lucas, Miss Lee, Miss B. Lambe, Miss M. Lambe, Mrs. Banks-Martin, Mrs. Money, Mrs. McMullen, Mrs. Mason, Mrs. Maillet, Mrs. Mathews, Mrs. Moss, Mrs. MacMillan, Miss May, Miss Mallinson, Miss Masters, Mrs. Pailthorpe, Mrs. Purbrook, Mrs. Fraser-Parkes, Mrs. Perfect, Mrs. Pinney, Mrs. Pattison, Mrs. Pettiford, Mrs. Phillips, Mrs. Purvis, Mrs. Parish, Miss Perfect, Miss Parke, Miss Peters, Miss S. Peters, Miss Pettiford, Miss Purrett, Mrs. Rose, Mrs. Ridley, Mrs. Robertson, Miss Ridley, Miss Roffey, Miss Rae, Miss Rennison, Miss Rimmer, Miss Rudland, Mrs. Saville, Mrs. Symonds, Mrs. Seabrook, Mrs. Singer, Mrs. Sutton, Mrs. Savill, Mrs. Stone, Miss Symonds, Miss C. Symonds, Miss Saville, Miss Slade, Miss M. Slade, Mrs. Tiddeman, Mrs. Taplin, Mrs. Thomson, Mrs. Tilling, Mrs. Temple, Mrs. Tewsley, Mrs. Vandy, Miss Vellacott, Mrs. Ward, Mrs. A. Williams, Mrs. Willford, Mrs. Wright, Mrs. Woods, Mrs. Worrall, Mrs. Wallace, Miss N. Williams, Miss Wilkinson, Miss Wood, Miss Watkinson, Miss Warren, Miss Willson, Miss Whipps, Miss Wright.

MATERIALS USED.

Bandage Cloth, 6,413 yards ; White Flannellette, 1,988½ yards ; Shirting, 1,516 yards ; Calico (unbleached), 1,430 yards ; Tiffany, 993 yards ; Grey Flannel, 885 yards ; Butter Muslin, 670 yards ; Wool for Knitting, 845 lbs. ; Wincey, 586 yards ; Madopallam, 396 yards ; Cotton Wool, 324 lbs. ; Cretonnes, 259 yards ; Khaki Flannel, 238½ yards ; Turkish Towelling, 178 yards ; White Flannel, 176 yards ; Khaki Drill, 147 yards ; Gauze, Surgical, 137 rolls ; Holland, 48 yards ; Cambric, 48 yards ; Scarlet Flannel, 23½ yards ; Jaconet, 5 yards ; Lint, one roll.

SUMMARY OF ARTICLES DESPATCHED FROM THE DEPOT.

Treasure Bags, 1,452 ; Socks (pairs), 1,380 ; Handkerchiefs, 926 ; T. Bandages, 884 ; Shirts, 795 ; Eye Pads, 538 ; Gratton Caps, 526 ; Mittens (pairs), 461 ; Shoulder Bandages, 435 ; Abdominal Bandages, 434 ; Triangular Bandages, 415 ; Belgians' Garments, 390 ; Many-tail Limb Bandages, 386 ; Anti-Vermin Pants, 325 ; Wool Scarves, 311 ; Pillow Cases, 300 ; Sterilizing Towels, 220 ; Helpless Night Shirts, 205 ; Davis Slings, 203 ; Pyjama Suits, 200 ; Bed Jackets, 196 ; Chest Bandages, 187 ; Hip Bandages, 180 ; Operation Stockings (pairs), 171 ; Operation Veils, 170 ; Washing Pads, 170 ; Wool Caps, 166 ; Cup and Jug Covers, 160 ; Face Towels, 140 ; Stump Bandages, 135 ; Night Socks, (pairs), 114 ; Helpless Bed Jackets, 110 ; Jaw Bandages, 109 ; Sailors' Vests, 103 ; Anti-Vermin Shirts, 100 ; Old Linen Night Shirts, 100 ; Body Belts, 92 ; Eye Shields, 80 ; Medicine Cloths, 80 ; Housewives, 75 ; Pneumonia Jackets, 72 ; Lavatory Cloths, 60 ; Tray-Mats, 52 ; Glass Cloths, 50 ; Kit Bags, 41 ; Hot Water Bottle Covers, 40 ; Mine Sweepers' Gloves (pairs), 36 ; Ward Bags, 30 ; Stretcher Bearers' Bags, 30 ; New Zealand Foot Bandages, 30 ; Helpless Feeders, 30 ; Sunshields for Egypt, 30 ; Nightingales, 28 ; Slippers (pairs), 26 ; New Zealand Massage Bags,

14 ; Blankets, 8 ; Cushions, 7 ; Bed Pan Covers, 6 ; Ward Suits, 6 ;
Sheets (pairs), 6 ; Knee Caps, 6 ; Men's Jackets, 4 ; Bed Quilts, 2 ;
Round Swabs, 22,805 ; Flat Gauze Swabs, 18,161 ; Shell Swabs, 823 ;
Turkish Towelling Swabs, 575 ; Rollers, 9,126 ; Total, 65,528.

DESTINATIONS TO WHICH ARTICLES WERE FORWARDED.

Head Depot, 2, Cavendish Square; Red Cross Society, London ; Red
Cross Society, Chelmsford ; St. Johns Ambulance Warehouse, London ;
Sailor's League (Lady Jellicoe) ; Kitchener's Army (Purfleet) ; Mine
Sweepers ; Queen Mary's Needlework Guild, Friary Court ; Lady Smith-
Dorrien (Treasure Bag Depot) ; The Lady-in-Waiting to the Queen ;
Belgian Refugees ; Servians ; Duke Michael's Fund for Gloves for the
Troops ; Children's Aid Committee (London) ; Prisoners of War in
Germany ; Essex Regiment's Depot, Chelmsford ; Essex Territorials in
Egypt ; Lady Monro, for Troops at the Dardanelles ; Mrs. Wyllie, Ports-
mouth, for Hospitals in France ; Queen Mary's Naval Hospital, Southend ;
Naval Hospital, Newhaven ; New Zealand Hospital, Hornchurch ; V.A.
Hospital, Aston, Derby ; V.A. Hospital, Upminster ; 25, General Hospital,
B.E.F. ; 2nd Stationary Hospital, B.E.F. ; 3rd General Hospital (Wands-
worth) ; Indian Hospital, Brighton ; Ford Lodge Hospital for Belgians ;
Southampton Hospital Ship ; H.M.S. " Eclipse " ; H.M.S. " Mars " ;
3rd B. Royal Field Artillery, City of London ;

To all our Hornchurch men serving in France and Egypt and in the
Navy, whose names could be ascertained, parcels were sent each Christmas, also to several other men of the 4th Essex Territorials.

On several occasions parties of men from the New Zealand Convalescent Hospital, Grey Towers, were entertained to tea in the grounds of
Dury Falls, by Mrs. Gardner and the members of the Guild.

Photo]   NEW ZEALANDERS ENTERTAINED BY THE GUILD   *[Luffs, Hornchurch.*
AT DURY FALLS.

BALANCE SHEET.

RECEIPTS.	£	s.	d.	EXPENDITURE.	£	s.	d.
To Original House-to-House Collection ..	106	18	6	By Materials for the work	989	12	9
,, Entertainments, Odd Sales, &c. .	440	5	4	,, Two Tricycle Hospital Chairs ..	96	17	6
,, Donations ..	402	12	9	,, Balance at Bankers	80	0	0
,, Sale of Waste Paper	27	16	5				
,, Sale of Materials left over ..	36	13	0				
,, Room Collections .	152	4	3				
	£1,166	10	3		£1,166	10	3

The Balance of £80 was forwarded to King George's Fund for Disabled Sailors, Soldiers, and Airmen, and the two Tricycle Hospital Chairs were presented to the Star and Garter Hospital, Richmond, for Incurable Soldiers and Sailors.

PRESENTATION TO MRS. GARDNER.

On Wednesday, April 23, 1919, the members of the Hornchurch Hospital Supply Depot gave an " at home " and presentation to their organiser, Mrs. T. Gardner, in the Council Hall, Billet Lane.   The hall was most tastefully decorated with flags, evergreens, and daffodils, the platform being draped with flags set off with large palms.   A most enjoyable programme of music was arranged by Miss Pettiford, who accompanied and also gave some musical monologues.   Songs were rendered by Miss Burden and Miss Escreet, Miss M. Lambe and Miss Ridley recited, and Master M. Pinney gave a violin solo.

Mrs. McMullen occupied the chair, and opened the proceedings by welcoming the guests.

Mrs. Lambe then presented Mrs. Gardner with a tortoiseshell and silver inkstand, suitably engraved, and penholder to match. She expressed her pleasure of the duty falling to her of making the presentation on behalf of all the workers as a token of gratitude, as it was only by Mrs. Gardner's organisation of the Depot, and throwing open her house for the work, that the members were enabled to ' do their bit ' in making the hospital comforts and necessaries.

Mrs. Gardner replied, thanking the ladies very heartily for the beautiful stand, which would just match the blotter given to her on a previous occasion by the members.   She wished to thank the hon. secretaries (Mrs. Lambe and Mrs. McMullen), for the help they had given her in every way throughout, and especially thanked the workers for their regular attendance. Wet or fine on Mondays, Tuesdays and Thursdays, they had turned up ; and however willing she may have been to do her part, it would have been quite impossible without the help of the workers.

Mrs. Lambe then presented Mr. Gardner with a leather and gold letter case, saying he had helped the Depot in so many ways, besides giving up the room in his house, that the workers wished to make some small acknowledgment to him.

Mr. Gardner, in returning thanks, said he was delighted with the useful letter case, but felt that his part had principally been to efface himself when his house was occupied by the workers. He said he felt very proud of the war work done by the ladies of Hornchurch, and the number of articles they had turned out constituted almost a record.

After tea had been served Mrs. Arthur Williams presented the hon. secretaries, Mrs. Lambe and Mrs. McMullen, with some gifts on behalf of the members, in recognition of their work for the depot.

THE NATIONAL BRITISH WOMEN'S TEMPERANCE ASSOCIATION
(HORNCHURCH BRANCH).

" For never anything can be amiss
When simpleness and duty tender it."
Shakespeare :—Midsummer Night's Dream, v., i.

When, early in November 1914, Grey Towers became a military camp, Hornchurch, having no public hall, was entirely without adequate accommodation for entertaining those men (and they were many) of the Sportsman's Battalion who desired something different from the regular and ordinary camp routine during their hours of leisure. This presented an opportunity for work of a most useful character, and the ladies of the Hornchurch Branch of the National British Women's Temperance Association, realizing that it was work which they were admirably fitted to engage in, immediately made preparations for dealing with it to the best of their ability, having regard to the limited accommodation available. They approached the Pastor and Deacons of the Baptist Church in North Street, who generously granted them, without any charge whatever, the use of the Hall at the rear of the church, where a *Rest and Social Room* was established and equipped within a very few days of the arrival of the Battalion in the village. The Sportsmen were not slow to take advantage of the facilities thus provided for their evening's entertainment, after their arduous military training during the day, and were glad of the rest and quietness, and not less so of the food and refreshment so well and liberally supplied at moderate charges by the ladies of the committee and the friends who assisted them in the good work. The room was open every evening from 6 to 9.30 o'clock, Sundays included. Books, magazines, and papers were provided, and on week days cards and other table games. The room was also well supplied with writing materials, free of charge. Occasionally also vocal and instrumental music was provided. The Deacons and members of the Baptist Church, as well as many friends connected with the Parish Church and Congregational Church, co-operated with the ladies' committee, and every effort was made for the comfort of those who, night after night, filled the small hall to its utmost capacity. The men of the famous Battalion fully appreciated the kindly efforts made on their behalf and many personal testimonies of their gratification were recorded in the visitors' book.

The Sportsmen left Grey Towers in June 1915 and the Rest Room was closed until the Pioneers' Battalion (26th Middlesex) came in the autumn to occupy the camp, when it was re-opened. The stay of the Pioneers was, however, of only short duration, and while the Committee were in the midst of preparations to give those splendid fellows a Merry Christmas, orders came for their removal to another camp and they left Grey Towers on December 21st, 1915.

On the arrival of the New Zealanders in January, 1916, the room was again reopened, and the gallant Colonials made good use of the accommodation provided for their comfort, until the opening on March 5th, 1916, of Te Whare Puni, in Butts Green Road, established for their special use and benefit by New Zealand friends, rendered the continuance of local effort unnecessary.

THE VILLAGE NURSING FUND.

The Hornchurch Village Nursing Fund, established in 1897, which provides and maintains a qualified nurse, whose services may be obtained by all parishioners, continued its useful and beneficial work during the war period, notwithstanding the fact that, at times, the funds were dangerously low, probably owing to the heavy demands made upon subscribers by war-time charities. In support of the funds a Fête and garden party was held on Saturday afternoon, July 26, 1919, in the grounds of Dury Falls, by kind permission of Mr. and Mrs. Gardner, when two dramatic performances were given on the lawn by the children of the local branch of the Young Helpers' League, under the direction of Miss Marjory Lambe, and also two concerts arranged by Miss Gladys Pettiford. In addition there were other attractions in the shape of al fresco competitive games, as well as a sale of work, and many inviting tea and refreshments tents. The whole event was eminently successful and resulted in the Fund benefiting to the extent of £46.

The picturesque group produced on page 209 was taken on this occasion, and represents the children of the Young Helpers' League in the dresses in which they appeared in the plays.

The Committee and Staff are :—Chairman, Mrs. Gardner ; Committee, Mrs. Allen, Mrs. Conly, Mrs. Dale, Mrs. Greatorex, Mrs. Jones, Miss Keighley, Mrs. Low, Mrs. Pailthorpe, Mrs. Saville ; Hon. Treasurer, Mr. E. Spenser Tiddeman ; Hon. Secretary, Mrs. E. Spenser Tiddeman ; Nurse, Miss Laura Rudland.

Photo]   Luffs, Hornchurch.

YOUNG HELPERS' LEAGUE PERFORMERS, JULY 26, 1919.

THE SOLDIERS & SAILORS FAMILIES' ASSOCIATION.

The Soldiers' and Sailors' Families Association, founded in 1885 by Queen Alexandra, had a Branch Division for the district of Romford, formed at the time of the South African War in 1899–1900, Mrs. Gardner being the Hornchurch representative. That Branch was still in existence in 1914, and at once resumed activities. Mrs. Gardner, with the assistance of the Rev. A. J. Parry, investigated the claims of the dependents of Hornchurch men who were serving in H.M. Forces at the commencement of the Great War, and various payments, amounting to a considerable aggregate sum, were paid weekly to meet pressing and immediate needs. This arrangement was continued until December 1916, when the work was transferred to the War Pensions Committee instituted by the Government, consisting of representatives of the Urban, Rural District, and Parish Councils and various local Associations. (*See page* 224).

HORNCHURCH PAROCHIAL WAR RELIEF FUND.

One of the first matters which concerned the parishioners after the declaration of war, was to consider the question of raising funds, and the most desirable methods for using the money so raised in relieving any distress which might arise in the parish consequent on the war. At a public meeting held in the Girls' Schoolroom, North Street, on August 12, 1914, the Parochial War Relief Fund was formed with this object, and a Committee appointed to administer it. The first meeting of the Committee was held on the 26th August, and after full discussion it was unanimously agreed that, as it was understood that families and dependents of sailors, soldiers, and territorials would be provided for by the Sailors and Soldiers Families' Association and the Territorial Association respectively, the best object to which the money to be raised could be put, would be the relief of cases of distress in the parish of Hornchurch, caused through the war, and outside the scope of the Prince of Wales's Fund.

It was reported at this meeting that the ladies of the parish had already collected upwards of £100 for providing comforts for wounded sailors and soldiers, and that about £50 had been collected at the various places of worship for the Prince of Wales's Fund.

The following Committee was appointed :—

Mr. L. Selby, London, County and Westminster Bank, Romford, *Hon. Treasurer.*

GENERAL COMMITTEE :

Mr. E. A. Pearce, Franklyn House, Hornchurch Road, Romford, *Chairman.*

Mr. Walter Halestrap, North Street, Hornchurch, *General Hon. Secretary.*

VILLAGE AND SOUTH WARD :

T. Gardner, Esq., J.P., C.C., Dury Falls, Hornchurch, *Chairman.*

Mr. S. Goodenough, Thanet Villa, Stanley Road, Hornchurch, *Hon. Secretary.*

HAROLD WOOD WARD.

Rev. Bernard Hartley, Crofton, Harold Wood, *Chairman.*

Mr. H. B. Ayres, St. Ronans, Harold Wood, *Hon. Secretary.*

NORTH WEST WARD :

Mr. C. T. Brooker, Craigdale Road, *Chairman.*

Mr. L. W. Wilmot, 74, Malvern Road, *Hon. Secretary.*

At the end of the war it was found that only a very few disbursements had been made from the funds of the Parochial War Relief Fund, and that there remained in the hands of the Treasurer the sum of about £150.

HORNCHURCH WAR SAVINGS' ASSOCIATION.

" How shall we do for money for these wars ?"*
" Levy great sums of money through the realm
For soldiers' pay in France."†

Shakespeare.

In response to the appeal to the Country, made by the Government through the National War Savings' Committee in London, a War Savings' Association was formed in Hornchurch, with an influential committee of ladies and gentlemen, under the presidency of Mr. Thomas Gardner, J.P., C.C.

The Rev. Herbert Dale undertook the duty of Hon. Secretary.

The first meeting of the committee was held at the Chaplaincy on August 28, 1916.

The help of the Masters, Mistresses, and teachers of the private and Council Schools in the parish was freely given in the work of collecting the contributions of the scholars for the purchase by instalments of War Savings Certificates. An adult section was also formed, so that residents in the district could become members of the Association. The method of working adopted by the committee insured success. Money was collected for war purposes, and the total weekly collection was immediately expended in the purchase of Government War Savings Certificates, which were lodged with the hon. treasurer, Mr. C. H. Baker.

As soon as a contributor had completed the purchase price of a certificate, viz., 15s. 6d., an ante-dated certificate was issued in exchange for the money paid. The advantage of this system was two-fold ; the Government received the money as soon as it was collected, however small the individual contribution, and the contributor became possessed of a War Savings Certificate dated, in very many cases, some months before the final instalment of the purchase money was paid.

The continued ill-health of the Rev. Herbert Dale compelled him to relinquish the heavy secretarial work of the Association at the end of October 1917.

He was relieved by Mr. W. J. Fuller who took up the duty in November, 1917 and carried on the work (assisted by Mr. G. C. Dohoo) until the Association was terminated on July 31, 1919. £2,134 7s. was paid over to the Government for war purposes, and 2,754 certificates were issued to members of the Association.

The Hornchurch Association was affiliated with the National War Savings Committee of London. In accordance with the rules of that body the accounts were audited, and a certified copy was sent to London at the end of each half-year. Mr. T. J. Beck and Mr. T. G. Burden audited and certified the whole of the accounts of the Association.

*Richard II., II., ii.
†2 Henry VI., III., i.

THE EMERSON PARK AND GREAT NELMES HORTICULTURAL SOCIETY.

Although circumstances arising out of the war affected adversly the normal activities of the E.P. and G.N. Horticultural Society, it was able to carry on a considerable amount of educational and propaganda work, and the Spring and Autumn Shows continued throughout the war period. After 1916, however, it was found necessary to discontinue the summer show and exhibition, owing chiefly to the difficulty of obtaining tent accommodation. Notwithstanding this, it was felt undesirable to abandon altogether the annual summer fixture, which, for so many years past, had been held at Nelmes. The committee, therefore, decided to hold a fete and garden party, with special provision for children's sports and games, and to endeavour to make the events of benefit to the various war charities, which at that time were so badly in need of funds. With the assistance, therefore, of its many members and friends, two most successful gatherings were held in the grounds of Nelmes, by kind permission of Mr. Alfred Barber, and these not only proved popular social events, but were also the means of helping the funds of some of the most deserving war charities.

The first of these events was held on Saturday afternoon, July 7, 1917, the children's sports being held in the field in front of Nelmes Mansion. There was a record attendance of over 500 people, the sports entries numbering 320. The New Zealand Convalescent Hospital Band (by permission of the Commanding Officer), gave selections of music, and there was a concert on the lawn in the evening. The result was a net profit of £13 4s. 9d., which was distributed as follows :—St. Dunstan's Hostel for Blinded Soldiers and Sailors, £8 16s. 6d., the Hornchurch Branch Queen Mary's Needlework Guild, £4 8s. 3d.

In 1918 the Fête took place on Saturday, July 6, and was largely a repetition of the previous year's function, but was very much more successful in its results, a sum of £52 19s. 6d. being presented to St. Dunstan's Hostel. As on the former occasion there was a concert in the evening, and the New Zealanders' Band again attended.

Mr. L. D. Ascoli acted as Organizing Secretary on both occasions, and was ably assisted by Mr. W. E. Clippingdale, the indefatigable Hon. Secretary of the Society, and a number of ladies and gentlemen, including Mrs. Home, Mrs. Parsons, Mrs. Watling, Mrs. Burden, Miss Edith Smith, Miss Winifred B. Masters, Messrs. S. H. Home, A. E. Watling, W. K. Walker, T. Smith, senr., T. Smith, junr., S. S Carthew, J. D. Johnson, F. Davis Bull, C. N. Cox, L. H. Hatting, J. R. S. Dixon, Herbert C. Hindom, Clive Parsons, W. J. Gibbins, W. C. Harris, C. E. Dunlop, and by the Hornchurch Section 3rd Romford Boy Scouts, under the direction of Scout Master C. E. Hazell.

ST. DUNSTAN'S HOSTEL FOR BLINDED SOLDIERS AND SAILORS.

During the war period special efforts were made to aid the funds of St. Dunstan's Hostel for Blinded Soldiers and Sailors by a combined Choir composed of members of the various religious denominations in the parishes of Hornchurch and Upminster, under the direction of the Hornchurch and Upminster Collecting Committee connected with the Hostel.

The musical programmes given by the choir were, for the most part, performed in Hornchurch Church and Upminster Congregational Church, and included selections from the Messiah and other oratorios, some records of which will be found in the "Parish Church" Chapter of this book. The Collecting Committee also arranged for several whist drives and dances, and were enabled to hand over to the Hostel, as a result of all their efforts, the sum of £67 2s. 7d. The committee was as follows :—Mr. H. W. Alden, Mus. Director, Organist, Parish Church, Hornchurch ; Mr. H. C. Johnson, Accompanist, Organist, Congregational Church, Upminster ; Mrs. W. E. Clippingdale, Accompanist, Organist, Congregational Church, Hornchurch ; Mr. Wm. Duncan, Hon. Secretary ; Mr. W. E. Clippingdale, Chairman.

Mr. Duncan died on November 8, 1918, after which the Chairman, Mr. Clippingdale, also took over the duties of secretary.

NATIONAL INSTITUTE FOR THE BLIND.

In addition to the work recorded in the previous chapter, the National Institute for the Blind was represented in Hornchurch, the joint district secretaries being Miss Winifred B. Masters and Mr. F. Davis Bull, through whose instrumentality several schemes for the collection of funds were set on foot. These included a Flag day in October 1918, and a performance at Gladstone House in February 1919, when a children's costume play, written by Miss Masters, and produced under her management, was given. She and Mr. Bull, as representatives of the National Institute, also co-operated in the arrangements connected with the fête held at Nelmes on July 6th, 1918, described on page 212.

GLADSTONE HOUSE WHIST DRIVES.

In November 1914, a meeting was held at Gladstone House, with the object of arranging a series of whist drives for the benefit of some of the War Charities, and as the outcome of that meeting five fixtures were decided upon, and the following Committee appointed :—Messrs. T. W. Catherwood (chairman), F. H. Barnes, T. G. Burden, W. E. Clippingdale, W. E. Cogar, J. B. Conly, W. H. C. Curtis, J. R. S. Dixon, C. E. Dunlop, J. M. Ewing, J. D. Johnson, E. S. Robinson and A. Stebbings.

The whist drives took place on November 28, December 19, 1914, January 23, February 20, and March 20, 1915, and were well supported, each event proving not only eminently satisfactory financially, but a great success socially. As a result the following contributions, totalling £22 17s. were made to War Charities selected by ballot, viz. : Belgian Relief Fund, £5 ; Serbian Relief Fund, £9 14s. ; Wounded Allies Relief Committee, £3 3s. ; British Red Cross Society, £5 10s.

Mr. J. D. Johnson acted as M.C., and Mr. A. Stebbings as Hon. Secretary and Treasurer, and it was largely due to their initiative and energy, and the hearty support given by Mr. W. H. C. Curtis, that the events proved so successful from all points of view.

EMERSON PARK CHILDREN'S SUNDAY SERVICE.

" Love sought is good, but given unsought is better."
Shakespeare :—Twelfth Night, iii., i.

For the past fifteen years a Service for the children of Emerson Park Estate, conducted on distinctly undenominational lines, has been held every Sunday afternoon in the private school room, Ernest Road (kindly lent by Mrs. Barnard), during the winter months, and in the summer time on the lawns of the various residents, by their kind invitation. Every endeavour is made at these services to teach practical Christianity, more particularly by fostering sympathy and kindly deeds for others.

Among the many sympathetic agencies developed in the parish by the exigencies of the great war, the benevolent activities of the children attending these services must not be overlooked, as the manner in which these little people worked to assist in many of the efforts made to ameliorate the lot of those stricken by the war is deserving of all praise. Commencing in 1915, the third Sunday in each month was set apart as " Wounded Soldiers' Day," when the young people brought contributions of money, eggs, chocolates, cigarettes, jam, honey, flowers, etc., which were despatched to the wounded soldiers in Currie Ward, London Hospital. For many months Mrs. Davis, of London, who attended the hospital weekly, acted as the direct almoner of the childrens' gifts, and each bedside was visited, and the simple gift of the boys and girls handed to the wounded men with a word of cheer and comfort. Messages, drawings, and paintings were put upon the eggs by the little people, and letters were written to the brave boys. A continuous flow of correspondence was started in this way, and many were the letters of thanks and appreciation sent to the children by the gladdened recipients, into whose lives joy was brought by the loving thoughtfulness of the little donors. *In 1916 nearly 600 eggs alone were contributed in this way.*

While wounded men were constantly coming and going from Currie Ward, one patient, Jimmie Howcroft, remained throughout, and a very close bond of friendship grew up between him and the Emerson Park boys and girls. "Jimmie," as they called him, saw active service at the front for about six months as an observer. He had a splendid record of brave and unselfish service, and had been highly commended. One day, however, owing to engine trouble, his machine nose-dived to earth, and as a result his back was broken. For nearly four years he lay in Currie Ward, quite helpless, and often torn with pain, an example of noble self-sacrifice, but there was always a smile on the brave lad's face when receiving his visitors, and his faith in God was just wonderful. Many of the boys and girls visited him, and a quite a number sent him letters every week, and gifts of flowers— specially grown for "Jim." As recently as March 11th, 1920, a letter was written by "Jimmie" to his little friends at Hornchurch, and, as no words of mine can testify half so well to the loving and tender work of these "ministering children," I reproduce it in full :—

Currie Ward,
London Hospital,
March 11th, 1920.

To my friends at Hornchurch.

During the three and a half years I have been lying here, in Currie Ward, I have received so many, many kindnesses from the Emerson Park children, and I have learned so much about them from their visits to me, and through Mr. Chilver, that I am greatly interested in their welfare and their proposed new meeting place.* I felt I must write you on the occasion of your meeting to thank you, the fathers and mothers, and friends of the boys and girls who have been so good to me.

Every Monday morning for more than 12 months, Mr. Chilver has visited me and brought great cheer to my heart, and our happy conversations I shall never forget. He comes heavily laden with flowers, fruit, eggs, jam, and many other good things, contributed by the children, which are the evidences of their loving thoughts and kind consideration ; they are also evidences of real practical Christianity. The gifts, and the most interesting letters from the little people—read to me weekly—bring a great joy into my life, and the children's wonderful consistency—in face of the fact that it is not possible for me even to acknowledge them, except through Mr. Chilver—is not only a great credit to them, but is a splendid tribute to the lessons of thought for others and self-sacrifice taught by Mr. Chilver and his friends.

Undoubtedly one of the most important of our duties is the training of the juvenile mind to look up to God as their Father and Friend, and of all tasks this is one of the most difficult, for we have to get our minds on to their plane, and in doing so, we do not descend to their level, but we ascend to their height. Knowing Mr. Chilver and his friends as you do, you will agree that the spiritual training of the children could not be in better or more sympathetic hands than theirs.

*It is proposed to build a new Children's Service Hut in Herbert Road, Emerson Park, on a plot of land, kindly given by Homesteads, Ltd. The Vicar, the Rev. Charles Steer, and the Pastor of the Baptist Church, the Rev. Thomas E. Howe, are co-operating with Mr. Chilver, and his Committee, to raise funds for this purpose, and are appealing to all lovers of young folk to help them in their laudable endeavour.

Now I must conclude by thanking all who have brought so much light and joy into my broken life, which I have tried to pass on to others. If any little word of mine can help on the scheme suggested for providing a comfortable bright room where the boys and girls can learn more of the Jesus I love, and Who is so much to me, I am glad.

Yours sincerely,

JIMMY HOWCROFT.

Among the many other war charities assisted by the children were the Belgian Refugees' Fund, the British Red Cross Fund, the Y.M.C.A. Hut Fund, and Queen Mary's Needlework Guild.

Mr. R. W. Chilver has had charge of this good work since its inception, and among those who have ably assisted him may be mentioned Mrs. Barnard, Miss Eva Errington, Mr. T. A. Bridges and Mr. Edgar V. Curtis.

HORNCHURCH AND DISTRICT MINIATURE RIFLE CLUB.

The Hornchurch and District Miniature Rifle Club possesses one of the best open-air rifle ranges in the county. If adjoins Hornchurch Station, and being on ground which was formerly a gravel pit, it is partly surrounded by what are practically low cliffs ; there is therefore very little fear of accident.

There are ranges of 25, 50 and 100 yards, all the firing points being under cover.

The Club was initiated at a meeting at the Drill Hall, in January, 1912, Mr. Thomas Gardner being elected president, Mr. A. G. Sibthorp, hon. secretary and treasurer, and Mrs. Gardner hon. secretary of the ladies' section. Sergeant Major Young was appointed range officer.

On Whit Monday, 27th May, 1912, the range was inaugurated, Mrs. Gardner performing the opening ceremony.

Apart from the privileges enjoyed by the members, and the general usefulness of the Club, the range was of real national importance during the war, for here the 1st Sportsman's Battalion went through their smallbore training in 1915, and in 1916 the men of the New Zealand Contingent stationed at Grey Towers Camp had full use of the range.

In the same year the Upminster Platoon of the Essex Volunteer Regiment qualified at this range for their firing tests, and from 1917 onwards the local company of the Cadet Battalion of the 4th Essex Regiment was granted free use of it for firing practice.

At the commencement of the War, Sergeant-Major Young rejoined his old regiment, the 4th Essex, and Mr. G. M. Horey became honorary range officer, and with the assistance of Mrs. Horey—Captain of the Ladies' Team—" carried on," and made all the arrangements for the many useful purposes which the range has served during the last three years.

Mr. C. L. Parker succeeded Mr. Sibthorp as hon. secretary and treasurer in January, 1916.

The Club is affiliated to the Society of Miniature Rifle Clubs, and to the Essex County Rifle Association.

During the period of the war, no fewer than 70 members joined H.M. Forces.

PARISH COUNCIL.

" Speak to the business, master Secretary :
Why are we met in council ? "

Shakespeare :—King Henry VIII., ii.

The following served as members of the Parish Council during the war, either for the whole or part of the period.

Messrs. A. A. Apps, H. B. Ayres, C. H. Baker, F. H. Barnes, A. E. Chaplin, W. E. Clippingdale, W. E. Cogar, T. Crawford, F. Creek, A. G, Dohoo,* J. S. Everson, A. Ferguson, H. J. Finch, W. Halestrap, T. Hunter. A. Knight, E. Lambert, W. H. Legg, A. H. Macklin, E. A. Pearce, J. J. Pyner, M. E. Ricketts, H. B. Sell, W. J. Westaway.

CHAIRMEN AND VICE-CHAIRMEN.

Chairmen.	*Vice-Chairmen.*
1914. Mr. E. A. Pearce.	Mr. W. H. Legg.
1915. Mr. W. H. Legg.	Mr. A. Ferguson.
1916. Mr. W. H. Legg.	Mr. A. Ferguson,
1917. Mr. A. Ferguson.	Mr. F. Creek.
1918. Mr. A. Ferguson.	Mr. F. Creek.
1919. Mr. E. Lambert.	Mr. W. Halestrap.

Mr. William, C. Allen, Clerk and Chief Assistant Overseer.
Mr. W. A. Warman*† Junior Assistant Overseer.

Apart from the general routine work in which the Council were engaged, some of which concerned the official war regulations issued from time to time, their principal war work was connected with the Government Allotment scheme and the fire brigade. The allotments are fully dealt with in the chapter following this. The fire brigade was kept in a state of great efficiency during wartime, and every provision was made to meet any emergency which might arise through the repeated air-raids ;‡ special equipment, smoke distinguishers, and gas masks for firemen were provided, and a motor for the fire engine. Many of the Special Constables were trained as extra firemen.

Seven members of the fire brigade joined H.M. Forces, viz. : A. G. Collin, C. H. Fancy, T. G. Frost, B. Lake, B. Newman, C. Newman, and R. F. Stroud, two of whom, T. G. Frost, and B. Lake, were killed in action. In the eastern district of the National

*These joined H.M. Forces.
†Mr. W. A. Warman was called up with the 4th Essex Territorials at the outbreak of war, and served through the Gallipolli campaign, and in Palestine until the second Battle of Gaza, rising to the rank of Corporal. He then joined the R.A.F., obtaining a Commission as Lieutenant and a pilot's certificate. He was killed, after a fall of 2,000 feet, just outside Alexandria on 13th October, 1918.
‡A further reference to the Fire Brigade is made on page 225.

Fire Brigades Association, a Fund, known as a Death Levy Fund, is raised for the relatives or dependents of firemen in the case of death, a levy of 1s. per member being made for this purpose. By means of that Fund, a sum of £36 was raised for the dependants of each of the firemen, who made the Great Sacrifice in the war.

Firemen A. Reeves and W. G. Axtell left their usual occupations for work of national importance, for part of the war period.

Firemen who served during the war period :—

Chief Officer, E. G. Bratchell ; Second Officer, H. Alabaster ; Firemen, W. G. Axtell, G. Barker, H. Fry, T. Flucker, C. Green, W. R. Green, J. Mallam, W. J. Mumford, A. Pill, A. Reeves, H. Stokes.

The undermentioned officers and men were presented with long-service medals in 1920 :—

Silver Medals—20 years service.

Chief Officer, E. G. Bratchell ; Second Officer, H. Alabaster ; Firemen, A. G. Collin and C. Green.

Bronze Medals—10 years service.

Firemen, W. J. Mumford and A. Reeves.

The Council erected new Council offices in Billet Lane, in 1915, the building of which was commenced in April and completed in October of that year.

ROMFORD RURAL DISTRICT COUNCIL.

Members representing Hornchurch Parish on the District Council during the war.

Mr. Edgar G. Bratchell, Village Ward (Chairman 1916 to 1920).
Mr. Thomas Crawford, Village Ward.
Mr. Edwin Lambert, North-west Ward.
Mr. A. F. Harrison, North-west Ward.
Mr. Alexander Ferguson, South Ward.
Mr. D. Shuttleworth, Harold Wood Ward.

THE ALLOTMENTS.

" We go to gain a little patch of ground."
Shakespeare :—Hamlet iv., iv.

The granting of small plots of land, commonly known as allotments, for the cultivation of vegetables, was one of the wisest and most popular of war time measures, and did much to relieve the food situation. This scheme was considered so important that it was mentioned as one of the chief reasons for the re-enactment of the Daylight Saving or Summer Time Act of 1916. Many articles appeared in the Press, urging the importance of increasing the home production of food-stuffs by private individuals, and by means other than through the instrumentality of the farming industry.

In the year 1916 there was a serious shortage in the crop of potatoes, and this, combined with the fact that foreign supplies were almost entirely cut off, led to stocks being almost exhausted by the spring of 1917. About that time the food supplies of the country generally began to be seriously threatened by reason of the activities of enemy submarines, and, as a consequence, a sub-department of the Board of Agriculture and Fisheries was formed, called the Food Production Department, whose duty it was to stimulate and control the home production of food-stuffs. This department encouraged in every possible way the allotment movement throughout the country.*

Hitherto, allotments in Hornchurch had been provided by the Parish Council, by hiring fields, and sub-letting ten-rod plots to individuals, mostly of the labouring and artizan classes. The new department issued an Order under the Defence of the Realm Act, known as Regulation 22 (Cultivation of Lands Order), which empowered Borough, Urban and Rural Councils to enter into possession of any land lying idle and vacant without any liability to pay rent to the owner, and sub-let it to individuals for the raising of crops of food stuffs.

The Order did not apply to Hornchurch, as the Council was only a Parish Council, but application was made to the Food Production Department for powers to be given them. After many rebuffs, persistency won, and it is interesting to record that *Hornchurch Parish Council was the first Parish Council in England to receive powers under the Cultivation of Lands Order.*

A Committee was formed of members of the Parish Council, with Mr. Walter Halestrap as Chairman, and no effort was spared to acquire all suitable land available in the Parish, and to encourage in every possible way its proper and efficient cultivation. It was, however, largely owing to the indefatigable efforts of Mr. William C. Allen, Clerk to the Council, that the work was so wonderfully successful, and grew from a very small beginning into quite an important village industry.

The demand for " Plots," as the war-time allotments were generally called, exceeded the supply, especially in the North-West Ward of the Parish, in spite of the fact that all vacant land was seized by the Council, and that new fields for permanent allotments were opened up. The number of these latter rose

*The following extract from the " Daily Chronicle " of 2 Feby., 1920, will convey some idea as to the national importance of the war-time Allotment Scheme :
THE WASTE PLACES THAT BROUGHT FORTH FOOD.
1,270,000 Tons Raised by Allotment Holders.
In 1919 the number of allotment holders in England and Wales reached a total of 1,750,000. It is estimated that they produced 1,270,000 tons of food, of which the following are the most important !—Potatoes 740,000 tons, cabbages and cauliflower 350,000 tons, onions 43,000 tons, parsnips 39,000 tons, peas 31,000 tons, beans 23,000 tons, vegetable marrow 16,000 tons, carrots 12,000 tons, beet 12,000 tons, rhubarb 7,000 tons, soft fruit 3,000 tons.

219

to 254 in the parish, and the war-time plots were 256, making a total of 510 ten-rod plots.

The policy of food production was followed up with great energy by the Council. To stimulate interest, prizes were given for the best cultivated plots, lectures were arranged in the different Wards, and eminent scientists gave their services to explain the scientific side of vegetable culture.

To guard against potato disease, spraying was undertaken by the Council. It was estimated at the end of the first year that no less than 200 tons of potatoes had been raised from ground that previously had been lying waste. In addition to this, other crops, such as beans, peas, green-stuffs, etc., were produced.

Owing to the unprecedented rise in the price of seed potatoes, the Council each year bought up large supplies in bulk, and retailed them at cost price, about 20 tons per annum being sold in this way in parcels of from 7lbs. to 1cwt. each.

The allotment movement naturally grew to tremendous proportions, and Associations sprang up all over the country, ultimately becoming united under the title of the National Union of Allotment Holders. Hornchurch and Romford united for the purpose of forming a branch of this Union. (So strong did the Union become that it impressed its importance on the House of Commons, which brought in legislation to extend the tenure of allotments after the end of the war.)

The great value of the allotment movement lay in the fact that the labour used in raising the food-stuffs was " spare time " labour ; that is to say, the labour of men who were otherwise employed during the day, and who utilized their leisure hours on the plots. It was remarkable, too, that all classes took to the movement, men of sedentary occupations and good position working on the land from patriotic motives ; and this work was not confined to men only, as women—the wives and daughters of the allotment holders—were often seen working with them, and rendering valuable assistance.

" He also serves his country who stays at home and digs," was the clever paraphrase of a popular quotation used by the " Daily Express " at the head of an article on the cultivation of Allotments in its issue of February 23, 1918, and those who through age, physical disability, or other legitimate cause were debarred from taking up arms, had not a little satisfaction in the knowledge that their honest spade work was not only securing greater comforts for themselves and their families, but that it was their contribution, however small, towards winning the war.

The Council also undertook the supply of glass preserving jars at cost price to enable parishioners to preserve fruit for the winter months, a total of 5,760 glasses being distributed in this way.

Mr. William C. Allen was offered, and accepted, a seat on the County of Essex Horticultural- Sub-Committee to represent Allotment holders, on which Committee he served during the whole period of its existence.

ROMFORD AND HORNCHURCH ALLOTMENT ASSOCIATION.

This Association was founded as the Romford and North-West Hornchurch Allotment Association at a meeting held at the Albert Road Schools in the autumn of 1917, the principal initiators of the movement being Councillors E. Lambert and W. H. Letts.

The President from the commencement has been Sir John Bethell, Bart., M.P., the first chairman being Mr. Ward, of Albert Road, and the Hon. Secretary, the late Mr. Smith, of Park Lane.

Various attempts were made to form a similar association in the village, and ultimately, as a result of a meeting held at the Council Hall, Billet Lane, in February, 1919, under the presidency of Mr. Thos. Gardner, J.P., it was decided, as indicated in the previous chapter, to join forces with the Romford Allotment-holders. The Association willingly agreed to change its name and rules, so that any person residing in the Urban District of Romford, or in the parish of Hornchurch, should become eligible for membership.

The Association is affiliated with the National Union of Allotment holders, and with the Royal Horticultural Society. The membership in March, 1920 was 750, the executive consisting of Mr. F. J. Sheail, chairman ; Mr. J. Seaman, Hon. Secretary ; H. B. Sell, Assistant Hon. Secretary ; and 15 Committeemen, the village being represented by Messrs. W. E. Clippingdale and F. B. Gatehouse.

Besides being active in forwarding the Allotment movement in the district, and safe-guarding the rights of members in regard to security of tenure of plots, trespass, etc., the Association has greatly increased the facilities for local food production by obtaining supplies of seeds, manures, &c., at a cost far below that otherwise possible. The Association has, therefore, already justified its existence, and although a " War-baby," bids fair to become a vigorous child of Peace. Despite all pessimistic prognostications to the contrary, the allotment movement has come to stay. A tangible indication of this is that since the signing of the armistice the membership of this Association nearly doubled itself.

LOCAL COUNCILS, COMMITTEES & ORGANIZATIONS ACTIVE DURING THE WAR PERIOD.

The following explanatory notes of some of the local Councils, Tribunals, Committees, etc., may not only prove interesting, but in some respects instructive, as indicating the large volume of war time work done in this parish and district by public and semi-public bodies.

THE ROMFORD RURAL DISTRICT COUNCIL, presided over by Mr. Bratchell for five years in succession, carried out a large amount of national, as well as local work during the war period. Many of the most important Committees mentioned hereafter were appointed by this Council, and came under its administration. The Romford Rural District consists of the parishes of Upminster, Hornchurch, Cranham, Wennington, Great Warley, Havering, Noak Hill, Dagenham and Rainham.

THE ROMFORD RURAL LOCAL TRIBUNAL dealt with 3,449 cases of application for exemption from military service, and the Local Government Board expressed, in eulogistic terms, its appreciation of its work. The Tribunal consisted of Mr. E. G. Bratchell (Chairman), Mr. W. G. Ketley and Mr. E. Lambert (Hornchurch), Mr. T. D. Hollick (Upminster), Mr. W. J. Gay and Mr. J. A. Parrish (Dagenham).

THE FOOD CONTROL COMMITTEE.—Important work was done by this Committee, the various rationing orders being carried out satisfactorily, and with little or no friction. Committee: Mr. E. G. Bratchell (Chairman), Messrs. E. Lambert, W. G. Ketley, A. Ferguson, A. Knight, and Mrs. McMullen and Mrs. Hawkins (Hornchurch), Messrs. W. J. Gay, W. G. Earl, J. A. Parrish, J. Dines and Mrs. Sisley (Dagenham), Mr. S. J. Holmes (Rainham), Rev. H. H. Holden and Mr. H. A. Martin (Upminster), and Mr. T. H. Scrivener (Warley). The Hornchurch Food Economy Committee was an offshoot of this Food Control Committee.

THE OLD AGE PENSIONS COMMITTEE.—This was originally a local Committee, whose duty it was to consider and recommend men and women for the old age pension, but, during the war, the Committee had also to recommend allowances for the dependents of sailors and soldiers, other than wives and children.

THE HOUSING AND TOWN PLANNING COMMITTEE.—This Committee had a very busy time during the war, and its future work is likely to be a great deal more strenuous. A town planning scheme is in preparation for the whole of the Rural District, and the Council propose to build at least 190 houses in the near future, 50 of them in Hornchurch.

THE MATERNITY AND CHILD WELFARE COMMITTEE.—The Maternity and Child Welfare Act 1918, empowered Urban and Rural District Councils to establish Baby Clinics, Crêches, etc., to provide doctors and nurses, where necessary, for expectant mothers, and to supply milk, etc., for children. The Rural District Council established two such clinics in the district during war-time (one at the Hornchurch Council Hall, Billet Lane, and the other at Dagenham at the Wesleyan School), the District Committee being as follows :—Chairman, Mr. E. G. Bratchell. Hornchurch, Messrs. E. Lambert, A. Ferguson, Mrs. Dendy, Mrs. Lambe, Miss Lee, Mrs. Perfect and Mrs. Symonds. Upminster, Mr. H. C. Martin. Great Warley, Mr. T. H. Scrivener. Dagenham, Messrs. W. J. Gay, W. G. Earl, Mrs. Earl and Mrs. Evans. Rainham, Mr. S. J. Holmes.

The Centre, in Billet Lane, was managed by the ladies of the Hornchurch Committee, with Mrs. Lambe as Secretary. Miss Davey, of Upminster, was the first Health Visitor appointed, and on her resignation in February, 1918, was succeeded by Mrs. E. H. Fawcett. The meetings were held fortnightly on Friday afternoons, at which Dr. Alfred Wright, Medical Officer of Health, attended for the medical examination of infants, and to advise mothers respecting ailing or sickly babies, and on the many minor ailments attending teething, malnutrition, etc. The fact that the centre met a long-felt want is proved by the attendance, which steadily rose from about seven or eight at each meeting to an average of 28. As the district is a scattered one, and many mothers have to come long distances to the meetings, the Council and Committee may feel a just pride in the result of their efforts.

In June 1918, the first Baby Competition was held, when several prizes were given in various classes. On July 4th, 1919, a much larger competition was arranged, when a great many prizes were awarded, the judging being done by Dr. Maude Bennett and Nurse Howlett, both of the Essex County Council. On the following Friday, July 11th, a Garden Party was held in the grounds of Hornchurch Lodge (by kind permission of Dr. Lambe), at which the prizes were distributed. This event was greatly enjoyed by the mothers and children, and not less so by the ladies and friends of the Committee.

The illustration here produced is from a photograph taken on that occasion.

The work of this Committee is still being carried on, and a third Clinic is now in process of formation at Upminster, with Mrs. G. Eve as Secretary, assisted by a Committee of local helpers.

THE ROMFORD JOINT HOSPITAL BOARD.—This is a Board consisting of five members of the Romford Rural Council, and three members of the Romford Urban Council, and is appointed to deal with cases of infectious diseases in the two districts, and to control the work of the Isolation Hospital, Rush Green. The Hornchurch members are Messrs. E. G. Bratchell and E. Lambert.

ROMFORD PETTY SESSIONAL DIVISION LOCAL WAR PENSIONS COMMITTEE.—The work of this Committee consists in relieving distress, etc., among the dependents of sailors and soldiers, by granting them aid in sickness, and to meet rent and other civil liabilities, as well as looking after the welfare of discharged sailors and soldiers. Mr. Bratchell and his wife represent Hornchurch Village, South Hornchurch, and Harold Wood on this Committee.

Photo]   [Luffs, Hornchurch.
GARDEN PARTY AT HORNCHURCH LODGE.

HOUSEHOLD FUEL AND LIGHTING COMMITTEE FOR THE ROMFORD RURAL DISTRICT.—This Committee was formed to administer the orders under the Household Fuel and Lighting Order in the Rural District area, with the exception of Hornchurch, Dagenham, Noak Hill and Havering, those places coming within the Metropolitan area for fuel and lighting purposes under the Act.

ROMFORD DISTRICT EMERGENCY COMMITTEE.—This Committee was formed for the purpose of arranging all details for the district in case of invasion by the enemy. Although the Committee was, happily, not called upon to put in operation the preparations made by it, a great deal of consideration and forethought had to be given to the subject, and many meetings were held from time to time. It was in connection with this work that Mr. Bratchell was sworn in as Special Constable.

HORNCHURCH FIRE BRIGADE.—The Brigade was always ready for duty during air raids, and on one occasion at least had rather an exciting experience. A Zeppelin raid had been signalled, and at almost the same time the Brigade was called to South Hornchurch, three stacks being on fire just behind the aerodrome at Suttons farm. It can readily be imagined what a brilliant target such a conflagration would have been to the Zeppelin gunners, and in what imminent danger the aerodrome would have been in, had the raiders passed over while the stacks were burning. Fortunately they took another route that night, otherwise the aerodrome and village would assuredly have been bombed. Mr. Bratchell has been chief of the Fire Brigade for the past twenty years.

SOME WAR WORKERS.

" You see how men of merit are sought after ! "
Shakespeare :—2 Henry IV., II., iv.

MR. R. BANKS-MARTIN, J.P., F.R.S.A.

Although the war work of Mr. R. Banks-Martin, of " Gracecourt," Woodlands Avenue, has been in great measure performed outside the borders of our own parish, his record is such an outstanding one, that I am sure his fellow-parishioners will feel that this volume would be incomplete without a brief resumé of his public activities. Soon after the outbreak of war he was elected Mayor of East Ham, which high office he held continuously from November 1914 to November 1918. The population of East Ham is now about 150,000, and it will, therefore, be realized how onerous and responsible were the duties which devolved upon him. With what zeal he responded to the many calls made upon him during the momentous years in which he occupied the civic chair, and the remarkable results achieved through his patriotic efforts and organizing ability, are well told in the following excerpt (with a few additions of more recent date), from the " *City of London Illustrated* " for August 1917 :—

"As chairman of the Recruiting Committee Mr. Banks-Martin's efforts have been beyond all praise. Into this important work he threw himself heart and soul, and with the assistance of his fellow-members and the military representatives, raised five most important military units—the 173rd Brigade R.F.A., the 178th (Howitzer) Brigade, the 16th Ammunition Column, the 141st Heavy Battery R.G.A., and the 32nd Battalion Royal Fusiliers. Numerically, the whole spells practically 4,000 officers and men, many of whom have rendered yeoman service at the front ; some have made the supreme sacrifice, while others have been badly wounded in the conflict. On the respective occasions of the 178th (How-itzer) Brigade and the 32nd Fusiliers being reviewed by the King at Aldershot, East Ham's Mayor had the honour of being presented to His Majesty.

Councillor Banks-Martin has also played a prominent and notable part in connection with the borough's war funds. He was chairman of the Local Committee of the Red Cross Fund, which raised £1,000, and of three Alexandra Days, when considerable sums have been collected. He inaugurated the local fund for the Belgians, which has reached a total of nearly £2,000. This genial architect also set a sports fund going for soldiers, which has accounted for nearly £150 for sports outfits for the units raised in East Ham. Then he took an energetic part in connection with the local hospital fund, for which, since his period of office commenced, over £300 has been raised by means of flag days. A fund concerning which the Mayor has a very warm corner in his heart is the Disabled Soldiers' and Sailors' Fund for those living in the borough, and some £350 has been raised in connection with this praiseworthy object.

In connection with the " Jack Cornwell," V.C. Memorial Fund, £6,000 has been raised for the purpose of building homes for Disabled Sailors, and providing naval scholarships, the Mayor being chairman of the Fund.

A fund was inaugurated by the Mayor for a Local War Memorial, £1,500 being raised for the provision of a monument to record the names of the fallen.

Altogether, under Mr. Banks-Martin's instrumentality nearly £11,500 has been garnered in, with the aid of a loyal band of assistants, to whom his Worship confesses his indebtedness, as he does also to the members of the Borough Council, whose cordial support makes his position as Mayor a very pleasant, if perforce it must sometimes prove an arduous, one. The Mayor is Chairman of the War Pensions Committee, the War Savings Committee, the Allotments' Committee, and also of the Local Food Control Committee, and has recently been appointed by the Lord Chancellor as chairman of the Local Advisory Committee of the Borough Justices.

East Ham's Mayor is a Captain of the Essex Motor Volunteer Corps in the local squadron organised by him last year ; is also chairman of the Local Tribunal, which deals with about forty cases a week, and has had the none too pleasant task of hearing and deliberating upon about three thousand five hundred claims since it was first set up. Mr. Banks-Martin takes a deep interest in matters educational, and is keenly alive to the great importance of commercial education, as it will affect the after-war struggle for commercial supremacy. On May 21, 1918, the King and Queen visited East Ham to inspect the war workers organisations, this making the fourth occasion the Mayor had the honour of being presented to the King during his four years of office.

The Mayoress is as keen as her husband in everything which tends to the welfare of the borough. She is responsible for the working of the local surgical branch of Queen Mary's Needlework Guild, which has about 350 members, entailing an expenditure of about £10 a week for making surgical bandages and dressings. The Guild supplies most of the local and some of the London hospitals, also sending up to the headquarters at Cavendish Square."

MR. WILLIAM HENRY BASS.

Peace has its heroes as well as War ! Mr. W. H. Bass, of South Hornchurch, can claim to come within that category, by reason of a courageous act performed by him under circum-stances which called forth not only quick determination, but more than ordinary cool personal courage.   On June 19, 1918, a lady fell off the up-platform at Dagenham Dock Station on to the line in front of an approaching train.   Although the train was at the time only a short distance away, Mr. Bass, who was standing close by, immediately jumped down, and, as the lady was picking herself up, pushed her from between the rails on which the train was running into the space between the two sets of lines, and managed to get both her and himself clear just as the engine passed them.

Mr. Bass is employed by the Midland Railway Company (London, Tilbury and Southend Section), and the Company, in recognition of his courageous act, presented him with a handsome silver watch, inscribed as follows :

" Awarded by the Midland Railway Co., to William Henry Bass, Engineers' Department, for courageous conduct in saving a woman's life at Dagenham Dock Station, June 19th, 1918."

The presentation was made by the Deputy General Manager of the Company at the Head Office, Derby.

The Carnegie Hero Fund Trust also recognised Mr. Bass's heroism by presenting him with their certificate, bearing the following inscription :—

The Carnegie Hero Fund Trust.
Founded, September 1908.

" Presented by the Trustees in recognition of Heroic Endeavour to save Human Life,
To WILLIAM H. BASS,
South Hornchurch.
June 19, 1918.

Dunfermline, 28 Novr., 1918.   JOHN ROSS, Chairman.
                                               J. B. DAVIDSON, Secretary.

Mr. Bass has been in the employ of the Midland Railway Co. for a period of 16 years, and in the spring of 1917, when a call was made by the Military authorities for civil labour, volunteered for service overseas, and after serving on the French Railway Lines received special commendation for his work.

MR. E. G. BRATCHELL, J.P.

In the days of peace, Mr. E. G. Bratchell set the pace in the national game of cricket,* his prowess in the field with bat and ball having earned for him the foremost place in our village annals for some years prior to the commencement of hostilities in 1914.   It was, therefore, only in keeping with the proper order of things, that, when the national game had to be temporarily abandoned for national work in connection with the war, the famous player should become the strenuous worker.

Mr. Bratchell was born at Upminster in the year 1868, and came to reside at Hornchurch at the age of nine years.   His public record is a remarkable one, no fewer than 31 local appoint-

*See *Village Cricket*, page 135, " Ye Olde Village of Hornchurch."

ments having been held by him during the war, many of which were of national importance. The public spirit he has displayed, and the extraordinary amount of hard work he has put in for the benefit of the community, is worthy of special mention in this village record, and I therefore append a list of his activities :

Chairman of the Romford Rural District Council, and Justice of the Peace for the County of Essex.

Chairman of the Romford Rural Local Tribunal, the Food Control Committee, the Food Economy Committee, the Old Age Pensions Committee, The Romford Rural District Council Housing and Town Planning Committee, the Maternity and Child Welfare Committee, The Hornchurch Food Economy Committee, and the Household Fuel and Lighting Committee of the Romford Rural District.

Vice-Chairman of the Committee for the prevention and relief of distress in the Romford Rural District.

Member of the Sanitary, Building, Finance, Highways and Byelaws Committee of the R.R.D.C., also of the Warley Joint Sanitary Committee, and the Upminster Cemetery Committee.

Member of the Romford Board of Guardians, also member of the Assessments, Building, House, Stores, Billeting and Military Committees of the Romford Board of Guardians.

Member of the Joint Hospital Board, and of the Romford Petty Sessional Division of the Local War Pensions Committee.

Member of the Romford District Emergency Committee.

Business Organizer of the Romford Rural District.

Special Constable.

In addition to these activities, Mr. Bratchell has served on many special Committees, and has attended as delegate a large number of Conferences, some of them at great distances.

SIR JOSEPH G. BROODBANK, KT.

Sir Joseph Broodbank has been associated with all matters connected with the war work of Harold Wood, and his many activities are frequently referred to under the Harold Wood section of this book. His national work was of an important character, and chiefly concerned his appointment on the Port of London Authority. As Chairman of the Dock and Warehouse Committee, he was responsible for all the arrangements for war traffic in the Docks of London, including the shipment of troops, stores, and munitions, and for the storage of the immense supplies of food, etc., controlled by the Government. He was also a member of the following Committees :—Port and Transit Executive Committee, Military Service Committee for the Port, and the Committee for the diversion of traffic from the East to the West Coast.

Sir Joseph was knighted in February, 1917.

MR. W. E. CLIPPINGDALE.

For many years Mr. Clippingdale has acted as Hon. Secretary to the Emerson Park and Great Nelmes Horticultural Society, and his contribution to the war work of the Parish has been largely in the direction of Horticulture and Food Production. Before the Food Production Department of the Board of Agriculture and Fisheries was formed, (which department was responsible for the Cultivation of Lands Order, which empowered local Councils to acquire land for allotment purposes), Mr. Clippingdale formulated a scheme for the compulsory acquisition of grass lands and gardening tools by local Committees, and the compulsory cultivation of such land by local residents under expert control and supervision. He presented this scheme in December 1916, and it was sent to the County Council, but was turned down as premature. Nevertheless, during the following spring the Cultivation of Lands Order came into force, with all its attendant benefits, as described in another page of this book.

In January 1918, Mr. Clippingdale was appointed by the Food Production Department as Horticultural representative for the Rural District of Romford, under the Essex Horticultural Sub-Committee, and held that position until the end of the war. He was elected a Parish Councillor in the spring of 1919, in the interests of Allotment-holders.

He also identified himself largely with the work connected with the St. Dunstan's Hostel for Blinded Soldiers and Sailors, and served as Special Constable from June 1915 until the disbanding of the force in 1919.

MR. G. C. ELEY, J.P.

Mr. Eley's many activities during the war were largely in the direction of education. He took a prominent part in the initiation of the Essex Cadets in connection with the Essex Educational Scheme, and addressed many meetings on the subject in various parts of the County, including Colchester, Saffron Walden, Grays, etc. He was a member of the Essex County Education Committee, and as one of a small Sub-Committee took an active part in arranging for the staffing of the Elementary Schools of the County, which became necessary owing to so many of the male teachers joining H.M. Forces. As Secretary of the Romford, Brentwood, and Grays District of the National Union of Teachers, he raised a considerable sum of money towards the Teachers' War Air Fund. He was the representative of the teachers of the district on the Romford Branch of the National Service Committee, and upon the Prince of Wales's Fund Committee. He was a member of the War Pensions Committee for the Romford Petty Sessional Area, Chairman of the Romford

Care Committee, and member of the Romford D.S.C., and Higher Education Committee. Mr. Eley is a Justice of Peace for the County.

MR. JOSEPH SCOTT EVERSON.

Mr. Everson's contribution to the public service during the war was as follows :—Overseer of the Parish, Member of the Hornchurch Parish Council and of the following Committees :—Finance, Fire Brigade, Allotments and North-West Lighting Committees ; Trustee to the Hornchurch Consolidated Charities ; Member of the Hornchurch Parochial War Relief Fund, and of the N.W. Hornchurch Advisory Committee.

Since the establishment of the Church Army Hut, in Park Lane, in March, 1920, Mr. Everson has served as Chairman of the Church Army Social Centre, and Chairman of the Finance Committee of the Centre.

MR. ALEXANDER FERGUSON.

Mr. Ferguson's membership of the Parish Council has extended over many years. In 1915 and 1916 he acted as vice-chairman, and was elected chairman for the years 1917 and 1918. He was chairman of the war Memorial and Peace Celebration Committees.

He also represented the South Ward of the parish on the Romford Rural District Council.

MR. CHARLES J. FIELDER, M.B.E.

Mr. Fielder was awarded the M.B.E. for personal services voluntarily rendered to the Admiralty in connection with the provision of small vessels for the fleet during the war.

MR. WALTER HALESTRAP.

Mr. Halestrap did very considerable public service during war time, served as Parish Councillor throughout the whole of the war period, and in 1919 was elected Vice-Chairman. He interested himself largely in the Allotment scheme, and acted as Chairman of the Committee responsible for carrying out the Government regulations issued from time to time.

MR. EDWIN LAMBERT.

Mr. Lambert put in a large amount of work in the local public interest during the war, the following being the principal appointments held by him :—Representative for the North West Ward on the Romford Rural District Council, and ex-officio member of the Romford Board of Guardians, Member of Hornchurch Parish Council, the Hornchurch School Managers,

the Romford Joint Hospital Board, the Romford County High
School Board of Governors, the Petty Sessional Division War
Pensions Sub-Committee, the Local Food Control Committee,
the Romford Rural Local Tribunal, the Local Economy Committee, and one of the Overseers of the Poor of the Parish.

The duties connected with the Local Tribunal, the Food Control Committee, and the War Pensions Committee were particularly onerous, the demand made upon the time of those
engaged on them being extremely heavy.

Mr. Lambert was elected Chairman of the Parish Council for
1919 and 1920, and previously served in that capacity in the
years 1910 and 1911.

MR. JAMES R. ROBERTSON.*

Mr. Robertson was a Member of the Romford Local Recruiting Committee, which carried out its duties under the direction
of the County of Essex Territorial Force Association. He also
served on the Romford Recruiting Advisory Committee. As
Civil Engineer in charge of the London Tilbury and Southend
Section of the Midland Railway, Mr. Robertson was responsible
for the maintenance of "lines of communication," and for
the carrying out of pre-arranged actions to assist the military
authorities in the event of emergencies, which fortunately
never arose.

MR. HARRY LAMBERT SYMONDS.

Apart from his service as Special Constable, and his connection with various phases of local war work, Mr .Symonds's
war-time activities were mostly outside the parish, and largely
connected with National Service, his chief appointments being :—

Ministry of Munitions :—(1) Member of Metropolitan Munitions Committee, (2) Member of Metropolitan Munitions Tribunal.

Ministry of National Service :—Chairman of London Jewellers
and Silversmiths' Munitions Committee.

Ministry of Reconstruction :—Member of Committee on Trusts.

Board of Trade :—Member of Imports Consultative Council.

MR. W. VARCO WILLIAMS, J.P., C.C.

Mr. Williams has identified himself with many of the local
voluntary efforts during war-time, and in addition has performed
important duties in the County and outside of it, the following

*In May, 1920, a vacancy occurred in the Hornchurch Electoral Division of
the County Council, owing to the death of Mr. Thomas Gardner. Mr. Robertson contested the seat with Mr. Edwin Lambert, Chairman of the Hornchurch
Parish Council. The election took place on 17 June, 1920, Mr. Robertson being
returned by a majority of 807 votes. (Robertson 1,568, Lambert 761.)

being among the principal appointments held by him :—Vice-Chairman of the Beacontree Bench of Justices for the County, Member of the Standing Joint Committee of Essex, and a Member of the Essex County Council, representing the Dagenham Division. He is also a Member of the Port of London Authority.

List of Women Workers.*

Barry, Maria Louisa, Canteen Worker, N.Z.Y.M.C.A., Hornchurch 1916—1918.
Beharell, Mrs., Rest Room Worker, 1914—1916.
Burden, Mrs, Rest Room Worker, 1914—1916.
Crouch, Dorothy Ivy, Canteen Worker.
Dohoo, Mrs. Helen, Hon. Secretary, St. John's Ambulance Association Classes, Oct./Decr./1916.
Douse, Mrs., Rest Room Worker, 1914—1916.
Farquhar, Mrs., Rest Room Worker, 1914—1916.
Frost, Mrs. Daisy, Cook, N.Z. Convalescent Hospital, Y.M.C.A., 1916—1919
Frost, Florence Kate, Cook, N.Z. Convalescent Hospital Y.M.C.A., 1916—1919.
Gardner, Mrs., Organizer Queen Mary's Needlework Guild,† and Rest Room Worker.
Haywood, Mrs., Rest Room Worker, 1914—1916.
Hinton, Mrs., Rest Room Worker, 1914—1916.
Jordan, Mrs., Rest Room Worker, 1914—1916.
Jordan, Dulce, Rest Room Worker, 1914—1916.
Jarvis, Gladys L., Canteen worker, N.Z.Y.M.C.A., and Q.M. Needlework Guild, Romford and Hornchurch Branches.
Major, Mrs., Rest Room Worker, 1914—1916.
Miller, Mrs. Lizzie, Special Police Women's A.C.
Perfect, Dora E., Rest Room Worker, 1914—1916, Hon. Sec. St. John's Ambulance Association Classes, Jan.—Mar./16. N.Z. Canteen Worker 1916—1917.
Perfect, Mrs. E. M. E., Rest Room Worker, 1914—1916.
Randel, Mrs. E. A., Y.M.C.A. Canteen Worker, Gidea Park, 1918—1919.
Singer, Mrs. Edith, Canteen Worker, N.Z.Y.M.C.A., Hornchurch.
Sibthorp, Elizabeth W., Canteen Worker, War Contingent Canteen, N.Z. Camp, Hornchurch.
Sibthorp, Grace, Canteen Worker, War Contingent Canteen, N.Z. Camp, Hornchurch.
Stuttle, Mrs. Elizabeth, Canteen Worker, N.Z.Y.M.C.A., Hornchurch, July 1918—May 1919.
Tiddeman, Mrs. E. Spencer, Canteen Worker, Hare Hall Camp, and High Holborn, 1915—1919.
Tiddeman, Marjorie Spenser, Canteen Worker, High Holborn, 1917—1919.

Men Workers—Miscellaneous.

Hawkins, James Reuben, Senr., Clerk A.P.C.,Warley Barracks and Clerk R.A.F., Feb. 1915—Oct. 1917. Army Agent, London, March 1915—1920.
Izod, Ernest F. S., Voluntary Munition Worker at Eley's Works, Edmonton.

*For further list of Women Workers see pages 117 and 118.
†For other workers in **Queen Mary's Needlework Guild,** see pages 203 and 204.

THE PARISH CHURCH.

" And he did bid us follow to the temple "*
" Heaven hath a hand in these events
To whose high will we bound our calm contents."†

Shakespeare.

In the ancient Parish Church of St. Andrew's, Hornchurch, were held many impressive and memorable services during the war period. The Vicar, the Rev. Herbert Dale, had established the custom in pre-war times of holding united services whenever any great national or public occasion arose, and at those times invitations were extended to the Ministers and congregations of the Nonconformist bodies in the Parish to take part. The war afforded many opportunities for the application of this laudable and broad-minded custom. Every year, on the anniversary of the declaration of war, or on the Sunday nearest thereto, a united service was held at which the Ministers of the Nonconformist Churches read the lessons, and the same procedure was also adopted on several occasions when thanksgiving or memorial services were held.

The Sportsman's Battalion, during its occupation of Grey Towers Camp, held regularly a Sunday morning church parade‡ at St. Andrew's, as did also the New Zealanders for some considerable time after their arrival, until they built their own church in the camp. St. Andrew's was the parish church of the N.Z. Contingent in England, and the Rev. A. J. Parry, assistant curate, and the Rev. Peter Miller, M.A., Pastor of the Baptist Church, became their honorary Chaplains. Mr. Parry was also acting Chaplain to the Sportsman's Battalion.

The services above mentioned and many other celebrations connected with the Parish Church are recorded at the end of this chapter, and for convenience for reference are arranged in diary form. I think this may be considered as fairly representing the special and public activities of the church and clergy during the war. I make no attempt to record in detail the social and other work which constitutes the daily round and common task of the parish priest in England. The Vicar and his curate were very hard worked men in those strenuous days, and there came a day when Hornchurch, like many other parishes in the Kingdom, was called upon to provide its quota towards the great and pressing spiritual needs of the army, and on May 11, 1917, the Rev. A. J. Parry accepted the King's commission as Chaplain of the Forces, and was ordered to proceed to Ballykinlar Camp, County Down, Ireland.

Towards the end of the year 1917, the resignation of the Rev. Herbert Dale was announced. Mr. Dale had been in failing

*Midsummer Night's Dream, IV., i.
†Richard II., vii.
‡The new heating apparatus, which was installed in the church in 1914, was largely paid for by the collections made at these parade services.

Ford's Real Photo, Ilford.

INTERIOR OF ST. ANDREW'S CHURCH, HORNCHURCH.

Showing at the top of the East window part of curtain used for darkening the Church.

All the Church windows were curtained at night as a protection against enemy air raids

health for some considerable time, and it was owing entirely to that circumstance that his retirement became imperative. In consequence of the war, however, the appointment of his successor could not be arranged, and at the request of New College, he continued his duties until June 24, 1918, on which date he formally resigned, after a ministry extending over a period of 16 years. He also resigned in 1917 the Chaplaincy of the Cottage Homes, which he had held since September 1907, and was succeeded in that office by the Rev. Bernard Hartley, Curate-in-Charge of Harold Wood.

His resignation was a matter of deep concern and regret to his parishioners, he having endeared himself to Hornchurch folk of all classes, his popularity being probably as great among Nonconformists, and with those who identified themselves with no particular religious body, as with his own Church people.

On June 30, the Sunday following the Rev. Herbert Dale's resignation, the Bishop of Colchester, the Right Rev. Dr. Whitcombe, a lifelong friend of the late Vicar, preached at the parish church. The Bishop's appreciation of his work and eloquence was very apt and appropriate, and a portion of his sermon is here reproduced as a fitting memorial of Mr. Dale's ministry in Hornchurch :

The Bishop said : " I cannot refrain from a personal reference ; it is the first Sunday since your late Vicar officially laid down the work which he has been doing here so faithfully and so vigorously, and I should be apparently devoid of sympathy and appreciation if I did not take this opportunity of voicing the gratitude of the diocese to him for the devoted labours of 16 years, and for the help and inspiration which he has given to you and to many outside this parish, of which, having had the privilege of being his neighbour and friend both here and before he came here, I am able to speak with personal knowledge and experience. It would, perhaps, be unusual and unfitting to sing his praises now, though I know not why it should be our custom to criticise people in their lifetime and reserve our encomiums until they have passed away. But he will forgive me if I venture to suggest to you that he shares some of the best and most striking characteristics of the Apostle of whom we have been thinking (St. Peter). The first is obviously his energy and enthusiasm. Whatever his hand found to do, or his voice to utter, he did it or said it with his might, and carried people with him by the impetuosity of his efforts, and the sincerity of his convictions. The second is his eloquence. It is a dangerous gift, the power of swaying and influencing others by the exercise of oratory, but if used wisely and with the highest purposes its value and effectiveness are boundless. This gift your Vicar has possessed in a remarkable degree. Two of the best speeches I ever heard in my life were made by him. One was before a diocesan conference, at Oxford, and one on the occasion of the Nelson centenary at Romford. The gift has been exercised with generosity and love, as by one who knew that though he spake with the tongues of men and angels, and had not charity, he was but as sounding brass or a tinkling cymbal ; consequently, you never heard from him harsh criticism of the faults of others, but warm appreciation, often too kindly, of whatever was good in their character and work. You join with me, I know, in thanking him for his unsparing toil and his warm personal affection, and together we wish him the happiness and rest which his strenuous life has so abundantly earned."

The high esteem and affection in which Mr. Dale was held prompted the people of Hornchurch to raise a subscription for a testimonial to him, which took the form of a beautifully illuminated address, and a packet of War Bonds to the value of £216, and in addition a silver canteen to Mrs. Dale, publicly presented in the School Room, North Street, on Friday, September 6, 1918. Mr. C. H. Baker, the people's warden, presided, and the presentations were made by Mrs. T. Gardner.

In addition to the parish presentation, Mr. Dale received a further packet of War Bonds from the people of South Hornchurch, 109 of whom subscribed towards the presentation, which was made at the Vicarage by a deputation from South Hornchurch Chapel.

THE LATE REV. HERBERT JOHN DALE, M.A.

The Rev. Charles Steer, M.C., who was serving as a Chaplain of H.M. Forces in France, received the appointment as Chaplain and Vicar Temporal of Hornchurch, in succession to the Rev. Herbert Dale, on June 24, 1918, but as his military duties prevented him from taking up his ministry at once, the Rev. Alfred Ernest Howe, M.A., Keble College, Oxford, was on July 5, 1918, appointed curate-in-charge during the interregnum.

Mr. Dale vacated the Chaplaincy in August 1918, and acquired the house in Butts Green Road, formerly known as Vrede Villa, which he designated "Chackmore," but he lived to enjoy his retirement for only a very brief period, his death taking place

Designed and Illuminated by H. Noel Paillthorpe.

ILLUMINATED ADDRESS PRESENTED TO THE REV. HERBERT JOHN DALE, M.A.,
VICAR OF HORNCHURCH, 1902-1918

suddenly on Sunday night, October 20, 1918, at the age of 70 years. This event caused widespread sorrow and regret, and all the parish mourned the loss of him who was so recently their revered and honoured Vicar. His funeral on October 24, at the parish church, was of a public character, and was attended by a very large concourse of people. The burial service, which was exceedingly impressive, was conducted by the Bishop of Chelmsford, assisted by the Bishop of Barking, Bishop Neligan, Chaplain to the N.Z. Forces, Rector of Ford, Northumberland, and formerly Bishop of Auckland, N.Z., and the Rev. A. E. Howe, curate in charge. The following clergy were also present at the service :---

The Rev. Canon Bayne, Honorary Chaplain to the Bishop of Chelmsford ; Rev. G. M. Bell, Vicar of Romford and Rural Dean ; Rev. E. G. Gardener, Domestic Chaplain to the Bishop of Chelmsford ; Rev. G. V. Sumner, Rector of St. Andrew's, Romford ; Rev. H. R. Phillpotts of St. Alban's, Westcliff-on-Sea (formerly Rector of St. Andrew's, Romford) ; Rev. A. J. Parry, Vicar of St. Peter's, Upton Cross (formerly Curate of Hornchurch) ; and the Rev. H. B. Curtis, Vicar of St. Barnabas, Little Ilford ; the Rev. J. Benson Evans, Pastor of the Congregational Church, Hornchurch ; the Rev. T. E. Howe, Pastor of the Baptist Church, Hornchurch ; and the Rev. S. I. Blomfield, Pastor of the Congregational Church, Upminster, were also present.

The coffin plate bore the following inscription :

HERBERT JOHN DALE,
Born June 28, 1848, died October 20, 1918.
Vicar of Hornchurch from 1902 to 1918.

A small Latin cross in brass was affixed above the plate, and a St. Andrew's cross below it.

On the Sunday morning following the funeral, October 27, the Bishop of Barking preached, and made a very touching reference to the late Vicar, as did also Bishop Neligan, who preached at the evening service.

Shortly after the appointment of the Rev. Charles Steer, he was taken prisoner of war by the Germans, and remained in captivity until October 30, 1918. He opportunely arrived in England about the time of the signing of the Armistice, and was present at the Parish Church at the Thanksgiving Services on Sunday, 17 November, 1918, when he preached at both the morning and evening services.

He formally commenced his ministry on 23 March, 1919, and was licensed by the Bishop of Colchester on 8 May.

1914.   CHURCH EVENTS.

August 9.—WAR SUNDAY.—War having been proclaimed with the German Empire on August 4, special intercessions were offered on Sunday, August 9, and a daily weekday service announced to take place at noon.

238

1914.

October 25.—A number of Belgian wounded soldiers quartered at Ford Lodge, South Hornchurch, attended 11 o'clock service, at which the Vicar gave them an address of welcome in French.

November 8.—FIRST SPORTMAN'S BATTALION—(23rd Royal Fusiliers).— First Sunday Service at which the Sportsman's Battalion officially attended Church on parade. The Vicar gave an address of welcome to the Sportsmen, and took as his text:—" Be thou faithful unto death, and I will give thee a crown of life."

November 15.—The Dead March was played in memory of Field-Marshal Lord Roberts, who died in France on the previous day, November 14. The Vicar preached in the morning on " Lord Roberts and the two young gunners," and in the evening the Rev. A. J. Parry preached on the topic " Order and Ardour," as illustrating Lord Roberts s career.

November 22.—At the Men's Service at 3-30, Monsieur Faes, a Belgian Refugee, from Antwerp, played two violoncello solos.

Christmas Day.—The Vicar preached from the text :—" The Government shall be upon His shoulders, and He shall be called the Prince of Peace," and introduced the words of a beautiful poem, entitled, " On earth—Peace," from " Punch " (December 23, 1914), which is here reproduced by permission of the Proprietors of " Punch."

Judge of the passionate hearts of men,
  God of the wintry wind and snow,
Take back the blood-stained year
    again,
  Give us the Christmas that we know.

No stir of wings sweeps softly by,
  No Angel comes with blinding light,
Beneath the wild and wintry sky
  No Shepherds watch their flocks
    to-night.

In the dull thunders of the wind
  We hear the cruel guns afar,
But in the glowering heavens we
    find
  No guiding solitary star.

* * * * *

But lo, on this our Lord's birth-day,
  Lit by the glory whence she came,
Peace, like a warrior, stands at bay,
  A swift, defiant, living flame !

Full-armed she stands in shining mail,
  Erect, serene, unfaltering still,
Shod with a strength that cannot fail,
  Strong with a fierce o'ermastering
    will.

Where shattered homes and ruins be
  She fights through dark and des-
    perate days ;
Beside the watchers on the sea
  She guards the Channel's narrow
    ways.

Through iron hail and shattering
    shell,
  Where the dull earth is stained
    with red,
Fearless she fronts the gates of Hell
  And shields the unforgotten dead.

So stands she, with her all at stake,
  And battles for her own dear life,
That by one victory she may make
  For evermore an end of strife.

1915

January 3.—DAY OF SOLEMN INTERCESSION.—A day of solemn inter- cession on behalf of the Nation and Empire was observed throughout the kingdom. The Parish Council and other local bodies attended Church at 3 o'clock in the afternoon. The Vicar preached and the Rev. Benson Evans, Minister of the Congregational Church, read the first lesson, and the Rev. Peter Miller, M.A., Minister of the Baptist Church, the second lesson. During the Services for the day £25 13s. od. was collected for the Sick and Wounded Fund.

April 18.—THE BISHOP OF CHELMSFORD.—First visit of the Bishop of Chelmsford, Dr. J. E. Watts Ditchfield, who preached at the Church Parade of the Sportsman's Battalion, at 9-30 a.m., taking as his topic :—" A Man." He also preached at the 11 o'clock service.

1915.

August 4.—FIRST ANNIVERSARY OF THE WAR.—On Wednesday, the 4 August, the first anniversary of the Proclamation of War with Germany, two special services were held. A service of prayer, with address, at noon (simultaneously with the Service at St. Paul's, which was attended by the King and Queen and Queen Alexandra), and at 8.15 in the evening.

September 16 (Thursday).—MEMORIAL SERVICE.—A Memorial Service was held at 4.15 in the afternoon in memory of Company Quartermaster Sergeant Charles Henry Baker, jun., and of 27 other parishioners who had fallen since the war began.

(C. H. Baker, jun., was a Sidesman of the Parish Church, and Superintendent of the Boys' Sunday School).

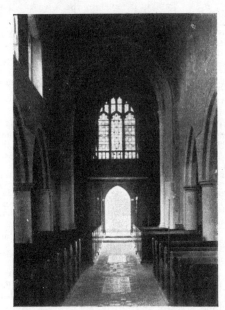

Photo]   [Lutis, Hornchurch.
WEST END OF CHURCH, SHOWING OPEN BELFRY.

October 24.—THE KING'S APPEAL.—The King, during the preceding week issued an Appeal to the youth of England to enlist. It was read in Church this morning and afternoon, all the congregation standing, and at the close of it " God Save the King " was sung. The evening service having to be discontinued, owing to the lighting restrictions, a course of Mission Services was opened this evening in the Cinema Hall, Suttons Lane, at 6 30 p.m. The King's Appeal was read in the course of the service.

November 7.—CHURCH DARKENING.—The generosity of a parishioner having enabled the Church to be so effectually darkened as to satisfy the requirements of the lighting regulations for protection against Zeppelin raids, the evening services in the Church at 6.30 p.m. were resumed.

240

1915.

November 28.—PIONEERS' BATTALION.—(26th Middlesex). First Parade in Church of the Pioneers' Battalion at 9.45 a.m.

December 5.—THE BISHOP OF CHELMSFORD preached at the evening service, taking as his subject: " The Message of the Church to the Nation."

December 19.—The last Church Parade of the Pioneers' Battalion.

1916.

January 2.—DAY OF SOLEMN NATIONAL PRAYER.—The first Sunday in the New Year was appointed a "day of homage and of reverend national recognition of the Hand of God in our National and Imperial History." At 3.15 p.m. a solemn United Service was held, at which the Rev. Benson Evans and the Rev. Peter Miller, M.A., read the lessons. The address was given by the Rev. A. J. Parry, who took as his text :—" Arise, let us go hence." Collections throughout the day were for the Order of St. John of Jerusalem, and the British Red Cross Society, and amounted to £17 10s.
(Muffled peals on the bells were rung on this day throughout England to emphasize the National sense of the loss it had sustained in the death of the brave men who had given their lives in the war.)

January 8 (Saturday) was also used to pay the solemn tribute of muffled bell-ringing.

January 16.—THE NEW ZEALANDERS.—At 9.45 a.m., was held the first church parade of the New Zealand Contingent. Topic of the Vicar's address :—" The Lord be with you." – Ruth ii. 4.
On the following Sunday, January 23, at their Church Parade, he took as his subject :—" Play up and play the game."

February 27.—The Bishop of Chelmsford addressed the New Zealanders at their Church Parade.

April 23.—Easter Sunday.—Celebration of the first Anniversary of Anzac Day (April 25). The New Zealanders in camp at Grey Towers Park paraded at Hornchurch Church to the number of 868 officers and men, when a special service* was held in commemoration of their comrades who had fallen in action during the war.

Whit Tuesday.—June 13.—LORD KITCHENER'S DEATH AND THE BATTLE OF JUTLAND.—A special Memorial service was held on Whit Tuesday, June 13, in honour of Lord Kitchener and the gallant men who sank with him in H.M.S. " Hampshire," off the Orkneys, on the night of June 5, 1916, and for those who perished in the Battle of Jutland on May 31, 1916. The organist, Mr. Alden, played Spohr's " Blessed are the Departed," as an opening voluntary, and the choir, preceded by the Vicar, Rev. H. Dale, and accompanied by the Rev. Peter Miller, and the Rev. Benson Evans, then entered, singing Lord Kitchener's favorite hymn, " Abide with me." A very touching and impressive Memorial Service followed, the Rev. Peter Miller and the Rev. Benson Evans reading the lessons. The Vicar preached from 2 Samuel iii., 30. " Know ye not that a Prince and a great man is fallen to-day in Israel." Before the sermon, the Dead March in " Saul " was played, and after the sermon Beethoven's Funeral March. The Holy Table was covered with the red and white ensigns, and muffled peals were rung before and after the service.
The great bell was also tolled from 12 noon to 12.30, at which time the Memorial Service to Lord Kitchener, attended by the King and Queen, was being held at St. Paul's Cathedral.

*See page 171 for full report of this service.

241

Q

1916.

June 13.—Burial of Private Vasau, a Christian soldier from Niue Island, one of the South Sea Islands, attached to the New Zealand Contingent, who died from pneumonia at Grey Tower Camp. The funeral was conducted by the Rev. J. Benson Evans, Minister of the Congregational Church.*

Photo]   [C. Stanley Holton.

GRAVES OF PRIVATES VASAU, MOKI RANGITIRA, FILITONA
AND TALEVA, IN HORNCHURCH CHURCHYARD.

The lower photograph shows the graves decorated with flowers by the parishioners,
and with the wreath sent by the High Commissioner of New Zealand,
on Anzac Day, 1919.

July 3.—Burial of His Highness the Prince Rangitira (known as Prince Moki), Private 16/1088, New Zealand Expeditionary Force, Base Depot. Prince Moki, who was 21 years of age, was a son of the ruling chief of the Island of Niue. He had seen active service in Egypt and on the French Front. He died of pneumonia at Grey Towers Camp.

*There were, at this time, a number of natives of the Niue Islands in camp at Grey Towers, but the climate of this country was very trying to them, and many of them suffered in consequence, several dying from pneumonia and other chest diseases. In their native land they lived entirely on fruit, and during their stay at Grey Towers, the Rev. A. J. Parry daily collected for them bananas and other fruit from the people of Hornchurch. He also conducted a service each morning in the hospital, the service being translated by one of the Niuemen, who was a native catechist.

1916.

It is said that Niue Islanders were converted to Christianity by missionaries of the Congregational Church. On this account the Burial Service (as in the case of Private Vasau) was conducted by the Rev. J. Benson Evans. At the Service a large number of the Prince's comrades sang a funeral hymn in the native language and to native music. The Rev. Herbert Dale was present at the Service as one of the mourners.

July 23.—The Vicar's address at the morning service was entirely devoted to a reference to Private Stuart K. Barnes, 2nd Battalion London Scottish Regiment, the report of whose death in action on the Western Front, on July 14, had just been received. Stuart K. Barnes was Captain of the Hornchurch Company of the Church Lads' Brigade before joining H.M. Forces.

August 4.—Second anniversary of the declaration of war.* Church Parade of the New Zealanders was held at the Parish Church at 11 o'clock, at which Canon Burton, Chaplain to the N.Z. Forces, was the officiant. The Rev. Herbert Dale preached, taking as his text : " God spake unto the children of Israel that they go forward."

September 6.—The bells of the church were rung this Wednesday evening in recognition of Lieutenant William Leefe Robinson's distinction, he having . been awarded the V.C. for attacking and bringing down Zeppelin L21, on the night of September 2nd/3rd.

September 21.—The 44th anniversary of the Rev. Herbert Dale's ordination as Priest. Harvest Festival. Preacher, Rev. W. J. Sommerville, Rector of St. George's, Southwark.

September 24.—This morning thanksgivings were offered for the safety of the parish and church, bombs having been dropped the night previous in the near vicinity during the raid in which Lieutenant Frederick Sowrey brought down Zeppelin L32, at Billericay.

October 1.—This evening during service, the Special Constables were called out from the church for duty, a Zeppelin raid being in progress. Just before midnight, L31 was brought down in flames by Lieutenant W. J. Tempest, at Potter's Bar.

November 2 to 7.—The National Mission of Repentance and Hope was held from November 2 to 7 inclusive. This was an event of far-reaching importance for the Church of England. It discovered both the weakness and the strength of the Church in the national life. At Hornchurch the Bishop's Messenger was the Rev. Canon H. K. Sanders, Vicar and Rural Dean of Woodford.

The Rev. A. J. Parry, Curate of Hornchurch, was sent by the Bishop as his Messenger to the parishes of Stanford-le-Hope and Moulsham, and also to Shoeburyness Garrison.

December 31.—Parochial Service of National Thanksgiving and Intercession at 3.45 p.m. The Rev. J. Benson Evans, Pastor of Congregational Church, read both Lessons. The Rev. Herbert Dale preached, taking as his topic :—" The blade, the ear, and the full corn of English History." Collection for the British Red Cross Society amounted to £8 9s. od.

1917.

February 4.—The Vicar preached on the topic : " The religious obligation of economy in food, and self-sacrifice in buying War Loan."

February 25.—The Vicar took as his topic for his evening sermon : " Rationing as a bearing of one another's burdens."

March 11.—Visit of the Rural Dean, Rev. G. M. Bell, who preached on " Individualism and Fellowship," taking as his text i. Cor., xii., 12.

*The Parish Commemoration was held in the open air in the evening. See page 194.

1917.

May 3, at 7.30 p.m.—Gaul's Holy City was performed in the Church. Soloists: Mrs. Drossi, Madame Laura Lawrence, Mr. H. E. Steed and Mr. W. Titley.

May 6.—ANNIVERSARY OF THE KING'S ACCESSION.—Church Parade at 11 a.m., of the 4th Cadet Battalion of the Essex Regiment, under the command of Captain G. C. Eley. 130 officers and lads attended, accompanied by their band and colours.

At the evening service the Rev. A. J. Parry preached his last sermon before taking up his duties as Chaplain of His Majesty's Forces at Ballykinlar, County Down, Ireland. The Vicar, on behalf of some of the parishioners, presented him with a cheque for £40 on his departure.

August 5.—Commemoration Service on the fourth Anniversary (August 4) of the commencement of the war, at which the Roll of Honour of the men of Hornchurch who had made the Great Sacrifice was read.

September 28 (Friday).—Confirmation by the Bishop of Chelmsford at 2 p.m., at which three New Zealand soldiers were presented by the Rev. Mackenzie Gibson, C.F.

November 18.—Confirmation by the Bishop of Barking at 3 p.m.

1918.

January 3 (Thursday.)—Performance of the Christmas music from the Messiah at 7 p.m. by the Greater Choir, at which a collection for the St. Dunstan's Home for Blinded Soldiers and Sailors was taken, amounting to £13 13s. Soloists: Miss Anderson, Miss Muriel Burden, Miss Thear, Mr. F. Hammond, and Mr. J. Challis. Organist and choirmaster, Mr. H. W. Alden.

January 6.—DAY OF NATIONAL PRAYER AND THANKSGIVING.—Special Parochial Service at 3.15 p.m., at which the Rev. Canon Bayne preached on the topic " Dedication of ourselves," St. John XVII., 19. The first Lesson was read by Canon Bayne, and the second Lesson by the Rev. J. Benson Evans. Collection for the British Red Cross Society amounted to £23 10s. od.

February 11.—The Rev. A. J. Parry was to-day nominated by the Bishop of Chelmsford to the Vicarate of St. Peter's, Upton Cross, Essex, and appointed Honorary Chaplain to H.M. Forces.

March 3.—A Carol Service was held at 3 p.m., the music being sung by the Romford Carol League, under the direction of Mr. J. Challis. The collection on behalf of St. Dunstan's Home for Blinded Soldiers and Sailors amounted to £6 6s. 7d.

March 31 (Easter Day).—At the evening service a solemn Te Deum was sung in commemoration of all Parishioners fallen in the war.

April 14.—Special Intercession Services, by request of the Bishop of Chelmsford, owing to the serious war news received from the Western Front.

May 12.—Return of Lieut. Philip Dale, the Vicar's elder son, after having escaped from Ludwigshaven, through Holland, he having been a prisoner of war in Germany for two years and seven months. He was taken prisoner at Loos on September 26, 1915.

June 23.—Last address given by the Rev. Herbert Dale as Vicar of the Parish. This was given at the Children's Flower Service in the afternoon. Hospital Sunday. Total collections (including boxes), £115.

June 24.—Resignation of the Rev. Herbert Dale, after a ministry of 16 years, as Chaplain and Vicar Temporal of the Parish of Hornchurch.

June 30.—The Bishop of Colchester was the officiant and preached the sermon, taking for his topic "St. Peter and the late Vicar," St. John XXI., 17 (see page 235).

244

1918.

July 5.—The Rev. Alfred Ernest Howe, M.A., Keble College, Oxford, appointed Curate-in-Charge of Hornchurch, pending the appointment of a Chaplain and Vicar Temporal to succeed the Rev. H. Dale.

August 4 (Sunday).—Fourth Anniversary of the declaration of War. The Parish Church was the scene of a memorable service, at which men and women of all shades of religious belief met together for Divine Worship, and to join in one common act of thanksgiving and intercession. The service, which lasted nearly two hours, was held in the afternoon. It was attended by members of the Parish Council, and of the Fire Brigade, the latter in uniform. Many men were present from the New Zealand Convalescent Hospital at Grey Towers, and also several of the nurses, whose red capes contrasted strongly with the blue uniforms of the men. The Altar was draped with the Union Jack, and the pulpit, reading desk, and the easternmost pillar of the south arcade with the national flags of the Allies.

The service opened with the processional hymn " To Thee O God we fly," followed by the special service officially appointed for the day, which was read by the Curate-in-Charge, the Rev. A. E. Howe, The hymn, " All people that on earth do dwell," having been sung, the Baptist Minister, the Rev. Thomas E. Howe, read the First Lesson (i. Kings, VIII., 54, *et. seq.*) The Anthem " Save them, O Lord " was then rendered by the choir, after which the Second Lesson was read by the Rev. J. Benson Evans, Minister of the Congregational Church, Emerson Park.

The sermon was preached by the Right Rev. Bishop Neligan, Chaplain to the N.Z. Forces, who took for his text the words, " God is our Refuge and Strength " (Psalm XLVI., 1-3).

At the conclusion of the sermon the National Anthem was sung, and the Roll of Honour of parishioners fallen in the War was read by the Rev. Herbert Dale, M.A. The " Last Post " was then sounded by the buglers of the New Zealand Forces, and during the singing of " For all the Saints " a collection was taken for the Essex Prisoners of War Fund. The service concluded with the episcopal benediction and the recessional hymn, " Praise my soul the King of Heaven." The collections during the day amounted to £19.

September 6.—Presentation to the Rev. Herbert Dale and Mrs. Dale (*see page* 236).

September 29.—Harvest Festival. Bishop Neligan preached at the Evening Service.

October 29 (Sunday.)—Death of the Rev. H. Dale.

October 24 (Thursday.)—Burial of the Rev. H. Dale in Hornchurch Churchyard (*see page* 238).

November 11.—Armistice Day.*

November 17.—Armistice Sunday.*

December 8 (Sunday).—A United Service of Intercession was held in the Parish Church in connection with the General Election, which took place on the following Saturday, December 14. This was probably the first time such an unusual service was ever held in the old Church, but the idea was one worthy of imitation. The Curate-in-Charge, the Rev. A. E. Howe, preached the Sermon, taking as his text the words," Seek ye first the Kingdom of God and his righteousness, and all these things shall be added unto you." Matthew VI., 23. The Vicar-designate, Rev. Charles Steer, M.C., C.F., took the Service, and the Pastor of the Hornchurch Baptist Church, the Rev. Thos. E. Howe, read both Lessons. The congregation was not a large one, but it was representative of all the religious bodies in the Parish.

*See Chapter " From Armistice to Peace."

245

Drawn by A. B. Bamford.

CHANCEL FROM THE NORTH CHAPEL, SHOWING
THE AYLOFFE TOMB.

1918.

December 29.—Commemoration Service for those who had given their lives in the war, at which the Roll of Honour was read.

1919.

January 12.—Bishop Neligan preached at the morning service (St. Luke II., 49.)

February 5 (Wednesday).—Performance of the Christmas music from the Messiah in the Church at 8 p.m., by the United Choirs of Hornchurch and Upminster, at which a collection, amounting to £5 3s. 1d. was made in aid of the St. Dunstan's Hostel for Blinded Soldiers and Sailors. Soloists : Miss Plessy Coomber, Miss W. Anderson, Mr. John Challis, and Mr. H. E. Steed. Organist and Conductor, Mr. H. W. Alden.

April 24 (Thursday).—Vestry Meeting held in the School Room, North Street. The first Vestry presided over by the Rev. Charles Steer as Vicar of the parish.

April 30 (Wednesday).—Performance of the Easter Music from the Messiah in the Church at 8 p.m. by the United Choirs of Hornchurch and Upminster, at which a collection amounting to £7 was made in aid of the St. Dunstan's Hostel. Soloists : Miss Annie Cross, Mme. Wilhelmina Lawrence, Mr. Lawrence Platt, and Mr. Fred Hammond. Organist, Mrs. W. E. Clippingdale ; Conductor, Mr. H. W. Alden.

June 1.—United parochial Service in Mill Field, at 3 p.m., to celebrate the home-coming of soldiers and sailors returned from the war.*

June 29.—Thanksgiving service for Peace.*

July 6.—National Thanksgiving Day for Peace.*

July 19.—National Celebration of Peace.*

August 9.—Parish Celebration of Peace.*

November 2.—All Souls Day, Special Service at which the Roll of Honour was read.

November 11.—Remembrance Day, First Anniversary of Armistice Day.*

December 4.—Church Social at the School, North Street, and official welcome of the parish to the Vicar, the Rev. Charles Steer, M.C., and Mrs. Steer.

December 14.—First visit to the Parish of the Right Rev. Dr. Inskip, Bishop of Barking.

CLERGY AND CHURCH OFFICERS AT THE END OF THE WAR PERIOD.

Vicar.—The Rev. C. Steer, M.A., New College, Oxford.

Assistant Curate.—The Rev. A. E. Howe, M.A., Keble College, Oxford.

Churchwardens.—Messrs. Walter Dendy and C.H. Baker.

Sidesmen.—Messrs. E. Allen, C. T. Beharell, A. W. Boulton, E. G. Bratchell, T. G. Burden, W. G. Card, J. H. Dockrill, J. Dockrill, R. Dockrill, H. P. Dorey, E. Fry, G. Fry, T. Gardner, W. Halestrap, W. E. Langridge, C. T. Perfect, A. F. G. Ruston, H. L. Symonds, and S. Biddle.

Parish Clerk and Sexton.—Lieut.-Colonel Arthur Cooke, New College, M.A., M.B., Ch. B. Oxon, M.A., Camb., F.R.C.S., &c.

Deputy Clerk and Sexton.—Mr. John Purrett.

Deputy Churchwardens.—Messrs. R. Dockrill and W. E. Langridge.

*See Chapter "From Armistice to Peace."

PRESENTATION TO MISS KEIGHLEY.

An interesting gathering took place in the Council Hall, Billet Lane, on Thursday afternoon, March 27, 1919, for the purpose of making a presentation to Miss Keighley in appreciation of her valuable services in the parish. The gift consisted of a handsomely fitted dressing case, a wallet containing £33, and an album with the names of nearly 400 subscribers, and the following inscription :—

" We, the undersigned, wishing to mark in some way our high appreciation of your very useful and long-continued labour for the benefit of others in the parish of Hornchurch and neighbourhood, ask your acceptance of the accompanying token of our regard. And we desire also to express the hope that you may long continue with us, and have the blessings of both health and happiness."

Mrs. Gardner, who presided, said they had met to offer to Miss Keighley their most grateful thanks for all the work she had done in the parish. Miss Keighley had made her home in Hornchurch for a great many years, was known to one and all, and was always trying to do the best she could for rich and poor alike. When their dear old vicar, the late Rev. Herbert Dale, had to retire owing to failing health, a great deal of Miss Keighley's work had to end as well. Miss Keighley knew how much they all appreciated the work she had done during many years, but some of them thought the parishioners would like to give her a tangible expression of their regard. The result was that they had obtained the gifts that were to be presented that afternoon. They hoped Miss Keighley would continue to live among them, and to do, at any rate, some of the work to which she had been accustomed.

Mr. W. Varco Williams, J.P., C.C., made the presentation, and said the subscriptions not only represented the pounds of the prosperous, who were few, but the pence of the poor, who were many. He felt sure the value of the gift would be added to by the knowledge that it represented the strong, sincere and deep appreciation of all Miss Keighley had done for Hornchurch during the many years she had resided there, and wherever she went she would carry with her the appreciation that was felt for her by the people of Hornchurch.

Miss Keighley, in acknowledgment, said she would need a great deal more eloquence than she had to enable her to adequately express how overwhelmed she felt by their kind words and beautiful gifts. She did not know how to thank them, but she did thank them with all her heart. It was always her joy to help her cousin, the late vicar, in his work. She only wished her work was worthy of their estimate of it, but she felt that they realised what she would have done if she had been able to do it. She would greatly cherish their gifts, which would be most valued possessions.

During the proceedings songs were sung by Miss Burden, and pianoforte selections were played by Miss Pettiford.

SOUTH HORNCHURCH CHAPEL.

South Hornchurch is to many modern Hornchurch folk an unexplored land, and, apart from those who live on its extreme borders, there are probably few parishioners who know very much about its people, whose homes lie scattered around the ancient manor house of Brittons, whose former glories are now only historic memories. Within a short distance of the mansion where the great family of Ayloffe lived in such magnificence, there now stands a small church, erected in 1864 as a church of ease to the Parish Church of St. Andrew's, and known as South Hornchurch Chapel. For over twenty-two years Mr. J. T. Attwooll has been its " unordained parson," fulfilling all the duties and responsibilities of a clergyman in all but those rites of the Church which are forbidden by the liturgy to laymen. His actual office is that of Lay Reader, which he holds by direct authority from the Bishop of the Diocese, the appointment being under the control of the Chaplain and Vicar Temporal of Hornchurch. He wears the badge and blue silk neck ribbon of his office.

Never were Mr. Attwooll's services more needed or more appreciated than during the Great War. The Roll of Honour for South Hornchurch contains the names of 96 men—a splendid contribution from so small a community—and it has been Mr. Attwooll's special care to keep in touch, as far as possible, with these men and their families during the whole of their service. It has been his custom to read the full Roll of Honour on the first Sunday of every month. Twenty-four of these brave men have made the great sacrifice, and through Mr. Attwooll's initiative there now hang on the walls of the Chapel beautiful blue and gold silk bannerets in memory of six of their number. These were presented by the relatives of the fallen men, and at their dedication a special prayer, composed by Mr. Attwooll, was used.

On Sunday evening, March 30th, 1919, a special memorial service was held in the Chapel for the twenty-four soldiers and sailors who had died in the war. The Rev. Charles Steer, M.C., had arranged to make this the occasion of his first formal visit to the Chapel as Vicar of the Parish, and was to have preached the sermon. He was, however, unfortunately unable to be present, owing to illness ; the whole service was therefore taken by Mr. Attwooll, who also presided at the organ. The chapel was crowded with relatives and friends of the men who had so nobly died for their country, and there were also present many of the men who had been demobilized from active service. Miss Halliday sang from Handel's Messiah," I know that my Redeemer liveth," and the Reader in charge took the same beautiful words —John xix, 25-26 for his text, and at the close, the large congregation standing, the Dead March in Saul was played, followed by the reading of the names of the men who had died.

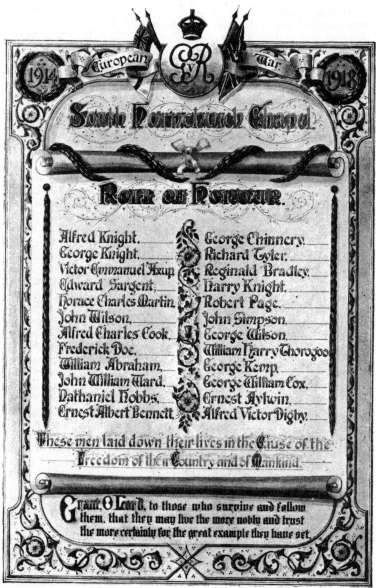

European War

1914   1918

South Hornchurch Chapel.

Roll of Honour.

Alfred Knight.	George Chinnery.
George Knight.	Richard Tyler.
Victor Emmanuel Axup	Reginald Bradley.
Edward Sargent.	Harry Knight.
Horace Charles Martin.	Robert Page.
John Wilson.	John Simpson.
Alfred Charles Cook.	George Wilson.
Frederick Doe.	William Harry Thorogood.
William Abraham.	George Kemp.
John William Ward.	George William Cox.
Nathaniel Hobbs.	Ernest Aylwin.
Ernest Albert Bennett.	Alfred Victor Digby.

These men laid down their lives in the Cause of the Freedom of their Country and of Mankind.

Grant, O Lord, to those who survive and follow them, that they may live the more nobly and trust the more certainly for the great example they have set.

Designed and Illuminated by H. Noel Pailthorpe.

ILLUMINATED ROLL OF HONOUR IN SOUTH HORNCHURCH CHAPEL.

On Sunday afternoon, December 14, 1919, the Right Rev. Dr. Inskip, Lord Bishop of Barking, on the occasion of his first visit to the Parish, dedicated in the Chapel a beautifully illuminated Roll of Honour to commemorate the sacrifice, heroism, and devotion of the brave South Hornchurch men who had fallen in the war. After the dedication, the Bishop, who was attended by the Vicar, the Rev. Charles Steer, delivered an appropriate address. The Roll, which is here reproduced, is the work of Mr. H. Noel Pailthorpe.

Mr. Attwooll's work in South Hornchurch is worthy of all commendation, and proof of his appreciation was afforded in December, 1917, when a presentation was made to him by the members of his congregation on the completion of twenty-one years' ministry among them. This took the form of a purse of money and an illuminated address, the presentation being made by the Chapel Warden, Mr. W. Cutler, who paid a sincere tribute to Mr. Attwooll and his work, and expressed the affection and esteem in which he was held by those for whom he had laboured so earnestly over so long a period.

CHAPEL OFFICERS.

Warden.—Mr. W. Cutler.

Sidesmen.—Messrs. T. Bradley, J. Cracknell, H. J. Harris, J. Holbrook, George Knight, E. Rust, G. Sealey, W. Smith, W. Pomfrett.

HAROLD WOOD.

That part of our huge parish known as Harold Wood has every reason to be proud of its war record, for, as far as can be ascertained, the number of men who joined H.M. Forces during hostilities, or were already serving before the outbreak of war, was no less than 206.* Those who were left at home did their utmost to " carry on " in various ways to help the men who had gone out from the village to the many battle fronts. A number of the women residents, especially the younger ones, did long and useful service in the offices of the Army Pay Corps and the Army Records at Warley. Others maintained the local postal delivery service, while some took up work on farms, or in the City, in place of men who had been called up. During the latter years of the war, too, many Harold Wood men did work at Woolwich and other munition factories.

HAROLD WOOD WAR WORK GUILD.—In January, 1917, a Guild of ladies was formed with the object of making comforts for the Troops. The following served on the Committee :— Miss D'Aeth, Mrs. Hartley, Miss Harvey, Mrs. Rae, and Mrs. Rowlatt. During the two years, 1917 and 1918, a large quantity of useful comforts were made. The War Work Guild was registered as a War Charity, and therefore was able to make

*The population of Harold Wood Ward, at the last census in 1911, was 1,100.

William C. Inman, P.A.S.I.

HAROLD WOOD WAR MEMORIAL HALL.

house-to-house collections in aid of its funds ; in addition, very considerable help was received from whist drives, concerts, etc., which were organized on its behalf. £73 worth of wool and other materials was used by the Guild, and the following is a list of the articles sent to the receiving depôt :—179 helmets, 755 hospital bags, 240 pairs mittens, 373 mufflers, 333 pairs socks, 116 operation stockings and 296 sun shields.

SPECIAL CONSTABULARY.—During the war period Harold Wood had its squad of Special Constables. The following is a list of those parishioners who performed this particular form of war service :—

Sergt. H. B. Ayres*
H. E. Ayres (A.)
A. Baldwin*
W. Barker (R.)
E. F. Bays
—Bridges (R.)
H. Bryant (A.)
Sergt. A. Clyde (A.)
Sergt. F. Creek*
C. Fancy (A.)
—Ford (A.)
J. W. Grout*
H. Hicks*
R. G. Howe*
Sergt. D. Lewtas*
E. Lloyd (A.)
D. Maitland (A.)
— Major*
— Manning (A.)
L. Page (A.)
Cpl. P. J. Park (N.)
W. Pond (A.)
T. Putman*
—Rainbird (A.)
G. H. Rainbow (A.)
S. Rea (A.)
M. E. Ricketts*
T. Rose*
C. Russell (A.)
C. Saltwell (A.)
A. P. Shave (A.)
W. Slyfield*
W. Smith*
J. West (A.)

Very few soldiers were billeted in Harold Wood. In the autumn of 1917 a small contingent of Royal Engineers visited the Ward, arriving on September 28, to erect telephone wires from Harold Wood to the aircraft station in Hall Lane, Upminster Common. Several men employed on the land were billeted here, as were also a certain number of young women land workers.

The people of Harold Wood did their share towards the support of sufferers through the war. In addition to sending a collection of over £6 from the Church to the Prince of Wales's Fund in August, 1914, a sum of £8 11s. 6d. was collected for the relief of distress, occasioned by the war, but not dealt with by that Fund.

ALLOTMENTS.—In order to help provide food, especially in 1918 when vegetables were so scarce, many residents took up allotments, and nearly all the available uncultivated land was broken up and made to yield crops. In Harold Wood the number of allotments cultivated was 52.

HAROLD WOOD CHURCH.—A weekday service of intercession was held, practically without a break, from September, 1915, to

A=joined Army, N=joined Navy, R=resigned, *=served to the end of the War.

August, 1919, at which the names of Harold Wood men serving in the Forces were read out, and prayer offered on their behalf.

In spite of the frequent air raids that took place over Essex, only on one occasion was a Church Service interrupted by a raid. This was on Friday, September 28, 1917, at the harvest festival. The warning was given during the service, when the hymn, " Jesu, Lover of my Soul " was sung, and the congregation quietly dispersed.

UNITED SERVICES.—Several times during the war united services were held, when members of the Established Church and Nonconformists met together and joined together in prayer to God in those dark days of anxiety and distress, and later in thanksgiving to Him when Peace was at last signed and bright hope shone again. The first of these services was held on January 2, 1916, and others at stated and specific times as occasion arose. The service in the afternoon of Sunday, January 6, 1918, will long be remembered. This was the day appointed by Royal Proclamation as a Day of National Prayer. The Church was crowded, as indeed were churches everywhere on that occasion. The preacher was the Rev. Harry Williams, Minister of the United Methodist Church, Manor Park. If ever earnest prayer went up from a nation to God it did on that day. His answer to it was seen in the marvellous holding of the great German offensive in the following spring, and later the turning of the tide, and the subsequent collapse of the German, Austrian, Bulgarian and Turkish armies that decided the war.

On Armistice Day, November 11, 1918, a well-attended service of Thanksgiving was held in the evening, at which the address was given by the Curate-in-Charge, the Rev. Bernard Hartley, M.A.

At a united service, held on January 5, 1919, the preacher was the Rev. J. H. Squire, M.A., B.D., Minister of the United Methodist Church, Seven Kings.

To commemorate the signing of the Peace Treaty on June 28, 1919, a Thanksgiving Service was held on July 6, which was followed on Sunday afternoon, July 27, by a special united service of Thanksgiving, when the address was given by the Curate-in-Charge, and prayer offered by Mr. F. Creek, one of the leaders of the United Methodist Church in Harold Wood. The collection at this service was given to the St. Dunstan's Hostel for Blinded Sailors and Soldiers. At other United Services the collections were in aid of the Essex Branch British Red Cross Society.

MEMORIAL SERVICES.—Two services in honour of the men of the district who had laid down their lives were held (besides three others arranged by private request). One of these was on August 4, 1917, when a list of nine names of men who had made the Great Sacrifice was read, and the other on December 29, 1918, the day appointed by authority for the Commemoration of the Fallen, when the number had increased to twenty-two.

LETTERS TO SAILORS AND SOLDIERS.—A letter and an appropriate card was sent from Harold Wood Church to every man whose address could be obtained, at Easter or Christmas, or both, in each of the years 1916, 1917, and 1918. Many replies were received, testifying to the pleasure the men felt in being remembered in this way.

LECTURE.—Mention may be made here of an interesting lecture given by the Rev. Harry Williams, on the work of the Y.M.C.A. at the front. The lecture was given in the United Methodist Chapel, in August, 1917, and afterwards repeated, by request, at the Church Room, on October 17, of the same year.

PEACE CELEBRATIONS.

A School Treat was given in a field, lent by Mr. Sam Mallinson, on July 5, 1919, and on August Bank Holiday, the Ward celebrations took place, which provided a very pleasant time for all the residents and for numerous visitors from the surrounding district. The arrangements had been made by a large committee, and all the principal residents had a share in making the celebrations successful. There was a fine display of decorations, and in the evening there were some pretty illuminations. The proceedings were opened in the afternoon in a meadow opposite the Village Institute by Mrs. Bryant, wife of Mr. E. Bryant, J.P., of Harold Wood Hall, supported by Sir Joseph G. Broodbank, J.P., and Lady Broodbank. She was presented with a choice bouquet by the little granddaughter of Mr. George H. Matthews. A programme of 32 races had been arranged, and the various events caused great interest and excitement. The tugs-of-war were particularly strenuous, and the races for veterans were a great feature. Prizes were offered for fancy dress, and there was close competition, some novel and attractive costumes being worn. There was a beauty competition, bowling for a pig, and various other diverting contests, which were all entered into with great spirit. Tea was served to residents in the Village Institute, a very large and happy party enjoying an excellent meal, and there was a tea tent in the meadow for the convenience of visitors. In the evening concerts were given in the Village Institute, and the outdoor revels were continued, in spite of a short shower. The prizes were distributed by Mrs. Bryant. The programme was brought to a close by a display of fireworks. The celebrations afforded keen enjoyment to all who shared in them, and those who made the arrangements had every reason for self-congratulation at the success of their efforts.

HAROLD WOOD MEN WELCOMED HOME.

On Saturday, September 5, 1919, at the Village Institute, Harold Wood, the ex-service men connected with the village were entertained to dinner, the whole expense of which was generously defrayed by Sir Joseph Broodbank. A company of about 250 sat down, including the men, their wives, and sweethearts. The arrangements were ably carried out by a Committee, consisting of Messrs. R. Warren, hon. treasurer; T. Putman, F. Miller, G. Rainbow, and A. J. Bryett, the latter as hon. secretary.

Sir Joseph Broodbank occupied the chair, supported by Lady Broodbank, Mr. Edward Bryant, J.P., and Mrs. Bryant, Lieut.-Colonel A. G. L. Pepys, M.C., Commanding the 44th Regimental District, Warley; Colonel A. R. Bryant, Essex Regiment; Lieut. Bryant, R.F.C., Mr. and Mrs. James Matthews, Mr. George H. Matthews, Mr. and Mrs. F. Creek, the Rev. B. Hartley, and others. After the dinner a concert took place. The artistes were the Misses Elsie Berry, Joan Fowler, Barrett, Messrs. R. Howe, L. Jones, G. and J. Barrett, E. Cooper, Fred Wilson, and G. Pratt (accompanist).

Sir Joseph Broodbank said he had been acquainted with that hall for some 21 years, but he had never known it put to a better use than it had been that evening. They owed much to the indomitable spirit of our people, personified and intensified in its finest form in the doings of their Navy and Army. To that Harold Wood had contributed in no small measure. No fewer than 206 men left that village, and of that number 140 had returned, 40 were still serving, and 26 had been killed or had died of wounds or sickness. The record family was that of Mr. Pemberton, senr., whose four sons and one son-in-law had served. Two of these were still serving, and they were all living. Harold Wood welcomed all who had come back, and mourned for those who had not returned. Their achievements were all the greater because they had never murmured or desponded under temporary defeats or boasted in the hour of victory, and they never knew how truly noble they were in it all.

Colonel Bryant remarked that those who had served had always appreciated the thoughtfulness of those who, at the beginning of the war, sent out blankets, and later cigarettes, etc. Since the commencement of the war the county of Essex had raised 27 battalions of infantry—an excellent record.

Colonel Pepys presented Military Medals to Sergt. A. E. Creek, R.F.A., for courage and devotion to duty during a violent enemy bombardment; Corpl. T. F. Putman, K.R.R., for exceptionally good work when in charge of a Lewis gun at Neuve Eglise; and Corpl. F. V. Roper, Post Office Rifles, for devotion to duty at Poelcapelle, when, as the result of his bravery and resource, a German farmhouse was captured with 50 prisoners and four machine guns.

The Rev. B. Hartley expressed thanks to Sir Joseph Brood-bank for providing the dinner, and referred to the excellent work he had performed during the war with the Port of London Authority.* Mr. F. Creek also thanked Sir Joseph and Lady Broodbank, and the vote was accorded with musical honours.

THE WAR MEMORIAL.

The people of Harold Wood entered heartily into the matter of providing a suitable war memorial for the men of their Ward who had died in the war, and actually completed their scheme while their neighbours in adjacent Wards were in the talking and planning stage. Early in the year 1919 twelve determined men belonging to the Established Church, the Non-conformists bodies, and the Village Club, with equal representation, met together to formulate a scheme. They then called a public meeting at which Sir Joseph Broodbank presided, and pro-pounded their scheme, which was to acquire the Entertainment Hall and equip it for a Village Institute and Club. The idea met with favourable reception, and it was resolved to carry it out, provided the requisite money could be raised. A Committee was appointed consisting of :—Messrs. A. J. Bryett, F. Creek, Rev. B. Hartley, Messrs. F. Macey, G. H. Matthews, F. Miller, T. Putman, G. H. Rainbow, T. Rose, —. Stokes, R. Warren, and W. Willats, and an appeal made to the public was so successful that a large sum was assured in a short space of time. Mr. Edward Bryant, J.P., the owner of the Entertainment Hall, had been approached with reference to the acquisition of the Hall, and had agreed to sell it to the Committee, but he was so impressed by the spontaneous response made by the villagers to the appeal for funds, and by their evident desire to perpetuate the names and memories of the heroic men who had made the great sacrifice, that he generously offered to present the Hall as his contribution to the memorial. Any doubt that may have hitherto existed as to the success of the undertaking was at once removed, and steps were immediately taken to work out the details connected with the scheme. These involved certain structural alterations to the hall itself, and the erection of memorial stones of similar design on either side of the entrance, the designs for which were prepared by Mr. William C. Inman, P.A.S.I.

*Sir Joseph Broodbank's special war contribution was in connection with the Port and Transit Executive Committee, of which Committee he was a member from its initiation. That Committee had the responsibility for the last four years of the war of controlling all the Port operations throughout the Kingdom, and upon them depended the rapid loading and discharging of vessels and foodstuffs. How great was their responsibility, can be readily realized, more especially after the submarine menace became so intense.

On Saturday afternoon, November 15, 1919, the memorial stones were unveiled and the Institute declared open, the ceremony being performed by Mr. Edward Bryant. There was a large attendance of interested and sympathetic parishioners and friends.

Mr. Bryant was supported by Rev. B. Hartley, M.A., Mr. F. Creek, Mr. James Matthews, Mr. George H. Matthews, Mr. R. Warren, Mr. T. Rose, Mr. F. Macey, and others. The first part

THE DEDICATION STONE.

of the ceremony took place inside the hall, and commenced with the singing of " O God our help in ages past," which was followed by an interesting address from the Rev. B. Hartley on " The Spirit of Sacrifice." After this the company left the hall, and Mr. Bryant proceeded to unveil the memorial stones. Prayer was offered by the Rev. B. Hartley, and

the Chairman then read the inscriptions on the stones, which
are as follows :—

The Harold Wood Memorial Institute.

Dedicated at the end of the Great War, 1914-1919, by the inhabitants
of Harold Wood, in grateful commemoration of the glorious heroism and
high sense of duty of all those who served in the sea, land, and air forces,
and in lasting memory of those who made the great sacrifice.

ROLL OF HONOUR.

W. Barber	P. Hayward
J. C. S. Beard	C. T. King
E. D. Brown	C. W. Little
H. Clyde	J. Little
A. C. Creek	P. Livermore
R. J. Crow	W. A. Martin
W. S. D'Aeth	F. L. Matthews
H. G. Dix	J. Peto
W. Fitzjohn	W. H. Taylor
E. A. Garrett	E. S. Turner
E. Green	W. A. Warman
L. Grout	A. S. Warren
W. F. Guy	J. W. G. White

A number of wreaths and floral tokens from the relatives
of those mentioned in the roll of honour were then placed at the
foot of the stones. The company then stood silent for half a
minute, and the " Last Post " was sounded.

The Chairman said they were assembled there that day to
unveil the memorial stones on which were recorded the names of
the heroes of Harold Wood who had given their lives in defence
of their country, and by their action had helped to save them
all from the terrible oppression they would have experienced
had the enemy conquered them. The ceremony followed closely
upon the Empire's tribute to the memory of their glorious dead.
It was sad to feel that these noble and gallant men were no
more, but they must live in admiration of their action, and
thankfulness and gratitude to them for helping to make the
country free, and once more a land of civilization and happiness.

The hymn, " For all the Saints who from their labours rest,"
was sung, and the Harold Wood Choral Society gave, " Soldier,
rest ! " (Sir Walter Scott).

Mr. G. H. Matthews, who proposed a vote of thanks to the
Chairman, said it was especially appropriate that Mr. Bryant
should perform the ceremony of unveiling the stones, for had
it not been for his generous aid they could not have had the
memorial in the complete form in which they saw it that day.
They were now able to perpetuate the memory of the dead, and
also to do something for the living. Although most of them
knew everything about the war memorial, he would just re-
capitulate its history. In the first place, a small committee met

to consider what would be the best form of memorial, and it was decided to try to get a club and institute to combat the dulness of village life. Mr. Bryant was approached, and he said he would sell the hall and its contents for £500. Everybody knew that the sum was much less than the value of the property. Subscriptions were invited, but when Mr. Bryant heard how sympathetically the appeal had been received, he told the Committee he had decided to present £500 to the fund. That, of course, meant giving them the hall and contents entirely free of cost. It would be of interest to many to know that, including Mr. Bryant, there were 170 subscribers, and that the total sum raised was £1,238 18s. 5d. In addition there were subscriptions to the welcome-home and the peace celebrations. With the thanks he offered to Mr. Bryant were also associated the thanks of the men who had returned from the front, and who were pleased to have a club and an institute as a war memorial.

The Chairman, replying, said when it came to his knowledge that the Harold Wood people had set their minds on having the hall, there was only one thing to do, and he had very much pleasure in presenting the building to the Committee for the benefit of Harold Wood. (Applause). He declared the hall open for the inhabitants of Harold Wood.

Miss F. Davis having sung "Land of Hope and Glory," Mr. F. Creek and Mr. H. B. Ayres outlined the aims and objects of the Institute, which it was stated would be useful for all kinds of social and recreative purposes.

In the evening a concert was given by the following artistes :— Mrs. Bryant, Misses L. Bryett, O. Rae and F. Davis, and Messrs. Hammond, R. Cooper, R. Howe, and Rea. Mr. Pratt was at the piano, and Mr. Bryett was musical director.

THE NONCONFORMIST CHURCHES.

" All places that the eye of Heaven visits
Are to a wise man ports and happy havens."

Shakespeare :—Richard II., I., iii.

THE BAPTIST CHURCH.*

The members of the Baptist Church in North Street, and its various organizations, began early to feel the drain upon its workers and young adherents consequent on the War. The Sunday School lost many of its teachers, and practically the whole

*A full record of the Baptist Church in Hornchurch will be found in " Ye Olde Village of Hornchurch," pages 87 to 91.

of the members of the young men's Bible class were early called to the Colours. The homes of many members were affected, and the empty chair betokened that the family circle had been broken into, and that the lad or lads, were away at the War.

Many letters from lads training in the towns and villages up and down the country, as well as those received from overseas, told of kindness received, homes thrown open, and hearty welcomes given, and in response, homes and hearts were soon opened to the soldiers who came to our own village. The Sportsmen, " Navvies," New Zealanders, and the men of the Royal Flying Corps, the Royal Air Force and No. 2 Transfer Centre, were invited to the church services on Sunday, and to its meetings during the week. Every Sunday, in addition to the ordinary services, a special bright Song Service was organized from 6 to 6.30, before the evening service, and at its close all lads were invited to a social hour held in the vestry, during which coffee and refreshments were served under the combined direction of Mr. W. H. C. Curtis and Mr. E. D. Alley. Favourite hymns, anthems, and solos were sung, reminding the boys of the Sunday home circles far away. The pulpit on Sunday was often filled by the boys' favourite " Padres."

On Monday evenings the bright and earnest Christian Endeavour Meetings were thrown open to all who cared to come, and of the New Zealanders alone about 100 men availed themselves of the temporary membership offered them. One or other of them—as in the home land, frequently took the leadership at these meetings, and contributed papers on various subjects, and at the business meetings they were always ready with helpful and practical suggestions. Greetings were sent to the lads' own Home Societies, and many appreciations were received from them of the comfort and consolation afforded the old folks at home that their boys in England were being helped.

During the early years of the war the Baptist School Room was thrown open by the Church every evening in the week as a Rest Room* for soldiers quartered in the village. Refreshments and the brightly furnished room, with conveniences for writing, reading, games, concerts, and musical evenings, were a boon to the men, especially on the dark winter nights, when there were few outside attractions.

Many of the Baptist Church members kept open house for the entertainment of the men stationed, for the time being, at Grey Towers and the Aerodrome, and Christmas and other parties were arranged and cordial welcome given to many.

On Monday evening, September 25, 1916, the Rev. Peter Miller, M.A., who had been Pastor of the church for eleven years,

*The Rest Room is described in detail on page 207.

gave his farewell address on his departure to take up the pastorate of the Baptist and Congregational Union Churches at Kimbolton and Spaldwick, Hunts. Mr. Alfred Yeo presided. Mr. Miller had identified himself largely with the religious and public life of the parish, and his departure was a matter of keen regret, not only to the members of his own congregation, but to many other parishioners who recognized in him a man of strong and sincere religious conviction and a fearless and convincing speaker on subjects concerning the social welfare of the people. He was a leader in the Temperance cause, and a powerful advocate of total abstinence.

On its becoming known that Mr. Miller had accepted another Pastorate, a movement to make him a parting gift was initiated. Subscriptions were contributed by members of the congregation and other friends, and at the farewell gathering a purse of money was presented to him by Mr. H. J. Major, the church treasurer, on behalf of the subscribers.

At a somewhat later date another presentation was made to Mr. Miller by members and friends of the National British Women's Temperance Association, which took the form of a study chair, and a tea tray to Mrs. Miller. This presentation was made in the Baptist School Rooms on November 14, 1916, by Mr. Thomas Gardner, and advantage was taken of the occasion to invite a number of the men from Grey Towers Convalescent Hospital to attend the presentation, after which they were entertained to tea and a concert.

After the departure of the Rev. Peter Miller, the church was without a resident Pastor until May 1918, when the Rev. Thomas E. Howe accepted the Pastorate.

Recognition services and meetings in connection with his appointment were held on Sunday and Thursday, May 12 and 16, 1918, which were largely attended. On Sunday the sermons were preached by the Pastor, and the Rev. G. H. Lawrence, D.D., of New Zealand.

On Thursday there was a service in the afternoon, when the sermon was preached by the Rev. W. Cuff, late of Shoreditch Tabernacle. A social gathering followed, and tea was served, and in the evening a public meeting was held, at which Mr. S. W. Bradbridge presided. Those taking part in the day's proceedings in addition to the names already mentioned, were :—Rev. Herbert Dale, M.A., Vicar of Hornchurch ; Rev. N. Hardingham Patrick, Superintendent of the Baptist Sustentation Fund, Eastern District ; Rev. Stanley I. Blomfield, Upminster Congregational Church ; Rev. J. Benson Evans, Hornchurch Congregational Church ; Rev. W. H. Shipley, Grays Baptist Church ; Rev. E. Ruslin, Romford Baptist Church ; Rev. E. S. Hadler ; and Mr. J. Connaton Hart, of Blackheath.

Mr. Bradbridge in an appreciative reference to Mr. Howe's work in the past, said that he was present at his previous recognition at Bermondsey 22 years ago. The Rev. Herbert Dale's remarks were indicative of the broadmindedness and good fellowship which he had always displayed in connection with the nonconformist bodies in the Parish. He addressed the congregation as " his dear Hornchurch folk," and took as the foundation for his remarks the words of St. John :—" Little children love one another." He said " To-day we are standing as the world had never before stood since the birth of Christ. Not only the church, but the individual, the parish and the whole community were in the melting pot. Out of that must come either a broad, deep, and a strong foundation of a new world amongst the nations in the Kingdom of God, or the reign of brute force. The new Pastor and his people were going forth into a future of magnificent possibility, but also of grave responsibility. He rejoiced that in the closing days of his own ministry in Hornchurch he was permitted to express, as a lesson driven home to him more forcibly than any other, the truth that we must love one another with a pure heart, bearing one another's burdens, and thus fulfil the law of Christ. For the Pastor and the people amongst whom he was to work, he asked God's blessing, and as the outcome of his own experience, he knew there was no greater, higher, or more vital teaching than that contained in St. John's words " Little children, love one another."

At the conclusion of Mr. Dale's address, Mr. Howe expressed his appreciation of the welcome extended to him by the Vicar of the parish.

In the addresses which followed by Mr. Bradbridge and Mr. Patrick, references were made to Mr. Howe's work in London, where for the past 22 years he had carried on his ministry at Ilderton Road, South Bermondsey, during which time he had received into the church fellowship 937 members, and left his church, not only free of all debt, but with a membership of 266, the highest in its history.

The Rev. Peter Miller, M.A., and his successor, Rev. Thomas E. Howe, were indefatigable on all occasions in extending the right hand of fellowship to all service men.

The Baptist Church had to bear its share of the loss occasioned by the war, and several of its brightest and most promising young members made the Great Sacrifice. At the latter part of 1919, as a memorial to the fallen, a pipe organ was installed in the Church, and a white marble memorial tablet, backed by a black marble base, was placed on the north wall of the church. The organ was dedicated on November 20, 1919, and the memorial tablet was unveiled by the Pastor, the Rev. Thomas E. Howe, on Sunday evening, November 30, 1919, the following being a reproduction of the inscription :—

BAPTIST CHURCH HORNCHURCH.
In Affectionate Remembrance of
THE FOLLOWING BRAVE MEN
ASSOCIATED WITH THIS CHURCH
WHO FELL WITH HONOUR IN THE GREAT WAR,
1914-1919.
F. CANTLE,
S. FARDELL,
J. LONG,
G. MAIDMENT,
P. MILLER.
"GREATLY BELOVED."

HORNCHURCH BAPTIST CHURCH ROLL OF HONOUR.

Pte. W. Alliston ; Seaman E. Ballentyne, R.N. ; Pte. Frank Sipthorp Cantle ;* Captain W. Collister ;* Lieut. H. P. Chilver , M.C. ; Pte. Percy Curtis ; Stoker W. Curtis, R.N. ; Pte. Frederick George Doe ;* Private Sydney Ernest Fardell ;* Pte. Charles Fardell ; Bombr. W. A. Fennell ; Pte. G. Goult ; Pte. A. Goodchild ; Sergt. Eric Gawler ; Sub-Lieut. James Hamilton, R.N.R. ; Seaman Wm. Hare ; Lieut. Sidney Harvey ; Corpl. T. A. Howe ; Lieut. B. J. Jackson ; Seaman John Letten ; Pte. Joseph James Long ;* Pte. George Maidment ;* Pte. Peter Miller ;* Pte. W. Nice ; Pte. Cecil Oliver ; Pte. Joseph Pamment ; —. Carev Spurgeon , Lieut. W. B. Stoner ; Corpl. Ronald Tippen ; Pte. Louis Willey.

In March 1918, during the great German Offensive, the pre-war Secretary of the Sunday School, Lieut. Harold Percy Chilver, distinguished himself by conspicuous bravery in action, and the church members were gratified later to learn that the King had awarded him the Military Cross for his gallantry and devotion to duty.

Mr. F. W. Thompson, who was Church Secretary for a period of nineteen years, resigned in December 1919, and a Testimonial, in appreciation of his long and faithful service, was presented to him on February 11, 1920, consisting of a leather suit case and a leather attaché case. He was succeeded by Mr. R. W. Chilver.

DEACONS AND OFFICERS OF THE CHURCH.

Deacons.—Messrs. E. D. Alley, W. Alliston, H. Barker, R. W. Chilver, A. Ferguson, H. J. Major.
Secretary.—Mr. R. W. Chilver.
Treasurer.—Mr. H. J. Major.

*Those marked * were killed in action, but, as will be noticed, only five of the seven names so marked appear on the War Memorial Tablet. The remaining two names are to be inscribed.

HORNCHURCH CONGREGATIONAL CHURCH.*

The Congregationalists in Hornchurch had no place of worship of their own prior to 1906. In May of that year the members of that religious denomination held their first service in the small schoolroom at " Cosy Cot," Ernest Road, and in the following month a properly constituted Church was formed. In October of that year Gladstone House, Berther Road, was acquired for the services, and there the work was carried on until 1909, when the present Church in Nelmes Road was built. The opening ceremony took place on the 23 of September, 1909, on which occasion the sermon was preached by the Rev. Ewart James, M.A., of Southend.

The Rev. H. J. Cubitt, B.D., of Romford, was appointed first Pastor in charge, and was followed by the Rev. George Stewart, and the Rev. Richard Nicholls. The latter, resigning in October 1912, was succeeded by the Rev. J. Benson Evans, who commenced his ministry on May 4, 1913, continuing his pastorate throughout the whole of the war period.

In addition to the organized war work in connection with the Church, most of the members of the congregation participated in the various organizations and activities prevailing in the parish during the war period. The Pastor, too, with the Minister of the Baptist Church, joined in the many united parochial services held in the Parish Church from time to time over the whole period of the war, records of which will be found in the Parish Church Section of this book.

Many members of the congregation joined H.M. Forces, the following being a list, as far as can be ascertained, of those who served during the war :—

H. T. Banyard, 2/Lieut., 3rd Corps, R.E.
H. L. Brown, 2nd Air Mechanic, R.A.F.
C. H. Cox, Trooper, 2nd City of London Yeomanry.
E. J. Daniels, Pte., M.G.C., Sept., 1917 to Oct., 1918, France. Killed in action Oct. 22/1918, age 19.
A. G. Dohoo, Capt., R.A.S.C.
F. Douse, Captain, 4th Batt., 8th Middlesex Regt.
L. Draycott, Able Seaman, 3rd " Hawke " Batt., R.N. Div.
S. N. Evans, Lieut., 19th London Regt.
W. R. S. Fox, Lieut., R.A.F., killed in action Aug. 22 1918, age 22.
S. Harvey, Pte., 21st Batt., R.F.
E. J. Haywood, Pte., Queen's Westminster Rifles.
W. A. Haywood, Pte., 11th Essex Regt., missing, presumed killed in action.
D. F. Kendall, 2/Lieut., R.A.F., killed Aug. 1918.
G. Maidment, Cpl., 18th K.R.R., killed Nov. 11/1916.
A. J. Mills, Gunner, R.G.A.
H. Sutton, Pte., 11th Batt., K.R.R.
G. T. Webster, 2/Lieut., 203 Machine Gun Coy., died Dec. 7/1917, from wounds received in action, age 29.
B. G. Weevers, Cpl., R.N.A.S. and R.A.F., Victualling Section.
S. Willey, Pte., H.A.C.

*For the full history of the Congregational Church in Hornchurch, see page 87 to 94, " Ye Olde Village of Hornchurch."

In March 1920, a movement was initiated to raise a memorial to the memory of those fallen in the war, which took the form of a bronze mural tablet. This was unveiled on Sunday evening, May 30, 1920, by the Rev. J. Benson Evans, in the presence of a large congregation.

The Rev. J. Benson Evans said :—

" This evening we are going to unveil the Memorial Tablet which commemorates the great sacrifice made during the war by those men who were connected with this Church.

The tablet is the outcome of a labour of love on the part of the " Ladies' Working Party," and it expresses the sentiments of us all. For we all feel that our gratitude to the brave men who fought and fell in the defence of our country should take a visible and permanent form. We shall not be true to our own feelings, and certainly we should not be fair to those men if we did not erect a memorial to perpetuate their names within the walls of the Church in which we and they worshipped together. I knew so well, and esteemed so highly, those brave fellows who made the great sacrifice to defend the priceless blessings of freedom and righteousness, and as I speak of them this evening they stand very vividly before my mind's eye.

But though this unveiling service is a profoundly solemn service, I don't want to make it a sad one, for I don't wish to harrow the feelings of those who are only too conscious this evening of the loss they have sustained. May the " God of all Comfort " be their strength and stay, and the fountain of their consolation and hope.

This memorial, handed down to posterity, will show that the people of 1920 were not ungrateful to those who, abnegating themselves, gave *all* in the cause of liberty amongst Nations. No tablet or memorial can adequately express what we owe to them. There is a danger, and it is a very lamentable danger, of some people forgetting the heroic services and sacrifices which our young manhood rendered in the hour of our Nation's peril. Let not the reproach be upon us—after the most merciless war in history (during which our hearths and homes were in jeopardy)—that we failed to honour our dead and help the broken and disabled. We do not forget those who fought and suffered hardships and were able to return to their homes when the war was over, but this evening we concentrate our thoughts in grateful memory on those who gave their lives for their country. No grander death can be imagined than that on the battlefield in a just and righteous cause, and while we sympathise most feelingly with the bereaved, we rejoice with them that their loved ones died so nobly.

They gave all. What can a man do more ? We thank God to-day for what they did, and we shall thank *them* some day when we shall meet them in the glorious re-union in the Home above."

After the anthem, " What are these," Mr. Evans, standing by the Tablet, said :—

" We erect this memorial to the Glory of God and in memory of the brave men who so readily came to the help and defence of our country in its hour of peril and dire need, and who gave their lives for God and His righteousness, for humanity and its liberty, for King and Country, and for us and our homes.

And now, in the name of the Father, the Son and the Holy Ghost, I unveil this Memorial Tablet. The names recorded on it are :—

ERNEST J. DANIELS.	DENYS F. KENDALL.
WALTER R. S. FOX.	GEORGE MAIDMENT.
WILLIAM A. HAYWOOD.	GEORGE T. WEBSTER.

May these names remain sacred in our memory for evermore."

Mr. Evans then offered a prayer, which was followed by the hymn " For Ever with the Lord," and after the Benediction "The Last Post" was sounded at the entrance of the Church by Bugler Sidney Roye Pailthorpe, Sir Anthony Browne's (Brentwood) School Cadet Corps.

This concluded a most impressive service.

The Rev. J. Benson Evans resigned his ministry in April 1920, in consequence of ill health. A farewell meeting in connection with his retirement took place at the Congregational Church on Tuesday, April 13, 1920. The Rev. Charles Vine, B.A., of Ilford, presided, and spoke in highly appreciative terms of Mr. Evans's work as Pastor, and also in connection with the London Congregational Union.

In expressing his gratification and thanks for the presentation of an illuminated address and cheque, made by Mr. A. C. Williams, the Church Secretary, on behalf of the members of the congregation, Mr. Evans remarked that this was the fifth presentation which had been made to him during his pastorate of seven years. He reminded them that when he resigned his pastorate at Croydon it was his intention to retire from the ministry, and it was only the strong representation made to him by the Hornchurch Deacons that decided him to defer his actual retirement, and to resume his labours as their Pastor.

In making the presentation Mr. Williams remarked that the increase in their membership was felt soon after Mr. Evans came to the Church, and that the growing prosperity was maintained all through the term of his pastorate, and was largely due to his sympathetic encouragement, particularly during the difficult period of the war.

Mr. Evans's ministerial life had extended over a period of 42 years, and in the four Churches in which he had laboured he had had the privilege of receiving no fewer than 2,000 new members.

The Rev. Charles Steer, Vicar of Hornchurch, the Rev. E. Ruslin of Romford ; Rev. T. E. Howe, Baptist Minister, Hornchurch ; and the Rev. H. Oliver, Congregational Minister, Upminister, all spoke in appreciation of Mr. Evans's work in Hornchurch.

During the pastorate of the Rev. J. Benson Evans the debt remaining on the Church was removed, the last payment being made in November, 1919.

In connection with the Church there is a Literary and Social Society, and Young People's Guild, also a Ladies' Working Party, who, through their efforts, presented the church in March 1920, with a piano for the use of its various societies.

DEACONS AND OFFICERS.

Mr. G. E. Draycott, *Deacon.*
Mr. James Bauckham, *Deacon and Treasurer.*
Mr. Arthur J. Mills, *Deacon and Financial Secretary.*
Mr. Albert C. Williams, *Deacon and Church Secretary.*

THE ELEMENTARY SCHOOLS.

THE VILLAGE SCHOOL.

War-time conditions made the carrying on of elementary school work exceedingly difficult. In our Village School there were many changes in the staff. Owing to the needs of the military service, scholars left earlier than they would otherwise have done, in order to help at home, or to go out to work ; the children, too, missed the home influence of fathers and elder brothers, and were not a little upset by air raids. Notwithstanding all these things, their conduct was, on the whole, exceedingly good.

Various kinds of war work was done by the children. The boys broke up a large piece of their playground, and used it for growing vegetables, and the girls made comforts of different kinds to send out to the fighting fronts, and to the navy.

During 1917, at the request of the Government, the children collected nearly a ton of horse chestnuts for munition making.

A War Savings' Association was started in September 1916, and carried on until July 1919, several pounds being collected weekly from the scholars, who also subscribed liberally to numerous war charities.

The following members of the staff joined H.M. Forces :—

Mr. C. A. Jervis, from Nov. 9/1914, to March 19/1919. He saw service in Malta, Egypt, Gallipoli, and was in France from the 1st battle of the Somme. He was taken prisoner in March 1918, and was behind the German lines until the Armistice.

Mr. W. A. Raven, from April 30/1917, to the Armistice.

Mr. H. G. Whitehead, from Feb. 22/1917, to Feb. 20/1919, serving in France, and with the army of occupation.

The Head Master, Mr. F. Edwards, was a Sergeant in the Romford Division Essex Special Police for over four years.

In August 1919, there were 375 scholars on the books.

STAFF.

Boys' Department.—*Head Master*, Mr. F. Edwards, *Assistants*, Mr. H. G. Whitehead and Mrs. L. R. Carter.

Girls' Department.—*Head Mistress*, Miss E. H. Spragg. *Assistants*, Mrs. Durrant and Miss Britton.

Infants' Department.—*Head Mistress*, Miss W. E. Pearce. *Assistants*, Miss Cooper and Miss Watson.

SOUTH HORNCHURCH SCHOOLS.

During the war about 100 old South Hornchurch boys did their part in the fighting as soldiers or sailors on the various fronts and at sea, and interesting letters were received at the School House from many of them stationed in France, Salonica, Palestine, Mesopotamia, and Siberia. Four of them gained commissions, and five laid down their lives for King and Country. Others did their best in munition work and in food production.

A number of the "old girls" also shared in the work by joining the W.R.A.F. and the W.L.A., while others worked in munition factories and on food production.

At Christmas 1914, part of the proceeds of the School Concert was given to the funds of the Hornchurch Depôt of Queen Mary's Needlework Guild.

Each year on Empire Day and at Christmas the Overseas Club Fund for tobacco and comforts for soldiers and sailors was liberally supported by the scholars, and many cards were received thanking the children for their thoughtfulness.

A subscription was made to the "Daily Express" Cheery Fund to supply a football to the Railwaymen working in France. Other funds supported by the children were the Fund for Relief of Belgian children, and the Funds of the Royal National Lifeboat Institution.

A Branch of the Hornchurch War Savings' Association was held in connection with the School, and many Certificates were taken by the scholars.

In the School gardens food production was kept well to the front, and in 1918 over 1¼ tons of potatoes were raised, besides large quantities of other vegetables. The elder scholars also did their share towards food production by orking in the fields during the busiest times, before morning school commenced and again in the evening, and in 1918 the elder boys were allowed six weeks extra summer holiday to enable them to assist in the gathering in of the harvest.

Mr. A. V. Gentry, assistant master, joined H.M. Forces and served from September 1914 to July 1919, in England, France, and Flanders, rising to the rank of Lieutenant.

SCHOOL STAFF DURING THE WAR.
Head Master.—Mr. H. J. Harris, A.C.P., F.R.H.S.
Certificated Assistants.—Miss E. L. Cox, Miss E. L. Pearce.
Uncertificated Assistant.—Miss D. E. Utley.

HAROLD WOOD SCHOOL.

The children of Harold Wood School were in no wise behind those in the neighbouring schools in their zeal for war work. During the food shortage, at the suggestion of the Essex Education Committee, the elder girls dug up and cultivated a large piece of their playground, and each produced, in addition to other vegetables, about ½ cwt. of potatoes, paying for their own seeds. The boys, too, in their school gardens, produced about three times the normal quantity of potatoes. The children also collected about a ton of horse chestnuts, and over 2,000 lbs. of blackberries, the latter in response to the Government's demand for this fruit for the controlled Preserve Factories. The gathering of such a large quantity of these wild berries is an achievement of which the scholars may well be proud.

In everything relating to the war the children did their best, and did it cheerfully. They subscribed generously to the funds for Church Army Huts, the Y.M.C.A. Huts, the Overseas Fund for providing sailors and soldiers with cigarettes, tobacco, and other comforts, the St. Dunstan's Hostel for Blinded Sailors and Soldiers, and for the Belgian Refugees.

About forty "old boys" joined H.M. Forces, and no fewer than ten of them laid down their lives. Letters were frequently received from men on active service, and were always answered promptly by the Headmaster. It must have been no small matter to keep up the steady stream of correspondence which this necessitated, but it was a labour of love which always received Mr. Rose's earnest care and attention.

Mr. Rose, being over military age, served as Special Constable for three years in the Harold Wood Section of the Essex Special Constabulary.

There were at the end of the war period, 145 scholars on the attendance books.

STAFF.

Headmaster.—Mr. Thomas Rose.
Certificated Assistant.—Miss L. Frost.
Uncertificated Assistant.—Miss E. Blaxter.

PARK LANE SCHOOL.

During the Great War the children of the Park Lane School were encouraged to assist the various charities and war funds which came into being, and subscriptions were raised for the Belgian Relief Fund, the Serbian Relief Fund, the British Red Cross, the Y.M.C.A., Sir Arthur Pearson's Institute for the Blind (St. Dunstan's), and others, and the response was always exceedingly good.

The school joined the Hornchurch War Savings' Association and weekly subscriptions were taken by the teachers and forwarded to the Hon. Secretary.

At the close of 1915, the Park Lane Cadet Company, 4th Cadet Battalion, Essex Regiment, was formed, the Head Master, Mr. G. C. Eley, accepting a commission as Captain, and being responsible for the training of the lads, who were old boys of the school. In connection with this a social club was formed, meeting twice a week at the school, until the end of 1918, when the company was amalgamated with other Romford Companies of the same battalion.

War work included the collection of waste paper and of 15 cwts. of horse chestnuts, and the cultivation of allotments by both boys and girls on the site chosen for a new Boys' School in Malvern Road.

Christmas parcels were sent out to the "old boys" serving with H.M. Forces.

It is worthy of record that the women teachers did excellent work during the war, and the boys, without the restraining influence of men teachers and fathers, behaved exceedingly well. Even during the somewhat trying times of the air-raids there was no undue excitement or restlessness. The Headmaster co-operated with the parents of some of the scholars in specially caring for the lads whose fathers were on active service.

Although hampered by the gradual enclosure of open spaces for allotment purposes, an endeavour was made to keep going the organized games and physical training of the lads, and Football Cricket and Swimming were continued during the whole of the period, 1914–1918, a work in which the women teachers cordially and loyally assisted.

War Staff (Boys' School.)

Mr. G. C. Eley, *Head Master.*
Mrs. F. G. Shave, *Certificated Assistant.*
Mrs. Chapman, *Certificated Assistant.*
Mrs. Drever, *Certificated Assistant.*
Mrs. Bonny, *Uncertificated Assistant.*

Every member of the Assistant Staff of the Boys' School enlisted voluntarily early in the war.

Mr. A. C. Potter joined the battalion of the King's Royal Rifles, raised by Sir Herbert Raphael, M.P., in the district, was promoted to the rank of Company Sergeant-Major, saw service in France, and was awarded the D.C.M. for specially gallant conduct at the taking of Flers.

Mr. C. Lovett joining the R.G.A. as a private, was rapidly promoted through the different grades, and gained a commission as 2nd Lieut. His active service was in France and Belgium.

Mr. F. G. Groot enlisted in the R.N.V.R. stationed at the Crystal Palace. After a short period he became a signaller, and within a few months was appointed to the position of Naval Schoolmaster and attached to Shotley Barracks.

Many of the old boys of the school were killed, and their photographs, where possible, were obtained, framed by the scholars themselves, and hung in the school. Among those who laid down their lives was Harry Ford, who lost his life in H.M.S. "Bulwark," blown up in the river Medway on November 26th, 1914. Another was Herbert George Hills, who was on H.M.S. "Hampshire," which sank off the Orkneys June 5, 1916, with Field Marshal Lord Kitchener and his Staff.

An ex-scholar, John French, was awarded the V.C.

THE COTTAGE HOMES OF THE PARISH OF ST. LEONARD, SHOREDITCH.

" Those that do teach young babes,
Do it with gentle means and easy tasks.
Shakespeare :—Othello IV., ii.

No record of war-service by Hornchurch people would be complete without reference to the part played by those little " strangers within our gate," the past and present children of the Cottage Homes. To all who have made acquaintance with this model village in Hornchurch Road, midway between the village and Romford, it will be easily understood that of the hundreds of one-time boys who issued from the Cottage Homes to join the " outer-English " of Canada, and the colonies generally, a goodly number must have borne arms in defence of the principles inculcated in that institution. Indeed, we are not without proof of this, since there is official record of 172 " old boys " who put themselves in touch with the School after joining the colours. This forms the basis of a Roll of Honour, to which almost weekly additions are even now being made. Quite a number of these lads were amongst the first to enlist. Their delight on revisiting the old " home " can better be imagined than described, and the story of the personal achievements of these young men must have yielded much gratification to the staff responsible for their upbringing. The case of one—Pte Richard Grey—serves as an illustration. In an interesting correspondence with the superintendent, continued until the time of his death in France, he revealed that two or three years more in Canada would have seen him a man of independent means. That such an untimely fate awaited this fine fellow, places him in the category of those thousands who, having much reason to live, hesitated not to sacrifice his life in the cause of the Motherland.

Scatter a thousand or so young lads in the whirlpool of life, here and abroad, and it is not an easy matter to keep a record of their later doings, unless they are prompted to communicate with the Homes, but from what is known we may construct a generous estimate of service under arms by " old boys " from the Cottage Homes.

In our admiration of these young men, we must not overlook the efforts to be of service manifested by the younger ones still in residence at the Homes at the time the drums of war disturbed the air, and during the progress of the world struggle. To the local branch of Queen Mary's Needlework Guild, the little girls at the Homes gave most enthusiastic support, striving mightily to " do their bit." How far these little ones identified themselves with the work of providing comforts for the fighting men, may be answered best by those responsible for the movement, to whom the pile of woollen garments, socks, helmets, scarves, etc., were dispatched as fast as the busy little fingers could turn them out.

Nor were the boys without their contribution. It fell to them to lead the Sportsman's Battalion to their Camp at Grey Towers. The band, under the direction of Mr. H. W. Alden (bandmaster), met the battalion on its arrival at Romford Station, with a letter to Col. Lord Maitland, offering the service of the lads, which was gladly accepted. To see those little chaps, whose stride was only half the length of that of the men of the battalion, stepping it out, was distinctly inspiring, although one cannot help feeling that the men found short stepping somewhat trying.

So much for the efforts of the girls and boys in their separate capacities, but September, 1916, provided an incident which called forth their conjoint appreciation. Captain W. Leefe Robinson was well known to the children by name, and the relief of the youngsters, when one of the enemy aircraft had flown its last flight, coupled with the knowledge that its doom had

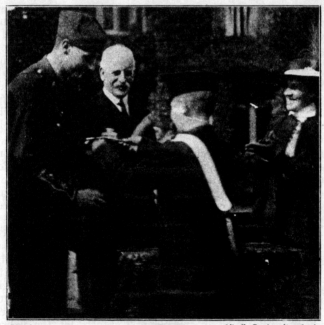

Photo]   *[E. E. Carter, Romford.*

PRESENTATION TO CAPT. W. L. ROBINSON, V.C. BY THE CHILDREN
OF THE COTTAGE HOMES.

been wrought by a Hornchurch officer, prompted the children to subscribe their pence which, with aid from the staff, resulted in the purchase of a souvenir for the gallant officer whose deed had magnetised their minds. Mr. Steed, the superintendent, was successful in securing the presence of Capt. Robinson at the Homes for the presentation of this token—a silver inkstand—and that day will be memorable to every child present. Two pictures of this event illustrate these pages.

Photo]   [E. E. Carter, Romford.

SINGING "GOD SAVE THE KING" AT THE CONCLUSION OF THE PRESENTATION CEREMONY.

Another act of thoughtfulness on behalf of these young-sters is disclosed in the following extract from a letter to the Superintendent, from the late Chaplain to the Homes, the Rev. Herbert Dale :—

" Please thank the children very much for the 153 coins and the sum of 14s. 4d., they have so generously contributed to the National Memorial to Lord Kitchener. It was very good of them, and I think that, however old they may grow up to be, they will always be glad (whenever they think of it), that they did it."

When it is borne in mind that the possession of a coin of any sort, however small, is a rare occurrence with these children, their contribution becomes a sacrifice, and without sacrifice there is no real merit in giving.

In conclusion, let us remember that here, practically on a line of defence, the children of the Homes lived days and nights of possible peril with a confidence and trust in those responsible for their care, which, in its expression, disclosed the admirable management of the institution. That these children were better and safer where they were housed than in the districts from which they hailed, was demonstrated as the months of war rolled on, for none of them suffered at the hands of the enemy, and all enjoyed the unfurling of the flag of victory on Armistice Day, which was to them, and all others who witnessed it, a sign that war had ceased.

The following are the names of former inmates of the Homes who made the great sacrifice in the War :—

Benjamin Bentley, Thomas Bentley, John Burgess, Albert Dean, Charles R. Foames, Richard Grey, Archibald Johnson, Sidney Kemp, Frederick Pope, Robert Robertson, John Street, Thomas Treacher, Alexander Watson, Thomas Welch.

WAR WORK AT THE RONEO WORKS.

" Experience is by industry achieved,
And perfected by the swift course of time."
Shakespeare :—Two Gentlemen of Verona i., iii.

Hornchurch played a not unimportant part in the supply of munitions during the war, through the instrumentality of Roneo Ltd., whose large works in Hornchurch Road are situate on the extreme western boundary of the Parish. " Roneo " is a household word in commercial circles, and the reputation of its office appliances is world-wide. We can therefore claim, with some little pride, that in these Works we have a village industry of great importance.

During the war practically the whole out-put of the factory was devoted to war purposes. Thousands of Duplicators, and many tons of ink and other supplies were provided to the order of the British and Allied Governments, as well as to many fighting units at home, on the seas, and overseas.

The factory was early in the war " commandeered " by the Government, and worked as a " controlled establishment."

The first actual war work undertaken was the manufacture of field kitchens for the new army, and ultimately the manufacture (in whole or in part), was successfully carried out of the following items :—Dial sights, automatic machine gun parts, fuses, grenades, shell parts, aeroplane details, and trench stoves.

A large number of employees belonging to the Territorials or Army Reserve, were called up at the outbreak of war, whilst others voluntarily joined the services, about 500 men leaving the employment of the Company for active war service. Of this number 26 lost their lives, and four were awarded the Military Medal. The majority of the discharged sailors and soldiers, who in pre-war days served the Company, have now returned to their former positions at the Works.

275

ONE OF THE WAR WORKSHOPS AT THE RONEO WORKS.

Owing to the shortage of male labour, over 300 women and girls were engaged during the war, and successfully filled the places of the absent men.

Despite air-raids, the difficulty of obtaining raw material, and other drawbacks, the factory *worked continuously, day and night, for over two years*, in order to keep up the supply of munitions—a most creditable performance !

" Flag " days, and other war funds, were liberally supported by the employees, and the former factory hands on active service were kept supplied with tobacco, cigarettes, and other comforts.

The Works also possessed a clever Concert Party, run entirely by its employees, which was always ready and willing to render assistance when local entertainments had to be arranged, and many War Charities and Funds were benefited by their kindly efforts.

The Works syren was one of the principal means of warning the whole neighbourhood of the approach of air-raiders, and members of the Works Fire Brigade were always on duty on these occasions, though fortunately their services were not required.

THE POLITICAL CLUBS.

" Faith, there has been much to do on both sides   .   . ."*
" Let our alliance be combin'd,
  Our best friends made, and our best means stretch'd out."†
" Let us devise some entertainments for them in their tents . .
  We will with some strange pastime solace them,
  Such as the shortness of the time can shape."‡

Shakespeare.

THE HORNCHURCH CONSERVATIVE AND LIBERAL UNIONIST CLUB.

The Hornchurch Conservative and Liberal Unionist Club, Constitution House, North Street, was established in the year 1908, and at the outbreak of war was managed by the following officers and Committee :—

> *President* :   Mr. W. Varco Williams.
> *Chairman* :   Mr. J. M. Ewing.§
> *Vice-Chairman* :   Mr. C. E. Dunlop.
> *Hon. Secretary* :   Mr. A. E. Palmar.
> *Committee* :   Messrs. H. Bailey, G. Blake, G. Blanks, E. Boyle, G. Butler, W. J. Drake, S. A. G. Davis, J. Emmerson, F. Hall, A. Kerr, J. Lungley, J. M. Mailer, W. E. Mohring, J. R. Pearce, A. R. Revill, L. O. Rowe, H. Sibthorp, H. White.

*Hamlet ii., ii.
† Julius Cæsar, iv., i.
‡ Love's Labour Lost iv., iii.
§ Mr. E. G. Bratchell was elected Chairman in 1919 on the resignation of Mr. J. M. Ewing.

Owing to the Secretary being employed on war work in France, this position was, subsequently, filled by Mr. W. Fairbairn.

Several members of the Club joined H. M. Forces at the beginning of the war, but the other members still carried on, and, on the arrival in Hornchurch of the Sportsman's Battalion, in November, 1914, it was arranged to give special facilities to any of the troops who desired to make use of the Club premises. They took full advantage of the offer, a large number of the battalion becoming temporary members, and in return for the hospitality shown them, they entertained the civil members at several Bohemian Concerts, which were greatly appreciated. After the Sportsmen left the village in June, 1915, the Club experienced a very quiet period, owing to several of the remaining members, hitherto exempt, being called to the colours under the military Service Act, but during that time various collections were made by the Club for War Charities. However, on the arrival of the New Zealand Troops, arrangements were made similar to those formerly affecting the Sportsman's Battalion, and the response was very encouraging, as at one time there were between 50 and 60 New Zealanders registered on the books of the Club. Many members also made it a practice to invite parties of the soldiers to their homes, and some were entertained on regular evenings to weekly " at homes," which were thoroughly appreciated by the gallant colonials. Billiard and Snooker tournaments were also arranged for the special benefit of the New Zealand Forces, with the result that four handsome silver cups, presented respectively, by Messrs. J. M. Ewing,. E. A. Bailey, E. C. Comber and A. E. Palmar, have been taken back to New Zealand as mementos of the time spent in Hornchurch.

Bowling matches were arranged on the Bowling Green, attached to the Club, and many keen and interesting contests were arranged under the management of Mr. W. Fairbairn, who also acted as Captain of the Club team.

In addition to weekly collections for the Red Cross Funds, whereby a substantial amount was subscribed, the Club held a very successful whist drive, in aid of the funds of the St. Dunstan's Hostel for Blinded Soldiers and Sailors, and this ensured a welcome donation to the funds of that institution.

On the departure of the New Zealand Forces, various members of the Sergeant's Mess, in recognition of the good fellowship extended to them during their stay in the village, presented to the Club a handsome Silver Challenge Cup, to be held for competition among the members under any conditions that the Committee might impose, and a farewell entertainment was also arranged at the Club House. It was decided by the Committee that the Cup should be competed for in a combined Billiard and Snooker Championship of the Club. The first winner of the trophy was Mr. T. H. Smith.

According to the records of the Club, the following members made the supreme sacrifice during the Great War :—

Frederick W. Collin, W. J. Cressey, G. W. Franklyn, C. W. Frost, W. G. Frost, T. G. Frost, B. R. Fry, A. T. Hills, J. A. Lungley, C. J. Macey, T. Mayne, W. J. Tickner, and F. C. Utley.

THE LIBERAL AND RADICAL ASSOCIATION GLADSTONE HOUSE.

The Hornchurch Liberal and Radical Association was formed in 1903, its objects being the diffusion of Liberal and Radical principles, and the registration of electors; all Liberals and Radicals residing in, or connected with, the Parliamentary Division being eligible for membership.

For a time the Association had an office in the High Street, but in 1911 the building, known as Gladstone House, with the land adjoining it in Berther Road, was purchased, the object being attained by the formation of a Limited Company, promoted by the Association, under the title of Gladstone House (Hornchurch), Limited. In this building a great deal of work has been carried out, and the Association claims its share in the three Liberal and Radical victories at the General Elections of 1906, and January and December, 1910, as well as in the return of the Government Coalition Liberal Candidate, Captain A. E. Martin, in the General Election of December, 1918.

Gladstone House contains a hall, in which meetings, etc., are held, also a library, and Committee and billiard rooms. Many members of the Association joined H.M. Forces during the war, including the Club Secretary, Mr. R. F. Stroud. The membership prior to the war was about 200.

There is also a junior section for youths, the Hon. Secretary of which is Mr. G. H. Bradley.

With the exception of the work connected with the General Election of 1918, all political activities were suspended during the war, the only functions carried on by the Association being of a social character, the chief of these being a series of evening social entertainments for the New Zealand soldiers encamped at Hornchurch. These entertainments were carried on continuously from November, 1916, and were brought about in this wise :—

When Grey Towers came into use as a convalescent hospital for wounded and otherwise war-stricken men of the New Zealand Contingent, the sight of the broken men in our roads and lanes soon appealed to the hearts and sympathy of many of our parishioners, and it was not long before the members of the Liberal and Radical Association sought how they might entertain and interest these heroic men who had fought in Gallipoli and France. At the suggestion of Mr. W. H. C. Curtis and Mr. E. D. Ally, a meeting was held at Gladstone House, at which an influential committee was formed to organize a series of social meetings, to which the occupants of the camp should be freely invited. Subscriptions were readily forthcoming to cover the expenses, and the socials commenced in November, 1916. The earlier meetings took the form of homely parties, with games, music, dancing, and refreshments, and were thoroughly enjoyed by the guests and their hosts. Later on, in consonance with the wishes of the men themselves, dancing and music predominated. The socials were immensely popular, and week by week the hall was filled to its utmost capacity.

So successful were the entertainments that in 1917 the invitations were extended to two nights each week, and were so continued till the close of the camp. Many friendships were made, and thousands of the men, now returned to their sunny southern homes, must have had weary hours brightened and filled with pleasure at these socials, and doubtless in far away homes on lonely farms and sheep runs, the name of Gladstone House is recalled and its entertainers are remembered with gratitude. Too much praise cannot be given to the long list of ready helpers, prominent amongst whom should be mentioned :— Mr. W. H. C. Curtis and Mrs. Curtis, Mr. and Mrs. R. W. Chilver, Mr. and Mrs. G. E. Draycott, Mr. L. Draycott, Mr. W. H. Goodchild, Mr. G. Gregg, and Mrs. Gregg, Mr. and Mrs. H. J. Major, Mr. J. J. Martin, Mrs. W. E. Cogar, and the hon secretary and treasurer, Mr. W. E. Cogar.

HORNCHURCH CRICKET CLUB.

Hornchurch Cricket Club* has a history, dating back to the year 1784, and in the early part of the 19th century was right in the forefront of Essex cricket. This was notably demonstrated by the fact that in 1830 they challenged all Essex, and fully justified their claim and position as champions by easily defeating a selected eleven of the County at Woodford Wells on the 1st July, 1830.

In the following year they challenged the Marylebone Cricket Club. When it is borne in mind that the M.C.C. was the foremost Cricket Club in England, that it published the first code of laws for the game, and that it was then, as now, the ruling and arbitrary authority in cricket affairs, we can form some idea of the place Hornchurch held in the cricket world, when such a Club considered them worthy opponents, and accepted their challenge for two matches. In the first match, played at Lord's

*For full record of the Club see " Ye Olde Village of Hornchurch," pages 135-142.

Cricket Ground, in London, on June 10th, 1831, Hornchurch put up a very creditable show, the result being a draw, which could not be said to be by any means in favour of the M.C.C., the scores being :—M.C.C. 71 and 58, and Hornchurch 61 and 7 for no wicket. This match was referred to in the press as follows, and incidentally places on record the many triumphs won by Hornchurch in and around London.

" That spirited little Club of Hornchurch, having been successful for several seasons in conquering all they have had to compete with, amongst which were the Islington Albion, East Surrey, Chelsea, Dartford, and others of minor importance, have now had the courage to challenge the Marylebone Club, which match commenced on Thursday last, the 10th inst., in the presence of a large assemblage of amateurs, amongst whom were the celebrated Pilchs, Caldecourt, etc., who were surprised to witness the stumps of the *crack club* lowered for so few runs by a country parish club, particularly those of Cobbett and Bayley. Mr. John Stevens's play was the admiration of the whole company, as he is one of the old school, and between 60 and 70 years of age."

In the return match, played at Langtons on August 25th, 1831, before a company of about 3,000 people, Hornchurch were badly beaten, the scores being :—M.C.C. 78 and 118, and Hornchurch 54 and 39.

Their defeat by the M.C.C. in no way disheartened our famous village players, for in 1832 we find them playing in great style at Langtons Park against Ingatestone. This match was thus reported :—

" The Hornchurch gentlemen were put in first, their opponents winning the toss, and at half-past three o'clock only four of their wickets were down, and the score standing at 237, the Ingatestone gentlemen thought proper to relinquish the match."

In the same year Hornchurch defeated Chelmsford, and in 1834 at Navestock they obtained an easy victory over West Essex in the first innings, the scores being West Essex 39, Hornchurch 118.

When Colonel Holmes built and occupied " Grey Towers," in 1876, he became possessed of part of the grounds of " Langtons " (including the famous cricket pitch), and it was thereafter known as Grey Towers Park.

The record of the Club in more recent years, though, perhaps, not so distinguished as in earlier days, was very creditable. At a dinner, given in 1910, at the Drill Hall, it was announced that over a period of 21 years, under the Captaincy of Mr. J. R. Robinson, 381 matches had been played, of which 183 had been won, 138 lost, and 60 drawn. Three centuries were scored in these matches, viz. :—By Mr. G. B. Bratchell, 100 against East Ham Atlas ; Mr. H. W. Stride, 106 not out, against Leyton ; and Mr. H. J. Harris, 105 not out, against Dagenham. Mention was also made of the almost phenominal batting and bowling of Mr. E. G. Bratchell, who had consistently played for the Club since 1890, and had bowled 3,040 overs, capturing 1,115 wickets at a cost of 8,328 runs ; his average being 7.46. He had also scored more runs off his own bat than any other member, his total being 2,726. This veteran player, in the following year (1911), made a century, 103 not out, in a match against Harold Wood.

The occupation of Grey Towers by the First Sportsman's Battalion, in November, 1914, together with other incidents connected with the war, made it impossible for members to indulge in the national game, and consequently in the years 1915 to 1918, no matches were played. An effort was made to re-start play in 1919, and, although the Club had no ground of its own, eight matches were arranged and played ; seven of which were won and one lost. A suitable ground for the future has, however, been secured through the generosity of Mr. Thomas

Photo]   [Luffs, Hornchurch.
HIGH STREET UNDER SNOW.

Gardner, and Mr. J. B. Gill, the owner and tenant respectively of the field adjoining Dury Falls in Wingletye Lane, which has been lent rent free.

The officers for the year 1920 are as follows :—
President, Mr. Thomas Gardner, J.P., C.C.
Vice-Presidents, Mr. J. R. Robertson, Rev. Charles Steer, M.A., M.C., Mr. W. Varco Williams, J.P., C.C.
Captain, Mr. E. G. Bratchell ; Vice-Captain, Mr. L. A. Culliford.
Hon. Secretary and Treasurer, Mr. T. A. Griffith.

As might have been expected from such good sportsmen, a fine response was made by the Club to the nation's call, and no fewer than 19 old members of the Club joined His Majesty's Forces during hostilities, four of whom made the Great Sacrifice. Of the new members who joined the Club in 1919, three had served with the Colours.

HORNCHURCH CRICKET ROLL OF HONOUR.

*Baker, C. H., Jun., Q.M.S., 4th Essex (Territorials).
Baring, J. H.
Bratchell, E. G., Jun., Signaller, R.G.A.
Castellan, V. E., Major R.F.A. (T.F.), O.B.E.
*R. Dawson, Pte., Essex Regiment.
*Fulcher, F., Corporal, 9th Essex Regiment.
*Franklyn, G. W., Jun., 2nd Lieut., 23rd London Regiment.
Gentry, A. V., Lieut., 2/23rd London Regiment.
Grant, W. J., Lieut., R.E.
Kirkman, H. C., Pte., Artists' Rifles, O.T.C.
Lovett, C., 2nd Lieut., R.G.A.
Mather, A. A., Sergt., 17th Royal Fusiliers.
McMullen, J. A., Lieut., R.A.F., M.B.E.
Parry, Rev. A. J., Chaplain to the Forces.
Robinson, E. H., Lieut., 3rd London Regiment, R.F.
Ruston, A. F. G., Major R.E.
Sanderson, Dr. A. F.
Stroud, R. F.
Thompson, C. W., Pte. R.A.S.C.

NEW MEMBERS.

Culliford, L. A., Capt., R.E., M.C.
Griffith, T. A., C.Q.M.S., M.T., R.A.S.C.
Steer, Rev. C., Chaplain to the Forces, M.C.
Those marked * were killed in action.

BELGIAN WOUNDED SOLDIERS AND REFUGEES.

Within a few weeks of the commencement of hostilities, a number of wounded Belgian soldiers arrived in the village, and were quartered at Ford Lodge, South Hornchurch. They remained there for several months, and frequently attended Service at the Parish Church. They were also made welcome at many of the concerts and entertainments held in the village during the winter of 1914/15.

Owing to the invasion of Belgium by the Germans, a large proportion of the civil population came over to England, and many Belgian refugees found sanctuary in our village. A number of these were without any means of support, and for a considerable period were housed and fed through the generosity of some of our parishioners, who subscribed weekly sums towards their maintenance. Mr. S. F. Gibson of " Woody Bay," Devonshire Road, acted as Hon. Secretary to the small Committee which undertook this hospitable work.

GERMAN PRISONERS.

" You have a vice of mercy in you
Which better fits a lion than a man."
Shakespeare :—Troilus and Cresida v., iii.

In the days to come, one of the most interesting recollections of wartime will be the German prisoners, who, for so long, were a feature of our countryside. The once familiar sight of these men, with their distinctive *discs* of red and blue patches worked into their uniforms, will soon be only a memory, but it will be a memory which will serve, when, round the fireside on a winter evening, we talk of the things which happened at home during the Great War. How, when taking a walk through the fields in our immediate neighbourhood, we would suddenly come upon a group of captured Huns, tilling the ground, or in-gathering the harvest, according to the season of the year, and how it was borne in upon us by their prosperous appearance that they were well content with their lot, and apparently in no hurry to return to their own land, at any rate, while the danger and risks of war still prevailed. Then, too, when travelling on the railway, we would sometimes catch a glimpse of them in the open fields, and invariably they would pause in their work to watch the passing train and its passengers ; their easy-going demeanour indicating the absence of anything approaching slave-driving, or even harshness.

The people of our village, who frequently used Upminster en route for the Halt, will remember the little group of Germans who were always to be found on the down platform on that station every evening, awaiting their train to Ockendon, where the local German Prisoners' Camp was situated. On such occasions an efficient armed guard was mounted over them, but it was no uncommon thing to meet with German prisoners working on the land, or walking along the lanes, without any visible guard whatever. One sometimes questioned the wisdom of this, but it was rarely that anything untoward happened, for the simple reason that the Bosche knew when he was well-off, and that working on the farms of England, with good food, and a comfortable shelter, was a far better and safer job than fighting Britain's sons on the battlefields of France and Belgium.

THE CONTROL AND RATIONING OF FOOD.

" So distribution should undo excess,
And each man have enough."
Shakespeare :—King Lear, Act IV., i.

During the first two years of the war there was very little scarcity of food, although prices of all commodities rose appreciably. Shops continued to display their attractive and toothsome wares as in pre-war days, and it seemed possible, if not probable, that this state of things would continue indefinitely. All this, however, was shortly to be changed, and in the closing months of the year, 1916, we were to experience inconvenience, if not actual shortage.

The first real food scarcity began to be apparent in the early months of 1917, when a shortage of potatoes was seriously felt. Towards the end of the Spring, it was particularly pronounced, and big queues outside greengrocers' shops were soon general.

284

The shortage was increased to some extent, owing to the extraordinary demand for seed potatoes, as large quantities of tubers, which, in ordinary times, would have been reserved for table use, were sold for seed purposes. Prices rose rapidly, until 3d. per lb. was demanded for potatoes for domestic use, and when matters had reached this stage, the Government stepped in and fixed the maximum retail price at 1½d. per lb., and this price was maintained until the new season's crop came on the market. It was very difficult to obtain potatoes at all for some time, and I well remember that for nearly three months my own household went entirely without, and our experience was, by no means, exceptional.

Bread and Flour.—In March, 1917, the quartern loaf reached the maximum price of 1s.,* but it did not long remain at that price, as, although the actual cost did not decrease, the selling price was reduced to 9d., the State bearing the 25% reduction as a war charge, which amounted to £50,000,000 per annum.†

Neither bread nor flour for domestic use were ever strictly rationed during the war period. A voluntary rationing system was put in force, and it was left to the honour of the people themselves whether or not they exceeded the recognised consumption per week, which was 4lbs. per head, to include both bread and flour. This was considered by the majority of people sufficient for moderate living. Although the private individual was treated thus liberally, a strict rationing order was enforced in connection with the supply of bread, cake, and pastries in hotels, restaurants, and other public places of refreshment. This order was particularly strict as regards afternoon teas, which, for a considerable time, were limited to a cost of 6d. per head.

For a period extending over the last two years of war, or thereabouts, it was forbidden to use white flour, and the Government took over the entire control of flour distribution.

Sugar.—The first article of domestic consumption to be strictly rationed was sugar.‡ Up to the early months of 1917

*In 1800 the price of the quartern loaf was as high as 1s. 5d.
†On April 12, 1920, the 4lb. loaf was again raised to 1s., owing to the abolition of the Government subsidy.
‡The upward trend of sugar retail prices since 1914 is shown in the following table :—

	Granulated. Per lb.	Loaf. Per lb.		Granulated. Per lb.	Loaf. Per lb.
	s. d.	s. d.		s. d.	s. d.
1914	0 2	0 2¼	1918, August	0 6¾	0 7¾
1915	0 3½	0 4	1919, October	0 7¾	0 8¾
1916	0 4¼	0 5	1920, April	0 10	0 10½
1917	0 4¾	0 5½	1920, May	1 2	1 2½
1918, March	0 5½	0 6¾			

From *Daily Mail*, 26 May, 1920.

there was no real shortage of sugar, but during the spring of that year, some difficulty was experienced in obtaining supplies, and as the year advanced this commodity became scarcer; and, in order to prevent the loss of fruit, special supplies were set aside for preserving purposes, certain quantities of sugar being allowed to persons growing their own fruit, over and above what was obtainable in the ordinary way for household requirements. This got over a temporary difficulty, but there were others to follow, which were not so readily disposed of, and after a little while the scarcity became so serious that the Government found it necessary to control supplies, and the public was thereupon rationed, sugar henceforth only being obtainable by coupon ; ½lb. being the quantity allowed per head per week. A facsimile of the Government notice, enforcing this regulation, is here reproduced.

I think very few of us ever realised what a large part sugar played in our everyday diet until we experienced the lack of it, and future generations will probably never quite grasp what a sugar shortage means to a community. Those who have had this personal experience will, however, have many reminiscences of how they schemed and scraped to make the ½lb. dole last the week round, and will remember with what rejoicing the Food Controller's announcement was received that an extra 4ozs. per head would be granted for the Christmas week of 1918. "What a small thing to be delighted about," someone will say in the dim and distant future, but it meant a very great deal to the housewife in those lean days.

Towards the closing months of the year 1917, matters connected with provisions generally became acute, such commodities as butter and margarine especially being most difficult to obtain. The formation of queues outside provision shops were common and everyday scenes in all towns and in some villages. Hornchurch suffered little in this respect, the chief reason being that so many residents obtained their household supplies in the neighbouring town of Romford. Scenes in that town were not a little distressing, long queues of women and children daily waiting hours at a stretch, for a pitiful half-pound of margarine, which substitute for butter was looked upon with scorn in better days. Queues were not confined to provision shops, but were to be seen outside butchers', fishmongers', green-grocers', and all shops where food of any sort was sold. During winter these queues were pitiful, and the fortitude of the women, who so patiently endured such trying ordeals, was worthy of all praise. These episodes of the war will doubtless be always remembered with not a little bitterness, mingled with relief that they are now experiences of the past, never it is hoped, likely to be repeated.

MINISTRY 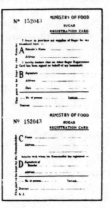 **OF FOOD**

SUGAR DISTRIBUTION SCHEME
NOTICE TO HOUSEHOLDERS

ON OR BEFORE
FRIDAY 26TH OCTOBER
YOU SHOULD RECEIVE YOUR

SUGAR REGISTRATION CARD

FILL IN THE NAME AND
ADDRESS OF THE
RETAILER WITH WHOM
YOU WISH TO REGISTER
AT **"A"**

THEN TAKE THE CARD
INTACT TO YOUR
RETAILER NOT LATER
THAN MONDAY,
NOVEMBER 5TH.

ENTER YOUR NAME,
ADDRESS & THE DATE
AT **"B"**

YOUR RETAILER WILL
FILL IN HIS NAME
AND ADDRESS
AT **"D"**

YOUR RETAILER WILL DETACH THE LOWER HALF OF THE CARD AND
RETURN IT TO YOU.

DO NOT TAMPER WITH YOUR CARD.

ANY PERSON FORGING OR ALTERING A SUGAR CARD IS LIABLE TO A
FINE NOT EXCEEDING £100 OR SIX MONTHS IMPRISONMENT, OR BOTH.

Up to Christmas, 1917, there had been no scarcity of meat, the Christmas markets were as well filled as ever with prime beef, and there was no lack of mutton and other kinds of butchers' meat. Turkeys, geese, and poultry were likewise as plentiful as in former years though very much higher in price. At the beginning of the new year of 1918, however, things took a sudden and surprising turn, and apparently, without cause or reason, the markets became almost denuded of meat of all kinds, and prices rapidly advanced, beef reached the, then, unprecedented price of 2s. per lb. Things went from bad to worse, and on Saturday, 5th January, matters reached a climax, and those, who, on the following day, were able to enjoy their Sunday meat dinner were in the minority. Rabbits on that occasion fetched as much as 4s. 6d. each, and many who purchased them at that extortionate figure considered themselves fortunate individuals. And so it came to pass that a meat rationing order came in force on February 25th, 1918, for London, Middlesex, Hertford, Essex, Surrey, Sussex and Kent, which was afterwards extended to the whole country. Under this order, every adult was entitled to 1s. 8d. worth of meat per week, to include, (in addition to butchers' meat), suet, poultry, game, rabbits, hares, bacon, ham, sausages, and tinned meat. Children were allowed half the above quantities.

On the same date butter and margarine were rationed, ¼lb. of butter or margarine being allowed for every adult and child. This was afterwards increased to 1oz. of butter and 4oz. of margarine.

Lard was also rationed a little later on, 2oz. being allowed per week per head.

The conditions affecting these rationing orders were modified and altered more than once before the war ended, but not to any appreciable extent.

In November, 1918, tea and jam were rationed, 2oz. of the former and 4oz. of the latter being allowed per head per week. New Ration Books were issued in this month to cover all the rationed articles. This book was quite an elaborate production, the pages being multicoloured and in design like miniature wallpaper.

The various rationing orders were willingly and cheerfully submitted to, and it was generally felt that the rationing of necessary foods was a wise and fair method of dealing with the country's supplies, largely modifying the queue system, which had not only been a hardship to the individual, but often times an inconvenience to the public.

The following are some of the Maximum prices paid for articles during the war periods :

MAXIMUM FOOD PRICES.

Bread 1s. per 4lb. loaf, butter 5s. 6d. per lb., margarine 1s. 4d. per lb., bacon 3s. per lb., meat 2s. 8d. per lb., milk 1s. per quart, condensed milk 1s. 6d. per tin (in pre-war times 6½d.) eggs 11d. each, rabbits 1s. 9d. per lb., sugar 8d. per lb., tea 4s. per lb. (ordinary quality), tapioca 1s. 2d. per lb., potatoes 3d. per lb., cauliflowers 1s. 6d. each, cabbages 9d. each, apples 3s. per lb., dessert pears 2s. 6d. each, tinned fruit 4s. 4½d. per tin, Brazil nuts 3s. 3d. per lb., walnuts 2s. 6d. per lb., chestnuts, 1s. 10d. per lb., jam (mixed fruit of very poor quality) and marmalade 1s. 3d. per lb., cocoanuts 1s. 10d. each, oranges 9d. to 1s. each, lemons 8d. each, butter beans 1s. 2d. per lb.

The following are interesting items which appeared in the Press, concerning the prices of food :—

Daily Express, December 16, 1918. :—

PRICES FALLING.

"The monthly return in the "Labour Gazette" shows a slight average decline in the prices of all the principal articles of food during November. The general level on December 2 was 129 per cent. above that of July 1914, as compared with 133 per cent. in November."

Daily Mail, December 16, 1918 :—

THIS WEEK'S FOOD GUIDE.
MORE MEAT AND SUGAR. COUPON-FREE ARTICLES.

"Several rationing concessions to make the Christmas table more cheery are in force this week, and should be remembered by the housewife when doing her shopping. They are :

MEAT coupons numbered 7 (this week's) are doubled in value, equalling 8d. worth each. All edible offal, and also suet, is coupon free.

POULTRY, GAME, and RABBITS are coupon free until January 4.

SUGAR, ½lb. extra on every coupon for next week, but that week's ration may be bought this week in advance.

APPLES from to-day are 9d. per lb. irrespective of size or description.

Next week's butter, margarine, and jam may be bought this week, but not meat.

Lard is no longer rationed.

Iced and sweet cakes and pastries, muffins and crumpets are now on sale, and new bread is permitted from December 23 to 28."

Evening Standard, March 18, 1919 :—

"The latest figures for the following countries show the increases in the price of food since July, 1914 :—

	Per cent.		Per cent.
Great Britain	130	Norway	175
France	144	Italy	153
Paris	137	India	51
Denmark	86	New Zealand	41.6
Sweden	220	South Africa	44

289

T

Daily Express, May 7, 1919 :—Extract of statement made in the House of Commons by Mr. G. H. Roberts, the Food Controller :—

"Up to July 1917 food prices in this country increased as rapidly, or even more rapidly than elsewhere, but since that time they have increased far less rapidly here, and have begun to fall much earlier than elsewhere. The prices prevailing in October 1918 were :—

BREAD.—United Kingdom 9d. per 4lb. loaf, France 8½d., Germany 11½d., Sweden 11½d., United States 1s. 5½d., Austria 1s. 10½d. Except in the two last mentioned cases the price was affected by a bread subsidy.

BEEF.—United Kingdom 1s. 5½d. per lb., United States 1s. 9d., France 2s. 11d., Germany 2s. 2d., Sweden 3s. 2d., and Austria 5s. 1d.

BUTTER.—United Kingdom 2s. 5d. per lb., United States 2s. 8d., France 4s. 1d., Germany 5s. 5d., and Austria 10s."

"Prices are still soaring. According to the "Labour Gazette" the average increase in retail prices of the principal articles of food on Nov. 1, 1919, was 131 per cent., as compared with July, 1914 ; the corresponding figure for Oct. 1 being 122 per cent. on the basis of the pre-war standard of consumption."

Four Food Controllers were appointed in succession during the war period, viz. :—Lord Devonport, Lord Rhondda, Mr. J. R. Clynes, M.P., and Mr. George H. Roberts, M.P., the last two belonging to the Parliamentary Labour Party.

HOUSEHOLD FUEL.

Although coal was very costly during the whole period of the war, it was not rationed or controlled until the winter of 1918. The rationing was, however, not illiberal, the allowance for 12 months being one ton (or its equivalent in gas or electric light) for every living-room, and in addition, 15,000 cubic feet of gas per house (or its equivalent in electric light), for lighting purposes. The price of Household Coal for the winter of 1918 was 43s. 6d. per ton, in and around London, and the price afterwards rose or fell in accordance with the following table :—

July 1919.—Increase of 6s. per ton.
December 1919.—Decrease of 10s. per ton.
January 15, 1920.—Increase of 2s. per ton.
March 1, 1920.—Increase of 1s. 6d. per ton.
May 12, 1920.—Increase of 14s. 2d. per ton.

In August 1920, the price of best Household Coal was 61s. 2d. per ton. [Prior to the war this quality Coal could be bought at about 30s. per ton.]

The great need for economy in fuel was emphasized by posters and press notices, issued by the Government from time to time, one of which, concerning the use of cinders, is reproduced below :

"CINDERS—Save them all ! Every year millions of scuttles of cinders are wasted. Cinders are partly burnt coal, and their heat value is 3lbs. of cinders to 1 lb. of Coal. UNLESS YOU SAVE THE CINDERS YOU ARE LOSING A LARGE PART OF YOUR COAL RATION.

Statistics prove that the average waste is nearly two weeks' coa
supply for each household. Think what it means to go two weeks without
coal—and then determine to sift your cinders.

If you have no sifter, pick the cinders carefully out of the debris under
the grate. Everything will burn again except the ash dust. The saving
you thus 'make will give you many bright glowing fires. GREAT
ECONOMY IS STILL NECESSARY WITH COAL!"

MATCHES..

There was a great scarcity of matches during the last two
years of the war, and this, probably, caused more inconvenience
than any other shortage of domestic articles. Smokers particularly will have reason to remember the time when they had
to treasure up every individual match, and when they went
back to the old fashioned custom of using spills for lighting pipes,
etc. Mechanical pipe lighters also came into general use, which
made those who possessed them somewhat independent of the
matchbox. For many months prices were controlled, and no
matches were provided in public places of refreshment. Whereas,
in pre-war days, a packet of matches containing 12 small boxes,
was obtainable for three-halfpence, the controlled price was
1d. per box, and for a long time only one box a week was allowed
per household. Higher prices were charged for larger boxes
and for wax vestas. The war-time match was a " venomous little
beast," and had a nasty habit of spurting fire into the eyes, and
of breaking off short when struck on the box, and as many of
them were not impregnated, they more often than not flickered
out immediately after lighting, which was the more annoying,
seeing that every single match had its value, notwithstanding
its quality.

WAR REGULATIONS.

" And what come may.
Time and the hour runs through the roughest day."
Shakespeare : Macbeth i., iii.

Many were the Regulations affecting every-day life which
came into operation during the war period :—

LIGHTING.—Owing to the frequent visitations of Zeppelins and
enemy aeroplanes to the Eastern Counties, stringent orders
were issued with regard to the lighting of shops and dwelling
houses. In our own village all the street lamps were, for a time,
shaded by blacking over the upper parts of the lanterns, and,
eventually, the lanterns were removed altogether, excepting
at dangerous corners, and during the last two years of the war,
these were also removed.

Shops were subject to the following regulations :—

(a) One lamp only to be allowed in each shop window, such lamp
not to exceed 25 candle power.

(b) These lamps to be carefully shaded, or reflected on to the goods
exhibited.

291

(c) The window lights under no condition to show any appreciable light to the pavement.

(d) All window lights to be extinguished by 8 p.m.

Private residents were requested to keep all blinds drawn, and all bright lights screened.

In consequence of these restrictions, our streets were dreary in the extreme, and in the winter months absolutely dangerous on moonless nights. But to feel the real dreariness of unlit streets one had to go into the towns, and our own neighbouring little market town of Romford lost all its attractiveness in the all-pervading gloom which settled down on it after sunset on a winter's night.

GARDEN FIRES.—Garden and rubbish fires were also strictly forbidden after sunset, and many people who were indiscreet enough to permit such were summoned before the Magistrates and fined.

PUBLIC HOUSES.—Before the outbreak of war, public houses in our neighbourhood were open from 6 a.m. till 11 p.m. on weekdays, and from 1 p.m. to 3 p.m., and from 6 p.m. till 10 p.m. on Sundays. Some time after the war commenced, closing was made compulsory at 10 p.m. on weekdays, and 9.30 p.m. on Sundays.

In the latter part of 1915, a further order was issued by the Board of Liquor Control prohibiting the opening of public-houses before 12 noon on weekdays, and making the following general regulation for opening and closing, which was effective until the end of the war period, viz. :—

Week days : 12 noon till 2.30 p.m.
6.30 p.m. till 9.30 p.m.
Sundays : 1 p.m. till 3 p.m.
6 p.m. till 9 p.m.

All houses might, however, be kept open from 6 a.m. till 10 p.m. for the sale of non-intoxicants and food.

A further order was introduced prohibiting treating within a certain area in and around London, which included Hornchurch.

DAYLIGHT SAVING OR SUMMER TIME.

" It shall be what o'clock I say it is ! "
Shakespeare : Taming of the Shrew., Act. IV., iii.

It took a world-war to bring about a useful innovation, orginated by Mr. William Willett, who had agitated for its adoption for many years with the greatest enthusiasm, and which had been before Parliament more than once without success It was in 1908 that the first Bill was introduced in the House of Commons, to give us an extra hour's daylight during the Summer months. This was known as " The Daylight Saving Bill," and, as Mr. Willett was not a Member of Parliament, the Bill was introduced by Mr. R. Pearce, M.P. It was referred to a

Select Committee, and was approved with certain changes. The Bill was again introduced in 1909, and its second reading was carried by 130 to 94 votes. but on again being sent to a Select Committee, a report in its favour was rejected by a majority of *one vote*, owing to " great diversity of opinion " and the fear of " serious inconvenience."

I well recollect attending a great meeting at the Guildhall, some two or three years before the outbreak of war, at which Mr. Winston Churchill, M.P., amongst others, spoke in favour of Mr. Willett's scheme. Most of the great cities and boroughs throughout the kingdom had pronounced in favour of this novel idea, and were represented at the meeting, but English prejudice dies hard, and Mr. Willett again failed to get his measure through Parliament, and died without witnessing the triumph of the scheme for which he had striven so hard. What peaceful persuasion failed to do, however, a great war brought about, and in the year 1916, the " Summer Time Act " (1916) was passed, by which it was decreed that in the night of Saturday/Sunday, May 20/21, all public clocks should be advanced one hour, and that in the night of Saturday/Sunday September 30/October 1, they should be put back one hour.

The following is a copy of the official announcement which appeared in the Press of May 18, 1916 :—

" DAYLIGHT SAVING LAW.—*Home Office Instructions for altering the Clock.* – The Summer Time Act (Daylight Saving) received the Royal Assent yesterday. Last night the Home Office issued the following notice to the public.

Important. Alteration of Time. In the night of Saturday-Sunday, May 20th-21st, at 2 a.m., the time on all railways, at all post offices, and other Government establishments will be put forward one hour to 3 a.m.

The altered time will be used for all ordinary purposes during the summer. For instance, licensed houses, factories, and workshops, and other establishments where hours are regulated by law, will be required to observe the altered time.

The Government requests the public to put forward all clocks and watches by one hour during the night of Saturday, May 20th. Normal time will be restored at 2 a.m. on the night of Saturday-Sunday, September 30th-October 1st.

The chief object of this measure at the present time is to reduce the number of hours during which artificial lighting is used in the evenings, and so save to the nation part of the fuel and oil for lighting, and release large quantities of coal which are urgently needed for other purposes arising from the war.

By order of the Home Secretary."

Although the above act provided only for the year 1916, Parliament made other enactments in the ensuing years, giving the following dates for the duration of " Summer time," viz. :—

1917 :—April 8 to Sept. 16.
1918 :—March 24 to Sept. 29.
1919 :—March 30 to Sept. 28.
1920 :—March 28 to Sept. 27.

THE AUDIBILITY OF CONTINENTAL GUN-FIRE IN ESSEX.

> " Ah me ! what act
> That roars so loud, and thunders in the index ?"
>
> *Shakespeare :* Hamlet, III., iv.

Hornchurch people will have many disturbing recollections of the audibility of Continental gun-fire during the war. The sound of the guns was heard with great distinctness on many and various occasions, more particularly during the summer months. It was, at times, very pronounced, and in my own individual case could be most distinctly heard and felt inside a built-out pantry at the rear of the house. This gun-fire often continued throughout all hours of the day and night, but, for the most part, it was intermittent.

Careful and elaborate observations were taken by Mr. Miller Christy, and contributed by him in three papers—covering the periods 1914 and 1918—to the Quarterly Journal of the Meteorological Society.* As many of the experiences recorded by him were almost identical with those experienced in Hornchurch, I give below (with his kind permission), some extracts from his records, including a few entries of special incidents, and some of his general remarks. On many occasions I experienced exactly the same sensations as those described by Mr. Miller Christy, and I have no doubt that many of our neighbours, especially those living on the higher parts of the parish, have similar recollections. The records here reproduced will, I feel sure, be very valuable, and may prove of even greater value to future generations than to those who lived through the years of the Great War.

" I have heard the sound of the fighting in Flanders repeatedly since an early period of the war. I did not, at first, realize what the sound really was ; but, as soon as I did so, I became interested in the fact and commenced to make notes of my own observations. I began also to gather, by means of a somewhat voluminous correspondence, records of observations by others, and I thus accumulated in time a considerable number of records which are incorporated in the present paper.

" Living on fairly high ground and not far from the East Coast, I enjoy specially favourable opportunities for hearing the gun-firing in Flanders. My house stands in the parish of Chignal St. James, between two and three miles north-west from Chelmsford, in Essex, and about 125 miles north-west from Ypres—taking that as a fairly central point in Flanders around which exceptionally severe land fighting has taken place. The house occupies a fairly elevated position (about 155 feet above sea-level), amid purely rural surroundings, with no higher ground in the immediate vicinity. Moreover, there is no higher ground between the house and Ypres. To reach my ear, the sound has to traverse about 25 miles of Flemish soil, about 75 miles of the water of the North Sea, and just 25

*Vol. XLII., No. 180, October, 1916 ; Vol. XLIV., No. 188, October, 1918 ; Vol. XLV., No. 190, April, 1919.

miles of Essex land. The fact that more than half the entire distance is across the sea, no doubt, favours the hearing of the gunfire. However this may be, the sound has been heard repeatedly, not only by myself, but also by very many of my neighbours who happen to live on ground as high or higher. The same may be said of many other persons living on high ground in other counties.

"The sound of the firing varies considerably. Sometimes one hears slow and deliberate firing, at the rate of from three to twelve shots a minute, each shot being quite loud and distinct. On these occasions, the firing heard is, I take it, that of the British "Monitors" and other warships bombarding, with their heavy guns, the German positions on the Belgian coast, about Nieuport, Ostend, and Zeebrugge. It is, however, difficult to prove this ; for, on some occasions when I have heard this kind of firing, no report of any such bombardment has appeared in the newspapers ; while at other times, when such a bombardment has been reported, I have heard no heavy firing (the weather conditions having been, perhaps, unfavourable, or myself absent from home).

"Usually, however, the firing I have heard has been much more rapid, much less distinct, and apparently more distant. No doubt the sound is that of fighting farther inland—say, around Ypres, Dixmude, or Arras. It varies in rapidity from, perhaps, four or five shots to the minute up to more than one hundred. This sound is, as a rule, quite faint, though easily perceptible and quite unmistakable. There is no sharp explosion, as when a gun is fired close at hand. What one hears resembles more nearly a dull and distant thud, which one seems to *feel*, rather than to hear. At any rate, that is the best description I can give of it. I have never heard the incessant rumbling described by some other observers elsewhere.

"Further evidence as to the origin of the sound is to be found in the fact that, in a room, or a verandah, or any other annexe to a house, it might often be heard more distinctly than out of doors, provided the aspect was southerly or easterly. Thus, I often heard the fainter kind of firing with unusual distinctness while in my bedroom, or writing in my study or standing in my porch, all of which face southerly."

1915.

September 11.—*Chignal St. James.*—"The loudest and most distinct firing I have heard at any time since the war began ; one could hear the actual explosions, rather than feel the usual faint thud ; began about 1 p.m., and continued steadily for nearly an hour, averaging about 20 shots to the minute (counted) ; recommenced for short periods several times during the afternoon."

1916.

June 24.—"From 8 p.m. till 11.30 (when I went to bed), firing very violent. It was not very loud, but exceedingly rapid—the most rapid, beyond comparison, I have yet heard. It was not the usual rapid succession of dull thuds, but was so incessant that it resembled a sort of constant faint vibrant fluttering or muttering, such as had been described to me previously by others living on much higher ground elsewhere, but I had not heard before. (Obviously the great British artillery assault, which begun on this day.)"

July 2.—"Firing again heard all day, though somewhat faint, until the late evening, when it became exceedingly intense and rapid, resembling a faint, vibrant, fluttering rumble, in which single shots were seldom distinguishable. It was most remarkable and impressive on an otherwise perfectly still evening."

"During the first fourteen weeks (May 1 to August 6), gunfire, which I am confident was really Continental was heard here, clearly and distinctly, on practically every day. It varied considerably in both loudness and nature. Thus, the sound of the fighting at Vimy on Sunday, May 21, was heard with remarkable ease and was reported to me from various other places in the south of England. What was heard then was, however, as nothing when compared with the loudness of the sound heard, especially in the evenings, from June 24 (when the great British artillery assault on the Somme began) till July 2. Moreover, during most of these nine days, the sound, as heard here, differed widely (as explained above) from that heard here at any other time since the war began. Its volume was positively amazing, considering that Chignal is about 155 miles from (say) Albert."

1917.

June 3.—" Firing of intense rapidity, but not remarkably loud, from before rising until after retiring. The whole air seemed full of a sort of vibrating flutter, with occasionally separate louder reports. A quite phenomenal day, something like those between June 24 and July 2 last year. Wind (a light breeze) West or South-west." [The firing to-day was heard clearly on the Surrey Hills (see *Daily Mail*, June 4). It was due, no doubt, to the heavy fighting recorded to-day at Wytschaete and elsewhere.]

June 14.—" Firing heard regularly every day since the 3rd, especially in the evenings. This evening, about 8, it became extremely violent and rapid—a continuous, vibrating, fluttering rumble, in which specially-loud single shots were distinguished now and then."

July 14.—" Guns very active all day, especially in the evening—a sort of throbbing rumble, not very loud, but sufficiently rapid and pronounced to be, at times, *really annoying*. At 9.7 p.m. a very distinct crackling explosion lasting two or three seconds, and certainly beyond sea. The pheasants in the wood round the house crowed vigorously, one in my garden continuing to do so for more than twenty minutes. I have seldom heard them crowing of late, there being fewer than formerly, and those which remain having become accustomed, I suppose, to loud distant noises."

July 27.—" Prodigious firing all last night—more rapid and more distinct, if rather less loud, than hiterto—so vehement that it prevented sleep. One heard it as a kind of incessant thumping, which vibrated most unpleasantly through the house, especially the eastern end. Wind West."

GENERAL REMARKS.—" This year I heard the oversea firing first on 22nd April and last on 6th September. Thus, it continued audible throughout a period of nineteen weeks and four days. This was longer than in either 1915 or 1916.

" During this period, there were very few days when the sound of the gunfire was not audible distinctly, and quite unmistakably. My impression is, indeed, that it was heard more loudly and far more continuously during 1917 than during either 1915 or 1916. Presumably, the atmospheric conditions were, in some way, more favourable to audibility in 1917 than in the two preceding years.

" One point which has struck me particularly during the past summer has been the small influence which the direction of the wind has upon the transmission of the sound ; for the firing has been heard here when the wind has been blowing from every point of the compass. I remarked particularly that, during the period when the firing was heard most loudly the wind blew generally from a more-or-less Westerly direction. It was only when a roaring and blustering wind blew strongly enough to drown the sound of the guns, that the firing could not be heard easily. This was often the case during July and August, when a high wind from the South-west was very persistent."

" REGULAR SEASONS OF AUDIBILITY AND INAUDIBILITY.—" In my report of observations made during the summer of 1916, I called attention briefly to the fact that there appeared to be every year a regular and well-defined ' Period of Audibility,' and that this was followed by a longer ' Period of Inaudibility.' In my report of observations, made during the summer of 1917, I was able to confirm and amplify my conclusions on this point, and also to define, to some extent, the average duration of the two Periods. The existence and regular sequence of these two Periods have been con firmed, in every detail, by the additional observations I now record for the summer of 1918. My conclusions have also been confirmed by others elsewhere, and have been discussed in detail by Mr. F. J. W. Whipple.

This year I heard the Continental gunfire first on 8th May and last on 26th August. The ' Period of Audibility ' lasted, therefore, for fifteen weeks and five days."

" This enables me to complete the tabular comparative statement I gave last year, showing the duration of the Periods of Audibility in each year of the war. The result stands as follows :

1915.—From about 1st May to about 31st August = 17 weeks 3 days.
1916.—From about 1st May to about 15th August = 15 weeks.
1917.—From 22nd April to 6th September   .. = 19 weeks 4 days.
1918.—From 8th May to 26th August   ..   .. = 15 weeks 5 days.

It appears therefore, that in 1918 the Period of Audibility was short—only five days longer than in 1916, when it was shorter than in the previous year, and some four weeks shorter than in 1917, when it was longer than in any other year."

PLAGUE AND PESTILENCE.

The gaunt spectres of war, famine, and pestilence have ever gone hand in hand. The last of this trinity of evils manifested itself in the latter days of the war in the mysterious malady, known as Spanish Influenza, which ravaged not only the Continent of Europe and the British Isles, but the whole of the civilized world, and raged from the summer to the winter of 1918, reaching its most serious stage, as far as London and the home counties were concerned, in November and December of that year. It was said that this disease was caused by the scarcity and poor quality of food, and that it carried off by death more victims than did the great war. Many believed it to be the plague, but, whether or not this was so, the malady was in some cases as suddenly fatal as was the great plague of London in 1665.

I have not been able to obtain monthly statistics, but during the year 1918, the total number of deaths from all causes in the Romford Rural District (of which Hornchurch forms part), for the twelve months was 344, of which 85 were directly attributable to influenza, or approximately 25%. In the parish of Hornchurch alone, the number of deaths from all causes for the same period was 136, and, reckoning on the same basis of percentage as that given for the Rural District, the deaths attributable to influenza would be 34 for the parish.

THE GENERAL ELECTION OF 1918
(ROMFORD DIVISION).

Will you tell me how to choose a man ?*
Haply a woman's voice may do some good,
When articles too nicely urged be stood on.†

Shakespeare.

The old Parliament was dissolved on November 25th, 1918, having been in existence since December 10th, 1910 (a period of eight years), longer than any other since the Long Parliament in the reign of Charles I., which lasted from November 3rd, 1640, to April 20th, 1653.

The nomination day for the new Parliament was fixed for December 4th, and polling day for the whole Kingdom, Saturday, December 14th, 1918.

This was the first election, under the Representation of the People Act of 1918, under which the old Romford Division was split up. *It was also the first election at which women were admitted as Parliamentary Electors.*‡

There were three candidates nominated for the new Romford Division, viz. :—

LETTS, WALTER HENRY, railway clerk (Labour), Proposer, George E. Button ; seconder, S. Philpot. Assentors : G. E. Jackson, W. Partridge, C. C. Taylor, H. J. Rand, F. A. Hewett, A. L. Baker, T. White, and E. Fletcher.

MARTIN, ALBERT EDWARD, film producer and farmer (Coalition), Proposer, Albert J. Joslin ; seconder, J. P. Carvell. Assentors : A. T. Hall, A. Beard, W. Hutchins, R. C. Orgles, W. G. Brown, W. G. Best, W. Banwell, and R. S. Snell.

WHITING, ARTHUR.—Trades Union official (Labour), Proposer, S. A. Hawkins ; seconder, E. Lambert. Assentors : W. J. James, J. C. Ross, E. G. Ketley, Rachael E. Hawkins, T. M. Moss, A. C. Rudge, J. Felton, T. Gregory, C. A. Rushton, and H. Clark.

A. E. Martin (Coalition Liberal), was elected, the result of the polling being :—

A. E. Martin (Co.L.)	10,300
W. H. Letts (Lab.)	5,044
A. Whiting (Lab.)	2,580
Coalition Liberal Majority	5,256

The new Parliamentary Division of Romford, includes the following parishes :—

Romford, Hornchurch, Upminster, Cranham, Wennington, Great Warley, Havering, Noak Hill, Dagenham, Rainham, and Barking Town Urban District, with a total population on July 1st, 1914, of 78,494, and an electorate of 37,055.

*2 Henry III., ii.
†Henry V., ii.
‡The first woman elected to Parliament was Madame Markievicz, a Sinn Fein, elected at the General Election, December 14, 1918, for the St. Patrick's Division of Dublin. She did not, however, take her seat in the House of Commons. Viscountess Astor, elected at a Bye-Election for the Sutton Division of Plymouth, 15 November, 1919, was the first woman to take her seat at Westminster. She made her " maiden " speech before a full House on February 24, 1920, in a debate on Liquor Control.

The total number of Parliamentary Electors for the Parish of Hornchurch, at this Election, was 4,540, viz. :—

North West Ward	1,927
Village Ward	1,670
Harold Wood Ward	500
South Ward	443
	4,540

The Old Romford Division, which was the largest in the Kingdom, had a population at the last census (1911), of 312,864, and an electorate in 1917 of 62,878.

Sir John H. Bethell, Bart., was the last member, he having sat continuously for the Constituency in the Liberal and Radical interests from 1906 to 1918.

NATIONAL FEDERATION OF DISCHARGED AND DEMOBILISED SAILORS AND SOLDIERS.

Approved warriors and faithful friends.
Shakespeare :—Titus Andronicus, I , i.

OFFICERS OF THE BRANCH :
Chairman : Rev. Charles Steer, M.C.
Vice-Chairman : Mr. E. Tucker.
Hon Secretary : Mr. Cecil Bullock.
Hon. Treasurer : Mr. Frank Luff.

Of the Associations for ex-service men, the first to take root in Hornchurch was the above-named Federation, usually known by its initials, N.F.D.S. & S., its badge being an ivy leaf.

At first the Hornchurch Branch was a sub-branch of Romford, but, by mutual agreement, it attained a separate existence on reaching a membership of 125. This occurred in September, 1919, and by the beginning of 1920, the membership was 150.

The Federation is a non-party organisation, limited originally to men who had served in the ranks, but later opened also to ex-officers, with the following objects in view :—

1. To remedy inequalities and injustices in the matter of Service Pensions, with special attention paid to both National and Local Administration.
2. To watch over the welfare of disabled men.
3. To assist with the rehabilitation of ex-service men in Civil Life.
4. To protect the interests of the Widows and Orphans of fallen men.

In addition to the above objects, the Branch endeavours to provide for the social well-being of its members, taking a keen interest in any project for the improvement of conditions of life, or for the promotion of good fellowship and sport.

The local energies of the branch have included an agitation to secure temporary housing for the men who have returned to find the house famine a real and pressing hardship ; the urging, with some measure of success, of the Local Authorities

HORNCHURCH BRANCH NATIONAL FEDERATION OF DISCHARGED AND DEMOBILISED
SAILORS AND SOLDIERS.

to provide allotment gardens, the support of the Peace Festivities, (when a large amount of work fell upon the Hon. Secretary) ; and the provision of several concerts and other entertainments at a time when there was no other organisation doing this in the village.

The files of the Branch show that a large number of Pension and other cases were taken up and satisfactorily dealt with, during the first six or eight months of its existence. Valuable work was also done in the provision of suitable men to sit on the United Services Fund Committee, the new Local Pensions Committee, and similar public associations.

The Federation has stood firm against all attempts to capture it for any party in the political world, preferring to use its influence impartially in the cause of equity and justice.

THE CHURCH ARMY HUT, NORTH-WEST HORNCHURCH.

The value of the Church Army and Y.M.C.A. Huts in the Military Camps, in England, on the Western Front, and elsewhere, has been so wonderfully proved during the war, that an effort has been made by these societies to continue some of the same kind of work in peace time for the villages. There being a good-sized Church Army Hut in the Camp at Grey Towers, the Vicar, the Rev. Chas. Steer, thought it desirable to get permission immediately from the Church Army Authorities to use it for a Social Centre in the parish, rather than let it be taken elsewhere. After considerable negotiation, a site was found in the North-West Ward, at the corner of Malvern Road and Park Lane. The population of that part of the parish is stated to be rather over 4,000, and there had hitherto been no common building or meeting place of any sort except the Council School. By the help of various residents in the Village Ward, and with the active co-operation of the people living near the spot, enough money was raised to enable the building to be commenced early in January, 1920.

Starting with the idea of simply removing the shell of the hut, it was found necessary to spend a considerable amount of money in re-building and decorating it, and when this was done the result was eminently satisfactory. The opening ceremony, which included a concert, was held on Saturday, March 6th, 1920,* when the Hut was crowded, and comments on the nature of the building were most encouraging. The management of the Social Centre is in the hands of two experienced ladies, Miss Hilda B. Callender and Miss Chapman (sent down from Church Army Headquarters), with an Advisory Committee of local residents.

* The Hut was formally opened and dedicated by the Bishop of Colchester on Saturday afternoon, May 29, 1920.

The need for such a place in the district for the purpose of public worship has been amply demonstrated by the large congregations present on each Sunday evening since its has been opened, while its value as a Social Centre is demonstrated by the large numbers of young men and young women, as well as of older folk, who may be found there on any evening of the week, either playing billiards (or waiting patiently for a turn at the table), playing other indoor games, or sitting round the tables chatting over a cup of the excellent coffee provided at the canteen.

Should such institutions prove to be a success, there can be no doubt that their place in the life of England will, for the future, be a marked and certain one. The people, and especially the young folk are crying out for such places where they can meet on the level, without the usual accompaniments which have hitherto been found in the old style of public-house, and it is sincerely hoped that the Village Ward will, before long, be in possession of such an institution.

EDWARD THE CONFESSOR LODGE OF FREEMASONS.

The Edward the Confessor Lodge of Freemasons, founded in 1916, combines at one and the same time the earliest and latest historical association with our old village, for not only is this recently consecrated Essex Lodge named after the Confessor, but its members claim him as a brother Freemason. The ancient history of Freemasonry in Hornchurch is, moreover, not exhausted by this linking up of the Craft with the great Saxon King and Saint, for it can be shown that a previous Masonic Lodge existed in Hornchurch as far back as the year 1734. It is thus referred to in masonic records :—

" The Lodge was consecrated in 1734 and met at the Red Lion, Hornchurch, its number being 182. When Grand Lodge held its great revision in 1740 this number was altered to 169, and this was again changed in 1755 to 103. Under this number, for reasons unknown and unrecorded at Grand Lodge, it was erased in the year 1769, having thus existed for a space of 35 years.

The foundation of the Edward the Confessor Lodge arose out of an informal meeting of four Hornchurch Freemasons in 1916, and as the outcome of their deliberations a meeting of Freemasons resident in the locality was held on March 27, 1916, at Suffolk House, in the High Street, at which it was decided that a Lodge should be founded in Hornchurch. The usual formalities then followed, and in due course a warrant was applied for and obtained.

In December, 1916, the Edward the Confessor Lodge was consecrated by Bro. the Right Hon. Mark Lockwood, P.C., C.V.O., M.P. (now Lord Lambourne), Provincial Grand Master of Essex.

This ceremony took place at the Great Eastern Hotel, Bishops-gate, London, E.C. The Provincial Grand Master was assisted by Bros. W. Rains Webster, Prov.S.G.W. ; Owen H. Clarke, Prov. J.G.W. ; Rev. J. Bishop Marsh, Prov.G.C. ; Thos. J. Ralling, P.G.D., Prov.G.Sec. ; Victor Taylor, Prov.G.D.C. ; R. Haward Ives, P.P.G.W. ; and A. W. Martin, Prov.G.Tyler.

The ceremony of installation was performed by the Prov. Grand Secretary, Bro. T. J. Ralling, P.G.D. who installed Bro. Charles J. Beharell as the first W.M.

The Worshipful Master appointed and invested his officers as follows :— Bros. Alfred Robertson, S.W. ; John Braid, J.W. ; J. W. Ewing, Treasurer ; Rev. A. J. Parry, P.P.G.C., Secretary ; E. Featherstone Griffin, as acting I.P.M. ; E. F. Williams, D.C. ; James Bauckham, S.D. ; W. J. Eales, J.D. ; Charles Living, I.G. ; John Downton, Junr., Steward.

At the conclusion of the Lodge proceedings there was a dinner in the Hamilton Hall, under the presidency of the W.M. The toast of " The Provincial Grand Master " was accorded musical honours, the New Zealand members of the Forces present (and there were many) rendering it in the Maori language.

This was probably the first occasion on which the Maori language was ever used at a Masonic consecration in England. The New Zealanders at Hornchurch had a very close relationship with the Edward the Confessor Lodge, and it is of interest to record that the first initiate of the Lodge was one of their officers, viz. :—Bro. Gordon H. Forsythe, Captain and Adjutant of the New Zealand Convalescent Hospital, Grey Towers.

Afterwards nine other New Zealanders from Grey Towers were initiated or became members.

The Rev. Charles Steer, M.A., M.C., Vicar of Hornchurch, was appointed Chaplain in 1919.

Three Provincial Honours have been conferred upon members of the Lodge since its foundation, viz. :—W. Bro. Charles J. Beharell, Provincial Senior Grand Deacon, invested in 1917 ; Bro. the Rev. Charles Steer, Provincial Grand Chaplain ; and W. Bro. Alfred Robertson, Provincial Grand Superintendent of Works, both invested in 1920.

The Freemasons War Hospital at Fulham was released by the War Office authorities in 1920, and it was then decided to convert it into a permanent Hospital for Freemasons. The Edward the Confessor Lodge accepted an invitation from the Committee to become one of the " Founding Lodges " of the Hospital, which is now designated the Freemasons Hospital and Nursing Home.

The meetings of the Lodge since its consecration have been held in the Council Hall, Billet Lane, but the members came to a decision in 1919 to purchase the Hall in Billet Lane, formerly

Designed by Sir Charles A. Nicholson, Bart., F.R.I.B.A.

The Parish War Memorial.

**About two hundred men from this Parish made the Supreme Sacrifice
on the Field of Honour for KING and EMPIRE!**

"Thou in this shall find thy monument,
When tyrants' crests and tombs of brass are spent."*

. . . .

"So long as men can breathe, or eyes can see,
So long lives this, and this gives life to thee."†

Shakespeare.

*Sonnet cvii. †Sonnet xviii.

304

used by the Conservative Club, and this will in due course be consecrated and used for the purpose of Masonic meetings.

The Lodge suffered a loss through the death of Bro. Joseph Wilson Dunlop, which occurred on 1st March, 1920.

Eight members of the Lodge served in H.M. Forces during the war, in addition to the New Zealanders.

WORSHIPFUL MASTERS OF THE LODGE.

1916. W. Bro. Charles J. Beharell.
1917. W. Bro. Alfred Robertson.
1918. W. Bro. John Braid.
1919. W. Bro. Ernest Featherstone Griffin.
1920. W. Bro. John Mooney Ewing.

HORNCHURCH PARISH WAR MEMORIALS.

In addition to the War Memorials already mentioned in these pages, a scheme for a Parish Memorial was adopted, and a proposal for a Church Memorial was being considered at the time this book was about to be published.

Some difficulty was at first experienced in coming to a decision respecting the Parish Memorial. Places with a smaller and more compact area have found it an easier matter to decide on something which commended itself from the outset, as in the case of the Harold Wood Ward. After various meetings had taken place, it was decided that the Parish Memorial should take the form of a Village Cross, to be erected on the small plot of ground on Church Hill, immediately outside the Church gates, where hitherto there has stood a postal pillar-box. The site is one which could not be improved upon in all Essex, situated, as it is, by the roadside, at a point passed daily by hundreds of people, and at the entrance to the Churchyard, hallowed by its associations to a large proportion of the population.

The work was put into the hands of Sir Charles Nicholson, Bt., F.R.I.B.A., and the dignified and noble yet simple cross which he has designed, is exactly the right monument for the purpose and for the spot. The names of all those who gave their lives during the war are to be inscribed upon the base of the cross, which will be of Clipsham stone. The names are to be cast on lead plates and affixed to the base, the grass plot being railed in by oak posts and light chains.

It was thought desirable by many parishioners, especially those who had lost relatives in the war, that there ought to be some memorial inside the Church. The Vicar, therefore, had a plan drafted by Sir Charles Nicholson, for the restoration of the Ayloffe, or north Chapel, (part of which had hitherto been used by the clergy as a Vestry), and it is hoped that sufficient money may be subscribed to complete the Memorial in accordance with the design and plans submitted.

305

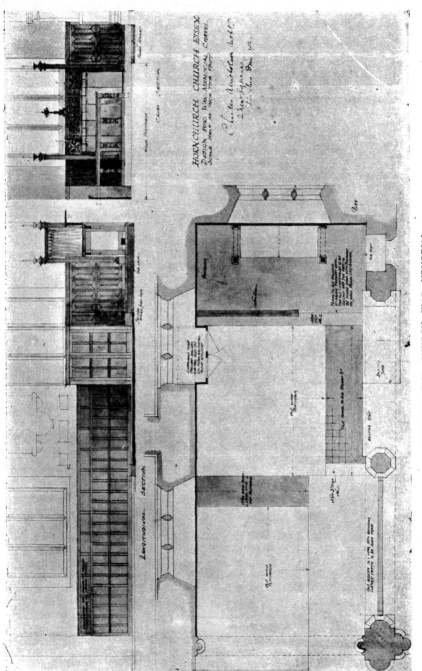

PLAN OF THE CHURCH WAR MEMORIAL.

The work involves the removal of the fine old piece of carved oak screen, which served to shut off the Vestry, and placing it behind the choir stalls as a choir screen. By this means the Chapel will be fully opened out, and by turning the pews to an eastward position, and placing an altar beneath the east, or Edward the Confessor-window, the whole of the structural alterations would be complete. The north and east walls of the Chapel, to a height of about 3ft. 6in., are to contain panels of oak on which are to be carved, and picked out in red and gold, the names of those parishioners who laid down their lives in the war, and it is also intended that other panels shall be devoted to the perpetual memory in Hornchurch of those military units which were encamped in this village during the war period.

As will be seen from the records contained in this book, no small share in the defence of the Homeland was taken by Hornchurch, particularly through the prowess of those airmen from our Aerodrome at Suttons, who brought down the first three Zeppelins destroyed in this country by direct aircraft attack ; while the continuance in our midst of the New Zealand Convalescent Hospital and Camp for such a long period, has forged a link between this ancient village and the new country overseas which will not easily be severed. The Sportsman's Battalion (23rd Royal Fusiliers), and the Navvies' Battalion (26th Middlesex Regt.), are two other units whose records will find a place upon the panels.

The plates here reproduced show the design for the Parish Memorial Cross, and the plan for the Memorial Chapel.

It is hoped that through the medium of this book the intention to erect these Memorials will be brought to the notice of a large number of the men of the various units which were encamped in Hornchurch, many of whom may wish to identify themselves with the suggested proposals, and may desire to join with our parishioners in providing the necessary funds for the proper and efficient carrying out of the work involved. Contributions may be forwarded to the Rev. Charles Steer, the Vicarage, Hornchurch, for the Church Memorial, and to Mr. Cecil Bullock, 2, The Avenue, Hornchurch, for the Parish Memorial.

MR. THOMAS WILLIAM WEDLAKE.

On October 21, 1917, there passed away, in his 89th year, our oldest inhabitant in the person of Mr. Thomas William Wedlake. His association with the village was as honourable as it was prolonged. He bore a name which, in the early years of the 19th century, became prominent throughout the agricultural world, and he continued up to the time of his death in the iron foundry business, made famous by the wonderful ploughs and other agricultural implements invented by his uncles, Thomas and Robert Wedlake, the founders of Fairkytes Foundry in

307

1784. The importance of that industry was commemorated on August 7, 1833, by the presentation at the White Hart, Romford, of a handsome silver tea urn, weighing 160 ounces, to Mr. Thomas Wedlake, by Christopher Tower, Esq., M.P., of Weald Hall, on behalf of the farmers and agriculturists of the Eastern Counties.

Mr. T. W. Wedlake was born in the High Street, on November 17, 1828, and held many public appointments. For many years he filled the office of People's Warden at the Parish Church..

MR. THOMAS GARDNER, J.P., C.C.

His life was gentle, and the elements
So mix'd in him that Nature might stand up
And say to all the world, ' This was a man!'*
A loyal, just, and upright gentleman.†

Shakespeare.

Frequent reference is made in these pages to the many activities during the war period of Mr. Thomas Gardner, of " Duryfalls," whose lamented death took place on Ascension Day, May 13, 1920, in his 70th year. The printing of this book was, at that date, nearing completion, and an opportunity was therefore afforded of including within its covers an appreciation of his public work in Hornchurch and in the county. Mr. Gardner came to Hornchurch in the year 1885, and was married on Feb. 16, 1887, at Alrewas Church, near Lichfield, to Miss Emma Bird, eldest daughter of Mr. Edward Johns Bird, of Orgreave Hall, Alrewas, near Lichfield. In August, 1900, he was made a Justice of the Peace. He was elected a member of the Essex County Council for the Hornchurch Division (which includes the parishes of Hornchurch, Upminster, Cranham and Warley), in March 1898, retaining his seat up to the time of his death, and always being re-elected without opposition. He identified himself largely on the Council with educational matters, being one of the original members of the Essex Education Committee, Chairman of the Romford District Committee, and Chairman of the Hornchurch School Managers. He took the greatest possible interest in the local schools, and prior to the control of the Elementary Schools passing to the County Council, served as Chairman of the Hornchurch School Board, being first elected to that office in the year 1889. On many occasions he and Mrs. Gardner entertained all the children attending the three parish schools, and teachers and scholars alike will sadly miss the kindly interest and attention which he always bestowed upon them and their work.

He served for many years on the Parish Council, and was Chairman of that body from 1897 to 1900.

*Julius Cæsar, v., v.
†King Richard II., I., iii.

He was a Sidesman of the Parish Church, and acted as Treasurer of the Church Restoration Fund in 1896-7. He was also a Feoffee of Roger Reede's Charity, having been elected to that office in 1905.

Outside the parish his interests were many and varied. He was Chairman of Messrs. Gardner, Locket, and Hinton, Ltd., of 3, Fenchurch Avenue, London, coal contractors and lightermen, and Vice-Chairman of the River Lee Conservancy Board,

MR. THOMAS GARDNER, J,P C.C

and a member of the Essex Sewers Commission (Havering and Dagenham Levels), an office held direct from the Crown. Amongst the many important positions filled by him in the City of London may be mentioned the following :—Member of the Court of the Waterman's Company, and Master of the Company, 1885-6 ; Member of the Council of the Association of Master Lightermen and Bargeowners, and President in 1897 ; Member of the Committee of the Bargeowners Protection Society, and Chairman from 1899 to 1920. He was also a Liveryman of the Drapers' Company, and one of the original members of the League of Mercy (King Edward's Hospital Fund).

Mr. Gardner was the oldest Hornchurch season ticket-holder on the L.T. and S.R. Section of the Midland Railway, and he often spoke of the time when he and one other passenger were the only Hornchurch first-class season ticket-holders on the line.

There were few undertakings affecting the social welfare and general good of the community with which Mr. Gardner was not associated, and he was not only a liberal and generous supporter of all charitable objects and organizations, but took a large and active personal share in the actual work connected with such undertakings.

During recent years " Duryfalls " has been a centre of the social life of the parish, and its beautiful and well-kept grounds have frequently been thrown open to the parishioners for their pleasure and enjoyment. Many functions have taken place there in the cause of charity, while others have been of a social character, on which occasions Mr. and Mrs. Gardner were the hosts of the village. During the war, too, the occupants of Grey Towers Camp were often entertained by Mr. and Mrs. Gardner, and many New Zealanders will have taken back to their own country pleasant recollections of their hospitality and of happy hours spent at " Duryfalls."

Mr. Gardner associated himself with all forms of recreation and sport in the district, and was president of numerous clubs and societies, including the Hornchurch Cricket Club and the Miniature Rifle Club.

The affection and esteem in which he was held could, in some measure, be estimated by the very large concourse of people assembled at the Church, and in the Churchyard, at his funeral on Thursday, May 17, 1920. The coffin was borne from " Duryfalls " upon a wheeled bier, and was followed on foot by the mourners and a long procession of friends and parishioners. The village schools were closed for the day, and the children and their teachers, who had known and loved Mr. Gardner so well, awaited the funeral cortège outside the Churchyard gates, to pay their last tribute of respect to his memory. On the altar rails, the choir stalls, the pulpit, and lectern were hung some of the many beautiful floral tributes sent in loving and affectionate memory of the deceased. The service was fully choral, and was taken by the Vicar, the Rev. Charles Steer, the lesson being read by the Curate, the Rev. A. E. Howe, and the committal sentences at the graveside by the Rev. G. M. Bell, Vicar of St. Edward's, Romford, and Rural Dean of Chafford. The Rev. H. H. Holden, Rector of Upminster, the Rev. A. J. Parry, Vicar of St. Peter's, Upton Cross, the Rev. Bernard Hartley, Curate-in-charge of Harold Wood, and the Rev. T. E. Howe, Pastor of Hornchurch Baptist Church, were also present.

By his kindly disposition and genial manner, Mr. Gardner had endeared himself to all sections of the community, and his memory will be long cherished by the people of Hornchurch.

FROM ARMISTICE TO PEACE.

What hear you of these wars ?
I hear there is an overture for peace !
Shakespeare :—All's well that ends well, IV., iii.

THE ARMISTICE.

There will probably never dawn another day quite like Armistice Day, November 11, 1918. After the long years of war, every hour fraught with pain, sorrow, and anxiety, there were few who were not war-weary, and when, at 11 o'clock on that memorable morning, the guns thundered forth the signal that the Armistice had been signed, the sense of relief was indescribable, a something which had to be felt, and only those who had lived through those strenuous times, knew exactly what the experience was like. I was in the Strand when the great news came through. A newsboy came rushing along the sideway shouting " Peace signed," and this, although somewhat a perversion of fact, caused him to be besieged by a good-humoured crowd, anxious to get a first sight of the good news in print. I managed to secure a " Star," where, under the " stop press " news, I saw the announcement for which we had all so long and anxiously waited. This was probably one of the smallest daily newsheets issued during the war, consisting only of four pages, measuring 15″ by 12″, and will give some idea to what straits the publishing world was reduced by reason of the war-time paper shortage. I have reproduced the first page of the " Evening News " of that date, showing the announcement and terms of the Armistice.

HOW THE CROWD GREW.

I then stayed in the streets and watched the news spread and grow, and it was a truly interesting and marvellous experience. First, a few people appeared at the office windows and on balconies, then there was a sprinkling of girls, men, and boys on the pavements in front of shops and offices, then some people afoot and on 'buses came along waving small flags. Then all this was intensified, gradually at first, then rapidly, until the streets were seething with a cheering flag-wagging populace with smiling faces, one and all giving vent to the feelings which had for so long lain dormant. Here and there one saw the quivering lip and moist eye ; indeed it was difficult for anyone, notwithstanding the joy in the air, to prevent the finer emotions coming to the top, and it was good that it should be so. Presently every conceivable conveyance, 'buses, motor-cars, carts, wagons, and heavy lumbering lorries, were positively piled up with people, shouting and waving flags and making all the noises peculiar to the London joy-crowd. Everybody took " French leave,"

The Evening News 630

London's Predominant Evening Journal. Largest Net Sale in the United Kingdom.

LONDON. MONDAY. NOVEMBER. 11. 1918   ONE PENNY.

THE END OF THE WAR.

The Prime Minister made the following announcement to-day:—

The Armistice was signed at Five o'clock this morning, and hostilities are to cease on all Fronts at 11 a.m. to-day.

FOCH CALLS THE "HALT!"

TROOPS NOT TO PASS BEYOND LINE REACHED AT 11.

"CEASE FIRE" ON ALL FRONTS.

EVACUATION BY ENEMY EXTENDED TO 31 DAYS.

The following messages were issued to-day through the wireless stations of the French Government:—

Hostilities will cease on the whole front as from November 11 at 11 o'clock (French time).

The Allied troops will not until a further order go beyond a line reached on that date and at that hour.

(Signed) MARSHAL FOCH.

German Plenipotentiaries to the German High Command, to be communicated to all the authorities interested—

Radio 3084 and G.Q.G. 2 No. 1386 received.

Armistice was signed at 5 o'clock in the morning (French time). It comes into force at 11 o'clock in the morning (French time).

Delay for evacuation prolonged by 24 hours for the left bank of the Rhine, besides the three days; therefore 31 days in all. Modifications of the text compared with that brought by Haldorf will be transmitted by radio.

(Signed) ERZBERGER.
—Admiralty, per Wireless Press.

HAIG WINS THE RACE FOR MONS.

CANADIANS ENTER TO-DAY AT DAWN.

LAST HOURS OF THE WAR.

RECRUITING STOPPED.

All Calling-Up Notices Cancelled. —Official.

PEACE!

"WE WANT KING GEORGE!"

Palace Guardsmen Carried Shoulder High.

NO MORE SHADING OF LIGHTS.

SPECIAL FIREWORK DISPLAY TO BE PERMITTED.

HOW THE KAISER ESCAPED.

RUSH INTO HOLLAND BY MOTOR CAR.

SHOTS FIRED AT HIS TRAIN.

HAGGARD AND BROKEN DOWN.

THE CROWN PRINCE

and mounted any vehicle upon which they could find room, and nobody minded. The most curious and amusing instance I witnessed of this kind was a large coal wagon, laden with sacks of coal, with some dozen or so of laughing and shouting girls and lads on top, absolutely oblivious to their surroundings. The sailors and soldiers, including large numbers of gallant Colonials, seemed, by right, to be leaders in all this rejoicing, and their uniforms, with the flags and bunting, lent colour to a spontaneous outburst of joy, which had surely never been equalled in our history.

THE NEWS AT HORNCHURCH.

On arriving home in the early evening, it was a pleasurable sensation to me to turn up the lights in every room, and to draw up all the blinds. It was a fine thing to be able to do this without the fear of a visit from one of our indefatigable Special Constables, who had seen to it in the days past that no single ray of light ever penetrated through our blinds after dark.

The great news had been received in the village, at the New Zealand Convalescent Camp, Grey Towers, and at Suttons Aerodrome, with every manifestation of joy, and many of our neighbours immediately journeyed to London so as to be " in the swim " of the general rejoicings. A Thanksgiving Service was held during the evening in the Baptist Church, North Street, but no street festivities or other public out-door celebrations took place, probably owing to the wet and inclement weather which prevailed.

ARMISTICE SUNDAY—November 17th.

> O God ! thy arm was here,
> And not to us, but to thy arm alone
> Ascribe we all.
>
> *Shakespeare* :—Henry V., iv., viii.

In all our rejoicings it was constantly borne in upon us that many of our dear ones, who had done so much to make our celebrations possible, were amongst those who would never return, and that a still greater number of brave men and lads were " out there," resting, it is true, after the storm and stress of battle, but away from kindred and home, and all they held most dear. Our truest act of remembrance of them, and of thanksgiving to God for our great deliverance, came on the following Sunday, November 17, which was observed all over the Kingdom as a Day of Thanksgiving for the success of our arms in the war. The services at the Parish Church, both morning and evening were characterised by great heartiness, and very large congregations were present. The morning service at 11 o'clock was attended by members of the Parish Council, the Special Constabulary, the Fire Brigade, and other parish

IN THE BELFRY, HORNCHURCH CHURCH.

organizations, as well as by a large number of wounded men,. accompanied by nurses, from the New Zealand Convalescent Hospital, with their band. The Church was beautifully decorated with the flags of the allied nations, the altar, lectern, and pulpit being completely draped with these international emblems.. The service was taken by the Rev. A. E. Howe, Curate in charge, the preacher at both services being the Rev. Charles Steer, M.C., Chaplain of H.M. Forces, and Vicar Designate of the Parish, only recently returned from Germany, where, for several months, he had been in the hands of the enemy as a prisoner of war. In his discourse he paid fitting and eulogistic tributes to the men of the Navy and Army, including the New Zealand and other Colonial forces, and referred in touching terms to the late Vicar, the Rev. Herbert Dale.

The National Anthem was sung immediately after the processional hymn. The whole service was soul stirring and memorable, the special prayers and hymns being most appropriate to the occasion. The hymns included the following :—" All people that on earth do dwell," " O God our help in ages past," " Onward, Christian Soldiers," " For all the Saints," " Now thank we all our God."

The bells, which had been so long silenced, again swung in the ancient befry, and rang a joyous peal ; Gransire Triples being rung by a Band of Ringers from Romford, viz. :—J. Horwood, treble ; R. Pye, 2 ; D. Keeble, 3 ; A. Pye, 4 ; L. Pye, 5 ; H. Dawkins, 6 ; J. Watson, 7 ; D. Phillips, tenor.

In the afternoon the Right Rev. Bishop Neligan, Chaplain to the N.Z. Forces, and formerly Bishop of Auckland, N.Z., conducted a Confirmation Service.

SUNDAY, JUNE 1, 1919.

On the afternoon of Sunday, June 1, a Church Parade, organized by the local branch of the Federation of Discharged and Demobilized Sailors and Soldiers, was held in the Mill Field. A large number of ex-service men from Hornchurch and Romford marched through the village, headed by the Village Band, and accompanied by the local Company of the Essex Cadets, the special constables, the local branches of the British Red Cross Society, and Queen Mary's Needlework Guild, to the Mill Field, where an open-air drumhead service was conducted by the Vicar, the Rev. Charles Steer, M.C., assisted by the Rev. A. E. Howe, Curate, and the Rev. T. E. Howe, Pastor of the Baptist Church, who read the lesson. Lieut.-Col. H. H. Slade was in charge of the Parade. There was a very large gathering of people, who joined heartily in the singing of the National Anthem and the special hymns selected for the occasion. The Vicar delivered a short address, in which he gave a hearty welcome home to the returned men, and at the conclusion a collection

[Lu*s, Hornchurch.

SERVICE IN THE MILL FIELD JUNE 1, 1919

[Photo]

was taken, amounting to £11 3s. 3d.. for the Charity Funds of the local branch of the Federation. The weather was beautifully fine, and nothing could have been more appropriate or fitting than the holding of such a service in the historic surroundings of the Millfield.

Following the Service, two men belonging to the Romford Branch of the Federation, were presented with decorations, awarded to them for distinguished service in the war.

PEACE.

Plant love among us.
Throng our large temples with the shows of peace,
And not our streets with war.

Shakespeare :—Coriolanus, iii., iii.

Including the Armistice period, the war lasted four years and 328 days.* Many anxious months elapsed between the signing of the Armistice and the conclusion of Peace, and it was not until May 7, 1919, that the Allies' Terms of Peace were handed to the German delegates in the Salon of the Trianon Palace, Versailles. Several extensions of time were granted the Germans, but the labours of the Peace Congress were eventually brought to a happy consummation by the signing of the Peace Treaty on Saturday, June 28th. This ceremony took place in La Galerie des Glaces, or Hall of Mirrors, at Versailles, where, in 1871, the Hohenzollern Empire was born and William I., of Prussia was proclaimed Emperor of Germany. On the present most memorable occasion no Royal or Imperial German was present, the sole representatives of what had recently been the great German Empire, being two undistinguished men, with no great reputation—Herr Hermann Mueller and Dr. Bell.

The delegates and signatories for Great Britain were Mr. David Lloyd George, Prime Minister, Mr. Bonar Law, Mr. Arthur Balfour, Lord Milner, and Mr. G. N. Barnes.

The ceremony commenced at 3.2 p.m., and at 3.47 p.m., M. Georges Clemenceau, who presided, declared the Treaty completely signed.

It was a few minutes after 6 o'clock that the roar of the first gun crashed out in London, announcing that Peace again reigned on the earth, and the cannonade which followed was distinctly heard in Hornchurch. At that time a garden party, given by the Church of England Men's Society to the local dis-charged and demobilized sailors and soldiers, was being held in the vicarage grounds, and as the guns thundered out their joyous message the people rose and sang the National Anthem, and a little later proceeded to the Parish Church and joined with many other parishioners in a short Thanksgiving Service.

*This is calculated to the date on which the Peace Treaty was signed, and not to the official end of the war, for which see page 328.

317

Merry peals of bells were rung both before and after this Service. A brief Service of Thanksgiving was also held in the Baptist Church, North Street, at which the Pastor, Rev. T. E. Howe spoke of the peace in terms of great hopefulness.

Although very little visible excitement prevailed, everybody was happy in the knowledge that war was no more, and their joy was unmistakable, and none the less sincere, by reason of an absence of anything of a boisterous nature. People with smiling faces congratulated each other in the streets, and, those who had them, put out their flags and bunting. Many bonfires in private grounds were lit in honour of the occasion.

On the following day Thanksgiving Services were continued in all public places of worship: The Rev. Charles Steer and the Rev. E. A. Howe made suitable references to the Peace in the morning and evening sermons at the Parish Church. Both services were opened by the singing of the National Anthem, and special hymns and petitions were used.

On Monday a bonfire was lit in the Millfield, at which a large crowd assembled.

PEACE SUNDAY, JULY 6, 1919.

In accordance with His Majesty's command, expressed by Royal Proclamation, Sunday, July 6, 1919, was observed as a National Thanksgiving Day for the restoration of Peace. At the morning and evening Services at the Parish Church special prayers and hymns were used, the sermon in the morning being preached by the Vicar, who took as his topic " Stability," Romans XII., 16. In the evening, the Rev. A. E. Howe preached on " Thanksgiving," Psalm 126, 4.

In the afternoon at 3 o'clock a special united Parochial Service was held, which was attended by the various local organizations. The sermon was preached by the Vicar, his topic being " The Triple Foundation of Peace," S. Matthew, XXII., 23. The collections throughout the day were for the Sick and Needy Fund, and amounted to £19 5s. 11d.

In consequence of engagements in connection with their own Services, the Ministers of the Baptist and Congregational Churches were unable to take part in this parochial service.

PEACE CELEBRATIONS.

Saturday, July 19, 1919, was proclaimed as a Bank Holiday for the celebration of Peace. A merry peal of bells rang out from the old church tower at 7 o'clock to usher in the day, and further peals were rang at 11 a.m. and 7 p.m., the band of ringers being :—John Dale (Foreman), Albert Fry, Arthur Fry, Daniel Phillips, John Ellis, Charles Barlow, John Jarvis, Charles Bone, Henry Grimwood and Arthur Eve. The village was gaily decorated with flags and bunting, and at 9 o'clock at night

BY THE KING.
A PROCLAMATION.

GEORGE R.I.

WHEREAS it has pleased Almighty God to bring to. a close the late wide-spread and sanguinary War in which We were engaged against Germany and her Allies; We, therefore, adoring the Divine Goodness and duly considering that the great and general blessings of Peace do call for public and solemn acknowledgment, have thought fit, by and with the advice of our Privy Council, to issue this Our Royal Proclamation hereby appointing and commanding that a General Thanksgiving to Almighty God for these His manifold and great mercies be observed throughout Our Dominions on Sunday, the Sixth day of July instant; And for the better and more devout solemnization of the same We have given directions to the Most Reverend the Archbishops and the Right Reverend the Bishops of England to compose a Form of Prayer suitable to this occasion, to be used in all Churches and Chapels, and to take care for the timely dispersing of the same throughout their respective Dioceses; and to the same end We do further advertise and exhort the General Assembly of the Church of Scotland and all Spiritual Authorities and ministers of religion in their respective church.s and other places of public worship throughout Our United Kingdom of Great Britain and Ireland and in all quarters of Our Dominions beyond the Seas to take part as it may properly behove them to do in this great and common act of worship, and We do strictly charge and command that the said Public Day of Thanksgiving be religiously observed by all as they tender the favour of Almighty God and have the sense of His Benefits.

Given at Our Court at Buckingham Palace, this First day of July, in the year of our Lord One thousand nine hundred and nineteen, and in the Tenth year of Our Reign.

GOD SAVE THE KING.

LONDON · Printed by EYRE and SPOTTISWOODE, LIMITED, Printers to the King's most Excellent Majesty.

there was a 'huge bonfire in the western part of Grey Towers Park, which was lit by Mrs. Steer, wife of the Vicar. There was no other local official recognition of the day, it having been arranged that the Parish celebration should take place on Saturday, August 9.

Prior to that day, however, the school children of the Village Ward, and the North West and South Wards, were fêted in various ways. This took place on Thursday afternoon, July 24, and altogether some 1,450 children were provided with free teas. The North-West children had theirs in the Y.M.C.A. canteen at Grey Towers Camp, and the remainder were regaled at their own school in their class-rooms.

The North-West children's celebrations were organised by a committee, the chairman of which was Mr. L. W. Wilmot, the hon. secretary, Mr. L. H. Potts, and the hon. treasurer, Mr. E. Day. Mr. H. B. Sell was chairman of the sports sub-committee, and Mr. G. W. Ruffell chairman of the finance sub-committee. There were about a hundred other workers, mostly ladies, who collected the necessary funds—entirely voluntary subscriptions—and arranged the teas. About 900 children were entertained with sports in the camp grounds, including flat races, slow bicycle, egg and spoon and threadneedle races, and a football match, and subsequently to tea. The Cottage Homes band played selections at intervals. The committee had also the assistance of the staff of Park Lane Schools. Each child was provided with a ticket, with four perforated corners—two for lemonade, one for sweets, and one for tea. The whole thing was done on a large scale, and reflected great credit on the committee and workers. After tea a concert was held, and an enthusiastic audience applauded heartily the efforts of the following artistes: Miss Tidbury, Miss May Jones, Misses Fielding and Liddon, Miss Knight, Miss Hayward, Messrs. G. Clark, W. Beere, Lieut. Moreland (juggling), Sergt. Lindley and the Mona Brothers.

The South and Village Ward celebrations were provided entirely through the generosity of Mr. and Mrs. T. Gardner. About 550 children were entertained at North Street Schools ; the South Hornchurch children being brought up on motor lorries by Mr. Poupart. Having first partaken of buns, the children went to the cinema in two sections, being afterwards amused with games of various kinds until tea-time. Following tea they assembled in the girls' playground, around the flagstaff, and went through a short programme. They first sang " Flag of Britain," an effort that brought forth considerable applause from the parents and others who were gathered there. Speeches were made by Mr. T. Gardner, J.P., C.C. and by the Vicar the Rev. Charles Steer, after which the children sang " Rule Britannia." The Schoolmaster, Mr. Edwards, proposed a vote of thanks to Mr. and Mrs. Gardner for so generously providing the teas. This was seconded by Miss Spragg, headmistress of the girls' school. The celebration concluded with the National Anthem, and each child was presented with chocolates on leaving.

PARISH PEACE CELEBRATIONS.

If some people doubted the wisdom of the Hornchurch Peace Celebrations Committee in deferring the parish festivities until August 9th, they had to admit themselves in the wrong, for the venture was considerably more successful than many of the more hastily planned projects in other parishes, and was attended with brilliant weather, in contrast to the irritating drizzle that nearly spoiled Peace Day.

The programme was a long and excellent one, including a dinner to old folks and widows, a carnival, sports, a concert, and various guessing competitions. There were sideshows, visitors being specially asked to see " Dora " the pig, offered as a prize in one of the competitions, also a " country fair " with its leaping horses, swings, roundabouts, and everything calculated to provide a happy day for young and old. During the afternoon the Cottage Homes' Band gave selections of music, and in the evening their place was taken by the Village Band, conducted by Mr. Reed.

The dinner, which was provided by the generosity of Mr. W. Varco Williams and Mrs. Williams, was held in the Drill Hall, and was attended by 220 old folks and widows, amongst the guests being our oldest inhabitant, Mrs. Mary Ann Smith from Appleton's Almshouses, who, notwithstanding her 93 years, was one of the merriest of those present. The dingy old hall was transformed by flags, flowers, and evergreens, into a really beautiful dining hall, and rarely, if ever, had it been seen to greater advantage. The tables were tastefully laid, and decorated with a profusion of pink roses and carnations, most charmingly arranged. The platform, too, was banked with palms and flowers, the whole effect being most picturesque.

In consequence of the serious illness of Mrs. Williams, Mr. Williams was unable to be present, but Mr. and Mrs. Fraser-Parkes (his daughter and son-in-law) welcomed the guests and presided at the dinner. At the conclusion a vote of thanks to Mr. and Mrs. Williams was proposed by Mr. Thomas Gardner, and seconded by Mr. E. Lambert, Chairman of the Parish Council. This was suitably responded to by Mr. Fraser-Parkes, and was followed by the singing of the National Anthem.

As the guests left the Hall, the men were presented with a packet of tobacco, and the women with a packet of tea, the gifts of a parishioner. The chairs were then removed from the Hall and placed on the side walks, where the guests were able to witness in comfort the passing of the carnival procession.

PARISH OF HORNCHURCH

..THE..

PEACE CELEBRATIONS

WILL BE HELD ON

SATURDAY, AUGUST 9th, 1919

In the FIELD BETWEEN HARROW DRIVE and GREY TOWERS CAMP

(By kind permission of the Officer Commanding)

OLD FOLKS AND WIDOWS DINNER

(Provided by W. Varco Williams, Esq., J.P., C.C.), at 1 p.m. in the DRILL HALL, High Street, Hornchurch.

NOTE. *Persons over 60 years of age and all widows desirous of attending must send in their names at once to the Clerk to the Council, Billet Lane, Hornchurch, when an invitation will be sent them.*

FANCY DRESS CARNIVAL

(Arranged by the D. & D. S. & S. Federation). Commencing at 2 p.m. Parade outside the Parish Church. Eight Classes, 16 Prizes.

Class 1. INDIVIDUAL ENTRIES LADIES.
Class 2. do. GENTLEMEN.
Class 3. LADIES TABLEAUX.
Class 4. GENTLEMEN'S TABLEAUX.
Class 5. SCHOOL CHILDREN.
Class 6. DECORATED PERAMBULATORS.
Class 7. DECORATED HORSES AND CARTS, CARS, LORRIES, etc.
Class 8. DECORATED CYCLES AND MOTOR CYCLES, etc.

Entries for the above to be sent to Mr. C. BULLOCK, 2 The Avenue, Hornchurch, by August 6th.

GAMES AND RACES

COMMENCING AT 2.30 P.M.

1. Parade of Carnival
2. 100yds. Flat Race, over 14 years of age, Scratch
3. 100yds. Flat Race, under 14 years of age, Handicap
4. Long Distance Race of about 3 miles
5. Sack Race, 50yds., open
6. Egg and Spoon Race, over 14
7. Egg and Spoon Race, under 14, Handicap
8. Bun Struggle
9. Obstacle Race, Open
10. 100yds. Veteran Race, over 50 years of age, Handicap
11. Derby Race, Jockeys under 6 years
12. Tilting the Bucket
13. Obstacle Race, open to Members of D.D.S.S. Federation
14. Tug-of-War, teams of 9
15. Ladies' and Gentlemen's Blindfold Driving Race
16. Four-legged Race
17. Sweep and Miller Fight
18. Wrestling on Horseback, Teams of six pairs

Good Prizes. Entries free, open to residents of Hornchurch only (including Camps), should be posted to Mr. H. Sell, Hon. Sec. to Fete Committee, 94 Craigdale Road, Romford, by Wednesday, Aug. 6th. Children's Entries on Ground.

DANCING in DRILL HALL from 7.30 p.m. Admission 1/-

CONCERT *in Marquee on Grounds, by the RONEO CONCERT PARTY at 7.30 p.m. Admission Free.*

COUNTRY FAIR, SWINGS, ROUNDABOUTS, GUESSING COMPETITIONS, &c.

The Cottage Homes and Hornchurch Village Bands

WILL PLAY THROUGHOUT THE DAY.

ADMISSION TO THE GROUNDS FREE. REFRESHMENTS AT POPULAR PRICES.

CHILDREN'S CELEBRATION

T. GARDNER, Esq., J.P., C.C. and Mrs. GARDNER having generously entertained the School Children of the South and Village Wards, and the North-West Committee the Children of the North-West Ward on the 24th July, no special provision for their entertainment will be made on this date.

(Signed) THE PEACE CELEBRATION COMMITTEE.

COUNCIL OFFICES, HORNCHURCH,
24th JULY, 1919.

Funds for the expenses of the Fete are urgently required, and contributions should be sent to Mr. C. H. Baker, Hon. Treas., High Street, Hornchurch, or W. C. Allen, Clerk to the Council, Billet Lane, Hornchurch.

GIFTS FOR PRIZES WILL ALSO BE WELCOMED.

Wilson and Whitworth Ltd., Printers, Romford.

The carnival was arranged by the Hornchurch branch of the National Federation of Discharged and Demobilized Sailors and Soldiers, whose secretary, Mr. Cecil Bullock, was mainly responsible for the organization of the procession. After a parade outside the Parish Church, the carnival proceeded by a circuitous route in the direction of the field adjoining Grey Towers Camp, where the festivities were held. The Cottage Homes' Band, was leading, and was followed by a long stream of people in fancy dresses, tableaux, decorated perambulators, carts, lorries, cycles, motor cycles, and other vehicles. Well to the fore was a weird procession of kilted soldiers, with painted faces, and labelled "The Jazz pipers from Jerusalem." Not far behind was a waggon bearing a tableaux, entitled "The Last Cartridge," depicting a wounded soldier firing his last shot. This was arranged by Mr. Cecil Bullock. Another represented the British Empire —a contribution of the Hornchurch Girls' Club. Then there was a motor lorry from the Roneo Works, crammed nigh to bursting with children and workers in fancy dress, and a car representing "The Old Woman who lived in a Shoe," by some members of the Mill Park Lawn Tennis Club. The Fire Brigade also took part.

For the best entries, prizes were awarded to the following :—

Ladies (individual entries)—1, Miss P. Manly (an allotment) ; 2, Miss Kathleen Tyrrell (gipsy boy) ; 3, Mrs. H. Harding (billiards) ; Gentlemen (individual)—1, Mr. S. Tickner (cow-boy) ; 2, Mr. R. A. Tickner (squaw). Ladies' tableaux—1, Girls' Club (British Empire). Gentlemen's tableaux—1, National Federation (Jazz pipers) ; 2, Mr. Tucker and Mr. Coulter (Wanted a house to let). School children—1, Miss Gertie Burrell (Dick Whittington) ; 2, Master C. Clippingdale (toreador), Perambulators—1, Mrs. Garnham ; 2, Mr Wall. Motors—1, Hornchurch Fire Brigade ; 2, Roneo Works. Cycles—1, Mrs. Howland ; 2, Mr. Lewis.

The judges were Mr., Mrs., and Miss Mason. Some 200 people took part in the procession.

The sports proved very popular, and 146 entries were received for these up to the time of the opening of the festivities, the number afterwards increasing considerably, as entries on the ground were allowed. They were open to residents of Hornchurch only (including Camps). The officials were : Clerks of the Course, Messrs. W. C. Allen and H. B. Sell ; judges, Messrs. Cox, Dixon and H. A. Macklin ; starters, Messrs. Smith and W. E. Clippingdale ; handicappers, Messrs. Gentry and Harris.

The prizes were presented by Mrs. Steer, wife of the Vicar.

The celebrations concluded with an excellent al fresco concert by the Roneo Concert Party, and a dance in the Drill Hall.

The arrangements were in the hands of a large and representative Committee, which included the Chairman and members of the Parish Council, Mr. William C. Allen, the Council Clerk acting as Honorary Secretary, and Mr. C. H. Baker as Honorary treasurer.

DINNER TO EX-SERVICE MEN.

Several public and semi-public functions were held by way of welcoming home the demobilised men, two of which have already been recorded in these pages, viz. :—A garden party, held in the Vicarage grounds on June 28, to which all local ex-service men were invited by the Church of England Men's Society, and the Church Parade and Drumhead Service held in the Millfield on Sunday afternoon, June 1. A little later about 40 men were invited by Mr. and Mrs. Dare, of the White Hart Hotel, to a dinner to celebrate the home-coming of their soldier son, Reginald Dare, from the war. There was, however, no arrangement made for a public dinner in honour of the returned

Photo]   [Qualis Photo Coy.
DINNER TO EX-SERVICE MEN, DRILL HALL, OCTOBER 18, 1919.

men, and what should have been the pleasurable duty of the community as a whole, was left to the initiative of the individual. The Drill Hall, High Street, was the scene of great festivity on Saturday evening, October 18, 1919, when Mr. and Mrs. C. H. Thurner, of Rock Mount, Mill Park, entertained 220 ex-service men of Hornchurch to a dinner, excellently served by Messrs. Joseph Lyons & Co. Mr. James Whitby occupied the chair, and during the evening the following toasts were given :—

His Majesty The King.—Proposed by the Chairman.
Our Absent Comrades.—Proposed by the Vicar, the Rev. Charles Steer, M.C.
The Hornchurch Boys.—Proposed by the Chairman. Response, Mr. Cecil Bullock.
Our Host and Hostess.—Proposed by Mr. Robert Green, J.P.
The Chairman.—Proposed by Mr. E. G. Bratchell, J.P.

324

The Vicar, in proposing the Toast, " *Our Absent Comrades*,"
which was honoured in silence, said :—" This is a toast which
is very near to our hearts. Those who are now enjoying such
splendid hospitality, have sat round less sumptuous boards
with comrades and pals who made light of the difficulties and
dangers of those days. Our dead comrades, I feel, are with us
in spirit, and are still associated with all that is high, noble, and
gallant, as they were in life."

The dinner was followed by a most entertaining programme
of music by Mr. Albert Carpenter's London Concert Party, to
which were invited the wives, sweethearts, and friends of the
guests, and the proceedings terminated with the singing of Auld
Lang Syne and the National Anthem.

The thanks of the guests to their hospitable host and hostess
was shown in no uncertain manner, and it is not too much to
add the hearty appreciation of the whole village to Mr. and Mrs.
Thurner, for their generous and public-spirited act.

The whole of the arrangements for the dinner and concert
were in the hands of Mr. Cecil Bullock.

During the evening two presentations were made by the
Chairman, Mr. James Whitby ; the first being a leather suit
case, subscribed for by the members of the Hornchurch Branch
of the National Federation of Discharged Sailors and Soldiers,
and presented to their first Honorary Secretary, Mr. Frank L.
Bullock, on his departure for Canada.

The second presentation was a handsome silver watch,
the gift of Mr. and Mrs. Thurner, to Mr. Cecil Bullock, who succeeds his brother as Honorary Secretary of the Branch.

THE GREAT SILENCE.

When you would say something that is sad
Speak how I fell !

Shakespeare:—Henry VIII., ii., i.

THE KING'S APPEAL TO THE EMPIRE.

The King invites all his people to join him in a special celebration of the anniversary of the cessation of war, as set forth
in the following message :—

Buckingham Palace.

November 6, 1919.

TO ALL MY PEOPLE.

Tuesday next, November 11, is the first anniversary of
the Armistice, which stayed the world-wide carnage of the
four preceding years and marked the victory of Right and
Freedom. I believe that my people in every part of the Empire
fervently wish to perpetuate the memory of that Great Deliverance, and of those who laid down their lives to achieve it.

To afford an opportunity for the universal expression of this feeling, it is my desire and hope that at the hour when the Armistice came into force, the eleventh hour of the eleventh day of the eleventh month, there may be, for the brief space of two minutes, a complete suspension of all our normal activities. During that time, except in the rare cases where this may be impracticable, all work, all sound, and all locomotion should cease, so that, in perfect stillness, the thoughts of everyone may be concentrated on reverent remembrance of the Glorious Dead.

No elaborate organisation appears to be necessary. At a given signal, which can easily be arranged to suit the circumstances of each locality, I believe that we shall all gladly interrupt our business and pleasure, whatever it may be, and unite in this simple service of Silence and Remembrance.

(Signed)   GEORGE R. I.

I have ventured to assert in another page of this book that there will probably never dawn another day quite like Armistice Day, and I feel sure it will be equally safe to predict that never will there be in our history two minutes so solemn and inspiring as those which immediately followed the striking of 11 o'clock on Tuesday, November 11, 1919. The expressed wish of the King to the nation that " *there may be, for the brief space of two minutes, a complete suspension of all our normal activities,*" was observed in a manner which left no doubt that there was, indeed, a real recognition in the great heart of the nation of the sacrifice made by her sons in the war. It was a wonderful thing to stand, as I did, before an open window in London, a few minutes before eleven o'clock on that morning awaiting the silence which was about to fall on the great city. When it came one seemed overwhelmed by the solemnity and momentousness of the occasion. It was a silence which could be felt ! Those two minutes were surely the most thrilling the nation has ever lived ! A nation standing with bowed and reverent mien before sacrifice. The following beautifully worded reference, eloquently descriptive of this national tribute, appeared in the " Daily Express " of November 12, 1919 :—

At the eleventh hour yesterday, there fell on the Empire the silence of its graves. Every centre of human activity was turned to stone. While these two short minutes went their long-drawn way, all who were left alive stood stock still—horse, foot, and engine. The people were no longer in the streets, in their clubs, in their houses, in the shops. They were in the Temple not built with hands, the street their nave, under the vault of highest Heaven. They were not afraid to pray, not ashamed of tears. Again, after twelve months of reaction, of fierce effort to forget we came together, as we came in grief and danger, terror and tribulation. We were not, for these two minutes, this man or that, ladyship or woman. We were just the people—the people to whom the King appealed with instinct so fine and sure, the people who fought and worked, suffered and endured ; the people who, by the mercies of God, escaped great perils, known, imagined, unimaginable ; the people who shall never see again the faces of their dead, never hear the remembered voice, never touch the warm, firm hand. Never ? Ah ! but we found our dead again at the eleventh hour yesterday, in that ancient sacrament, that imperishable hope—the communion of souls. These two minutes revived our soul. The memorial silence, the thoughts and prayers and tears have—we are sure of this—renewed a right spirit within us. It will show in our national life. But do not let us neglect so fine an instrument. *Let us, at the eleventh hour of the eleventh day of the eleventh month of every year hold this service of pity and thanksgiving.* Let us not sacrifice this purge of pettiness and selfishness. The year may come when the meaning is obscured, when observance is a sham. But not in our time, not while the unhealed scars of body and heart can still glow red and angry at a thought.

The Great Silence was observed publicly in Hornchurch Church, and was so timed to follow the Prayer of Consecration in the Service of Holy Communion. There was a large congregation, and it was a most impressive moment to all present. The Hymn " Peace, Perfect Peace " was sung immediately after the expiration of the two minutes.

WHEN THE WAR ENDED.

TWO SIGNIFICANT ANNOUNCEMENTS.

THE SIGNING OF THE PROTOCOL, AND THE RATIFICATION OF PEACE.

Paris, January 10, 1920.

" The signing of the protocol (pledging Germany to carry out uncompleted agreements and to pay the penalty for the Scapa scuttling) occupied three minutes ; the exchange by fourteen Powers of their Peace Treaty ratifications was over in fifteen minutes.

The signing of the protocol (says Reuter), took place in private. The other ceremony was held in public at the Ministry of Foreign Affairs, where M. Clemenceau had Mr. Lloyd George. Mr. Bonar Law, Lord Curzon, and the Lord Chancellor on his left hand.

One delegate of each of the Powers placed his signature to the procès-verbal to the effect that all documents of the ratification had been produced and found in order.

THE FRENCH PREMIER'S COMPLIMENT.

M. Clemenceau, after signing, saluted Baron von Lersner and Herr von Simon (the German delegates), telling them that he would give orders that afternoon for the repatriation of German prisoners. The French Premier also handed a letter to the German delegates, assuring them on behalf of the Allies, that the reparation of 400,000 tons of naval material for the Scapa Flow scuttling, would be reduced if it was found that such reparation would be damaging to the vital economic interests of Germany. This reduction, however, would not exceed 125,000 tons. The Allies did not consider the scuttling a war crime."

At the conclusion of the ceremony M. Clemenceau said :—

" The protocol and ratification of the Treaty concluded between the Powers of the Entente and Germany are signed. From this moment the Treaty comes into force, and it will be executed in all its clauses. The sitting is at an end."

Daily Graphic, January 12, 1920.

OFFICIAL DECLARATION OF PEACE WITH GERMANY.

" An Order in Council was published in last night's " London Gazette " declaring the date on which the Allied and Associated Powers ceased to be at war with Germany.

The Order recites the fact of the Peace Treaty having been ratified by Germany and three of the principal Allied and Associated Powers, including Great Britain, and of a procés-verbal of the deposit of ratifications having been drawn up and dated January 10. It proceeds :—

" And whereas treaties of peace with other belligerents not having yet been ratified, it is desirable to declare the date which is to be treatedl as the date of the termination of war with Germany before declaring the date which is to be treated as the date of the termination of the present war :

" Now, therefore, his Majesty, by and with the advice of his Privy Council is pleased to order, and it is hereby ordered, that the said tenth day of January shall be treated as the date of the termination of war, between his Majesty and Germany."

Daily Express, January 11, 1920.

————————

So now dismiss your Army when ye please,
Hang up your ensigns, let your drums be still,
For here we entertain a solemn peace.*
    God, if thy will be so,—
Enrich the time to come with smooth-fac'd peace,
With smiling plenty, and fair prosperous days !
Abate the edge of traitors, gracious Lord,
That would reduce these bloody days again,
And make poor England weep in streams of blood !†

Shakespeare.

* Henry VI., v., iv.
† Richard III., v., iv.

328

DIARY OF THE WAR.

1914.

June 28.—Archduke Franz Ferdinand and his wife assassinated at Sarajevo

July 28.—War declared by Austria on Serbia.

July 29.—Austrians attack Belgrade.

July 31.—Berlin receives news of Russian mobilisation.

August 1.—Germany declares war on Russia.

August 3.—Germany declares war on France.

August 4.—Germans invade Belgium.

August 4.—Great Britain declares war on Germany.

August 6.—Austria declares war on Russia.

August 7.—Fall of Liège.

August 9.—U.15 sunk by H.M.S. Birmingham. This was the first German submarine sunk in the war.

August 10.—France declares war on Austria.

August 12.—Great Britain declares war on Austria.

August 16.—Expeditionary Force landed in France.

August 23.—Mons retreat began.

August 23.—Japan declares war on Germany.

August 26.—Battle of Tannenberg.

August 28.—British naval victory off Heligoland.

Sept. 5.—End of Retreat from Mons to the Marne.

Sept. 6 to 11.—Battle of the Marne.

Sept. 22.—H.M.S. Aboukir, Hogue and Cressy sunk by submarine. Loss of about 1,500 lives.

Oct. 9.—Antwerp occupied by Germans.

Oct. 15.—Ostend occupied by Germans.

Oct. 16.—Battle of the Yser begun (ended Nov. 17—estimated German losses, 300,000).

Oct. 20.—Battle of Ypres—Armentières opens.*

Oct. 29.—Lord Fisher appointed First Sea Lord in succession to Prince Louis, of Battenberg.

Nov. 1.—Naval action off Coronel.

Nov. 3.—Sea Raid on Great Yarmouth by eight German Cruisers, one of which, the " Yorck," 9,350 tons, was sunk by a German mine on return journey.

Nov. 5.—Great Britain declares war on Turkey.

Nov. 9.—Emden destroyed by H.M.S. Sydney† off Cocos Island.

Nov. 14.—Death of Field Marshal Lord Roberts, at St. Omer, France, while visiting Indian Troops on the Western front.

Nov. 26.—H.M.S. " Bulwark " blown up in the Medway.

Dec. 8.—Naval battle off the Falklands.

Dec. 16.—Germans bombard West Hartlepool, Scarborough, and Whitby, killing 127 civilians.

Dec. 25.—First aeroplane raid on England.

1915.

Jan. 19.—Zeppelin raid : Yarmouth and district.

Jan. 24.—Naval Battle off Dogger Bank, German battleship " Blucher " sunk.

April 22.—Second Battle of Ypres began. Poison Gas first used by Germans.

April 25.—The Allied forces land in Gallipoli.

May 7.—The Lusitania torpedoed and sunk. Loss of 1,145 lives.

May 17.—Second Battle of Ypres ended.

May 23.—Italy declares war on Austria.

May 25.—Coalition Cabinet formed.

May 31.—First Zeppelin raid on London : East End.

June 4.—British and French advance in Gallipoli.

*Armentières was the first sector occupied by the New Zealanders in France.

† The " Sydney " was escorting New Zealand troopships.

329

June 7.—Zeppelin brought down in France by Flight Sub-Lieut. R. A. J. Warneford, for which act he was awarded the V.C. He met his death a few days later, while testing a new aeroplane.

June 22.—Austro-Germans recapture Lemberg.

July 9.—Conquest of German South-West Africa.

August 4.—Fall of Warsaw.

August 6.—New landing at Suvla Bay, Gallipoli.

August 18.—Russian naval victory in the Gulf of Riga.

Sept. 8.—Zeppelin raid on London : 20 killed, 86 injured.

Sept. 26.—Battle of Loos.

Oct. 3.—Allied troops land at Salonika.

Oct. 4.—Russian ultimatum to Bulgaria.

Oct. 5.—Allied Forces land at Salonika.

Oct. 9.—Belgrade occupied.

Oct. 12.—Greek Government declines to assist Serbia.

Oct. 12.—Nurse Edith Cavell brutally shot at Brussels by Germans.

Oct. 13.—Zeppelin raid on London and Eastern Counties : 56 killed and 114 injured.

Oct. 14.—Bulgaria at war with Serbia.

Oct. 19.—Lord Derby explains " Derby " recruiting scheme.

Oct. 29.—Prohibition of " treating " in Public Houses came in force.

Nov. 17.—Lord Kitchener visits Suvla Bay.

Nov. 22.—Turks routed at Ctesiphon, 18 miles from Bagdad.

Dec. 3.—General Townshend at Kut-el-Amara.

Dec. 15.—Sir Douglas Haig replaces Sir John French as British Commander-in-Chief.

1916.

Jan. 8.—End of British evacuation of Gallipoli.

Feb. 9.—General Smuts appointed to East African command.

Feb. 21.—Verdun battle begun.

March 10.—Germany declares war on Portugal.

March 31.—Zeppelin L15 sunk in Thames Estuary after being attacked in Essex by aircraft and gunfire. Crew surrendered.

April 24.—Irish rebellion. Dublin seized.

April 25.—Sea Raid on Lowestoft by German raiders.

April 29.—Fall of Kut-el-Amara, after siege of 143 days, surrender of General Townsend with 9,000 British and Indian Troops.

May 24.—British Conscription Bill passed.

May 31.—Battle of Jutland.

June 4.—Russian offensive under Brusiloff begun.

June 5.—Loss of H.M.S. " Hampshire " with Field Marshal Lord Kitchener and his Staff. Sunk by mine off the Orkneys, while on passage to Russia.

June 21.—Allied Note to Greece. Demands conceded.

June 24.—Compulsion for Military service for all men from ages 18 to 41.

July 1.—Somme Battle begun.

July 27.—Capt. Charles Algernon Fryatt, of the s.s. Brussels, court-martialled and shot at Bruges by the Germans.

August 6.—Italian offensive on Isonzo begun.

August 27.—Rumania enters war. Italy declares war on Germany.

August 29.—Hindenburg appointed Chief of German Staff.

Sept. 3.—Zeppelin L21 destroyed at Cuffley by Lieut. W. Leefe Robinson.

Sept. 15.—Capture of Flers, Martinpuich and Courcelette—**Tanks first used.**

Sept. 23-24.—Two Zeppelins brought down in Essex, L32 in flames (at Billericay), by Lieut. Frederick Sowrey, and L 33 intact, by Lieut. A. de Bath Brandon.

Oct. 1.—Zeppelin L.31 brought down in flames at Potters Bar by Lieut. Wm. J. Tempest.

Nov. 28.—Zeppelin destroyed off Norfolk Coast.

Dec. 1.—Allied troops at Athens attacked.

Dec. 5.—Mr. Asquith resigns.

Dec. 7.—Mr. Lloyd George Prime Minister.
Dec. 12.—General Nivelle succeeds General Joffre in command of French Army. General Joffre becomes President of Allies' War Council.
Dec. 14.—Allied ultimatum to Greece.
Dec. 20.—First Peace Note from President Wilson.

1917.

Jan. 31.—" Unrestricted " submarine warfare announced by Germany.
Feb. 24.—British recapture Kut-el-Amara.
Feb. 25.—Enemy destroyers bombard Margate.
March 11.—Bagdad taken by British, under General Sir Stanley Maude.
March 12.—Russian Revolution.
March 26.—Price of 4lb. loaf raised to 1s.
April 5.—America declares war on Germany.
April 9.—Battle of Arras. Capture of Vimy Ridge, 13,000 prisoners and 166 guns.
April 26.—Raid on Ramsgate.
May 14.—Italian offensive opens.
May 15.—General Petain in command of French Army.
June 7.—British victory at Messines Ridge.
June 12.—King Constantine of Greece abdicates.
June 13.—Worst aeroplane raid on London (daylight) : 157 killed, 432 injured.
June 16.—Zeppelin brought down off Kentish coast.
June 26.—First Americans arrive in France.
July 7.—Daylight Aeroplane Raid—22 machines over London. 59 killed, 193 injured.
July 14.—Bethmann-Hollweg, German Chancellor, resigns.
July 21.—Russians retreating.
August 14.—China declares war on Germany and Austria.
Sept. 3.—Germans capture Riga.
Sept. 10.—Kerensky assumes control of Russian Government.
Sept. 16.—Shilling loaf reduced to ninepence. The State bearing the 25% reduction as a war charge.
Sept. 24–Oct. 1.—Week of moonlight raids on London.
Oct. 4.—British victory with over 5,000 prisoners at Passchendaele Ridge.
Oct. 19.—Zeppelin raid : E., N.E. coast, and London : At least 4 raiders lost and others damaged.
Oct. 25.—Italian retreat from Plazzo to south of Auzza.
Oct. 26.—Brazil declares war on Germany.
Oct. 27.—Fall of Gorizia—enemy claims 100,000 Italian prisoners.
Oct. 31.—General Allenby takes Beersheba.
Nov. 1.—Count Hertling replaces Michaelis as German Chancellor.
Nov. 7.—General Allenby takes Gaza.
Nov. 17.—Jaffa occupied.
Nov. 20.—General Byng, with Tanks, breaks Hindenburg Line facing Cambrai.
Dec. 3.—Russian General Staff surrender to Bolsheviks.
Dec. 7.—Hebron captured.
Dec. 8.—America declares war on Austria-Hungary.
Dec. 9.—Fall of Jerusalem.
Dec. 11.—British aeroplanes raid Rhine towns.

1918.

Jan. 8.—President Wilson enunciates his 14 points.
Jan. 28.—Air Raid on London : 58 killed, 173 injured.
Feb. 10.—Trotzky announces Russia is no longer at war.
Feb. 16.—General Sir William Robertson resigns as Chief of General Staff. General Sir Henry Wilson succeeds him.
Feb. 21.—General Allenby takes Jericho.
March 2.—Russo-German Peace signed at Brest-Litovsk.
March 7.—" Northern Lights " and moonless raid on London.

March 21.—German attempt to smash British Army begins. The commencement of the last great German offensive.

March 23.—First long-range gun bombardment of Paris.

March 29.—General Foch appointed Generalissimo.

April 13.—Haig's " Back to the Wall " order to the British Army.

April 18.—Lord Milner becomes War Secretary.

April 22.—Great naval raid on Zeebrugge and Ostend.

April 24.—British retire from Villiers-Bretonneux, 9 miles from Amiens, farthest point reached by Germans.

April 25.—British retake Villiers-Bretonneux.

May 9.—Second naval raid on Ostend, H.M.S. Vindictive sunk as obstruction in Ostend Harbour.

May 19.—Last aeroplane raid on London, 32 " Hun " machines attacked, seven of which were brought down.

May 27.—Big German attack between Soissons and Rheims begins.

June 2.—German advance on the Marne checked.

July 12.—German dash for Paris.

July 15.—Foch regains definite initiative by counter-attack between Soissons and Chateau-Thierry.

July 20.—Germans recross the Marne.

August 2.—Fall of Soissons. Enemy still retreating.

August 5.—Last Zeppelin raid on England.

August 6.—Zeppelin brought down in North Sea.

August 8.—British attack begins on 20-mile front east of Amiens.

August 27.—British advance along the whole front.

August 29.—British and French take Bapaume and Noyon (Bapaume taken by New Zealanders.)

August 31.—Australians take Mont St. Quentin.

Sept. 1.—Australians take Peronne.

Sept. 6.—German retreat from the Somme line.

Sept. 12.—American Army success on the St. Mihiel salient. British success on Cambrai front.

Sept. 15.—Austrian Peace Note. Germany makes offer to Belgium.

Sept. 19.—British advance in Palestine.

Sept. 25.—Bulgarians ask for armistice.

Sept. 27.—President Wilson adds his " five conditions " to the 14 points.

Sept. 29.—Passchendaele and Messines Ridges retaken.

Sept. 30.—Bulgaria surrenders unconditionally.

Sept. 30.—Fall of Damascus.

Oct. 1.—French take St. Quentin.

Oct. 3.—Prince Max of Baden becomes German Chancellor.

Oct. 3.—Breach in the Hindenburg Line.

Oct. 6.—Prince Max asks Mr. Wilson to summon Peace Conference.

Oct. 7.—Mr. Wilson demands German evacuation.

Oct. 9.—Capture of Cambrai by Canadians.

Oct. 10.—Capture of Le Cateau.

Oct. 11.—German whole front breaking.

Oct. 13.—Germany accepts President Wilson's terms.

Oct. 17.—British land in Ostend, Lille and Douai recaptured.

Oct. 21.—German Government replies to Mr. Wilson protesting against the charge of " atrocities," and assuring the President that the new Government is democratic and constitutional.

Oct. 24.—Mr. Wilson retorts that if Allies have to deal with present Monarchial autocracy or militarists they must demand, not peace negotiations, but surrender.

Oct. 26.—Fall of Aleppo.

Oct. 27.—Germany says she awaits proposals for armistice.

Oct. 27.—Great Italian offensive begins.

Oct. 28.—Entente leaders meet at Versailles. Austria asks for separate peace.

Oct. 31.—Turkey surrenders and signs armistice.

Nov. 3.—Austria signs armistice.

Nov. 5.—British, French, and Americans launch simultaneous attacks from Valenciennes to the Meuse. Announced in Parliament that Versailles Conference had drafted armistice terms to be communicated to Germany on appliction under the white flag to Foch.

Nov. 6.—Germans in retreat on 100-mile front in France. Sedan entered. Announced that Plenipotentiaries left Berlin for Foch's Headquarters.

Nov. 7.—Mutiny at Kiel.

Nov. 8.—German Plenipotentiaries receive the terms of the Armistice.

Nov. 9.—Kaiser abdicates, the Reds seize the public offices in Berlin, and United Socialists under Chancellor Ebert form a Government.

Nov. 11.—Mons occupied by the British at dawn.

ARMISTICE SIGNED, 5 a.m.

HOSTILITIES CEASE, 11 a.m.

Nov. 17.—Armistice Sunday. National Thanksgiving in all Churches.

Nov. 20.—Surrender of submarines off Harwich.

Nov. 21.—German Fleet's surrender off Firth of Forth.

1919.

April 28.—**Birth of the League of Nations :**—Covenant of the League of Nations approved at a plenary session of the Peace Congress in Paris. Sir James Eric Drummond appointed first Secretary-General of the League.

April 30.—The Chancellor of the Exchequer, Mr. Austin Chamberlain, brought in his £1,500,000,000 Budget, and introduced Imperial preference for the first time.

May 3.—Partial abolition of War Food Coupons. After this date coupons were discontinued for meat, sugar, butter and margarine, but the Government still retained control as to supplies and prices.

May 7.—**The Allies Terms of Peace handed to the German Delegates in the Salon of the Trianon Palace Hotel, Versailles, Mr. Lloyd George, Prime Minister, Mr. Arthur Balfour, Mr. Bonar Law and Mr. G. N. Barnes being the delegates of Great Britain at the ceremony.**

May 15.—The remains of **Nurse Cavell** were brought from Ostend to Dover by the Destroyer " Rowena," on the evening of the 14th May, and on the following day were removed to **Westminster Abbey**, where the first part of the funeral service was held ; the last funeral rites taking place in Life's Green, in the precincts of **Norwich Cathedral**, on the afternoon of the 15th May. Nurse Cavell was a native of Norwich.

June 13.—Launch of the Victory Loan.

June 21.—The interned German Fleet at Scapa Flow scuttled by German crews, under Admiral Von Reuter's orders.

June 28.—**The Peace Treaty signed at Versailles in the Galerie des Glaces,** the Signatories for Great Britain being Mr. David Lloyd George, Prime Minister, Mr. Arthur Balfour, Mr. Bonar Law, Mr. G. N. Barnes, and Lord Milner.

July 5.—March through London of 15,000 to 20,000 men of the London Regiments.

July 6.—Sunday. National Thanksgiving Day for Peace.

July 8.—Remains of **Captain Charles Algernon Fryatt** brought from Bruges for burial. The body arrived in London from Dover and was taken to **St. Paul's Cathedral**, where the first part of the funeral service was conducted. It was then conveyed to **Dovercourt**, the burial taking place in Upper Dovercourt Churchyard.

July 19. **Peace Day. Proclaimed Bank Holiday for the Celebration of Peace. Victory March through London.**

Nov. 11.—**The Great Silence.** Solemn National observance of the **first anniversary of Armistice Day**, by two minutes silence on the striking of 11 o'clock a.m.

1920.

Jan. 10.—**Signing of the Protocol and Ratification of Peace at Paris. An order in Council published in the London Gazette, declared this to be treated as the date of the termination of the war with Germany.**

INDEX TO ILLUSTRATIONS.

334

INDEX.

A.

" Achi Baba " 168, 169.
Aeroplane Attacks, 133 to 136.
Air Raids, The, 120 to 138.
  ,, details of Casualties, etc., 136.
Allen, Wm. C., 217, 219, 221, 323.
Allen, Capt. C. H., 26.
Alley, E. D., 261, 264, 280.
Allington, Lady, 169.
Allotments, The, 218.
Anzac Day Celebrations, 171 to 183, 241.
Armistice to Peace, 311.
Artillery Volunteers, Hornchurch Battery, 12.
Ashburner, Lt.-Col., L. F., 154.
Attwooll, J. T., 249, 251.
Audibility of Continental Gun Fire, 294 to 297.
Ayloffe Chapel, 305.
Ayloffe, Sir Wm., 2.

B.

Babington, Major P., 138.
Baby Clinic, 223.
Baker, C. H., Senr., 8, 211, 217, 236, 247, 323.
Baker, C. H., Jun., C.Q.M.S., 43, 89, 240, 283.
Banks-Martin, Robert, 27, 225.
Baptist Church, The, 207, 260 to 264.
Barber, Alfred, 212.
Barrett-Lennard Sir Thos., 5.
Barstable and Chafford Troop, 5.
Barking, Bishop of, 30, 238, 247, 251.
Barnes, Francis H., 15, 217.
Barnes, Stuart K., 15, 17, 32, 44, 243.
Bass, Wm. H., 226.
Bassett, Sergt. Cyril, V.C., 175.
Bates, W. E., 150.
Bayne, Rev. Canon, 238, 244.
Bearblock, 6, 40, 86, 88.
Beharell, Charles J., 303, 304.
Belgian Soldiers and Refugees, 283
Bell, Rev. G. M., 238, 243, 310.
Bellairs, Comd. Carylon, 199.
Bendall, Lt.-Col., F. W. E., 37.
Bethell, Sir John, M.P., 194, 221, 299.
Betts, Sergt. Thos., 3.
Bill, family, 45.
Birdwood, Genl. Sir W., 177, 178, 179, 180,
Birdwood, Lady, 169.
Bishop, Benjamin L , 4, 17.

B.

Bowick, W. A. R., 46, 111.
Boy Scouts, 19.
Bradbridge, S. W., 262, 263.
Braid, John, 303, 304.
Bratchell, E. G., 217, 222, 223, 224, 227, 247, 281, 324.
Brand, W. H., 22.
Brandon, Lieut. A. de Bath, 122.
Bretton's, Manor of, 2, 249.
Breckels, J., 15, 17.
British Mercantile Marine, 111.
British Red Cross Society, 98, 108, 241, 243, 254, 315.
Broodbank, Sir Joseph, 228, 254, 256, 257.
Broodbank, Lady, 255, 256, 257.
Brookfield, Dr. Storrs, 25.
Brown, Brig.-Gen. C. H. J., 158, 166, 176, 178, 184.
Bryant, Colonel, 256.
Bryant, Edward, J.P., 255, 256, 257, 260.
Bryant, Mrs., 255, 256, 260.
Buckman, Miss Rosina, 167.
Burrows, Sergt. W. A., 25.
Burton, Canon H. D., 167, 243.

C.

Cadets, 4th Batt. Essex Regt., 28 to 32, 244, 315.
Calais, Siege of, 2.
Cantle, F. S., 48, 264.
Card, Capt. John Victor, M.C., 48.
Cavell, Nurse Edith, 330, 333.
Challoner, Mrs., 169.
Chamberlain, Miss Beatrice, 169, 170.
Chamberlain, Mrs. Joseph, 169.
Chapman, Lieut.Victor, 137.
Chelmsford, Bishop of, 238, 239, 241.
Chester Memorial, 9.
Chilvers, Lieut. H. P., M.C., 49, 90, 264.
Chilver, R. W., 214, 215, 216, 264.
Christy, Miller, 294.
Church Army Hut, 163, 301.
Church, The Parish, 233 to 247.
Church Events, 238 to 247.
Church of England Men's Society, 317.
Church Lads' Brigade and Cadets, 15, 16.
Church War Memorial, 304 to 307.
Clippendale, W. E., 212, 217, 221, 229, 323.
Civil Voluntary Effort in the War 196.

335

336

337